Digitized Lives

In chapters examining a broad range of issues—including sexuality, politics, education, race, gender relations, the environment and social protest movements—*Digitized Lives* argues that making sense of digitized culture means looking past the glossy surface of techno gear to ask deeper questions about how we can utilize technology to create a more socially, politically and economically just world. This second edition includes important updates on mobile and social media, examining how new platforms and devices have altered how we interact with digital technologies in an allegedly 'post-truth' era.

A companion website (www.culturalpolitics.net/digital_cultures) includes links to online articles and useful websites, as well as a bibliography of offline resources, and more.

T. V. Reed is Buchanan Distinguished Professor Emeritus of American Studies and English at Washington State University. He is the author of *The Art of Protest: Culture and Activism from the Civil Rights Movement to the Present.*

Digitized Lives

Culture, Power and Social Change in the Internet Era

Second Edition

T. V. Reed

Routledge
Taylor & Francis Group

NEW YORK AND LONDON

Second edition published 2019
by Routledge
711 Third Avenue, New York, NY 10017

and by Routledge
2 Park Square, Milton Park, Abingdon, Oxon OX14 4RN

*Routledge is an imprint of the Taylor & Francis Group,
an informa business*

First edition published by Routledge 2014

Library of Congress Cataloging-in-Publication Data
Names: Reed, T. V. (Thomas Vernon), author.
Title: Digitized lives : culture, power, and social change in the
    internet era / T.V. Reed.
Description: Second Edition. | New York : Routledge, 2019. |
    Revised edition of the author's Digitized lives, 2014. |
    Includes bibliographical references and index.
Identifiers: LCCN 2018032050 | ISBN 9781138309531 (hardback) |
    ISBN 9781138309548 (pbk.) | ISBN 9781315143415 (e-book)
Subjects: LCSH: Internet—Social aspects. | Information
    technology—Social aspects. | Social change.
Classification: LCC HM851 .R4336 2019 | DDC 302.23/1—dc23
LC record available at https://lccn.loc.gov/2018032050

ISBN: 978-1-138-30953-1 (hbk)
ISBN: 978-1-138-30954-8 (pbk)
ISBN: 978-1-315-14341-5 (ebk)

Typeset in Stone Serif
by Apex CoVantage, LLC

Contents

Illustrations

⊡ FIGURES

⊡ TABLE

Preface

Why Buy This Book?

Have you been tweeted, blogged, YouTubed, Snapchatted, Instagrammed, Kindled, interacted, texted, sexted, crowdsourced and socially networked to the edge of your sanity? Are you tired of being told that digital technology will solve all the world's problems, or that it is bringing an end to civilization? Do you want to make common sense of all this digital stuff without the hype, the paranoia or the jargon? Then maybe this book is for you.

There are many books that promise to tell all about the Internet and new communication technologies. Most fall into one of three categories. The most common type is the "how to" book that provides step-by-step ways to use the technology. While these tend to go out of date quickly, they can be useful, even when they call their readers "dummies." The second type is written in a form close to a rant by people either so enamored of or so afraid of new technologies that they profoundly exaggerate their positive or negative impact. The third type of book is written by experts who generally tell way more than most of us want to know about a small aspect of these new media technologies in a language that seems to have come from another planet (the planet Geek, to be precise, a planet I love and visit frequently, but do not live on). Only this third category is relevant to my aims in this book. Many of these works by experts are very important, and this book would not exist without them. But they are not for everybody. They are aimed at a fairly exclusive community of scholars and advanced communication students, not the rest of us.

This book is different. What I hope to do is provide a framework for readers to think about questions such as: Why use these technologies at all? If we do use them, how much use is good for us? And within those broad questions, more pointed ones, such as what are "new media" doing to our brains, to our sex lives, to our parent–child interactions, to our politics, to our education system, to our identities as individuals and as community members? In other words, how do these new technologies fit into the bigger picture of society and culture in the twenty-first century? This book is less interested in programs, apps and devices that come and go in the blip of a computer screen than in asking, in as clear and jargon free a way as I can, some enduring questions about what we can and should make of these technologies, about how we can take control of them rather than have them control us.

We all sense that the Internet and the ever-changing array of new digital hardware and software are changing the world, and changing us. But most of us aren't so sure what those changes are, and whether they are for the better or for the worse. Indeed, anyone who tells you they do know for sure what those changes mean is probably about as reliable as that email from the complete stranger who wants you to help him transfer his million dollars into your bank account. From the dawn of the Internet era, there has been a duel between the technophobes and the technophiles, the haters and the lovers of tech. Right at the dawn of the Net era in the early 1990s this exaggerated pro–con debate took off with books such as Neil Postman's relentlessly pessimistic *Technopoly* (1993), answered by Nicholas Negroponte's relentlessly optimistic *Being Digital* (1995). Avoiding these two speculative extremes that have been repeated often in the subsequent two decades of Internet life, this book seeks to examine some of what is actually going on in digitized spaces, noting both the dangers and the pleasures involved. Part of that work is recognizing that the digitizing world is only part of the world, surrounded by political, economic and social forces that shape what happens online more than the technology itself.

For many of the more than 3 billion of us now taking part in the digitized life (about one-half of the world's population), asking these questions is like a fish trying to think about water. We take that water for granted. It's just where we live. But just as the quality of water is vital to a fish's health, so too is it vital for us to think about the quality of digital culture, to try to sort out the healthy from the polluted or the toxic waterways, to try to make things a little less murky, a little more transparent.

Reportedly the great modernist writer Gertrude Stein, when asked by her lover on her deathbed the presumably metaphysical question, "Gertrude, what is the answer?" replied, "What is the question?" I'm on Stein's side of this exchange. I think most often good questions are more important than answers. I'd like readers of this book to enter a conversation about how to think more carefully and deeply about these new forces that we have unleashed upon the world. I have tried to identify some key questions to help you come to your own conclusions about how you are going to involve yourself in (or sometimes wisely run away from) what these new digital cultures offer. The great science fiction writer Theodore Sturgeon had a motto that more of us might take to heart: "Ask the next question." What does that mean? Good question. Well, one thing I think it means is always ask the question that leads beyond what you think you already know. That's what I hope my questions will lead you to do—ask the next question neither you nor I have thought of yet. As for those of you who have been assigned to read this book in a class, if you don't like your teacher's questions, or mine, ask your own. This is not a textbook where you are told just the facts, ma'am, or the scholarly Truth. This book is a set of provocations.

One question asked often about new communications media is whether or not they are creating a new "generation gap" between adults and youth, between members of the "digital" or "d-generation" and the **analog** one. If you are a reader under 30, you may well have grown up with digital devices utterly woven into your lives. You are what some call **digital natives**, as opposed to **digital immigrants** who come to new media as adults. Not all digital natives are young; aspects of digital culture now go back several decades. And not all digital immigrants are older, since not all youth grow up with digital devices. But generally speaking, the digital native/digital immigrant distinction has an age dimension that is rapidly fading. More important is the distinction itself. Think of it as analogous to being a native speaker of a language. If you grew up immersed in digital culture you probably developed something like a fluency with it, a sense of it as natural. You have a different relation to digital tech to that of folks who came to digital culture after having spent a good many years in the pre-Internet era.

Many digital immigrants have gotten very good at using new digital media, but just like someone who becomes fluent in a second language, they seldom have quite the same command as those who speak the language as natives. They don't feel quite as "at home" in digital spaces. So those of you under 30 reading this book may understand some things about digital life that your over-30 parents and teachers will never quite get. On the other hand, digital immigrants have some knowledge that digital natives do not, namely knowledge of the olden days Before the Web (BW) that may allow them to see some things about digital culture that are not as apparent to immersed natives. In any event, one hope for this book is that it will spark cross-generational dialogues about the pros and cons of various digitized experiences.

One key question we will return to again and again as we look at various new media and the cultures surrounding them is what is truly new here and what is not? And to understand what is truly new, as opposed to merely newish-looking or newly hyped, you need to know what went before (or at least more about the undigitized world). Hence the value of those who grew up BW. I have drawn many of my examples for the book from North America, both because it has been for some time the center of digital culture production, and because it is the terrain that I know best. But much of what I say here has broad application around the globe, and I have tried wherever possible to examine specific impacts in places outside of the countries I know most fully. Without unduly burdening the reader with footnotes, I have tried to cite the most relevant research sources on the topics I raise, but because many of these sources are locked behind pay walls I often do so through summaries in accessible newspaper and magazine articles. But I urge readers seeking more detail and nuance to seek out the original material if they have the means to access them through libraries or other resources.

This second edition of *Digitized Lives* is thoroughly revised, bringing new insights to older questions, updating a number of issues, and raising some vital new ones that have arisen or become more prominent since the first edition came out in 2014. This includes a whole new chapter on privacy issues, a major revision of the politics chapter in lieu of recent digital disruptions of electoral and social movement arenas, as well as revisions in all the other chapters to reflect significant events in a rapidly changing technical landscape. Revising and updating, however, does not mean surpassing all that came before. One of the downsides of our rapidly changing digitized lives is an increase in the prevalence of *presentism*. Presentism is the false belief that newer is always better, that all previous things, ideas and information are made obsolete by newer versions. This may be true of some new tech devices, or at least the tech companies who benefit financially from getting us to buy every new digital product would like us to think so. But it is seldom true of ideas. So if you see a source cited here that is more than a few hours old (or heaven forfend, a number of years old!), or a reference to an app that is no longer trending, do not assume the information provided is not useful. I have updated statistics wherever relevant, but perspectives provided on a previous phenomenon (apps or platforms no longer getting much or any use) may prove highly useful in analyzing Snapchat or whatever app is hot by the time my publisher gets this book into your hands or this e-book onto your phone. Rather than scoffing at old stuff, where appropriate use your own brain to further update this book by applying questions and concepts found here to newer developments in digital culture.

⎘ OUTLINE OF CHAPTERS

Chapter 1 looks at general questions about how technology shapes culture, questions about the extent to which technologies develop a life of their own beyond human control. It also introduces some crucial terms useful in thinking about the culture–technology relationship, and describes some of the ways readers might follow digital culture scholars in tracing the social impact of new media.

Chapter 2 deals with the often-overlooked forces that make digital culture possible, the production process that creates the devices and the networks that carry digitized cultural materials around the world. It also deals with another largely hidden part of digital culture, the environmental devastation resulting from the production, use and disposal of digital communication devices.

Chapter 3 takes up one of the most discussed aspects of digital culture, the impact of that culture on individual and collective identity, including the alleged real world/virtual world divide, issues of digital crossdressing (impersonating someone you are not), the rise of cyberbullying and the experience of being overwhelmed by the sheer amount of information thrown at us by digital media.

Chapter 4 takes up the changing nature of privacy in our highly networked *surveillance society*. It looks at the phenomenon of *dataveillance*, the increasing amounts of personal data gathered on us by social media corporations and by governments. This chapter includes some advice on how to minimize privacy invasion.

Chapter 5 continues the discussion of identity by looking specifically at how questions of gender, ethnicity, sexual identity and physical dis/ability have been reshaped by digital cultures. Is the digital world creating greater social equality or replicating or even extending existing inequalities?

Chapter 6 takes up the multifaceted question of sexuality as impacted by new media spaces, looking at online sex education, at various cybersex practices (from sexting to sex-bots), at controversies surrounding online pornography, and at the role of digital media in the epidemic of sex trafficking.

Chapter 7 looks at a variety of ways in which political cultures, from mainstream parties to dissident social movement protesters to revolutionaries to terrorists, have had their actions reshaped by digital technologies. The recent rise of digitally assisted authoritarianism around the world has changed the tone of this chapter considerably since the previous edition, with new issues arising around **fake news** delivered mostly by new media and the alleged rise of a **post-truth** politics. Suggestions on ways to combat fake news are offered as well.

Chapter 8 is devoted to digital games and the various controversies that have surrounded them, from allegations that they promote mindless violence to those who argue that games can be used creatively to solve many of the world's problems. The chapter also looks at the ways that digital gaming has contributed to the phenomenon known as **militainment**, the increasing fusion and confusion of militarism and popular culture.

Chapter 9 takes up another controversial area where digital technology is having a huge impact, the arena of education, from pre-school through graduate school and out into the wider world of lifelong learning. It also takes up the issue of lifelong education and the role of digital media, including the digital humanities and digital arts, in representing the world's rich array of past and present cultures.

Chapter 10 explores the vital question of who does and does not currently have access to digital cultures (about half the world), and what the reasons for this might be, including why some people intentionally and thoughtfully opt out of the digital world. It also looks at various digital divides involving not just access to digital life, but the varying quality of access as it shapes social and economic possibilities.

Chapter 11 concludes with a glimpse at some likely trends and more speculative possible future developments in increasingly digitized lives. What hopeful developments are likely, and what possible negative developments will societies need to avoid? At one extreme, some posit a possible **robot apocalypse** (takeover by intelligent machines with little or no use for human beings); at the other extreme, a world without serious disease or violent conflict. As with the rest of the book, this chapter tries to avoid both excessive hope and excessive hype, while examining some best and worst case scenarios and drawing on some speculative fiction books and films as aids to imagining various feasible futures.

▣ COMPANION WEBSITE

This book has an accompanying website—culturalpolitics.net/digital_cultures—that includes a bibliography with books, articles and relevant websites for further exploration of key digital culture issues, and a timeline on the evolution of digital cultures. The website is a resource and a reminder that this book can only introduce topics that deserve much deeper understanding. The website also has a response section where you can send me comments or questions about the book or about digital culture issues more broadly. I appreciate getting feedback (most of the time).

⮥ COMPANION WEBSITE

This book also contains a glossary of terms. Terms that appear in the glossary are highlighted throughout the text in boldface.

Acknowledgments

This book grew out of many years of teaching courses about digital culture at Washington State University and York University. Students in those classes contributed important insights to this book, and I thank them for educating me.

I also want to thank several individuals who played a valuable role as readers of the first edition, in particular Hart Sturgeon-Reed, Noël Sturgeon, Katie King and Jason Farman. And I thank Hart and Noël for additional comments for this second edition.

Lastly, I want to thank the amiable folks at Routledge who brought this new edition to press: Erica Wetter, Emma Sherriff and Sarah Adams, as well as Jane Fieldsend (from Florence Production Ltd) and all the other hardworking people who help keep the book world alive in this not quite completely digitized world.

1

How Do We Make Sense of Digitizing Cultures?

Some Ways of Thinking Through the Culture-Technology Matrix

Computers are incredibly fast, accurate and stupid. Human beings are incredibly slow, inaccurate and brilliant. Together they are powerful beyond imagination.

(Leo Cherne, Discover America conference, Brussels, June 27, 1968)

The Internet includes an unimaginably vast sea of data that is profoundly changing the range and nature of human communication. Not only has it greatly decreased the cost of communication and enabled heretofore-impossible distances to be crossed instantaneously, but it is also increasingly subsuming all other media into itself. Mail, phoning, film, television, music, photography, radio—all have been translated into digital form and made available in far more accessible ways to the roughly 3.5 billion people (now redefined as "users") around the world. No book can hope to fathom the immensity of the Net and other "new" information communication technologies (or ICTs, as they are known among professionals). But we can examine some of the key patterns of human social interaction made possible, fostered or transformed by these "new media." Note that this is the second time I have put "new" in scare quotes. Why? Because one of the recurring questions in the fields upon which this book draws is: What aspects and impacts of digital media are truly new? Are our interpersonal relationships growing more open or becoming more superficial? Are we becoming more politically informed or more politically divided? Are we building a more equitable economy or leaving many people behind as robots take over work? Are we being entertained more richly or being drawn more and more into empty distraction? Overarching all these questions is a bigger one: Is the real world being overtaken by a digital one?

There is no doubt that the digitizing world is full of new things, but not all of the hyped newness is of equal significance. Not every new app or platform or device is as revolutionary as its promoters would have us believe. So, part of the task is to distinguish wider patterns of significance, important newness from superficial novelty. To get at those questions, this book draws from a wider array of academic fields that examine the social impacts of information and communication technologies: Anthropology, sociology, psychology, political science, communication, rhetoric, ethnic and women's studies, cultural studies and half a dozen other disciplines. The interdisciplinary field that most directly addresses the set of issues raised in this book looks at **digital cultures**—the *social relationships* that occur through immersion in the realm of the Internet, video games, smartphones and other high-tech platforms and devices. Studies of digital culture ask how communication technologies reflect the wider social world, how they create new cultural relations and how those new online experiences in turn reshape the offline world.

Culture is one of the most complicated words in the English language, but for our purposes we can simplify it to mean the values, beliefs and behaviors that are typical and defining of a group. In this sense, we are all involved in many cultures. We can think of cultures as like the Russian dolls that have smaller and smaller dolls inside. At the broadest level we can talk about global culture, at the next level national cultures, then perhaps ethnic cultures and so on down the line to the cultures of small groups (clubs, workplaces, etc.) in which we take part. In terms of digital cultures, we can think in terms of Twitter culture, or Facebook culture, digital classroom cultures, smartphone cultures, digital activist cultures, gamer cultures and so on, each of which could be divided into smaller groups (e.g., *Grand Theft Auto 5* player or iPhone user cultures).

The analogy breaks down, however, in that Russian dolls are far more clearly demarcated than are cultures. Cultures are fluid, not neatly bounded entities. Recent anthropology theory argues that "cultures" should be seen as real fictions, as always artificial constructions of observers. The question of what typifies or is essential to a given cultural group is always subject to debate within that group. The boundaries or key characteristics of any imagined cultural group are always blurry, and often in process and changing. Cultural meanings are in fact never settled; they are always subject to contestation, both among outside observers and internal participants. This simply means that anything claimed about a given cultural group can be challenged, and that is a good thing. It keeps cultures from becoming static and keeps those who analyze cultures from becoming complacent or arrogantly sure of their interpretations.

At the broadest level, digital communication technologies have played a very significant role in our current international configuration of economics, politics and culture, the period of the last several decades that is generally referred to as neoliberal or "free market" globalization. Globalization is not a new phenomenon in history. There have been many forms and periods of significant global interaction for hundreds of years. Precisely what is new about our current era is up for debate, but among the new features of this particular phase of globalization is the spread of digital communication networks. Most scholars agree that our current brand of globalization would be impossible without the rapid movement of money, data, knowledge and non-material commodities across national borders via the Internet and other digital technologies.

To address some of the human-to-human issues surrounding our digitizing world, we need to get beneath the glossy surface of ever-cooler new tech devices to ask questions about what these devices are doing *to* us, and what we can do *with* them to make our lives and the lives of others better or worse. My aim is to avoid both the pro-tech hype driven by profit-hungry electronics corporations, and the equally dubious tech haters driven more by fear of the new than by clear thinking about some of the downsides of high-tech cultures. Instead this book tries to provide some useful ways to think through the many and varied social impacts of digital cultures, and hopefully provides some tools to help readers play a stronger role in shaping new technologies in ways that improve the world.

Few of the questions this book addresses have simple answers. One reason there are no easy answers about what new technologies are doing to us is that the subject is incredibly vast, and changing at a phenomenal rate. Though no one really knows how to count them with complete accuracy, halfway through the second decade of the twenty-first century there were close to 5 billion individual Web pages indexed by Google (and millions more unindexed). Moreover, between the time I wrote that sentence and the time you are reading it, millions more were created. If Facebook were a country, it would be the most populous one on Earth. YouTube broadcasts more in a day than all major TV networks have broadcast in their entire history. In the history of the world, counting every language, there have been about a hundred billion printed books; the amount of information contained in that number of volumes is uploaded onto the Web every month. How could anyone claim to know what is going on across all those sites and in all the other arenas that make up digital cultures? Trying to understand digital cultures is a little like trying to interpret the lyrics to a song that adds new verses every day. Sometimes the new verses seem to continue the song's main themes, but at other times the new verses go off in totally unexpected directions because the song has more than 3 billion co-authors.

As a result of the rapidly changing nature of new communication networks, the question of what new technologies are doing to us covers a territory that is riddled with contradictory evidence. Are they helping create a more just world, bringing down dictators and opening up societies, or are they giving hate-mongers a new, safely anonymous space to recruit? Are they giving women, ethnic and sexual minorities new platforms to be heard, or new ways to be vilified and marginalized? Are they offering new spaces for smaller cultural and linguistic groups to have a voice, or allowing dominant cultures (and the English language) to overwhelm everyone else? Are we creating a new "(digital) generation gap," or finding new ways for parents and children to communicate across differences and distances? Is the Web truly worldwide in terms of who can use it, or are we creating a world of digital haves and have-nots? Is the Web a space of free and open public discourse, or one controlled by governments and huge corporations? Is the Web creating new transnational, person-to-person understandings, or amplifying existing cultural misunderstandings? Is the Web a space where physically disabled people can enjoy the freedom of virtual mobility, or a space biased toward the able-bodied, leaving the disabled to struggle for full access? Is online sexual content destroying relationships and degrading morals, or offering liberating knowledge and new forms of intimacy? Are video games turning users into mindless virtual killers, or teaching valuable life skills? Is the Internet making us more knowledgeable, or just drowning us in a sea of trivia? Is the digital world one where we are more "connected," or one that stunts the face-to-face interactions that alone can carry true human connection? Are we becoming more liberated as individuals with many more social options, or being turned by government surveillance, politically biased "fake news" and corporate data mining into programmed human robots?

Clearly, a case can be made for each extreme side of each of these questions. But that doesn't mean that the truth is somewhere in the middle. It means that the "truth" of digital cultures is a set of ongoing processes, and will depend on the thinking and acting users do now, including decisions we make as citizens and as consumers about the further development and use of new technologies in the near future. It will depend on the personal decisions we make, on the collective political work we do to shape social policy about technology and on the lives we choose to pursue as participants in a rapidly digitizing age that is upon us, whether we like it or not.

So, digital cultures are very much in progress, and no one really knows what the more than 7.5 billion of us stranded on the third rock from the sun we call Earth will eventually make of this still relatively new set of technologies. We are dealing with two ongoing processes, the: The human development of digitizing technologies and the human use of those technologies. They are not the same thing because humans do unexpected things with the tools we create. And that is what a technology is, a *tool*. The roots of the word technology are in the Greek name for practical things that extend our human capacities. Some of our more famous technologies, the wheel, the printing press, have changed the world and human identities in unimaginably diverse ways. So too will our digital tools, with an emphasis on the unimaginable part. The tools will only be as good as the imaginations of the people who put them to use.

While we are still learning to make sense of the new media explosion, there is little doubt that it represents a major transformation in human culture, what one scholar has called a "fourth revolution in the means of production of knowledge" (Harnad 1991), following the three prior revolutions of language, writing and print. As with each of these previous "revolutions," much consternation has been generated by the arrival of the digital age. The Greeks worried that the invention of writing would fundamentally undermine the key human capacity of memory. The arrival of the printing press was viewed by some as a dangerous degradation of human communication. And so too have many lamented that digital media will bring the "end of world as we know it." The end of the world has been predicted since the beginning of *homo sapiens*, and this latest prediction is no doubt as wrong as all the others. But some things in the world certainly are changing. And the "as we know it" part of the phrase is undeniable. New media will not bring an end to the world, but they are deeply changing the way "we know it." New media (like the printing press) in the past have not brought an end to the world, but they do bring an end to certain ways of knowing, while adding new ways of knowing and new identities. And that is surely what is happening now; we are experiencing a (digital) revolution in how we come to know the world and ourselves.

Having raised the issue of knowledge, let me say a word about my approach to knowing about digital cultures. Objectivity is one of the great inventions of the modern world. It is a worthy ideal of the natural sciences and much scholarship in the social and human sciences. But, like all ideals, it is never fully attained. The idea of information and analysis presented without personal, cultural or political bias is a wonderful thing to strive for, because no one benefits from distorted information. Some think the way to achieve objectivity is to pretend to be a person without biases. Instead, I agree with scholars who argue that such a position just hides biases that all of us have. So my approach will not be to pretend to be neutral on all issues raised in this book (I will not, for example, give white supremacists equal credence with folks fighting racism online). Rather, I'll make my own positions (read *biases*, if you wish) explicit when I have a strong point of view and trust that readers will factor my position into their responses. Having said that this is a book with more questions than answers, I will also share my ambivalences and uncertainties along the way.

I believe all knowledge is **situated knowledge**, that it is produced and interpreted by humans always embedded in cultures, always able to see some things better, some things less well, from their particular place in the world (Haraway 2003 [1984]). This is not relativism—the claim that all cultural viewpoints are of equal value and validity. Situated knowledge (Haraway 1988) begins in the recognition that each of us has insights and blind spots based upon our background and our current location in various economic and cultural hierarchies. This position acknowledges the unequal power available to different individuals, and seeks to bring awareness of that inequality into the cultural conversation. It includes a search for a *deeper level of analysis that more closely approaches objectivity* by acknowledging our inability to *fully* transcend cultural perspectives. But an inability to *completely* leave aside our cultural viewpoints does not mean all viewpoints are equal. When we are called to jury duty, we are asked by the court if we can put aside biases that may prejudge the case. And if we do not do so, other jurors may challenge us. At the same time, the best judges and lawyers will seek to bring a variety of situated knowledges into the jury room in order to most fairly weigh evidence. Though things outside of a courtroom are far messier, a healthy democratic society functions in much the same way, through careful weighing of the facts, wise use of our differing respective knowledge bases, careful introspection into our limiting biases and a check upon us by our questioning fellow citizens. Facts matter, and not all attempts to account for the facts are equally valid. And the fact of unequal power and differing degrees of self-interest must be factored into the search for political truth and cultural understanding. That is what I have tried to do in this book, though I am sure I have done so imperfectly, as is inevitable among humans (and for that matter, among Artificially Intelligent entities, so far—see Chapter 5).

Before moving too deeply into this revolutionary world of digitized cultures, it is important to note who is *not* part of those cultures, i.e., most of the people on earth. Of the roughly 7.5 billion people on this planet, about half, 50 percent of us, have no access to the digital world at all. And millions of others have severely limited access compared with the taken-for-granted fast broadband access enjoyed by those of us with economic or social privilege. These **digital divides** in turn rest upon growing economic and social inequality in almost every country around the globe, and vast disparities of wealth between countries. In broad statistical terms, there are clearly great digital divides between the Global North and the Global South, as represented by these percentages across continents: 95 percent of North Americans have access, 85 percent of Europeans, 64 percent of Middle Easterners, 6 percent of Latin Americans, 49 percent of Asians and only 36 percent of Africans (Internet World Stats, www. internetworldstats.com/stats.htm). Access varies by country within continents of course, and by class, since even the poorest countries have economic elites. In the many countries with a dominant ethnic group and other minority ethnicities, minority ethnic groups almost invariably have poorer access, usually due to having lower incomes and fewer cultural benefits compared with the dominant ethnicity.

Why does this matter so much? Consider these statistics:

- 80 percent of people live in countries where the income gap is widening.

- The richest 20 percent of the population controls 75 percent of world wealth.

- 25,000 children die each day from poverty.

- Seven in a hundred people have a college education.

- A billion people in the world are illiterate.

- One in five people on earth has no clean drinking water.

- One in five owns a digital device.

(Statistic Brain n.d.; UNESCO Institute
for Statistics n.d.)

While statistics at the global level are subject to considerable variation depending on methods of measurement, a general pattern of profound poverty alongside great concentrations of wealth is undeniable. And, with some local exceptions, it is clear that economic and social inequalities in the world are currently being replicated, and often exacerbated, by parallel inequalities in access to the Internet's resources; this in turn means that the economic, political, social and cultural benefits provided by digital access are distributed in extremely unequal ways.

Scholars also recognize that digital divides are about more than access to devices and software. There are also divides centering on language and culture (which languages and traditions are prominently and fairly represented on the Web, and which are not), techno-literacy (who does and who doesn't receive culturally relevant education in using digital devices and resources), and censorship/openness (who does and who does not have their access significantly limited by governmental or corporate forces). All these various digital divides are crucial to keep in mind if we are to approach a realistic appraisal of what is going on in the online (and offline) worlds. (For more on digital divides, see Chapter 9.)

With these issues of huge scale and widely varying contexts in mind, let me be clear that I will not pretend to deal with all aspects of new communications technologies. My focus will be on cultural and social questions, on asking what can be done to make digital communication technologies serve the cause of richer representation for groups currently on the cultural margins, and how digital communication technology can be used to further economic and social justice for all. Thus, the three keywords in my subtitle—*culture, power* and *social change*. An emphasis on digital *culture* means focusing less on the gadgets, more on the human interactive dimensions of digital phenomena (though, as we will see, there is no way to fully separate the technical and the cultural). Focusing on *power* means centering questions about who currently benefits from digital cultures and who doesn't. It means asking to what extent and in what ways the digitization of a large chunk of life on planet Earth has helped lessen or has deepened economic, social, political and cultural inequality. Focusing on *social change* means suggesting how these new media could be used to further progressive change. These are issues upon which the very survival of the planet itself may depend. Such a focus, however, does not mean that other issues about the impact of digital cultures will be ignored. Any book on the vast arena of digital cultures must be selective, limited. Focusing especially on issues of social justice is the selectiveness I have chosen, but the series of case studies I highlight can to a great extent be generalized to better understand much of the wider realm of digitally enabled communication.

⧉ DOES TECHNOLOGY MAKE US MORE THAN WE MAKE TECHNOLOGY? TECHNOLOGICAL DETERMINISM VS. TECHNOCULTURAL ANALYSIS

The metaphor of Web "surfing" that entered the vocabulary of Internet life during the early days and has stuck around for quite a while provides one way of imagining the power of digital technologies. Apart from the fact that I grew up in California, the surfing metaphor makes sense to me because it is an image of folks struggling to control, and even artfully use, a force much bigger than they are. Surfing is a highly individualized sport, but it can also be done in tandem (on one board) and in groups (though separated along the same wave). A wave is not a bad metaphor for the Web in that it is a massive, moving force beyond the full control of any individual human. Any user has at some point wondered how the wave took them far off the course they had plotted (for example, how did you start looking up information on Albert Einstein and end up surveying the microbrews at a tavern in Toronto; big hint, the tavern is called Ein Stein). (Sometimes the fault is purely with the computer, not the user, of course. As a reminder of how dumb computer algorithms can be, I recently searched "wiki-leaking" in Wikipedia commons and was asked, "Do you mean wife-leaving?" No, I did not.) Despite distractions and the dumb brilliance of algorithms, many individual users and groups of users can surf the waves of the Web with a high degree of precision. Web waves, like those in an ocean, are endless and each one unique. Nevertheless, patterns can be charted, and a certain amount can be predicted. Cyberskeptics will warn that information tsunamis will soon drown us all, while cyberhypers will focus only on the pure joy of those many varied waves, each providing a rad ride. Somewhere between these extremes we can make sense of the ever-changing but readable relations that exist between people and technologies.

In less metaphorical terms, one of the most common ways of talking about the relationship between humans and the technical devices they invent is a theory called **technological determinism**. As the name suggests, this approach stresses the technological side of the technology–society relation. In its more extreme form, technological determinism argues that technologies are the single most important force driving human history, and that there is an almost automatic cause-and-effect relationship between the kind of technology a culture has and the essential qualities of that culture. Technological determinism grants technologies themselves independent causal power. Much of early discussion of cyberculture, for example, suggested that something inherent in the technology would lead inevitably to evil (dystopian) or highly positive (utopian) outcomes. Neither has happened because technology never acts alone. Critics of this deterministic approach argue that it exaggerates the extent to which social meanings and uses arise *automatically* from technological innovations. Most serious scholars now reject the extreme forms of technological determinism. However, much of the work that has been done to understand the impact of technological innovation across thousands of years of human history is immensely important, and makes clear that the society-shaping role of technologies should never be underestimated.

At the same time, it is clear that a central problem with techno-determinism is that it largely ignores the fact that technologies emerge from various social and culture groups, and that those groups play a profound role in how the technology is subsequently used. In other words, cultures create technologies, and the extent to which a given technology comes in time to alter culture is never a simple one of technology dictating to society. Technology is not a Frankenstein's monster or the Terminator running amok. It is a series of devices and practices in the hands and minds of users. We are all Dr. Frankensteins, we all have Terminator power (aka smartphones) at our command, and it is up to us whether our monsters and **cyborgs** help us to make a culturally richer, politically more just world or strangle the life out of us. In relation to how these technologies work in the world, I take a position stated succinctly many decades ago by one of the first thinkers to look closely at what communication media are doing to us and to the world, controversial media critic/prophet

Marshall McLuhan, who remarked, "We shape our tools, and afterward our tools shape us" (McLuhan 1994 [1964]: xxi).

McLuhan here is trying to avoid two kinds of mistakes in thinking about technologies of communication. On the one hand, he seeks to avoid technological determinism (though he was not always so careful to avoid this trap), and on the other hand, he seeks to acknowledge that each communication tool (from the pencil to the television to the PC) has certain likely uses built into it that can shape our actions in ways we may not intend or initially imagine. Keeping with the tool metaphor, think of the expression "to a hammer, the whole world looks like a nail." Hammers were designed to do certain specific things, and they are very good at those things. But they can't do everything because not everything in the world is a nail. And they can be put to ill uses not originally intended. They can, for example, like Maxwell's silver hammer in the Beatles song, be used as a weapon (so can a pencil, for that matter). So one key trick in thinking about any technology is to ask not only what can it do for us, but also what can it *not* do for us, what are its limits and what do we *not want* the tool to do. If we don't ask these questions, new technologies might just metaphorically, or should I say virtually, bash our skulls in, or at least hammer away in destructive ways at lots of things that aren't nails.

All technologies have some uses built into them. It is hard to play music with an electric blender, and hard to mix smoothies with an iPod. But technologies also always have unforeseen consequences. The Internet, to take a pertinent example, was designed with the needs of a small number of military personnel and scientists in mind. Hardly anyone in on the early development of what became the Internet conceived of it as the revolutionary medium of popular communication it has become. On the one hand, the technology had the potential use to which it is now being put built in, and so in some sense the technology has driven the development that became the modern Internet. But on the other hand, that development was a highly uneven, stop-and-start process that, while enabled by technical breakthroughs (especially the invention of the World Wide Web), was a thoroughly social and cultural phenomenon. Complex technological devices might be thought of as like a chessboard. Chess has many rules and restrictions; you cannot do just anything on a chessboard. But the number of particular outcomes that are possible on the platform, that simple board of squares, is virtually infinite. The military-scientific inventors of the Internet had no idea that it would one day be used to share videos of cats playing the piano (if they had, would they have had second thoughts?), but they did build in the possibility of doing so. Fortunately, as it turns out, the Net is big enough to contain *both* scientific brilliance and feline silliness.

What virtually all forms of critical digital culture analysis have in common is a rejection of pure technological determinism in favor of approaches that can be grouped under the rubric **technocultural**. As the term's blending and blurring of the words "technology" and "culture" suggests, technocultural approaches argue that technologies and cultures can never be neatly separated, because technical innovations are always created by individuals and groups deeply shaped by cultural assumptions and biases, and technologies are always used in particular cultural contexts that reshape them even as they partly reshape the cultural contexts.

Choices about which technologies are to be developed are always partly economic, partly political and partly social. In turn, choices about which technologies become popular are deeply social and cultural, as are the uses to which technologies are ultimately put. Decisions about which technologies get built and disseminated (and which do not) are shaped by economic systems, governmental action, social needs/desires and individual choices. The adoption and use of technologies is always a social process that is only partly predictable (as the makers of high-tech devices that bombed on the market know all too well). Once created, technologies are subsequently adapted, changed or replaced through further sociocultural processes. None of this can be easily determined in advance. This means that whether we have a technological utopia coming our way, or a technological apocalypse, is not something looking at technologies alone can ever tell us. We must also look at the human contexts that shape and reshape those technologies.

Among the more useful and interesting frameworks for thinking about culture and technology are **actor–network theory**, and a parallel **feminist technoscience** approach. Actor–network theory is associated with figures such as French philosopher of science Bruno Latour, and a similar feminist approach was developed most fully by Donna Haraway. Actor–network theory views technological devices as actors (agents), with something resembling human agency (power to impact events), but with the caveat that, like humans, technological actors are always caught up in larger networks of power and causality (Haraway 1997; Latour 1987). Technologies and humans are both entangled in economic relations, political relations, social relations and cultural relations. To further the metaphor, you could say that a given technical device, say the smartphone, is an actor in the world with a variety of identities (*personalizations* such as color, size, shape, ring tones, language, etc.) and behaviors that vary widely, but all act within a set of wider social and technical systems (networks) that shape and limit their nature and uses. Uses of the smartphone are wide but not limitless, and certain uses are far more likely given the specific social contexts and networks of their users (business people are more likely to think of them as work tools, while teens are more likely to think of them as socializing tools and so on).

Technocultural approaches to digital culture issues avoid the extremes of viewing technologies as running amok, out of human control, and the equally dangerous assumption that technologies have no likely social consequences, including unintended ones, built into them. The good news is that we are still early in the process of collectively determining what we will do with the (relatively) new digital devices and platforms that are the subject of this book. And, ironically, the devices themselves may provide us with some key tools we need to make good technocultural choices. At least until fully functioning artificial intelligences (AIs) come along that are as complex, subtle, creative and multifaceted as the human brain, it will still be fallible, culture-bound humans who, through individual and collective action, will determine the future path of technology (and culture). The best technocultural approaches offer a more dynamic way of thinking *with* our high-tech tools, approaches that regard ever-changing cultural, political, economic and social conditions as integral to, inseparable from, the media that help create those social conditions.

▣ COMPONENTS OF DIGITAL CULTURE ANALYSIS

How do the folks who study digital culture, the folks whose work I rely on in this book, go about their work? The complete study of digital cultures can be thought of as addressing four main components: **Production analysis**, which looks at the wider political, economic and social contexts shaping a particular digital culture; **textual analysis**, which closely examines the content and form in digital spaces—words, images, sounds, etc.; **audience/user analysis**, which tries to get at precisely what actual users are doing with digital devices and what meanings they are making of digital texts; and **historical analysis**, which measures the unique qualities of digital cultures in relation to previous forms of communication and as they change over time.

Understanding the production process enabling digital cultures means asking who actually makes digital devices, and under what economic and social conditions. Who are the *electronic company executives* and what are their working lives like? Who are the *software designers* and what are their working conditions? Who are the *hardware designers/engineers* and what are their working conditions? Who are the *assembly line workers* and what are their working conditions? These questions matter in regard to issues of just and unjust labor practices, and also because digital devices are never culturally neutral; they always have the particular cultural biases of their makers built in. Production analysis asks what cultural ideas are built into hardware, into software, into Web interfaces or the shapes of smartphones? What cultural ideas are built into various webpage genres, templates and styles? How do dominant cultural ideas influence design, and to what extent can folks from less socially powerful, more marginalized cultural positions influence the design and creation of our digital devices?

Textual analysis in its various forms (rhetorical, semiotic, psychoanalytic and so forth) examines the verbal (written and spoken words), visual (colors, layout, still and moving images) and aural (voice, music and other sounds) elements of websites, games and other digital spaces, as well as these qualities as manifested in digital devices such as smartphones, game consoles or tablet computers. Much digital text analysis focuses on what we most often mean by text, the written word, examining the verbiage on a Web page or the conversation in a chat room, doing the kind of close reading associated with literary analysis. But because digital cultures generally exist these days in multimedia form, textual analysis often also includes sounds and imagery, as well as words. Whatever its focus, textual analysis has to be extremely sensitive to differing cultural contexts. Color on a website or on an iPhone cover, for example, can convey very different things to people whose culturally derived associations with color symbolism differ. For example, in Brazil the color purple signifies mourning, in Asia luxury, in Britain royalty and in the US frivolity. Subcultures likewise may offer signifiers that counter dominant ones.

In addition, as with literary textual analysis, textual studies of digital cultures pay attention to the forms and formats in which digitized texts appear. Each genre and platform, from a less-than-140-character microblog to e-books running to hundreds of pages, from texts experienced on smartphones to ones read on a laptop to ones projected onto huge screens in classrooms or movie theaters, contain different implicit meanings and expectations and create differing experiences. Form deeply shapes content, which in turn shapes consciousness. Major debates in **digital culture studies**, for example, swirl around the issue of how the rapidly shifting, link-driven reading experience typical in online spaces may be shaping our ability to think linearly, or to pay attention to long narratives, or to follow complex, multilevel logical arguments.

Textual analyses are generally qualitative (involving close interpretative reading), rather than quantitative (based upon statistical data), but one sub-category of textual approaches, **content analysis**, takes a largely quantitative form, doing things such as counting the occurrences of female Asian American characters in a particular genre of video games. Content analysis at the numerical level alone is generally not very illuminating, but when combined with cultural analysis these data can give a more solid statistical base to interpretations. Contrary to the adage, "the facts" never "speak for themselves"; even the purest quantitative data are subject to (always debatable) interpretation. However, interpretation is generally more believable when backed by one or another kind of empirical evidence, and much of the best interpretive work in the cultural study of technology remains grounded in one or another archive of data that combines qualitative and quantitative elements.

Audience or user analysis takes a number of different forms and uses a number of different methods. These can be ranged in degrees of breadth vis-à-vis depth. The broadest amount of information can be gained through *surveys* or *representative sampling*, which can involve hundreds if not thousands of respondents. The Web itself has contributed immensely to the field of social surveying in general, and it is obviously an even more perfect tool for gathering information about specifically online cultures. A second approach uses *focus groups*, a method long used to study *old* media. Focus groups survey a relatively small number of people, typically fewer than 20, interviewing them in more depth and more interactively than is possible through a poll survey. Finally, the anthropological and sociological approach called ethnography is being applied to digital culture (Escobar 1996; Hesse-Biber 2011). Traditional ethnography involves living among while studying a cultural group. **Cyber-ethnography** (aka online or virtual ethnography, netnography, webnography, computer-mediated ethnography, etc.) applies this approach to digital culture groups. Typically cyber-ethnography takes one of two forms. In one mode, scholars act as "lurkers," observing online activities surreptitiously by visiting **cyberspaces** (work spaces, play spaces, socializing spaces) unannounced. The second main mode of cyber-ethnography involves researchers engaging in *participant observation* by openly joining an online community—a chat room or a **Massively Multiplayer Online Role-Playing Game (MMORPG)**—in order to study the group's experience from both inside and out. One group of scholars, for example, joined World of Warcraft, the largest online game community (with reportedly over 10 million players), playing for several months and then writing up, sharing, and publishing their analyses of the game and game experience from a variety of perspectives (Corneliussen and Rettberg 2008). There is much debate about whether honest disclosure that one is a participant-observer is preferable to lurking, since the presence of a researcher may skew the activity of other users, while lack of candor on this issue can raise charges of privacy invasion. Elaborate rules have been devised to mitigate some of these issues, but no clear consensus on the best approach has emerged.

User analysis tries to understand what *actually happens to people* as they utilize digital spaces and devices, both in the narrow sense of finding out what they are doing and the larger sense of uncovering what is being done to them. By the latter I mean trying to get at the personal and social impact of spending time using particular digital devices and platforms. How does a person's idea of geography change when they work primarily with mobile devices? What is the impact of digital surveillance on a worker whose every keyboard stroke is being read by the boss? What is the impact on one's sense of self, community and privacy of being in an always-connected state through a smartphone? And so on.

One particularly intense kind of audience, fandom, has received a great deal of attention in relationship to digital culture. While fandom has a long history prior to the rise of the Net, the online world has exponentially increased the amount and depth of fan activity. And because much of this activity is publicly visible, researchers have been given a richer look into how audiences interpret a range of popular culture topics (movies, celebrities), as well as providing data on how online practices may be changing the nature of fans in regard to their objects of affection and interest.

Historical approaches in effect surround all these other methods, since without knowing the history of technocultures, the history of cultural texts and the history of media audiences, it is impossible to really measure the specific impact of any element of new media production. Thinking historically, the alleged newness can be separated out into various degrees or levels across a continuum by addressing questions like these: 1) What does the new technology do that could not be done by earlier forms of communication? Prior to the Web and applications such as Skype, visual conversations across great distances were only possible on *Star Trek*; 2) What does the new technology do more easily, more cheaply or more effectively than earlier mediums? Downloading digitized music greatly increases access to a range of forms, and, even when done legally, generally reduces costs; 3) What does the new technology do that might be done as well or better by older mediums? When you see two friends walking down the street, each with a smartphone talking to other people, you may well ask whether they would be better off actually talking to each other via the ancient medium of face-to-face communication. These three questions certainly do not cover the full range of possible historical meanings and impacts of new media, but when kept in mind they can sort through a lot of hype and clarify a good deal about what is truly important and innovative in new communication technologies.

Few individual studies of digital culture substantially deal with all four elements, though they often combine two or more, but the richest view of the terrain of digital cultures emerges when all these elements are factored into the picture. I have tried to do that with the topics all-too-briefly surveyed in this book, but I urge those of you who wish to dig more deeply into any particular aspect of digital culture, starting perhaps with resources provided on the companion website, to keep this full array of factors in mind as you proceed.

⇲ TERMINAL CONFUSION?

Whenever a new field is devised to understand new social phenomena, that field generates new words to help define and clarify those phenomena. The nasty name for these new words is "jargon"; the more positive word is "terminology." To the uninitiated, these new terms often seem like unnecessary complications, if not downright gibberish. But to those in the field, they are helpful shorthand and absolutely crucial tools. The field of technology, and with it technology studies, is often criticized for generating particularly inscrutable jargons. Some of this criticism is no doubt deserved (the proliferation of acronyms and neologisms surrounding computer culture is truly baffling). But new terms also offer vitally necessary specificity and clarity. Every field has them; your plumber has a vocabulary every bit as esoteric as your computer technician, but we seldom criticize plumbers for a specialist vocabulary that runs from "adjusting links" to "zero soft" water because we know it helps them get the job done.

Just as you would probably allow a plumber the right to call not for that shiny metal thing with a kind of c shape on the end, but rather specify a crescent wrench, I hope you will recognize that the specialist vocabulary introduced in this book is not designed to obscure but to clarify, to create a shorthand language that makes it easier to communicate complicated ideas. While mostly defined as used, fuller definitions of many of these keywords (marked here by bold type) appear in the Glossary. I trust you will come to see most of them as useful tools rather than as attempts to colonize your brain.

One key term central to any analysis of digital cultures is the term **mediation**. In the context of communication theorists, mediation refers to the medium of communication used to exchange human thought and feeling. Communication theorists point out that *all* human interaction occurs through one medium or another. Every communication we engage in is mediated. The single most important communication medium humans have is verbal language. And like all media, languages are imperfect at conveying thoughts and feelings; language separates us even as it connects us. Anyone who knows more than one language knows that there are things that can be said and thought in one language that simply cannot be translated into another. (And the writer Franz Kafka once remarked that "all language is a poor translation," presumably of some pre-linguistic reality.) As any literature professor will remind you, form does matter; form does impact meaning. Each linguistic medium creates a particular world. Visual languages (images of various sorts) communicate some things words cannot (though the claim that a picture is worth a thousand words has not yet been statistically proven, to my knowledge). But in truth they are just two equally imperfect media of communication. The point here is that all communication between humans is shaped both positively and negatively by mediation; digital mediation is just another variation on this wider set of processes (Kember and Zylinska 2012). There is no completely neutral medium, no medium that does not enable or privilege certain kinds of interaction and limit other communicative possibilities.

Saying that all interaction is mediated, however, is a far cry from the famous, much misunderstood, claim by communication scholar Marshall McLuhan that "the medium is the message" (1994 [1964]). McLuhan meant not that the medium was the *whole* message, but rather that the medium profoundly shapes the message. The same idea conveyed by a speech, a book, a film, a TV show or a podcast will differ to some degree because we experience it in medium-specific ways. In addition, we know that even within the general arena of digitized communication, things such as the size of the screen (from tiny cellphone to giant projection) and the context of reception (home, office, public event) also shape the meaning. While a technology never *fully* determines how it will be used, there are strong tendencies built in that must be accounted for in any analysis of the human–technology relationship.

The form of communication most often spoken of as most real, authentic or unconstrained is face-to-face conversation. But not only is face-to-face communication shaped by choice of language and by visual cues (body language), both of which are deeply culturally shaped, any face-to-face moment is filled by thoughts and feelings shaped by all the other media we use (and that use us)—newspapers, books, television, telephones, radio, film, photography, music, painting and now by email, blogs, microblogs and vlogs, carried by mobile phones, video games, social media platforms and so on. Some or all of those forces of mediation are now with us when we meet face-to-face. That means there is no inherent reason to privilege face-to-face communication as somehow more real, more immediate. To most of us not utterly immersed in digitized spaces, face-to-face communication still feels more real, but that should neither lessen the reality of other modes of communication nor ignore that face-to-face communication is still via a medium. Nothing is *im(not)*-mediate; we are always already in a multimedia state when we talk face-to-face. This is not to downplay the importance of face-to-face interaction; it has unique qualities that cannot be replicated. And so does every other medium. Rather it is to remind us that we are never in a pure state of communication; all communication in technologically rich cultures is shaped by not only the medium we are using (including the human voice using the medium of one of many human languages), but also by all the other media that have shaped the person who enters into so-called face-to-face communication. Social media is a particularly inappropriate name for sites such as Facebook, since all media are social. Conversely, even when we are in conversation face-to-face we may well be having what might be more accurately called a face-to-Facebook communication, given the way that experiences with digital media are now woven into our other modes of communicating.

There are also a whole set of terms that unfortunately ignore the complexity of mediation and reinforce an absolute **real world/ virtual world** divide (a topic I take up in more detail in Chapter 3). For example, while less pervasive than it once was, the concept of cyberspace, along with the prefix "cyber" in general, is still fairly widely used. For a while everything seemed to be a cyber-this or cyber-that—cybercafes, cyberbullying, cyberdogs, etc. More recently, "e-ing" seemed to be preferred such that we now have e-books, e-commerce, e-waste (see Chapter 2), e-learning (see Chapter 8) and so on. But even if the term "cyber" is being superseded, the most common other candidate for an alternatives, "virtual space," or "digital space" again reinforce a more absolute split with the material world in some ways.

A partial solution perhaps is to always pluralize, to speak of many cyberspaces or virtual spaces, or digital spaces to at least remind us to distinguish among various different imagined spaces created by interacting with different devices and media (the Web, console games, smartphones, etc.), for differing purposes (shopping, learning, working, playing, voting, etc.), and through differing cultural lenses. So in the context of this book, I will use the term "cyberspaces" in the plural, along with other analogous terms (digital spaces, virtual spaces), to help assure that we do not too easily homogenize this complicated, real imaginary terrain as one continuous space, place or thing existing in some place floating above or otherwise outside the *real* world.

As a product of culture-laden people, digitized spaces are always very much woven into the rest of the world. They are a part of, not apart from, the real world. As spaces for the production of culture, digital environments have evolved some of their own special forms, styles, rules, structures and identities, but these seldom stray far from offline versions. The line between cybercultures and wider cultures is never absolute or stable; the boundaries are being crossed all the time in both directions. Wider cultures always shape or spill into cyberspaces, and cyberspaces spill out to wider cultural fields in a myriad of ways. On one hand, given the ubiquity of posting these days, for many the entire "offline" world seems to be just a text waiting to be Tweeted, YouTubed, SnapChatted, Facebooked or Instagrammed (Jurgenson 2012). And many face-to-face interactions these days revolve around "online" events. It might be surprising to some, but most of the world most of the time is offline, and much still happens there that never gets online.

Still, it is also true that ever increasing amounts of cultural content from other mediums (old media) are being drawn into digital cultural contexts. Older forms of mass media such as television, film, radio, newspapers, magazines and so forth are now often filtered through digitized spaces. This is part of the complex process known as **remediation**, taking one media form and transmitting/

transforming it through another (e.g., "old media" television programs digitized and broadcast onto a tablet or smartphone). This is a
two-way process in that incorporating older media reshapes the new
(websites that look like TV screens), while the old media adapt to
the new (TV news shows that look like websites). In these and many
other ways, there is no absolute split between virtual worlds and the
so-called real world, new media and old, or between digital spaces
and analog spaces. These "worlds" are actually always interwoven in
complex ways. This does not mean that virtual, digital or cyberspaces
cannot or should not be isolated to some extent for the purposes of
cultural analysis, but it does mean that it is crucial to remember that
such isolation is always somewhat artificial, always on another level
incomplete.

One key duo of terms that obviously shapes everything discussed
in this book is the Internet and the World Wide Web. Technically
speaking, the Internet is the physical basis that makes most cyberculture possible. It is the *network of linked computers* all over the world,
over which information, from emails to documents to websites, travels around the globe. The World Wide Web, on the other hand, is the
most popular Internet interface; it is the system of codes (HTML and
its variants) that make the information traveling along the Internet
visible and accessible to users. Since the Internet is the more common, popular word used to talk about what is online, much of the
time I will use it (and its shorthand, the Net) as a synonym for the
World Wide Web (and its shorthand, the Web). There has in recent
years been an argument made that the word "internet" should no
longer be capitalized, that a small "i" should be used because we do
not capitalize seemingly comparable words such as television. This
change has not yet been popularly adopted, so I will stick to capital-
izing, but this trend itself is another sign of domestication of technology as the Internet, or internet, loses its aura of difference, becoming
just another medium alongside others.

Another, hipper kind of domestication can be found in the many
tongue-in-cheek variations on Internet and Web that have arisen over
the years, including interwebs, Dub Dub Dub, Webternet, the tubes
or intertubes, or, for the truly esoteric, 1n73rw3b (in Leet, a code language used by some digerati) and many more. Regardless of the name
you prefer, it is helpful to keep in mind that while I may use them
interchangeably (especially the shorthand term Net), the Internet is
actually the material, physical basis that allows the so-called virtual
worlds to appear via the Web and other interfaces.

⊡ WHAT'S IN A NAME? NEW MEDIA/CYBER/DIGITAL CULTURE/ETC. STUDIES

Ironically, the field that has generated so many new terms to make sense of all this high-tech stuff has yet to agree on a term to name itself. Given that the field draws from the sciences (neuroscience, for example), the social sciences (psychology, anthropology and communications, for example) and the humanities (literary and cultural studies, for example), inability to agree on nomenclature is not surprising. Known variously as **new media studies**, **cyberculture studies** or **digital culture studies**, among others (Internet studies, computer-mediated communication, etc.), the field that tries to make sense of recent trends in electronic communication has not settled on a single name. This is partly because each possible name emphasizes some aspects of the phenomena while saying less about other aspects or dimensions. Fortunately, thinking about each of the most common names proposed for this area of study actually can be quite useful in revealing something about some key issues involved in thinking about newer communication technologies.

One major arena or approach goes by the name new media studies. This particular name immediately takes us back to the problematic question: "new" compared with what? The quick and easy answer is new compared with "old media" such as TV, radio, film, photography and print. But exactly when and how does a medium become new? When exactly does a new technology or a new medium cease to be new? The public version of the Internet is now close to three decades old. It is certainly not new to some people. Yet, new people are constantly being added to the user rolls. Does that make the medium new again? Doesn't the experience of newness change depending upon when one encounters the new? For "new" to be more than a marketing tool, it is crucial to always ask new compared with what, and new in what sense?

Emphasis on the media (the new devices and platforms) implied in the name can also bias study toward the "techno" side, and away from the "cultural" side of **technocultural analysis**. A related issue with the term "new media" is its entanglement with commercialism. Under modern consumer capitalism, "new" is always good, always better. How many ads use the phrase "new and improved," with the latter word hardly needed? So there is a certain prejudice in the term "new media" that tends automatically to connote progress, rather than leaving open the question of whether the particular newness in question is for better or worse. And overall, as discussed in Chapter 2, the endless search for newness is having devastating ecological consequences (Slade 2007).

Another way to talk about the newness of new media is to speak of their impact on "old media." The rise of the broadband, broadcast dimension of the Web, for example, has been accompanied by the declining popularity of the old medium of television among young (under 25) users. When young people do access TV programming, they increasingly do so via digital devices. The impact of digital music production and digital downloading on the old media of the CD is well known (from the Napster controversy to rise of services such as iTunes), and the old medium of radio has been given a new but different life on the Internet. Likewise, digital technology has taken over the old medium of film in a variety of ways, from the digitization of much Hollywood "filmmaking" to digital cameras used increasingly in independent films to video capabilities on smartphones. How does viewing movies on computers, tablets or phones change the experience? (Some studies of digital remediation compare this with earlier issues like how watching movies on TV differs from seeing them in public theaters.) In each of these cases, old media have undergone remediation into new media, have been reworked through a new medium (Jenkins 2008). They have not disappeared (yet), but have in various ways and in varying degrees been transformed by newer, digitally based media. How different is the experience of watching TV programs on your smartphone from watching them on a television set? Scholars debate how much and in what ways transferring content into a new medium changes the experience, but they agree that the medium matters to the message. So, while the term new can be misleading, and overemphasis on media form over the content can be a problem at time, the name "new media studies" points to a variety of key questions about (relative) new-*ness*, and to what is or is not truly new about cultures reshaped by digital media.

A second term, **cyberculture studies**, was popular for quite a while to name the field, but fell into some disrepute in the 2010s. On the one hand, the term rightly points to one of the key aspects of (much but not all) new media, the fact that it favors cybernetic systems, that is systems in which non-human devices or processes do things previously only done by humans. Robots are an extreme example of this; search engines such as Google are a more mundane, currently common form. The term raises two main problems. First, it tends to call up images of things beyond our control, of technology running on its own. And second, because "cyber" as a modifier partly arose from and remains associated with speculative/science fiction (cyberspace, cyberpunk, cyborgs, etc.), the prefix "cyber" often calls up associations with s/f that suggest futurity and strangeness, or suggest that these processes are part of an inevitable future. But "cyber" is still a popular prefix and continues to shape how people think about all things digital. And public perceptions or fantasies are themselves an important part of digital culture, part of what is sometimes called the **technological imaginary** (our imagined relations to technologies, as interwoven with what we actually do with them and through them).

The third common term for the field is **digital culture studies**. It, too, is both useful and somewhat problematic. Making something digital technically refers to a process by which information (verbal, visual, aural) is turned into a particular kind of mathematical code, the binary code of 0s and 1s. The ability to turn information into digital code is the technological breakthrough that enables computers and computer programs, the Internet, the Web, smartphones, video games, e-readers and most other forms of new media to exist. This is crucial to remember because taking a digital form, as often contrasted with an analog one, does entail certain possibilities and certain limitations. One famous example is the debate about the differing sound quality between digitized music and earlier analog forms such as vinyl records. Keen listeners may disagree as to preference, but they agree that there is a difference. The down side of the term "digital" is that in privileging this code language, we may be engaging in a subtle form of technological determinism as we suggest that this coding process is the essence of what we are studying, rather than the cultural processes shaped by but not determined by the mathematical coding that underlies various uses of digitized cultural phenomena. In other words, that something is digitized inherently tells us only some things; what is made of those digitized things depends on much more than the fact that 0s and 1s underlie it.

A slightly different approach to talk about new media/digital/cybercultures is to see them as the essence of an *information society* (or sometimes *networked society* or, as in my subtitle, the "Internet era") (Castells 2000; Fuchs 2008; Webster 2006). This term makes the broadest claim of all, suggesting that these new digital communication technologies and the cultures they help enable have become so important that they have redefined the entire social world. Now, the good news is that "society" plays a prominent role in that description, in a way that terms just privileging the technology do not. But the modifier "information" largely erases that benefit. First, when was there ever a society where information was not of central importance? Of course, those who use this term intend to indicate something more than what we traditionally mean by "information." They especially mean digitized information, and/or information carried on computer networks such as the Internet and mobile phones. But beyond this they mean to suggest that somehow the circulation of information has become *more* important than ever before. The phrase also credits (perhaps over-credits) information technology as a key force enabling the current form of neoliberal globalization. While it is true that the movement of ideas, money, products and labor transnationally would not be possible without the Internet and related communication technologies, there is nothing in the technology, for example, that determined it would be used, under revived "free market" ideologies, to increase economic inequality around the globe.

Those using the term "information society" also suggest that information has become a more central economic resource, a commodity, one that accounts for a greater amount of economic activity than ever before (accompanied by a corresponding decline in the importance of manufacturing). They suggest that with the greater importance of information comes greater social and cultural power for those with access to or control over the flow of information. There is certainly truth in this, and battles over the power of information are clearly central today. But at the same time, it is important to realize that material production, including the production of digital devices themselves, is still very much with us and very much part of societies around the globe. As we will see, to forget that the electronics industry is indeed an *industry* is to obscure, among other things, its environmental impact and its impact on workers. It is therefore probably more apt to talk about the significant growth of the information sector of contemporary societies rather than using the term "information society" to characterize the current world system overall.

While perhaps a bit frustrating, the fact that each of the most common terms used to describe this emerging field is problematic should not cause despair. Rather it indicates a certain healthy openness. Each term keys us into important aspects of the terrain, as do other variants including "Internet studies," "networked culture studies," "computer-mediated communication studies," "Web studies," etc. Each of these terms also proves partial, in both the sense of incomplete and biased, in relation to the overall dynamic experience of our digitizing world. To summarize, "new media" points us to the forms and devices—the Web, video games, smartphones, virtual reality suits, etc. "Digital" points us to the common, underlying and enabling mathematical coding process that animates all these devices. And "cyber" points us toward the way popular culture *imagines* these emergent communication developments.

In this book, it is the *culture surrounding and embedded in these devices and processes* that will be the main focus. But it is impossible to think clearly about these cultural formations without thinking about the devices, processes and encodings that intertwine with them. There is no way to abstract the cultural content from the new digital cybernetic media that enable them, nor should they be separated from the broader historical forces that create and recreate them. One obvious way history matters in all this is, again, highlighted by use of the word "new." Much of the hype around new media emphasizes this "new" side over the "media" part. But anthropologists of communication point out that the most common uses of "new" technologies may be to do "old" things. That is to say, new devices may most often just reinforce the same old existing patterns of communication and interaction. One of the most comprehensive studies of the impact of the landline telephone, for example, concluded that during the period of its "newness" in the United States, defined as from 1900 to 1940, "the telephone did not radically alter American ways of life; rather, Americans used it to more vigorously pursue their characteristic ways of life" (Fischer 1992: 5). Could this be true of our latest batch of ICTs? Are they far less new than we think? Are they merely reinforcing old ways of being, rather than, as so much of the hype suggests, radically changing our way of life? If the answer were simply "Yes," this book would probably not be necessary. So, for the sake of my publishers, among others, let me say that the answer is more complicated than a simple "Yes" or "No" can offer.

While the field-without-a-name is full of intense debates, not only over what to call itself, but also over many other more substantive issues, most of the best questions and best answers about the social and cultural impact of digitizing our lives do come from this variously named academic discipline (though journalists and other non-academic analysts have also contributed significantly to our understanding). Knowledge in all academic fields is incomplete and imperfect, and all fields worth being called scholarly are rich in debate. There is a growing amount of very useful research that is crucial to sort through if we care about what digital cultures mean now and are likely to mean in the future. Knowledge starts with information (facts, basic data), but knowledge is something more; it is making

sense of the information. It involves finding the right analytic framework to put data into meaningful and useful patterns that can lead to
intelligent action. What, for example, do we make of this fact: When
I spoke the word "facts" into my dictation program as I was writing/
speaking the previous sentence, the program initially wrote, "FAQs"?
What does that tell us? That my laptop is trying to take over writing
my book? Probably not, though in the not-so-distant future we will
have to deal increasingly with artificial intelligences that blur the line
between humans and techno-devices (my dictation program was at
least smart enough to "choose" FAQs over FAX as closer in relevance).
No, the less paranoid knowledge we could take from this incident is
the reminder that this book is inside the very thing it is trying to look
at from the outside, that these technologies are very deeply embedded in our everyday lives in ways from which we can only partly
distance ourselves, even when we try very hard. Is it possible, for
example, that my decision to write this book in relatively short chapters was, unconsciously, in part determined by my knowledge that
many observers claim our attention spans have been shortened by
spending time in the distracting world of hypertext links and micro-
blogged tweets?

Since each of the names for the field of study upon which this
book draws is illuminating, but incomplete and somewhat misleading, as well as for the sake of variety, I will use each of these modifiers—new media, digital, cyber and others—interchangeably when
naming the field of cultural study. At other times, I use the terms
with their more precise meanings to indicate devices (new media),
the technical form underlying the devices (digital), or the human/
non-human control elements (cybernetics) of these devices and processes or the appropriation of the term in popular discussion.

Many topics covered in this book are immensely complex, and
we will just be scratching the surface of them. This inevitably means
simplifying, but I try to avoid oversimplifying by pointing to compli-
cating factors and suggesting through the companion website where
readers can go to dig more deeply into each topic. That there are few
definitive answers stems partly from the fact that these new media
are evolving rapidly, and that means their meanings are still up for
grabs. We the users continue to remake these devices just as quickly
as designers and workers make them. Devices, apps, platforms come
and go. Some of the ones I mention in this book will already seem
quaintly historical by the time you read this. But these ephemeral
devices and apps represent deeper cultural processes. By drawing from
the rich existing scholarship on new(er) media using the range of

scientific, social scientific and humanities-based approaches sketched previously, it is possible to gain insight into these deeper processes that particular digital devices or programs embody (for a time), processes that continue beyond the passing moment of particular pieces of hardware and software.

2

How Is the Digital World Made?

The Designer/Worker/User Production Cycle

Most of the time for most users, the Internet simply magically appears through a click on a smartphone, tablet or laptop. Most of the time we don't think about how this magic is made possible, do not think about the complex production process behind that pretty little screen and the Internet that seems to hold all the world's knowledge. Before taking up questions about *what* goes on in digital cultures, it is important to think about *how* digital cultures are possible at all, to look at the history and present of the production process that enables an online world to exist in the first place.

⊞ THE INTERNET'S WEIRD HISTORY

The technocultural history of the Internet is a fascinating one that offers a rich example of the interplay of conscious design, unpredicted consequences and ongoing human adaptations. But first we might ask, is there really only one Internet that has been in existence since the 1970 or 1980s, as most histories tell it? Or is it more accurate to think of a series of Internets, because the nature, scope, uses and meaning of the Internet(s) have changed so much over time? The Internet is more like a process than a thing. At the very least the Internet we know today has evolved through several very different phases, and will go through more radical changes in the future.

Though there are many possible ways to characterize the phases or versions of the Internet(s), I think the following labels provide a shorthand pointing to most of the key stages or transformations, and they will provide the scaffolding for my version of this history: 1) the military/academic Internet (in the 1970s and 1980s);

2) the scientific/academic Internet (of the 1980s); 3) the avant-garde countercultural Internet (of the early 1990s); 4) an emergent public Internet (in the mid-1990s); 5) the commercial Internet (in the late 1990s); 6) the domesticated Internet (growing increasingly since the last decade of the twentieth century); and 7) Web 2.0/interactive Internet (beginning in the early 2000s). Each of these stages or versions overlaps with and partly incorporates elements of the earlier stages, and the boundaries between the phases are porous and somewhat arbitrary. But no matter how one chooses to name it/them, the history of the Internet(s) is a culturally complicated one that continues to evolve in only partly predictable ways. It is also a history that is more than a little bit strange.

The cultural history of the Internet is strange in large part because what has come to be the defining media form for our age evolved largely through a series of unexpected, unplanned transformations quite far from the original intentions of its creators. While a technological system as immensely complicated as the Internet has many and varied origins, it is clear that its initial uses were military and scientific. What has become the most public, extensive communications network in the history of the world was originally a top-secret, highly restricted communication system built by and for the United States military with support from mostly university-based scientists and engineers. The Defense Advanced Research Projects Agency (DARPA) of the US government created ARPANET to facilitate communication among military personnel and scientists working in or for the military. With the rare exception of one key figure in this developmental process, J. C. R. Licklider of MIT and DARPA, who as early as 1962 spoke of a "galactic network" that sounds quite a bit like the Internet that was to emerge decades later, the people responsible for what became a worldwide network of users had a very restricted idea of what their project would entail. This networked computer system was first referred to as the Internet in 1974 ("A Brief History of the Internet"; Edwards 1996).

The Internet began life as a top-secret secure network designed to allow the United States military command and control to survive a nuclear attack. The dispersed, decentralized nature of the Net that gives it such a powerfully democratic potential today was initially intended to allow communication to continue if vast areas of the network were destroyed in war. The transformation of this system into the largest, most open, public network of communication in history could be characterized as, in a very quirky way, technologically determined, in the sense that the technology overran its intended uses.

But there was nothing predetermined about the various phases the Internet has passed through. Those have very much been determined by sociocultural, not solely technical, factors, though the technical breakthrough of a more user-friendly way to access the Net was inarguably a key in the transformation.

The path by which the Internet has come increasingly to be a major medium of popular communication is a winding one with many unexpected turns. Another key step forward occurred in 1991, when the National Science Foundation in the US received permission from the military to link to the ARPANET, permission granted largely because of a close connection between many scientists and the military. While hardly a general opening to the public, this move proved crucial in expanding the Net beyond the military and more deeply into academia such that universities soon became an important force in the further expansion out into public space. The scientific/academic Net gradually drew in more and more users in more and more scholarly fields (and continues to do so), moving from the sciences to the social sciences to the arts and humanities. As the number of academic entry points grew, knowledge about this new online world began to slip outside of colleges and universities.

But no doubt the strangest-seeming detour along the route to the current Internet passes through the "hippie" counterculture. Among the first folks outside the military and scientific communities to take an active interest in the new communication possibilities deriving from networks of linked computers were some refugees from the 1960s counterculture (popularly known as hippies). The San Francisco Bay Area was famously one of the major meccas of hippie culture in the 1960s and 1970s, and that area was just adjacent to what became the symbolic center of digital innovation, Silicon Valley, just south of San Francisco. The proximity of those two communities, along with nearby centers of academic computer research such as Stanford and the University of California, Berkeley, were a matrix for the next stage of development of the Net. Counterculture-shaped figures such as Stewart Brand began to envision the Internet as a potential cyberutopia embodying the values of "peace, love and understanding" at the heart of hippie ideology. The Bay Area has a long history of bohemian communities (not only the hippies, but as one of the centers of Beat culture in the 1950s and others before that), a site with a more openly progressive political orientation than many other parts of the US. Those communities developed a serious social critique of America's obsession with wealth, war and selfish forms of excessive individualism (Turner 2006). Folks who had helped end racial segregation in the US and protested the disastrous Vietnam War, and who felt the soul of America to be lost in a sea of excessive consumerism believed a free, open new form of communication beyond the control of corporations and the government could radically change the country and the world for the better.

The combination of "freaks" (as counterculturalists preferred to call themselves) and "geeks" (as the technosavvy were beginning to be called) proved a potent mix for imagining and building early popular cyberspaces. It is important to keep in mind that this phase was still largely a written text phase; some sound and images were present but in nowhere near the levels we now take for granted. Much of the early utopian thought about *cyberspace* (the term came into wide usage at this point) that spoke of it being beyond gender, beyond race, beyond disability stemmed from the fact that many online communicators were invisible and inaudible to each other at this stage. All you had to go on were words not noticeably connected to particular human bodies. In two of the most influential early books on digital culture, Howard Rheingold (2000 [1994]) touted the possibilities of a virtual community that transcended all social and geographic borders, and social psychologist Sherry Turkle (1995) speculated that online communication would enhance self-exploration by allowing us to engage in masquerade, to play with identities not our own. Both of these books offer cautions as well as optimism in regard to computer cultures, but they were largely received as part of a wave of praise for the possibilities of life on screen. They represent a wave that pictured the Web as a place not just for scientists or computer "geeks" (before geeks became chic), but for anyone seeking an exciting new space to explore, create and change the world.

The counterculture origins of much early digital culture work have had a lasting impact. This history in part accounts for a strong anti-establishment, anti-authoritarian streak in much "geek culture," ranging from the libertarian efforts of the open-source movement to political hackers and WikiLeakers. But where these early adopters touted the utopian possibilities of virtual communities (they created one of the first of these, the Bay Area's WELL—Whole Earth "Lectronic Link") and the exciting new kinds of identities possible via the Web, others, partly in response to this optimism, saw only dystopian possibilities. Critics expressed fears that humans would all become mindless drones lost in computer screens with little sense of the real world and little connection to others. In subsequent years and with wider use of the technologies, this two-sided exaggeration has largely given way to more modest assertions about the cultural impact of digital cultures. But it is not hard to this day to find cyberutopian and cyberdystopian screeds on the bookshelves or Amazon.com.

The countercultural, avant-garde Web slowly opened up into wider circles over the course of the early 1990s. In order for digital culture to become a significant phenomenon, two key technical things had to happen to make the Net more user friendly. The first huge step in this direction has been mentioned: The creation in 1990–1991 of the World Wide Web. When British physicist Tim Berners-Lee invented the interface that he dubbed the World Wide Web in 1989, he had little idea he was creating the means for billions of people to communicate. He was responding to a very practical problem that had developed in his place of work, CERN (originally Conseil Européen pour la Recherche Nucléaire), the foremost physics laboratory in the world (home to the fastest and most sophisticated atom-smashing particle accelerator, among other things). Berners-Lee wanted to find a better way for scientists at the lab to communicate, and feeling, as he put it, rather "desperate," he pulled together a bunch of software and networked hardware (using a NeXT computer created by Steve Jobs shortly after he was unceremoniously kicked out of his own company, Apple Computers), and out of that messy matrix emerged the World Wide Web (Berners-Lee 1999).

At the time, the name World Wide Web was a ridiculously ambitious one, but it has proven to be a prophetic one. Berners-Lee has consistently been one of the most important promoters of the ideas that the Internet should in fact be worldwide, that access to it is nothing less than a "human right" and that it should be regulated only technically with no censoring interference by governments or corporations (see **Net neutrality** in the Glossary). The crude browser that Berners-Lee and his younger French colleague, Robert Cailliau, came up with, was the great-great-great-grandparent of Chrome, Firefox, Safari, Opera and Internet Explorer, and all the others that came to be the main entry points to the Internet. Due in part perhaps to the accident of its naming, the World Wide Web started on a self-fulfilling prophecy of becoming an ever-expanding network of computers moving first slowly, then at breakneck pace, beyond the confines of the military and the scientific community. With hindsight, such a development seems inevitable, but it was far from obvious to anyone, including Berners-Lee, that the Web would gain anything even remotely resembling its current ubiquity.

The second key development, the point at which the Web truly became the hub of popular digital cultures, came in the mid-1990s with the invention of truly easy-to-use browsers. First Mosaic in 1993 broke the ground, and then 2 years later Netscape produced the first truly user-friendly and widely adopted browser. Ever more user-friendly Web browsers emerged in rapid succession. Where early navigation of the Net had required a fair amount of technical knowledge, new browsers made cyberspaces far more accessible. By 1996, close to 90 percent of Web traffic occurred through Netscape, with the other 10 percent mostly taken up by Microsoft's browser, Internet Explorer. But that year, Microsoft started including Internet Explorer as part of its basic software package, and the first of several browser wars was under way. While the details of who won and who lost in this and subsequent browser battles is of little consequence, the wars signaled recognition that the public Internet was a phenomenon here to stay (as late as 1995 Bill Gates had dismissed it as a passing fad), including as a space where corporate profits could be made.

Indeed, corporate profits define the next major stage of Internet growth, the commercialization or monetizing (making a profit) moment. Put bluntly, a sector of the corporate world, first in the US, then in pockets around the globe, realized that the Internet could be used not just for business communication, but for business, period. Some had recognized the commercial potential of the Net from the beginning, but full commercialization evolved slowly until the mid-1990s. Then came the phase first glorified, then vilified, as the "dot-com boom." Just as the utopian phase of the early, avant-garde Net proved to be overly optimistic, so too the commercial phase proved overly ambitious in its claims, and the dotcom boom eventually came to seem like a dot-*con* job when the dotcom bubble burst. But this phase set in motion the development of the Web as a site of commerce that has of course continued to grow. After recovering from the dotcom bust, e-commerce has steadily increased its presence in the world, becoming a very significant part of the Internet. Slowly but steadily companies such as Amazon and eBay began to prove that the Net could be a profitable place for business. But even after the dotcom boom-and-bust cycle ended, the commercialization of the Net has been something of a rollercoaster ride. Initially, many major media corporations believed that they could turn the Web into a pay-per-use broadcast medium like television. What they did not realize was that a significant portion of the population that had grown up on the free, open and frontier-like Internet was not willing to relinquish that freedom for corporate control. The anti-authoritarian component of the digital world was soon at war with the commercial version, and that war continues in a variety of ways today.

There is no doubt that giant media corporations control a great deal of the content of the Web. Initially, the Time Warner/AOL merger seemed to promise a transformation of the Net into just another form of corporate media. But just as the Web slipped out of the hands of the military, and then of scientists, and then of avant-gardists, it has eluded complete takeover by media moguls as well. A kind of uneasy truce, mixed with occasionally open warfare, characterizes the relation between the free Web and the monetized Web. And between the giant media corporations and the advocates of a wholly free Web, there are mixtures, including small businesses able to compete more easily with larger ones because of this cheap communication medium, and sites such as Google and YouTube that provide free search and upload spaces, respectively, but along with heavy injections of advertising.

The free Web spirit also continues to limit commercial uses of the Net in other ways. When television networks came to realize that charging for their shows on the Web would be widely resisted, they used digital space to intensify the popularity of their shows through overt and covert Net advertising, including encouraging development of fan sites that, thanks to new media capabilities, were far more intense and extensive than fan communities of the past (previously confined primarily to print and snail mail). Likewise, old media such as newspapers found that they had to offer at least some content on their new websites for free if they were to lure users into a relationship for which they would later pay. Search engines, the lifeblood of the Net, also had to find a medium ground. Initially attempts by Google, by far the world's most widely used search engine, to put advertising on their site met with a great deal of resistance, especially when advertising seemed to merge with pure search responses. Eventually they compromised by more clearly delineating paid from unpaid search responses, and lost credibility whenever it was rumored that search rankings could be manipulated for a price.

The next major phase of the Net, generally referred to as Web 2.0, intensified debate about control and commercialization of digital spaces. First used by Darcy diNucci, and popularized by Tim O'Reilly, the term is meant to designate a more interactive set of networked relationships. The Web has long been the center of most digital culture, but the features designated by the phrase "Web 2.0" represent the fact that it has become even more central. The main devices associated with digital culture—desktop, laptop and tablet computers, cellphones and video game consoles—now all have the capacity to be networked via the Web. That greater interconnection is in fact part of the definition of "Web 2.0", along with claims of greater personal and collective interactivity via things such as social media sites (Facebook, Snapchat, Pinterest), blogs and microblogs (e.g. Twitter, Tumblr), wikis, electronic self-publishing (WordPress, etc.), video sharing sites (You Tube, Vimeo), mashups, crowdsourcing and so on. Clearly many of these things were available before the phase called Web 2.0, and to the extent that the term represents a new phase of the Net at all it is one more of degree than absolute transformation (Tim Berners-Lee rejects the term as misleading jargon). But for the purposes of this book, the term is useful shorthand for ways in which the Web as a site of cultural production and exchange has expanded and intensified in recent years making questions about just what digital cultures are all about all the more important. And it is a term that has shaped how people think about the Web and digital culture, has shaped what some call the "technological imaginary," our collective images of what a given technology is and can be.

Each stage of the evolution of the Net has left its mark. Each new phase has incorporated rather than fully supplanting the previous phase, and each of these phases or moments in the history of the Internet(s) has left some impression that can be uncovered with a little archeological digging. Successive versions never fully erase previous iterations, and clearly the history of the Interwebs is still very much in progress.

⇥ FROM DREAM TO REALITY TO DREAM: PRODUCING DIGITAL STUFF

When we unwrap and pick up a shiny new high-tech device—a laptop, a smartphone, a tablet, a game console—we don't have to think much about how it came to be there in our hands. But understanding the process of production is as much a part of digital culture as analyzing the conversations generated by a blog post. Dozens of technical design decisions, intentional and accidental, enable and shape digital cultures. Technical decisions are always also social, political, economic and cultural decisions. The material objects—tablet computers, digital music players—are the result of many non-technical decisions that are laden with cultural import. Why did those decisions get made the way they did? What business pressures were involved? What social and political policy decisions shaped the technology? What cultural values were built into or left out of the design?

Who participated or was consulted in the design decisions, and who was not?

We know the names and think we know the digital dreamers who founded electronic corporations in their garages or brilliantly invented digital products that shook the world. We know names such as Steve Jobs, the zen genius of Apple Computers, Bill Gates, the once maligned, now heroically philanthropic genius behind Microsoft, Larry Page and Sergey Brin, the "do no evil" geniuses behind Google, and, of course, Mark Zuckerberg, the Harvard geek genius turned billionaire head of the Facebook empire. The media pays a lot of attention to the dreamers and digital stars, but far less is paid to the thousands of workers who make the visions of these "geniuses" become reality. Moving from the shiny new box containing the latest video game or tablet computer back in time to that object's creation reveals some far less shiny realities.

At the very top of the labor chain, there are some folks who no doubt embody the popular image of digital brainiacs sitting on sunny decks atop sleek steel and glass buildings sipping lattes and thinking up new digital gadgets and games. These are the heroes (and fewer heroines) of the industry, the ones every tech-savvy kid dreams of becoming the way every kid with basketball talent dreams of being an NBA star. But, as with the tiny elite of players who make it to the big leagues, this stratum of digital workers is a tiny group. This level also includes a small but essential corps of venture capitalists, the moneymen (and most are men) who finance start-ups and inject cash at key moments for existing corporations.

Just beneath the superstars of the digital production world, there are large numbers of mid-level executives who come to work in casual attire and enjoy the benefits of lovely digital campuses with cafés and playgrounds. This level is part of what has been described as a *brotopia* in Emily Chang's book of the same name, a brotherhood of young men who came to represent geek chic, a world that, while slowly changing due to intense pressure from women in tech, is still male-dominated (Chang 2018). Most of the rest of the workers who create the digital stuff wealthier folks love to consume face far different, considerably less pleasant work conditions.

While creating video games or hot new tech devices is the dream job of millions of young people, the realities of most production in the electronics industry are often more like a nightmare. Most of the second-tier production of computers, cellphones, apps and digital game software is done by hundreds of **microserfs** (Coupland 1995) in tiny cubicles working on some tiny part of a project of which many only have a tiny understanding. Few of these folks get to have substantial creative input into the products. Given the rapid obsolescence of much digital hardware and software, these workers also often face long hours to meet tight deadlines, while the relative glamour of a new industry only briefly compensates for often mediocre wages.

The largest tier are the assembly-line manual laborers who produce the microchips and other hardware components, or package (and package and package) the digital devices. Most of this labor force is terribly underpaid, overworked and often handling or breathing toxic materials without proper protective gear. While some of this work is still done in the Global North, the vast majority is done by women, men and children in the Global South. Some of this work, involving staring for hours into microscopes to check for irregularities in microchips, has led workers to severe eye injury or blindness. Ironically, and contrary to images of robots in electronic industry advertising (watch, for example, 2011 Droid commercials on YouTube), most of these high-tech devices require old-fashioned, painstaking hands-on assembly. While the two upper tiers continue to be dominated by males, this third tier is mostly composed of Third World women who are often stereotyped as more obedient employees (Margolis and Fisher 2006; Pellow and Park 2002).

The occasional exception to this production process often gets more attention than the truth of the daily grind. Just as in the film industry, occasionally a low-budget, independent film will strike gold and make a huge profit, so too independent game or app designers now and then have a big hit that once again animates the myth of the lone genius or the do-it-yourself entrepreneur striking it rich through imagination and perseverance. But the overwhelming reality of the electronic culture industry, like that of the mainstream Hollywood film industry with which it increasingly competes, is the story of a few major mega-conglomerate media corporations (in this case mostly console makers Nintendo, Sony and Microsoft) controlling the work produced by a handful of major "content providers" such as EA, Konami, Ubisoft, THQ and Activision. These larger companies tap into and absorb smaller game design studios, frequently siphoning off the most talented designers and bringing them into the conglomerated world. The impact of this process might be compared to how the mainstream music industry works. In order to keep selling music, the music industry must tap into emerging independent music trends. But it does so not to create real innovation, but only to turn real innovation into a more mundane mass marketable commodity for sale to pop audiences with less demanding tastes, but a desire for the thrill of the seemingly new. Just like the way punk or rap developed toned-down mainstream versions, but even more quickly, many significant innovations in game design are absorbed by game corp giants who generally dumb them down (Dyer-Witheford and de Peuter 2009).

This least well paid and often exploited level of the digital production world is, not surprisingly, the most invisible one. The world's increasing income inequality, a process accelerated by the economic and cultural forces that go by the name "globalization," is written all over the realms of digital production. Those actually producing what hip designers imagine often work for poverty wages in dangerous conditions. Many live crowded into dormitories in situations approaching slave conditions, often working 16-hour days, and, when production deadlines loom, non-stop for several days. Apart from the occasional scandal when workers in a computer assembly factory in China or Bangladesh commit suicide or die in a fire because they were literally locked into the factory, these workers do not get much attention. And when scandals bring them to public attention, their work conditions are dismissed as aberrations and swept from popular memory as easily as the mind cleansing in films such as *Eternal Sunshine of the Spotless Mind* or *Men in Black*.

China Watch (2013) reports that

> Apple has zero tolerance for lapses in the quality of its products. If a quality issue arises, Apple will do everything it can to have it corrected immediately. But a lower level of urgency apparently applies in responding to labor rights abuses. Despite its professed high standards for the treatment of Apple workers, serious labor violations have persisted year after year.

China Watch and other labor rights organizations find it difficult to believe claims by electronics corporations that they are unaware of working conditions in the factories of their subcontractors. Corporate executives often deploy a tactic made famous by corrupt politicians: Plausible deniability. CEOs for giant electronics corporations such as IBM, Apple, Microsoft, Intel and the like generally express outrage, briefly, and assert that they do not know what goes in their company's supply chain. Creating some distance between the corporation and its actual producers is quite deliberate, done for both legal and public relations protection, given the inevitability that awful conditions will be exposed at some point. When challenged to clean things up, electronics corporations invariably spin out some story about more careful monitoring, better conditions and so forth, while at the same time, again plausibly but ultimately dishonestly, claiming that because other companies do it too they can only improve things a small amount without being driven out of business (Pellow and Park 2002; Smith, Pellow and Sonnenfeld 2006).

Critics admit that a concern with competitiveness is a real thing, but counter that this means the industry as a whole must be targeted, rather than periodically singling out one electronics corporation for momentary public shaming. Some who uncritically praise global markets argue that these underpaid, overworked, often endangered laborers are nevertheless better off than before, when many of them were penniless peasants. There is surely a grain of truth in this regarding some workers in the high-tech economy. But critics ask the next question: Are worse and slightly better but still horrendous the only options? Can we do no better as makers of a global economy? These processes not only exploit workers in the Global South, but they also come home to roost in privileged places such as North America and Europe, where the wages of workers are driven down by employers threatening to outsource jobs to the cheaper labor markets of Bangladesh, Malaysia, Mexico or Ghana (Gabry 2011; Pellow and Park 2002; Smith et al. 2006).

A similar question about workers in both the less industrialized, less technologized Global South and the overdeveloped, over-teched Global North is why, if certain jobs are really so bad, so many people fight to get them? Again, critics respond, the answer is fairly simple: Given the choice of starving with no job or taking a bad job, anyone in need is going to opt for the bad job. The less simple follow-up questions are how is it that the world economy has produced so many dangerous jobs and such vast income inequalities, and, more important, how might various forces, including technological forces, be marshaled to improve worker conditions and economic fairness around the globe? How do you justify a wage ratio in which CEOs in the US make 355 times more than laborers, 105 times more in Sweden or in Japan a "mere" 55 times more? The disparity among countries alone reveals that there is nothing natural or inevitable about this degree of inequality.

The electronics industry is by no means the only one relying upon exploitative labor practices, but electronics is in many respects the leading contemporary industry and thus reform of its practices would reverberate through the entire global economy. There are hundreds of groups and thousands of people working to provide more humane alternatives to current conditions. Politicians and govern-ment workers, educational institutions, unions and other worker soli-darity organizations and social protest movements in every part of the globe are working diligently to create a more equitable economy. But they are up against immensely powerful, highly mobile corporations, often supported by governments, with vast resources to fight against any reform that represents even the smallest threat to their profits. In yet another twist of the Internet plot, however, those very devices and processes created by high-tech corporations have provided more economical, accessible and communicatively richer means to orga-nize to resist corporate exploitation. It is quite possible to appreciate the designers of high-tech gadgets, cool apps and hot video games without ignoring the human costs of putting those designs into exis-tence. What is important to keep in mind is that valuing the hip entrepreneurs of digital production more than those who materially produce the things that make cybercultures possible is a political choice with political consequences for millions of people. Pressure to reform by providing better pay and more humane, safer work envi-ronments can only work when pressed upon the entire realm of elec-tronic production. And that pressure will have to come from many quarters, social movement activists, unions (local and transnational), governments, non-governmental organizations (NGOs) and consum-ers unwilling to buy devices produced by near-slave labor. Ironically and fortunately, the technology at the heart of all this process, the Internet, is a near perfect tool to organize and publicize such efforts to change the system.

⏩ MAKER CULTURE PRODUCTION: THE OPEN SOURCE DO-IT-YOURSELF DIGITAL WORLD

A fourth tier or category of digital culture production includes all the producers outside of the mainstream, large-scale digital production companies and processes. They fall into a couple of categories that might be summed up as users who augment mainstream digital pro-duction and DIY makers who challenge that increasingly monopolis-tic system led by major electronics corporations.

One of the most common claims about new media compared with old is that they are highly interactive and participatory. Indeed, "interactive" and "participatory" were cited as among the key com-ponents distinguishing the supposedly new Web 2.0 from the earlier Web. But people are questioning what constitutes *meaningful* inter-activity, and asking who benefits from most kinds of interactivity as defined by the major digital corporations. Interactivity and true power are not the same thing in digital worlds. To many in a new generation of users, much of this kind of interactivity seems like little more than cosmetic changes atop a template deeply controlled by the corporate overlords of the Net.

User-generated content has always been part of the Net, but in the early twenty-first century new technologies and broadband capabilities greatly expanded that potential. One critic coined the word **prosuming** (producing/consuming), another the equally awkward term "produsing" (producing/using) to name the process by which culture consumers have become culture producers via the Web. User-uploaded videos, iReports for major media outlets such as cable news networks, thousands of online product reviews and a host of other consumer-generated content represent what some see as a far more democratically produced cultural content. Undoubtedly digital cultures offer exciting new forms of interaction. An ordinary individual can be an eye-witness reporter, alerting the world to breaking news of a natural disaster or a political crisis. A layperson can act as a scientist or scholar participating in a crowd sourced research project. An amateur Sherlock can go online to help detectives solve real-world crimes. Certainly these forms of digital participation are popular and have impact in enriching lives and in diversifying the overall content of the Web. YouTube users generate more video content daily than all of network television in its entire history. Sheer volume, again, makes it very hard to characterize the nature and impact of such user generated cultural production.

Notwithstanding the positive side of some digital interactivity, others note that much of it primarily benefits the same few huge corporations that dominate the digital market. They argue that this is more con- than pro-suming. It underwrites immense profits for major corporations, not only ones such as YouTube and Amazon but also for companies whose products are endorsed, sometimes honestly, sometimes not, via online reviews and Facebook "likes." Some have critiqued this as merely the next step in product branding wherein companies, having already turned consumers into walking billboard advertisements through ubiquitous logos on clothes, are now going a step further by turning them into an unpaid labor force of content producers and advertisers. Consumer endorsements, real and fictionalized, have long been a part of advertising, but the Web has turned this form into a much larger phenomenon, though one lacking the compensation given to more formal endorsers (Karaganis 2007; Schäfer 2011).

No one denies that there can be something quite empowering in uploading cultural material of one's own creation onto the Web. But the more thoughtful realize that this kind of participatory culture does not seriously challenge the content dominance of the main *culture industries* (the major media corporations). The traditional giant culture-producing corporations have moved quickly to incorporate and profit from user-generated content. As Tobias Schäfer summarizes, so far it is "evident the new [digital media] enterprises emerge and gain control over cultural production and intellectual property in a manner very similar to the monopolistic media corporations of the twentieth century" (Schäfer 2011). This is hardly surprising since some of those "new" monopolistic media enterprises are the same old ones: Time Warner, Bertelsmann, NewsCorp/Wall Street Journal (owner now of Tumblr) and once idealistic new media corps such as Google that seem to have forgotten their promise to "do no evil" (Hillis, Petit and Jarrett 2013; Jarrett 2008; McChesney 2013; Schäfer 2011; Vaidhyanathan 2011).

As the once wide-open Net falls more and more into the hands of a small group of monopolistic digital corporations, the push for alternatives is growing. More and more young people are learning to code in school and out, and few of them dream of jobs in giant, impersonal, profit-distorted companies. Many see both the negative side of the production process and the increasingly standardized, unimaginative digital culture these behemoths are creating. A wider culture of local production—in food, in the arts, in virtually every aspect of life–is driving a major revolt against the big five digital companies. Crowdsourcing, an idea that originally seemed exciting and democratic, often leads to sameness and blandness, though it has also created some stunning things.

In response, a large do-it-yourself **maker culture** has arisen, assisted by some new technologies alongside new social spaces and attitudes. Many new community centers and other collective spaces (FabLabs, Makerspaces, Innovation Stations, etc.) have sprung up to encourage collaboration and mutual learning in the techniques of DIY digital production. Sites such as Code Academy make *coding* available to a very wide group of people, Git hub pushes *open-source software* that challenges expensive corporate software, low cost peer-to-peer sharing social media is an alternative to corporate media, various DIY production tools demystify digital processes, and *3D printing* represents the possibility of a far more decentralized, locally varied production process. In some ways maker culture is returning to the original meaning of "hacker." Before the term was co-opted to describe illegal activity, "hacking" meant digital improvisation, creative problem-solving and new ways to be creative.

Given an emphasis on the local and on variety, it is difficult to generalize about maker culture(s), but there are certain values that many makers share, including perhaps most crucially sharing itself. In fact one of the terms used to talk about maker culture(s) was the "sharing economy," though the term was itself quickly co-opted by commercial interests. But sharing and trading of software, templates, skills and much cultural production itself via barter, along with the reuse and recycling of materials, are important in most maker cultures. Maker fairs, hackathons (collaborative coding event often in support of social causes), game jams (game making contests) and similar events deepen networking communities. **Mesh media networks** (locally linked rather than going through the Internet) offer an alternative to the giant social media companies such as Facebook, Snapchat and Instagram. *Bandcamp* challenges commercial music sites such as Apple Music and Google Play Music by connecting listeners directly to artists without corporate intermediaries; *Patreon* similarly connects visual artists directly to supporters, bypassing the mainstream art market. Throughout maker culture there is a preference for *crowdfunding* instead of reliance upon corporate forces that organize and standardize taste, while taking a large chunk of the profits that might otherwise go to creators. Some argue for barter networks or cryptocurrencies to challenge the giant banks and financial networks. Taken together, these and related developments add up to the opportunity to create a whole new *sustainable economy* not dominated by giant corporations and polluting energy sources (Boler and Ratto 2014).

New, alternative cultural forms are up against deeply entrenched, fabulously well-funded existing cultural production monopolies. The old adage that the only people with true freedom of the press are the people who own presses is equally true in a slightly different way regarding digital culture. While in some sense, all users *own* the Web, the power of an individual not working for a large media corporation to disseminate cultural offerings to the Net's audience clearly pales alongside Viacom's ability to do so, especially if government rules continue to favor giant digital corporations and refuse to challenge the increasingly monopolistic nature of companies such as Google/ Alphabet, Facebook and Amazon. The occasional exception to the rule—the blog comment or video that goes viral—serves mostly to keep alive the fantasy of a level playing field, rather like the way that lotteries keep alive the highly unlikely possibility that tomorrow you may be a multi-millionaire. A far more level playing field is indeed a potential within the capabilities of the Net, but it is an as yet mostly unfulfilled potential that will take collective social action, not just individual luck, to fully realize.

DIY/maker culture is now a global phenomenon, and a growing one. Makers are increasingly the source of innovation in the digital world (Hertz 2014). At its most ambitious, maker culture imagines a major transformation of the world's economy, one that challenges the concentration of power in central governments and a few corporations. Just as alternative energy sources such as wind, solar, geothermal, biopower and others that can be locally controlled are challenging centralized, high-polluting fossil fuels, 3D printing offers an equally decentralized alternative to huge, monopolistic, often socially alienating and environmentally damaging factories. And at the level of cultural creation, an open-source DIY Web, based on a return to Net neutrality principles, promises far more interesting, varied and rich musical, visual and written art, and more vibrant cultures overall. Like the locavore movement in food production and consumption, digital maker culture promises a more mind-nourishing and soul-satisfying fare. Advocates of what some call *critical maker culture* understand the need to work collectively to break up digital monopolies at the same time that they develop locally based, environmentally sustainable and more democratic alternatives. Tied into long-standing dissatisfaction with corporate globalization, various non-market and mixed market/cooperative models are being widely embraced around the globe, which could move maker culture from the margins to the heart of society (Alperovitz and Bhatt 2013; Boler and Ratto 2014; Raworth 2017).

⊡ CLEAN ROOMS OR "DARK SATANIC MILLS"? TOXIC PRODUCTION E-WASTE AND ENVIRONMENTAL JUSTICE

Perhaps the biggest lie told about the electronics industry is that it is a "clean" business (companies widely circulate images of clean rooms where workers in white suits carefully handle precious circuit boards). While when looking at corporate headquarters, the industry *looks* clean—sleek white buildings, no smoke stacks billowing pollution up into the air—in fact both the manufacture and the disposal of electronic devices involve serious dangers to people and the environment. Looked at more closely, the electronics industry is not that far from what the poet William Blake called the "dark satanic mills" of nineteenth-century industrial production. It is no coincidence that large chunks of major electronic production sites are among the most polluted places on the planet. In Silicon Valley alone, birthplace of the electronics industry, there are 30 "Superfund sites," representing the US Environmental Protection Agency's highest level of toxic contamination (*Silicon Valley Toxics Coalition* n.d.). With digital devices now outnumbering humans on the planet, the situation is worsening.

In fact, at every stage—mining for components, assembly, use, disassembly—electronics has proven to be an extremely environmentally damaging industry. Mining for key minerals, and toxic assembly and disassembly processes, endanger the lives of workers, and toxic **e-waste** (electronic waste) presents major health issues for people and the environment all around the globe. In addition, the extensive use of electricity-hogging digital devices has a very high cost in energy resources, thus contributing to global climate change.

Computers, monitors, game consoles, cellphones, printers, cables and most other e-devices and peripherals contain significant amounts of toxic, often carcinogenic, elements. These include arsenic, barium, beryllium, bromated flame retardants such as polybromated biphenyl, cadmium, chlorofluorocarbons, chromium, copper, dioxins and furans, lead, mercury, phthalates, polychlorinated biphenyls (PCBs), polyvinyl chloride (PVC), which when burned create hydrogen chloride gas, and selenium, to name a few. A list of the hundreds of dangerous elements in high-tech devices, along with specific health hazards attached to each, would take up much of the rest of this book. Some of these toxins affect the workers who assemble devices, some can impact users, all impact those who disassemble devices (especially when components are burned), and all of us, though hardly equally, are impacted by landfills piling up obsolete e-devices that can leach into local water supplies and agricultural lands, as well as incinerators that send this material into the air where they can potentially drift over any community (Grossman 2007).

There is also danger in some of the mining that unearths the minerals used in digital devices. The case of one of these minerals is comparable to the "blood diamond" controversy in South Africa, implicated in genocidal war in the Congo surrounding the mining of coltan (used in the capacitors found in almost every kind of digital device) (Snow n.d.). Thousands, including many children, have died in the coltan wars, and ultimately those lives are lives lost to our electronic pleasure. After extraction, the assembly process of electronic devices likewise often takes place under horrendous conditions.

Among the most troubling of those conditions is failure to protect workers from exposure to dangerous chemicals. Conditions in Silicon Valley have historically been deeply inadequate, and conditions in other parts of the world are even worse (Pellow and Park 2002). Pictures of regimented rows of Chinese workers wearing medical gowns while assembling digital devices might suggest they are being protected, but in fact the gowns are to protect the chips and circuit boards from contamination by humans. In Europe, there are strong regulations on the books that putatively protect workers from exposure, but evidence makes clear those rules have frequently been bent or broken by less than scrupulous producers, and US rules are far more lax. And when those regulations become even mildly financially burdensome to electronics corporations, they generally export assembly jobs to countries with far more lax, or non-existent, protections for workers and the environment. This production process has been critically examined in satiric game form by Molleindustria's Phone Story (*Phone Story* 2011). This game was removed by Apple after 3 days in its App Store, no doubt causing more controversy and bad publicity for the company than the game itself. But there is no reason to put the blame just on Apple Computers; the entire industry contributes to these horrendously hazardous work conditions and environmental impacts.

While the appearance in recent years of electronic recycling depots is generally a good thing, they may give a false sense that e-waste is being dealt with seriously. In fact, the rapid obsolescence that digital products undergo (the average user life of a cellphone is less than 18 months, a laptop 2 years) has led to massive amounts of toxic waste, and a variety of failures to deal responsibly with that waste has compounded the problem. Overall, 50 million tons of electronic waste was produced in 2017, and over 70 million tons a year is expected by 2020. Less than 15 percent of that waste is recycled and a large percentage that is recycled is done so inadequately, in terms of handling the toxic materials and/or location of disposal sites. The US is the only industrialized country that has not ratified the Basel Convention, the international agreement that makes it illegal to export toxic waste. The US alone has over 50,000,000 obsolete computers, and US consumers toss away over 1,000,000 cellphones every year. Similar figures exist for Europe, Australia (30 million computers a year), the UK (900,000 tons annually of e-waste), Japan, China (70 million cellphones a year) and other major users of technology have proportionately comparable amounts of e-waste. E-waste is the fastest growing contributor to municipal landfill toxicity worldwide.

And all these figures are growing at a rate of between 4 percent and 10 percent per annum. The rapid economic development of India and China, two nations far from the saturation point in terms of digital devices, will greatly deepen the problem.

As with all other aspects of digital culture, the e-waste problem shifts with changes in digital design and marketing. While playing a

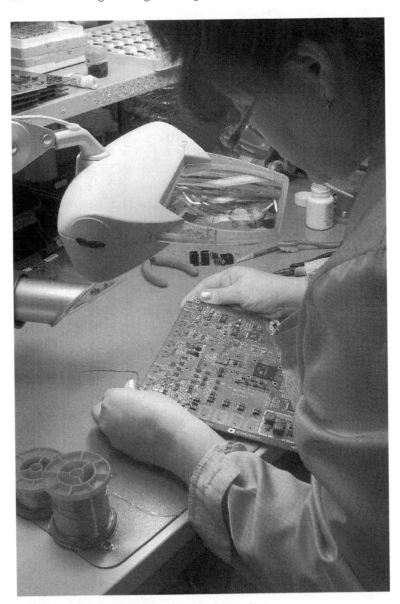

FIGURE 2.1 *High tech, handmade (Courtesy of shutterstock.com)*

positive role in expanding Net access to previously digitally deprived populations, the spread of smartphones around the entire globe threatens to increase the e-waste problem exponentially. The fact that the electronics industry has honed to an art form the practice of **planned obsolescence** (the purposeful creation of products that go out of date quickly to assure new sales) likewise compounds the problem (Slade 2007). The fast rate of obsolescence not only impacts the volume of electronic waste, but also decreases its chances of being recycled. For example, for several years recycling glass from computer monitors and TV sets was sufficiently lucrative to be a viable business. But the arrival of LCD, plasma and other flat screen technologies decimated that particular terrain of recycling, such that many former recyclers are now illegally dumping their old toxic TVs (Urbina 2013).

Electronics recycling and reuse efforts have a considerably mixed history. Much recycling has been done illegally, with few safeguards for those handling the materials. Reuse of devices by passing them down the line to less privileged users has grown over the years. But reuse is a mixed blessing environmentally in that older devices sent to less technologically developed countries or poorer areas of developed countries (with good intentions by charitable organizations) are generally more toxic than newer ones currently in use among wealthier consumers. This becomes yet another way in which the e-waste problem falls unevenly on poorer populations in the world.

As with so much of the world's pollution, the burden of e-waste falls upon the less developed world, while the vast majority of the waste results from use in the overdeveloped world, especially North America, Japan and Europe. The issue is therefore not only an environmental issue, but very much an environmental justice issue. Environmental justice is the branch of environmentalism that documents and fights against the fact that environmental hazards are far more prevalent in working-class neighborhoods and neighborhoods with high concentrations of people of color in the Global North, and in the poorest communities of the Global South. The vast majority of workers endangered by e-waste around the globe are the poor, women and people of color, because they do most of the toxic assembly and because, as noted, most of the e-waste is exported from the developed world and dumped on the Global South, where protections for disassemblers are largely non-existent. Most of the toxic waste from electronic devices ends up leaching into the land, air and water in the poorest parts of Africa, India, China and other parts of the less industrialized world. Go to YouTube and punch in "e-waste" and you will come face-to-face with countless images of young children, pregnant women and all other manner of human beings breathing toxic fumes, handling dangerous chemicals and generally being subjected to the deadly impact of the digitized lives of others they will never meet.

The Global North is not free of these problems either, though once again the greater burden falls on people of color there too. Many factories in Europe and the US employ immigrants at extremely low wages and often do not provide safety materials in all languages spoken by workers. Some disassembly work in the US is done under seriously unprotected conditions by free or nominally paid prison labor, a labor force that is disproportionately non-white, given deep racial inequities in the American economy and justice system. In the US, most incinerators used to burn toxic waste are in poor, mostly African American and Latino neighborhoods, or on Native American reservations. In parts of India, China and Africa incineration takes place not in facilities designed for that purpose, but in open fires in cities and villages where toxic smoke drifts through the streets (Pellow and Park 2002). It is far from unusual for pregnant women and very young children to be working near these toxic fumes for hours at a time. Birth defects, neurological disorders and a host of other diseases result from this process of recovering precious metals from digital devices.

In addition to electronic waste, vast amounts of electricity are consumed by various proliferating forms of computing, mobile

FIGURE 2.2 *A pile of circuit boards for recycling (Courtesy of shutterstock.com)*

phoning and gaming. For example, as far back as 2006 Nicholas Carr pointed out that in

> *Second Life*—whose parallel universe, though free at the most basic level, is populated by the avatars of Europeans, North American, and Japanese with annual real life incomes of $45,000 or more—the average [virtual] resident uses about 1,752 kilowatts of electricity a year . . . and generates CO_2 emissions equivalent to a 2,300 mile journey in an SUV.
>
> (Carr 2006)

And *Second Life* is just one of the many hundreds of large, online territories. Multiply that by multiuser online game sites, console games and the rest of the Web, and we are talking about a vast increase in the amount of directly and indirectly polluting energy used in a world deeply threatened by global climate change. If the Internet were a country, it would be the fifth largest consumer of energy in the world. Google alone uses as much energy as the entire nation of Turkey (Oghia 2017).

Many people—from engineers to artists to activists—are working on these issues. More efficient (digital) energy monitoring devices can be of some help, as well more efficient batteries for storing solar and wind-generated energy. Important **green computing** or sustainable IT efforts are also under way, due in large part to increasingly bad publicity that e-waste has received that has in turn led to pressure from consumers (Hilty 2008; Tomlinson 2010). It is already possible to build digital devices that have far fewer toxic components, that are more truly recyclable and more energy-efficient. Green computer research is also attempting to make devices more energy efficient, and more broadly digital technologies such as *smart grids* and *green grids* have the potential to make energy use overall more efficient (The Green Grid n.d.). But efforts to shift to less toxic materials for digital devices can be expensive, and few large electronics firms are willing to bear the costs. Perhaps they underestimate the environmental consciousness of consumers, who, if made aware of the environmental costs, might well be willing to pay a bit more for their e-devices until mass production brings the costs of green digital technologies in line closer to the costs of currently toxic ones.

Artists have brought attention to the issues in a variety of ways, from artworks made from recycled computer parts to esthetic clean-up art that creatively restores environments damaged by e-waste. Some artists have made e-waste a theme of their work, as for example in the photography of Chris Jordan, who has produced images that seem initially quite beautiful but upon closer inspection reveal the massive problem of e-waste dumping (Jordan n.d.). Use of recycled electronic components by artists such as Marion Martinez can both raise awareness of the e-waste problem, and suggest the need for creative solutions. Martinez, by using e-waste such as recycled circuit boards to create *chicana futurist techna arte* related to her Latina and Native heritage, evokes environmental stewardship as a spiritual value (Martinez n.d.). Some artists reshape the environment more directly through *environmental restoration artworks*, some of which, like the Gardening Superfund Sites project in Silicon Valley, have incorporated e-waste (*Gardening Superfund Sites* n.d.). Activists have also shown creativity through things such as *eco-toxic tours*, a somewhat satiric variation on eco-tourism that points up environmental hazards such as e-waste present around the globe.

Numerous non-governmental environmental organizations and environmental justice movement groups include e-waste in their work (Gabry 2011; Pellow and Park 2002). They continue to pressure governments for better waste regulations, more effective recycling programs, greater protection for assembly and disassembly workers and less toxic, more efficient devices, among other issues. In yet another ironic twist of the digital world, much of this work is carried out via the World Wide Web and using various kinds of digital devices. Environmentalisms in general, and environmental justice efforts in particular, have a significant online presence (see *cultural-politics.net/environmental_justice*). These efforts show promise, but as with so many environmental issues time seems to be running out, and much more is needed as unsustainable electronic production expands, threatening thousands of lives, rendering many environments uninhabitable and contributing significantly to overall environmental degradation and global climate change.

3

What's New about Digitized Identities?

Mobile Bodies, Online Disguise, Cyberbullying and Virtual Communities

Somewhere between the old adage "there's nothing new under the sun" and the commercial hype around every newly available app being a "revolution," the truth about what is importantly new about our increasingly digitized lives is revealing itself. Given the thousands of years of human history, it is in fact difficult to find wholly unprecedented experiences. But over that same history technologies have often provided the means for (while not wholly determining) large-scale transformations of human existence. As mentioned before, a number of scholars suggest there have been four major revolutions in human communication: The age of spoken language; the age of writing; the age of the printing press; and the age of mass mediated communication. Some divide this last stage into two, with old media (TV, radio, film) distinguished as a stage from new digital media of communication. Given that the digital age is only a few decades old, its place in the many thousand years of human history is clearly still emerging. But one of the clearer aspects of the digital age is that it entails a very rapid pace of change, so it is not too soon to speculate on what new things it is quickly bringing to the longer human story.

In looking at our developing digital age, I would put the general situation as follows: While there are few if any areas of cultural life solely or wholly created or determined by digital media, there are few if any areas of cultural life that have not been reshaped to one degree or another by digital media. There are at least four interrelated arenas of transformation impacted by digital technologies: Changes in the kind of devices with which we communicate (from landlines to smart phones, TVs to laptops, books to ebooks); changes in the relation among media (with TV, film, radio and print culture increasingly absorbed into online digital culture), accompanied by an increased ability to create media or talk back to media via DIY and interactivity; changes in how we interact with social systems, especially the economy (e-business, online shopping, new electronic corporations dominating Wall Street), and politics (political campaigns and governance waged via social media, info-bots and online fake news); and changes in our personal lives, as many are increasingly centered on digitized versions of these other three factors, including more and more of our activities and interactions (friendships, dating, jobs, banking, shopping, gaming and recreation) occurring in digital spaces and via digital devices.

Among the overarching elements brought forth by digitization that are impacting all these arenas is an enormously sped-up rate of change. Many changes take the form of augmented speed, ease and/or scope. In terms of communicating, the speed, range and cost of communication has improved, making it possible to connect with people all over the globe instantaneously and interactively at far lower cost than ever before. Increase in scope is clearly apparent in things such as the sheer amount of information available to those with online access. The amount of information potentially available at our fingertips (literally) has grown exponentially. It is as if we had given every Web user the equivalent of hundreds of encyclopedias.

These changes in technical capacity, speed and scale are clear. What is less clear is what the vast array of humans are doing with these new capacities. The short answer is that they are doing all the things that they have done before—making friends, making love, making money, making art, making protests, making war, making terror. But because the medium is (part of) the message, each of those makings has been changed to one degree or another by digital mediation. In many cases, the nature of those changes remains hotly debated. That is why I pose so many questions in this book.

In this chapter I want to focus on the issue of newness in relation to questions of personal identity and interpersonal relationships. Are we being deeply changed in who we are by the mechanisms of digital life? Do we behave differently toward others in online spaces? Do factors such as disguising our real identity or being anonymous online change how we behave, for good or ill? How do things such as *trolling, harassing* and *cyberbullying* differ from behavior offline? Are our interpersonal relationships growing more open or becoming more superficial? Are *virtual communities* really communities at all? Is the general sense of our lives as *globally connected and mobile* mostly a source of pleasure about the range of possibilities or anxiety about the loss of a core identity?

⊟ IS THERE A VIRTUAL WORLD/REAL WORLD DIVIDE?

Not surprisingly, given the vast number of people who now engage with digital media and the varying types and degrees of that engagement, there are not many generalizations one can make about the impact of digital life on identity. But there are a few patterns that are fairly pervasive. There are also probably even more myths or hyped claims about digitized life that don't hold up under scrutiny. Much of the *cyberbole* (hyperbole about cyber things; Woolgar 2003) stems from too stark a set of claims about the inherent difference between online life and away from screen life.

One of the overarching questions regarding the extent to which digital culture is significantly new and different circles around the idea of a *real world/virtual world divide*. This supposed divide has been one of the ways we fail to make good sense of the digital world, even one of the ways we make nonsense of it. Imagining a rigid real world/virtual world divide is problematic in a number of ways. Much of the problem stems from inadequate conceptual terms. One of the most enduring terms used to describe the world created by the Internet and related digital domains is the term "cyberspace." Recall that the term came into the English language via a science fiction novel, William Gibson's *Neuromancer* (1984). The book was prophetic in the sense that it described an online world that in some respects resembled the online world we later came to know (even though Gibson had never been on the then-nascent Web when he wrote the novel). But more important than the prophetic element was the power of the word. "Cyberspace" quickly caught on as the name for the place created by electronic communication. It became a ubiquitous term (and therefore perhaps part of a *self-fulfilling* prophecy in some ways), but it has also been very misleading. It is, after all, as its origin in a work of fiction should remind us, only a metaphor. In fact, Gibson points us in this direction by defining cyberspace as a

> consensual hallucination experienced daily by billions of legitimate operators, in every nation . . . A graphic representation of

data abstracted from the banks of every computer in the human system. Unthinkable complexity. Lines of light ranged in the non-space of the mind, clusters and constellations of data. Like city lights, receding.

(Gibson 1984: 69)

A major problem with this metaphor resides in the word "abstracted." "Cyberspace," or its cousin terms, such as "virtual space" or "digital space," tends to cut these spaces off from their connection to their supposed opposite, "the real world." While cyberspace doesn't exist in precisely the same way that Montréal or Melbourne or Mogadishu exist, it does have a physical, geographical basis that is far from abstract. Metaphors such as "cyberspace" tend to hide the Net's physical existence in favor of its imaginary existence. While cities and countries are also in a sense imagined places, we generally imagine their geographic location in a way that is more grounded, literally, than is our imagination of cyberspace. In the broadest sense, the geography of the Internet is three things at once: The place from which the user is accessing it, the user's experiences online in that space and a largely invisible space of connected servers, data centers and individual computers that enable the experience. We often forget the first of these spaces (lost in cyberspace), and seldom think much about the third space (because its materiality is also subsumed by our online experiences). This makes cyberspace a somewhat different kind of place, but it is still a place in the world. Moreover, as Mark Hansen notes, for example, we *filter* digital images through our body-mind such that we are never really *in* a digital reality (Hansen 2004). In some sense, we are always living a partly virtual life offline too, given the way our sensory system processes information from outside our bodies. The extent to which we process digitized information and digitized experiences differently from other kinds is much debated.

In a very real sense, all human reality is virtual reality. But not all virtual realities are the same. The experience of being lost in imaginary space is one not unique to this medium. Just as the name San Francisco calls up different images for each of us depending on our knowledge of that real, imagined city, there are as many cyberspaces as there are users of networked electronic communication devices. The difference is that few of us imagine cyberspace's geography in any physical way; its geographic grounding is weirdly dispersed and invisible, with most of us imagining it rather abstractly like Gibson's consensual hallucination.

As Andrew Blum puts it, playing on the term "ethernet," we misleadingly tend to think more in terms of "ether" than "Net" (Blum 2013). The seemingly placeless, ethereal world of the Web is not possible without millions of very earthbound terminals and CPUs, hundreds of thousands of miles of cords and fiber optic cables, thousands of Wi-Fi towers, hundreds of huge warehouses full of servers, millions of routers and switches, arrayed as a whole panoply of engineering esoterica like Dense Wavelength Division Multiplexing terminals and regen sites (see Figure 3.1). No matter how lost we may get imaginatively in cyberspaces, those seemingly virtual spaces are connected to this massive array of material objects anchored in geographically specific places. But, almost as if it were ashamed of the concrete reality behind the illusion of empty cyberspace, the electronic communication industry deeply buries behind secret closed doors much of this infrastructure. (For a glimpse inside, see the short documentary "Bundled, Buried and Behind Closed Doors" [Mendelsohn 2011] and visit Google's rather sanitized and aestheticized Data Centers Gallery [Google Data Centers Gallery n.d.].) This process of making the material basis invisible has negative consequences in terms of our ability to connect to the labor force that makes the illusion of disembodied cyberspace possible, and the environmental consequences of our digitized activities, as explored in Chapter 2.

This leads us back to the much used (and abused) terms in the title of this section, the *real world* and the *virtual world*. While this distinction is in certain respects unavoidable, it can also be deeply misleading. It is misleading because no one ever exists only in the virtual, only in cyberspace. As suggested above, we are always somewhere in the real world (even if we are moving through it with mobile smartphones in hand), using physical devices networked to other physical devices, whenever we imaginatively experience ourselves to be in a virtual world. Now, depending on the degree of *immersion* we feel, that sense of otherworldliness may be subtle or very strong. And it is important to take that illusion of virtuality seriously; it *is* to some degree a new kind of experience. But it is also not wholly new (whenever we read a novel we also enter a virtual world, just not a digitally delivered one). So, a key to studying virtual worlds is to remind users that they are never just in a virtual world, but also always in the material one. The dualism of real world/virtual world is wrong in both directions. The virtual world is part of the real world, and the real world is part of the virtual one. The founders of the widely-used file sharing site Pirate Bay (subject, like Napster before them, to

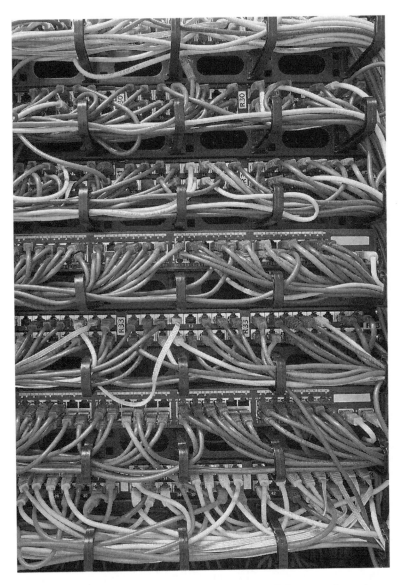

FIGURE 3.1 *A bit of the material Internet (Courtesy of shutterstock.com)*

a lawsuit regarding the issue of legal vs. illegal downloading) prefer the term "away from keyboard" life, noting that "the Internet is for real" (Klose 2013). For the purposes of this book, I will mostly use the term "online" to name these spaces, because it is the most commonly used term and is a somewhat more neutral term in that it merely designates connection to the Internet without unduly characterizing the nature of that connection. But when you read the word, please imagine "scare quotes" around it, because we are always in an offline world while online, such that the notion of two worlds is ultimately a false one.

Another reason to question the real world/virtual world concept is that, to a very large degree, the online world is a reflection of the offline world. But mirrored reflections are always distorting, from the basic fact that they show things in reverse to the huge, deeply weird reflections of funhouse mirrors. And with regard to digitally mediated worlds, the degree to which those reflections differ from offline representations can vary a little or a great deal. That is to say the mirroring is a range, with some parts of online reality differing little from offline, while others may be deeply different, and with many aspects in between. Sorting out this range, finding what has and has not changed in moving from non-digital to digital spaces is a major part of the work of not only this chapter but this book as a whole. The reflecting and refracting medium matters a great deal, but in another sense it is the same world whether represented via a digital medium or face-to-face. In general, if you don't like what you find on the Web, don't just blame the online world; blame the offline world out of which it came. There are many things unique to digital cultures; if there were not we wouldn't need this book. But that uniqueness is not otherworldly, it is this-worldly.

Much of the hype surrounding digital cultures, especially games and virtual reality simulators, is that they are deeply immersive in wholly new and dangerous ways. The assumption here is that users/players lose themselves in virtual worlds as never before in human history. Yet from ancient story telling around campfires to novels to movies, immersion in fictional worlds has always been a part of human experience. Might it be as immersive or even more immersive to enact scenes from a story where your own imagination fills in the details, rather than having them digitally simulated? Neuroscience may give us the answer to this question, but the research on the topic of immersion is immensely complex. The term turns out to have no stable meaning and many different dimensions that are hard to measure (Madigan 2010). This again reminds us that claims of newness or uniqueness regarding digitized experiences need to be approached carefully.

As discussed, when a technology is newly minted it often seems quite strange. In its early years, the Web was experienced as a very weird, almost miraculous space, or place. But over time (and in the case of new media the amount of time seems to be growing shorter and shorter), the new becomes ordinary, becomes taken for granted as just part of our world. This is part of what scholars call the **domestication of technology**, the process by which things that initially seem new and wild can quickly become familiar. All users have had that experience to some degree, and at this point in the evolution of digitized life, domestication has occurred pretty widely. So-called *early adopters*, many of whom seek out truly new things to do with new technologies, give way over time to more and more conventional users who subsume the new into older patterns of interaction. Domestication refers in common parlance to the home, and that is a convenient way to think about this process: It is becoming "at home with" the technology. In this case, domestication included the literal movement of digital devices from schools and offices into the home (into domestic space) partly via smaller and smaller devices, from bulky to smaller desktop computers to laptops and smartphones. Domestication is also an ongoing historical process, one that is repeated whenever a new group of users encounters a new technology, and whenever a group of existing users encounters a newer technology (as in the move from dumbphones to smartphones, where telephone-like communication was augmented by communication with the Web and other features of the Net).

Scholars of all things digital caution also against thinking of a particular device such as the cellphone as one thing that has gone through changes and variations (symbolized by physical transformation from devices the size of a cat to ones that now fit into the palm of your hand). Lisa Gitelman, for example, in her book *Always Already New* (2006), argues that we should not think of the telephone or even the cellphone as one "thing" that has changed over time (in size, shape, features and functions), but rather as something like an evolving process. Much the same can be said about many other forms of digital technology. They make sense more as processes than as things, or at least as a series of things, not one thing. Specificity in time (history) and place (geography) and social context (culture) all matter greatly in talking about ICTs. The danger in these kinds of domestication processes is that they can lead us to stop asking questions about what we really want and need from our technological devices, and whether they are enhancing or harming the parts of our lives they touch.

⧉ IS LIFE ONLINE A MOBILE MASQUERADE?

While, as I've argued, the strict real world/virtual world split does not hold up under scrutiny, being online can *feel* quite different from being offline, and there is little doubt that many online experiences change lives in significant ways. Even though the real world/virtual world distinction is misleading, there *are* clearly ways in which life online is different, if not absolutely new. One key area of interest surrounds the claim that cultural identities in the Internet era are becoming less stable, more mobile and malleable than they have been in the past, and that ICTs are playing a role in that destabiliza-tion. This claim has especially been made in relation to young people whose identities have not yet fully formed, and whose immersion in digital culture is often deeper (Stald 2008). Previous forms of mass communication already added complexity to contemporary life and weakened some traditional kinds of social identities, and that pro-cess has greatly intensified in the digital era. The sheer amount of information about other cultures and other ways of being provided by digital media can be deeply confusing and challenging to one's identity, especially among those in the still formative years of youth. Some celebrate this condition as liberating us from overly rigid roles and lifestyles, while others see this as a dangerous development whose flip side is people desperately turning to religious fundamen-talisms (every one of the major religions—Hinduism, Christianity, Islam, Buddhism and Judaism have seen an increase in fundamen-talist forms), and ideological fundamentalism (the rise in terrorism and authoritarian populism). Sociologists, cultural anthropologists, political scientists and psychologists are divided about how much of this is due to the rise of digital culture, but most see digitizing life as a factor.

In all discussions of digital identities, it is important to realize that there are vastly different degrees of involvement with cyberspaces, and patterns of difference across generations. The average teenager in the US spends about 4 hours a day in digital spaces, primarily a mix of social media and games. That is a significant amount and far more than the average adult spends. While this has been exaggerated as something turning youth into digital zombies, there are legitimate concerns about the impact of this much time online among young people who are just developing their identities. Howard Gardner and Katie Davis's *The App Generation* (2013), a well-researched, balanced study based on in-depth interviews with young social media users, found that some young people can become trapped in the limited template identities proffered by apps, while others find ways to get beyond these reductive default elements to use digital spaces very creatively. It depends in part on the degree to which they can separate their online from their offline lives. The differences, they suggest, lie in three areas: Identity, intimacy and imagination. Those who become overly reliant on *app identities* suffer in all three areas, while those who use their imaginations to transcend the limited categories and options typical of online identities, and who have strong offline interactions, flourish. While it is not inevitable, it is possible for online pseudo-intimacies to crowd out more substantial offline ones (true also of adults, by the way). They recommend that parents, teachers and other supervising adults encourage kids to think about differences between on- and offline life, and to be creative in using apps rather than simply following prompts like those that limit "relationship status" to three or four categories. In a comment that clearly extends beyond the "app generation" that is their focus, Gardner and Davis remark that "when we allow apps to restrict or determine our procedures, choices and goals, we become '*app dependent*' rather than '*app enabled*'" (Gardner and Davis 2013: 10). Perhaps the 25 percent of Americans who say they are "constantly online" most need to heed this advice ("Internet/Broadband Fact Sheet" 2018).

There is one area of digital life shared broadly by most users that may be having a society-wide impact. There is a strong case to be made that for many people a digitized life is a more mobile one, literally and figuratively. More than half of people worldwide with digital access do so wholly or mostly through a mobile phone, and overall 70 percent of time spent in digital spaces occurs through smartphones. The mobile phone, as its name obviously implies, has made us more mobile in our communicative interactions. As a result, studies suggest that this has changed our relation to space, including creating a physical world–virtual world fusion (not the same as erasing the difference). As Jon Agar notes, the invention of an earlier mobile device, pocket and wrist watches, changed our relation to time and space by making us more aware of time passing, more fixated on it and with the creation of local time zones more aware of time as globally relative (cited in Farman 2011).

On the one hand, we should not overstate the novelty since we have been extending our human capacities via technologies since our first ancestors built spears to hunt game and sharpened sticks to dig for root foods. Each new technological development changed us, and thereby changed the nature of humanity to some degree. The first writing on paper (papyrus) transformed our relationship to space in ways not dissimilar to the first mobile phone. Having words that were previously bound on immovable stone tablets be able to travel with us in the form of paper documents changed our sense of space just as surely as being able to take vocal communication with us as we travel has done. Prior to the cellphone, answering the phone and being asked, "Where are you?" would have led you to question the sanity of the caller. "Where am I? What do you mean? *You* called me. I am here at home on the phone. Have you been drinking?" (Farman 2011). (Having raised the question of sanity, this is perhaps the place to mention that many people have jokingly observed that the biggest danger from cellphones may be that it is no longer always possible on the street to tell a potentially harmful hallucinating person from an exuberant mobile phone user.)

What other things are our new mobile devices (phones, small game consoles, iPods, etc.) doing to our embodied sense of place, space and time? The ever-present possibility of connection to other places and people via smartphones impacts our sense of self in ways we are only beginning to understand. Space was already theorized to be shrinking in a globalizing world where fast travel and even faster communication shaped our imagination. But the mobile smartphone and related devices greatly deepens that sensation. The whole world can seem quite literally to be in our hands. As digital theorist Jason Farman argues, the mobile phone and other mobile devices have transformed how we relate to a whole host of things, creating a new kind of *mobile embodiment* that is in many ways more fluid, but nevertheless grounded in the material world in old and new ways (Farman 2011). Digital music players, for example, not only change our relation to sound, moving it from the home or concert venue into a host of new spaces, but they can also serve to give a new sense of public/private space. As anyone who has ever ridden a bus or subway knows, iPods or other music players can act as a kind of insulating device to ward off other people, to create a private space in public. Something of the opposite can happen around the use of mobile phones in public when people act as if they are in a private space while making their conversations (often annoyingly) public. Mobile devices, in other words, are among the digital phenomena that are redefining the boundaries between public and private spaces. More generally, they are changing our sense of self as we move through the world, and our sense of the relation between proximity and distance. Smartphones often give us a sense of feeling more connected to others across distances, for example, while at other times a friend next to you talking to someone else may feel more distant. The constant presence of a phone in one's pocket or purse can also diminish one's sense of loneliness, and/or it can diminish one's sense of privacy. And while communicative mobility can in some ways dislodge our sense of place (compared to older place-bound phones, for example), **locative media** enabled by digital apps such as Google Maps can actually deepen our sense of connection to place (Farman 2011).

Another influential body of work suggesting that identity has become more mobile in the digital era has been prominent from the early days of cyberculture studies. Brenda Danet's 1995 essay, "Text as Mask: Gender, Play and Performance on the Internet," was fascinated with the idea that the Web seemed designed for infinite play with identity (Danet 1995 [1998]). Particularly in the period when the Web was primarily a word medium, no one on the other end of a digital encounter necessarily knew who you were or what you looked like. Danet found that close to 80 percent of Web users she surveyed admitted to pretending to be a different gender, race or sexual orientation than they were in "real life." This number is no doubt inflated by the fact that at the time of her survey the brand-new Net was largely populated by adventurous early adopters of an avant-garde and countercultural bent. In any event, this notion of an anonymous space open to identity play was soon taken up by advertisers who famously began to talk about the Web as a place beyond race, class and gender (as if the virtual world had fully replaced the real one). Almost immediately the misleading nature of that claim was parodied in a famous cartoon in the *New Yorker* from 1993 featuring a dog at a keyboard, telling a canine pal, "On the Internet, nobody knows you're a dog" (Steiner 1993). Soon there was a whole industry of further parodies: "On the Internet nobody knows you're _____" ("a space alien," "a cat," "a pickle"; you name it).

Exaggerating the breadth and depth of these identity-bending phenomena was part of the general tendency in early cybercultures to stress that alleged gap between real and virtual life. Again, this was partly due to the fact that the medium was still new, primarily textual and still inhabited mostly by extremely adventurous folks not representative of wider populations. But beneath the exaggerated claims that people could be wholly someone else online, and that who we were offline would be unknown and irrelevant, there were very interesting questions being raised about the impact of digital cultures on identity.

Significant instances of identity-shifting phenomena, under concepts such as "racial cross-dressing" and **identity tourism**

(Nakamura 2002), continue and are actively studied. From relatively trivial forms, such as cyber fibbing about one's looks or job or age on online dating sites, to more serious, even criminal, acts of impersonation, it is clear that engaging with digital cultures can have an impact on self-image. But as the term "identity tourism" suggests, merely touring an identity is very different from profoundly inhabiting it. This is especially true of the kind of identity tourism Lisa Nakamura studied: A privileged person virtually inhabiting a body that has historically been subjected to discrimination (Nakamura 2002). Developing the deep **cultural competence** to understand another person's **subject position** (subject position is the way your race, gender, language, class, etc. position you in the world and unwittingly shape your world view) when it differs significantly from your own in terms of ethnicity, class, gender and so forth is not achieved by casual surfing or digital masquerading.

These early insights about identity in cyberspaces continue to be very important, though in less hyperbolic form. Identity cross-dressing remains a significant phenomenon in chat rooms, social media and dating sites and other online spaces. Rise of the slang term **catfish** to describe someone who systematically lies about who they are online testifies to this ongoing process. The popularity of the documentary film *Catfish* (2010), and the spin-off reality TV docudrama *Catfish: The TV Show* (2012+) in which participants uncover falsified identities, has revived interest in the question of how much identity trickery goes on online. And new questions about true identities online have arisen with the proliferation of **bots** masquerading as human users.

The claim that identities may be more fluid, more mobile, online than off continues to be approached from a number of other angles as well. Two scholars, for example, have written about the phenomenon they call **wikidentities**, claiming that social networking sites such as Facebook and Instagram have led many young people to take a very malleable view of their identities. The study suggests that young people often work collaboratively with online friends in fabricating their self-images, just as a wiki works to collaborate on a common project (Mallan and Giardina 2009). This is not a totally unprecedented phenomenon. There is a rich literature on the performance of identities over the centuries, and there have been eras in the past where the crafting of identity was for some a far more active, conscious and collective project than what goes on in social media today. So-called individual identities have always been socially constructed and managed. But online identity formation needs to be looked at on its specific terms, and does seem to bring something new into the world, at least in comparison with recent generations.

Talk about the fluidity and malleability of identity in certain arenas of digital culture must always also be counterbalanced with two other truths. First, it is very difficult to leave behind identities formed by history and deep processes of socialization. Even digital natives are subject to offline forces, particularly the influence of the folks who raise them, and the teachers who teach them, people who in turn have been deeply impacted by a host of forces far wider than any putatively worldwide Web. And second, our identities have always been performative, collective and variable. We are not the same people with our bosses as with our families, with our parents as with our peer age friends. Our identities have always been formed by complex interactions with others, not in some isolated identity chamber. Online worlds certainly provide rich grounds for experimentation with identity, and falsification is not uncommon; 25 percent of teen boys and 30 percent of teen girls say they have posted false information about themselves online, most commonly their age (Madden et al. 2013). But we should not exaggerate how many people partake of serious experiments in identity masquerade, nor over-emphasize the depth of transformation such actions entail in reshaping fundamental social identities. We simply don't know yet how deeply identities are being reshaped by online masquerade, digital cross-dressing and other forms of identity gaming.

We do know, however, that a great many people develop feelings of inferiority based on the kind of relentlessly upbeat accounts that typify social media posts by youth. Variously called Facebook Envy and Facebook Depression, this is a serious psychological phenomenon, driven by FOMO (Fear of Missing Out) and other imaginary feelings that everyone else's life is more interesting or exciting than one's own, based on heavily edited posts. This is part of a more general phenomenon we might call *life tourism*. Critic Susan Sontag once noted that taking photographs can have the effect of making us tourists of our own lives (Sontag 2001: 9). If that is true, then the craze for taking selfies and photographing, videoing and posting our lives via social media may be even more deeply turning some us from living our lives to becoming tourists of them.

A related impact on identity online comes from the formulaic packages that increasingly make up Web apps and platforms. Social media and other app users are subjected to what I call *template identity*. Bits of so-called personalization on social media sites hide the fact that identity parameters are defined very narrowly, limiting our identities to categories set up because they make sense to engineers and marketers, regardless of how well they represent the range of human emotion and thought. Emotions cannot be fully expressed through mere emoticons. And think of the mental impact of the fact that for a long time the only response available to a Facebook post was Like or Dislike. I remember the weird feeling of people "liking" a post in which I announced my mother's death. How mind twisting is that?

As long time Silicon Valley designer and one of the early creators of virtual reality Jaron Lanier demonstrates at length, users are in danger of becoming mere "gadgets" if they do not become more aware of ways in which design decisions, templates and other technical operations not visible on the surface of the Web subtly and not-so-subtly shape who we are and how we think (Lanier 2010). Technical configurations, out of concern for cost, laziness and sheer inertia tend to "lock in" many design elements that fundamentally limit human creativity in digital spaces. Lanier surmises we "like" online cat videos in part because "we know that Facebook is turning us into trained dogs. We know we are being . . . turned into circus animals. And we long for that independence that cats show" (quoted in Dowd 2017).

Lanier urges far greater degrees of involvement of everyday users in design decisions because his experience as an engineer has taught him that, because of the still mostly white male brotopia that is Silicon Valley, technicians represent a small, rather socially narrow portion of humanity. They tend to do things because they have technical logic, but that logic is not always human logic. Lanier further expresses concern that while crowdsourcing and wikis can have great value, there is in the ethos surrounding them a danger of downplaying the uniqueness of the individual voice, and disrespecting hard-earned forms of expertise that cannot and should not be replaced by a "hive mind." Though he doesn't use the phrase, what he is in effect describing is a move toward the crowdsourcing of identity. Lanier's books, while sometimes over the top in their rhetoric to get our attention (an increasingly difficult task in our information overloaded lives), are full of insights about the dangers of identity loss in digitized spaces that need to be brought more fully out into the public arena for discussion and debate (Lanier 2010, 2018).

At their best, digitized lives open onto a wonderful array of possible identities and interpersonal connections. At their worst, digitized lives are being driven into techno-niches and consumer templates by engineers and product marketers who present a narrowing of human possibilities.

⇥ ANONYMITY, DISINHIBITION AND CYBERBULLYING

If the idea of life online as disembodied has been overstated, there is another "dis," **disinhibition**, that is much more prevalent and relevant. Much of the early discussion of technology touted the benefits that online anonymity provided. Psychologists talk about disinhibition as a factor shaped by anonymity. The most famous forces of disinhibition are alcohol and drugs. Anyone who has ever attended a party where alcohol enlivened the event can testify that disinhibition can be a good thing. (For those of you who have never been in a situation in which alcohol or other drugs have been consumed, think of things you might have said in confidence to your closest friends or family members but would never say in public.) At the same time, anyone who has attended a party where alcohol consumption led someone (surely not you!) to make an absolute fool of themselves, or say or do something deeply offensive, knows that disinhibition can have highly negative consequences. The same pattern can be seen regarding the disinhibition provided by online **anonymity in digital culture**. Studies have shown clearly that people say things online when their identities are protected that they would never say if they were known and could be held accountable for their words. Anonymity has, for example, provided a cover for vast amounts of online hate speech.

One form of hateful speech that has proven especially pervasive is **cyberbullying**. Bullying is hardly a new phenomenon in the world, but the anonymity provided by digital spaces has added a new dimension that has made bullying easier. As a specifically digital transformation of an offline problem, it also expands the range of bullies beyond the physically intimidating, increases the size of the audience seeing the bullying (especially in the minds of the bullied), persists longer given its online presence and can take a wider variety of forms (from sharing embarrassing photos and videos, to excluding from online groups or creating hate groups or forums, to trolling/ stalking, fake profiles and "fraping" (impersonating) the bullied individual, to unwelcome sexting and other forms of sex/gender harassment, to blackmail). Often females and sometimes males are subjected to forms of body-shaming. Homophobic taunts are common, especially for boys, regardless of actual orientation. Unwelcome outing of LGBTQ I2 (that's the letter I and the number 2) inserted before the + students is common. Racial and ethnic harassment is also pervasive, as are attacks on immigrant status (actual or falsely assumed).

Here are some key statistics about cyberbullying:

- Around 1 in 3 students experience bullying through the academic year.
- Only 15 percent of students admit to being cyberbullied.
- 61 percent of overweight teens have reported being bullied online.
- 70 percent of K-12 kids have witnessed cyberbullying take place.
- Only 10 percent of cyberbullying victims will report to an adult about getting cyberbullied.
- Females are 2 times more likely to be victims of cyberbulling.
- Kids are 7 times more likely to experience cyberbullying from friends than strangers.
- Cyberbullying victims are 2 to 9 times more likely to contemplate suicide (Tulane 2018).

Some clever apps such as Stop!T and Rethink Before You Type have attacked this problem. But it remains a serious issue that costs lives and deeply damages many others. Eighty percent of young people interviewed about bullying said they were more likely to bully online than offline, though offline bullying is still more common. Fortunately the issue has received greater and greater attention in recent years and there are now more resources than ever before for students, teachers and parents, including websites and anti-bullying apps, as well as solid empirical research (Cyberbullying Resource Center n.d.; Kowalski, Limber and Agatson 2012; NSPCC n.d.; Teachers with Apps n.d.).

It is difficult to tell whether cyberbullying is increasing or decreasing, since more reporting is occurring due to greater attention being paid to the problem. But regardless of the overall numbers, it is a serious issue that hinders the academic and social lives of millions of children and teens around the world. Of the possible solutions available, it seems clear that mere punishment of bullies seldom solves the problem. In fact, it may compound it by reinforcing the kind of power dynamics that can lead to bullying. The best solutions tend to include empathy training via face-to-face encounters between the bullied and bullies (Carlisle 2015). Because the problem is also a global one, studies show that the nature of cyberbullying and the possible solutions vary depending upon national cultural context (Smith 2018).

While cyberbullying often flourishes because the perpetrators think they can remain anonymous, they are usually wrong. In thinking generally about online anonymity, it is important to realize that while online disinhibition is real, anonymity ultimately is often an illusion. Anonymity is usually a temporary condition that can almost always be turned into identification with the right investigative tools. Given that even some of the most sophisticated hackers seeking to remain anonymous have been tracked down if their activities are defined as criminal, what chance do the rest of us have of remaining anonymous if someone really wants to discover who made that comment, posted that image, did that cyberbullying? Putting too much faith in the anonymity of cyberspaces inevitably leads to perilous consequences, as a number of politicians, celebrities, hackers and ordinary folks have often discovered. It seems better to assume that there is no such thing as absolutely anonymous cyberspace.

The more positive side of disinhibition is that in some situations it can foster more honest conversations. The seemingly anonymous spaces on the Web have revealed a great many things about current social thought and emotion. Much of what has been revealed is far from flattering to our sense of humans as a rational, compassionate species (for example, the ability to anonymously report stories of domestic abuse, sexual harassment and sexual violence revealed the devastating consequences and widespread nature of these experiences). Some say it is better to have those expressions out in the open rather than repressed. Perhaps, but our unbridled *Ids* are no more the whole truth about us than are the more controlled expressions of our more moderated *Egos* (to use the convenient Freudian metaphors). Web anonymity reveals as many lies as it does truths. As always, we humans are stuck with the interpretive task of sorting out the true from the less true from the totally false. But digital cultures are certainly making the task of telling the true from the false more difficult. Digital cultures, riddled as they are with "fake news," "fake science" and "info-bots" pretending to represent real human opinions, have created a spiraling movement toward the most extreme forms of expression. On YouTube, to take just one example, recommendation algorithms have a bias toward the most extreme aspects of any topic you choose to look at, based on the marketing idea that you will stay hooked if you are shown more excitably bizarre things (often in *clickbait* form). This pushes all users toward the edges of thought and behavior (Tufecki 2018). Such a tendency is probably bad for human interaction in general, but in one particular realm it is clearly doing truly significant damage. The tendency to push people toward extremes in *politics* has become a threat to democracy in many parts of the world through the rise of authoritarian populisms very much fueled by the Web (see Chapter 7). Part of this is due to the use of a particular digital form, microblogging, a medium that often reduces thought to mindless slogans and easily spreads misleading or downright false statements. A study of the 2016 US presidential election, for example, found that inflammatory fake news on Twitter travelled faster and more broadly than accurate reports (Vosoughi et al. 2018).

ARE VIRTUAL COMMUNITIES FOR REAL?

From the earliest days of the public Internet, the possibilities of virtual communities have been much touted and much derided. While the utopian hopes for such communities have faded somewhat over the years, there is no doubt that new communities have formed online that would not be possible, or at least not as easily possible, offline. Some of these communities that simply could not exist at all are ones of particular importance to people who are place bound or who live in geographically isolated places. The Internet, for example, has deeply changed life for many immigrants, making it much easier to maintain connection to homeland countries. Diasporas (voluntary or forced exile communities) have much richer possibilities for communication across great distances. At the same time, given that many of these migrants are forced to move for economic reasons, digital divides mean that these communication possibilities are often severely limited for those communities that need them most.

Many other kinds of online communities built across previously unbridgeable distances of time, space and cost have been formed around politics, leisure and recreation and virtually every other aspect of life. The importance of these kinds of online community connections is undeniable. They certainly represent an enhancement of possibilities for those who take advantage of them. To see them as less real than other kinds of group connections is clearly a mistake from the point of view of those involved in them, and it would seem little more than prejudice against the new to see them as somehow less than other kinds of community. Especially given the availability now of visual communication apps and devices that provide a better simulation of face-to-face interaction, it is difficult to see what is lost in online communication.

More questionable perhaps are communities formed around people who could in fact meet in non-cyber spaces. Most critiques of virtual communities argue that some authentic human relation is lost when people connect only through online media. Sociologist Robert Putnam, in his widely-read book *Bowling Alone: The Collapse and Revival of American Community* (2000), lamented the alleged decline if not death of community and civic culture under contemporary social conditions, before the emergence of the Internet as a significant public space. While focused on the US, this analysis has been said to fit the situation in many other democratic societies. Putnam's claims have been challenged on many grounds, but it is interesting to note that his critique arose just as the Internet was taking off. It seems plausible that either much civil life was already in the process of moving online, or that a perceived deficit in community was quickly taken up by folks online. Recent political events, however, make clear that some kinds of "community" interaction may be shaped quite negatively by being carried out mostly online (see Chapter 7).

The claim that online communities are somehow less real also ignores the fact that, with the fairly rare exception of those communities mentioned previously that can *only* exist in digital spaces, few members of virtual communities limit themselves exclusively to online interaction. Hardcore video gamers, for example, often parodied as living excessive, obsessive online lives, love to get together face-to-face in spaces ranging from living rooms to giant arenas at gamer conferences. There is ample testimony (far beyond dating sites) of relationships beginning online and spilling out into various offline worlds of work and play. Much prejudice against virtual communities seems based on either fear of the new or nostalgia for some supposedly perfectly unmediated world that never existed.

▣ HOW MUCH ONLINE LIFE IS GOOD FOR US?

> I maintain myself on the puppet drug of personal technology. Every touch of a button brings the neural rush of finding something I never knew and never needed to know until it appears at my anxious fingertips, where it remains for a shaky second before disappearing forever.
>
> (DeLillo, *Zero K*: 55)

The kind of questions raised previously about virtual life have led to questions of just how much online life (if any) is good for us. Some of those of a technological determinist bent fear new media are robbing us of an essential humanness that can only be conveyed face-to-face. This claim, again, ignores the fact that no one spends all their time solely in digitized spaces, and exaggerates the digital dualism of online/offline.

While the differences have often been exaggerated, as I have suggested, it also would be a serious mistake to assume that there are *no* differences between digitally mediated life and other experiences. Sherry Turkle, for example, a pioneering digital culture theorist who once celebrated the fluidity of life online is now far less sanguine about the technological world than in her earlier work. She believes ubiquitous computing, constant connection via mobile devices and the evolution of more and more human-seeming robots (from toys to talking smartphones) have rendered many people better able to relate to digital devices than to people. Turkle argues in her book *Alone Together* (2012) that as we expect more from technology, we expect less from each other. She suggests that obsessive computer users are losing the capacity to be alone, and at the same time, are not really together (hence her paradoxical title). She believes that the kind of virtual intimacy we have via electronic devices is not an adequate substitute for complex offline human interactions. While she sees technologies getting better and better at mimicking human speech, mimicry is by definition only a stand-in for something richer, or dare we say, more real. The danger Turkle is pointing to is that digital natives, growing up on this form of digitized intimacy before they have an opportunity to develop deeper forms of intimacy with fellow humans, will never learn the difference, will never know that they have lost a vital part of personhood.

Nathan Jurgenson has countered Turkle by suggesting that, paradoxically, because many of us are spending so much time online, we have come to value offline family time, solitude and general disconnection more than ever. He claims that these times have become more precious precisely because we think we are losing them. Jurgenson points out that many people have come, in a kind of reverse digital snobbery, to brag about how much they resist being online. "People boast about their self-control over not checking their device [while dining with friends]," he writes,

and the table usually reaches a self-congratulatory consensus that we should all just keep it in our pants. The pinnacle of such abstinence-only smartphone education is a game that is popular to talk about (though I've never actually seen it played) wherein the first person at the dinner table to pull out their device has to pay the tab.

(Jurgenson 2012)

As Jurgenson argues explicitly and as Turkle too knows well, the offline/online division ("digital dualism," Jurgenson calls it) is an overly simplified one. And Jurgenson doesn't address the fact that the vast majority of the world's population still has never been online at all, or discuss the vast range in degrees of online life that individuals experience. Conversely, Turkle doesn't sufficiently acknowledge that once one has been online, the online world is part of one's "real life." Each author may have part of the truth here, and only the future will tell how users come to balance (more) digitized and (less) digitized realms of experience. But the bottom line is that away-from-keyboard communication is a vital human form of interaction that can never be fully recreated digitally and thus needs to be balanced against digitized life.

In any event, not only is most of the world still not online, but many people who could have access choose not to be digitized. There are a variety of reasons for not living a digitized life, many of which are discussed in Chapter 10, but the point is that we should not assume life online is a universal experience or one desired by all. And among those who have availed themselves of digital experiences, there is an increasing desire for a balanced approach that has led to things like the **Slow Technology Movement** (Ascharya 2012; "Slow Technology Movement" n.d.). Not against technology, and including many tech industry professionals, the movement argues for more careful and thoughtful engagement with digital spaces and cultures, recognizing that time away from digitized life can be essential to a richer, more complete life.

It is perhaps telling that many Silicon Valley tech leaders greatly restrict the use of digital devices by their children, and a number of them have placed their kids in digital tech-free schools (Weller 2017). There is one tech-free Waldorf school in the geographic center of the IT world, Silicon Valley, where 75 percent of the students are children of electronic corporation executives. If many of the foremost creators of digital culture feel a need to limit the amount and ways that their offspring use digital technology, surely it is worth the rest of us to carefully think through how much of a digital life is healthy.

The concept of addiction is vastly overused these days, but in relation to some aspects of digital culture it seems apt. As Tim Wu argues in his important book *The Attention Merchants* (2016), social media apps have incorporated and far extended the psychological techniques used historically to capture our attention in order to increase the addictive qualities of online life. This is turning many of us into *infomaniacs*, constantly checking our smartphones or logging onto our social media accounts. In the process of feeding this addiction, we also play into a far deeper issue addressed in the next chapter, the fact that all this time online is being monitored by corporations and governments in ways that may prove quite unhealthy indeed for all of us.

4

Has Digital Culture Killed Privacy?

Social Media, Governments and Digitized Surveillance

While some of these questions about online life seem to have both positive and negative features, I can find nothing positive to say with regard to the impact of digital technology on our right to privacy. If the Net, in conjunction with other digital technologies, has not quite killed privacy, it has dealt it a near fatal blow. And with the death of privacy goes a whole host of human rights. The Internet is *the greatest surveillance device ever invented*. The fourth amendment to the US Constitution and many other democratic documents guarantee the right to privacy because without it personal and political freedom is impossible. Yet, with remarkable rapidity the digital era has severely eroded most of the key spaces of privacy.

Wikipedia offers a useful general definition of privacy: "the ability of an individual or group to seclude themselves or information about themselves and thereby reveal themselves selectively." (https://en.wikipedia.org/wiki/Privacy) The dual emphasis in this definition on the *individual* and on *groups* is important here. Private spaces are central to the construction of personal identity *and* crucial to the collective negotiation of political ideas. Thinking about privacy means thinking about both *personal privacy* and what might be called civic or *political privacy*.

Why does privacy matter? That's a question asked only by people in democratic countries who take it for granted. Anyone who has ever lived in an authoritarian regime knows that privacy is a key component of freedom and of personal identity. Privacy is about choice, about the choice of what information to keep only to ourselves, what to share with just one friend or a parent, what to share with a larger circle of acquaintances and so on up until what becomes public or in the hands of a government agency. As anyone who has ever lived in captivity can tell you, when you lose privacy you lose a huge part of the self. And attacks on privacy have always been a part of attacks on freedom.

While particular notions of what should or should not be private vary from culture to culture and person to person, and from one historic period to another, the key issue here is the second half of the definition, "reveal themselves selectively." Privacy is about controlling what information about yourself or groups to which you belong is made available to others. By that definition, and regardless of what it is a particular person wishes to keep private, privacy has been deeply invaded and eroded by the corporate and governmental use of digital technologies. In digital culture, we have increasingly given away the power to selectively reveal information about us to others. This is a vital issue because privacy is both a key element in enabling us to shape our *personal identities* and a key element for establishing and maintaining *political freedom*. In most democratic societies around the globe, privacy is deeply tied to freedom of thought, freedom of speech and the right to protest.

The stakes are very high and the solutions very difficult because many of the most positive aspects of current and emerging digital cultures are closely tied to forces capable of developing into one or another kind of oppressive *surveillance society*. If this surveillance society comes fully online, it will do so not through some major political upheaval, though such events may be used as excuses to speed up the process, but most likely will evolve through a slow series of largely invisible (and in some cases unintentional) actions that take away our privacy and with it key human rights. Indeed, the dark irony of this brave new world, if it arrives, will be that it is brought on by our addiction to the very real pleasures and benefits of digitized lives.

The problem exists at the heart of the Web on most of the widely used resources—Internet Service Providers (ISPs) such as Verizon, Comcast, T-Mobile and AT&T, search engines such as Google, Yahoo and Baidu, social media sites such as Twitter, Instagram and Facebook, and e-tail sites such as Amazon. These and similar apps and platforms have instituted the phenomenon known as **dataveillance** (data as surveillance) to unprecedented levels (Vaidhyanathan 2018).

At the level of personal identity, ideas about what constitutes privacy seem to be changing at a pace difficult to fathom or control. It is hardly a secret that the Web is a site of much excessive self-disclosure, intentional and otherwise. Over 90 percent of US citizens polled felt that people had lost control over how personal information is being shared (Madden and Rainie 2015). Writers such as lawyer and law professor Lori Andrews and media studies scholar Daniel Trotter, among many others, have documented a host of disturbing examples of how Google, Verizon, Yahoo, Amazon, Facebook and other telecom and digital tech corporations are abetting a massive invasion of privacy: Insurance companies checking up on your health habits, credit card services checking your marital status, lawyers checking out what kind of a juror you would make, law enforcement gathering evidence on you without a warrant and a thousand other forms of data scraping that are possible in the new media world (Andrews 2012). The phrase "guilt by association" has taken on a whole new power in the world of social media "friending." But how many of us realize the full extent of those disclosures or the personal and larger social costs such disclosure may entail? And how many of us are taking action to change things?

In his book *Social Media as Surveillance* (2012), Daniel Trotter examines four areas where Facebook, Twitter, LinkedIn and other platforms are acting like Orwell's Big Brother, examining and seeking to control all aspects of our behavior: Interpersonal surveillance (as we spy on each other), institutional surveillance (as institutions such as universities and employers watch over us as we study or work), market surveillance (as businesses spy on customers, potential customers and everyone who offers any personal preferences online) and government surveillance (as authorities from the CIA down to local cops can spy on pretty much everything we do or even discuss possibly doing).

There is a central contradiction at the heart of Net culture. The primary good of the system, its interconnectivity and interactivity, is inherently connected to its profound vulnerability. We are amassing unimaginably powerful amounts of data about ourselves in a central repository utterly vulnerable to criminal, corporate and governmental abuse. There is a myriad of disturbing, systematic, largely invisible ways in which digital culture slashes through privacy. The amount of information Internet service providers, search engines, websites, social networking sites and other digital spaces have gathered on individuals is truly staggering. While modern bureaucracies have long gathered excessive amounts of information on citizens, the Internet has brought an exponential growth in the amount and kind of information available and centralized its collection and analysis.

⮊ WHAT RIGHTS ARE BEING LOST IF PRIVACY IS LOST?

Many people who grew up amidst this age of surveillance have come to see this as normal, rather than as a radical break from the privacy needed to lead a free and independent life in a democratic culture. And even those who grew up in earlier eras that prized privacy more fully are gladly handing over that privacy for the joy and ease of digitized lives. What's at stake in this transformation?

One useful rubric to better understand what is at stake in the loss of privacy enabled by the collection of data about us by ISPs and search engines (such as Verizon and Google) and social media corporations (such as Facebook and Instagram) is the Social Network Constitution developed by communications law expert Lori Andrews. Whether or not this particular mechanism is the best means for restoring privacy, the clear framework it offers gives a sense of what abuses are already happening, and is a useful starting point for thinking about the larger threat posed by this data gathering to our basic rights at citizens.

TABLE 4.1 *The Social Network Constitution*

We the people of Facebook Nation, in order to form a more Perfect Internet, to protect our fundamental rights and freedoms, to explore our identities, dreams, and relationships, to safeguard the sanctity of our digital selves, to ensure equal access to technology, to lessen discrimination and disparities, and to promote democratic principles and the general welfare, declare these truths to be self-evident:

1. The Right to Connect

The right to connect is essential for individual growth, political discourse, and social interchange. No government shall abridge the right to connect, nor shall a government monitor exchanges over the Internet or code them as to sources or content.

2. The Right to Free Speech and Freedom of Expression

The right to free speech and freedom of expression shall not be abridged (and an individual shall have the freedom to use a pseudonym), as long as the speech does not incite serious, imminent harm nor defame a private individual. Employers and schools shall be prohibited from accessing social network pages or taking adverse actions against people based on what they express or disclose on a social network, except in cases of imminent harm to another individual.

3. The Right to Privacy of Place and Information

The right to privacy in one's social networking profiles, accounts, related activities, and data derived therefrom shall not be abridged. The right to privacy includes the right to security of information and security of place. Regardless of active security settings or an individual's efforts to guard his or her digital self, social networks are private places.

4. The Right to Privacy of Thoughts, Emotions and Sentiments

Social networks provide a place for individuals to express themselves and to grow. A person's thoughts, emotions, and sentiments—and his or her characterization by others—shall not be used against him or her by social institutions, governments, schools, employers, insurers, or courts.

TABLE 4.1 *(Continued)*

5. The Right to Control One's Image

Each individual shall have control over his or her image from a social network, including over the image created by data aggregation. A person's image may not be used outside a social network for commercial or other purposes without his or her consent, nor shall it be used online for commercial or other gain without his or her consent.

6. The Right to Fair Trial

Evidence from social networks may only be collected for introduction in a criminal trial if there is probable cause and a warrant has been issued. Evidence from social network sites may not be collected for or introduced in civil cases unless the activity at issue occurred on social networks (such as defamation, extortion, invasion of privacy, or jury tampering). Evidence from social networks may only be introduced at trial if it is directly relevant to the crime or civil action charged and the probative value outweighs the prejudicial value, the evidence is relevant, the evidence is properly authenticated, and the evidence otherwise complies with all rules of civil and criminal procedure. In custody cases, social network information should be admitted only if it provides direct evidence of potential harm to the child.

7. The Right to an Untainted Jury

Jurors shall decide cases based on the evidence presented in court and not information or inferences acquired from social networks, search queries, or other sources.

8. The Right to Due Process of Law and the Right to Notice

An individual is entitled to due process, which consists of advance notice and the ability to control, correct, and delete the individual's online information. No information shall be collected or analyzed without advance notification of the individual. That notification shall include an explanation of the specific use and purpose of the collection and analysis of that information. There shall be a warning about possible repercussions of giving consent for the collection of that particular information. Access to a social network shall not be denied based on a decision not to consent to the collection, analysis, or dissemination of information. An individual shall have the right to know what entities are in possession of or are using that individual's information and he or she shall have a right to gain access to and obtain a copy of all the information regarding him or her.

9. Freedom from Discrimination

No person shall be discriminated against based on his or her social network activities or profile, nor shall an individual be discriminated against based on group data aggregation rather than on characteristics of that particular individual, unless the social network activities provide direct evidence of a crime or tort.

10. Freedom of Association

People shall have freedom of association on social networks and the right to keep their associations private.

© from Lori Andrews, *I Know Who You Are and I Saw What You Did: Social Networks and the Death of Privacy* (The Free Press, 2013).

◪ SOCIAL MEDIA AS SURVEILLANCE MECHANISM

To understand the extent of **data mining** that experts like Andrews worry about, it is important to realize that most of it goes on invisibly. The "privacy" settings on social media sites falsely lull people into thinking that their identities or photos or browsing history or other information are far more protected than they are. In point of fact, media corporations have almost unlimited legal access to the data they gather. And every time a person clicks on a "user terms agreement" they don't read they are adding to the chances of losing something precious.

How does all this work? It works like magic! But not in a good way. The essence of most magic is misdirection, and so it is in this case. Google gives us unlimited searches for all kinds of information, for free! Amazon allows us to examine hundreds of thousands of books and other products, for free! Facebook and Instagram connect us to family, friends, to the whole world, for free! YouTube provides endless numbers of amusing, amazing amateur and professional videos, for free! It's like magic. But like stage magic the real magic is in the misdirection. All this "free" stuff comes at the cost of your privacy as these giant corporations use sleight of hand and small print to amass unprecedented amounts of data about millions of us that add up to a tremendous, dangerous invasion of privacy. Ultimately, it is less like the magic show where we are entertained by showy illusion than it is the kind of magic show where shills walk through the audience picking people's pockets while they are entranced by the magician.

Every day millions of people have their personal information—age, income level, address, phone numbers, credit card numbers, medical information, sexual preferences, political views, massive amounts of consumer likes and dislikes, names of lovers, friends and relatives—routinely shared without their knowledge or explicit consent. Corporations such as Verizon, AT&T, Facebook, Google and others imperil safety, leave people open to fraud and blackmail and lessen political freedom through their data mining efforts. There are countless examples of criminals, governments and criminal governments accessing data gathered through our daily use of smartphones, search engines and social media. Every day thousands of people lose jobs or fail to get jobs, are denied admission to a college, lose custody rights, have their marriages compromised, lose health insurance, become victims of cyberbullying and sexual harassment or become victims of other crimes because of information gathered from their online activities. Identity theft is greatly facilitated by the sharing, knowingly or unknowingly, of data online. And so is old-fashioned breaking and entering. According to one study, 78 percent of thieves even use postings about vacations on social media to figure out when to target homes for home invasion break-ins. But criminal use may not be the most dangerous aspect of the problem of privacy invasion.

Whatever you imagine the surveillance capacity of modern technology to be, the truth is likely far worse than you imagine. Should it trouble us that Facebook, Amazon and Google know more about us than our best friends or spouses? This is not an exaggeration. One joint study by researchers at Cambridge University and Stanford found that data gained from Facebook "likes" proved better at judging a person's personality than their closest friends, their spouses and sometimes, even themselves (Aschwanden 2015).

If you want to get a small taste of how much information is being collected on you, log onto Google and use their Takeout tool to download the data they have on you from apps like Gmail, Maps and above all, Search. The amount will likely surprise, if not terrify you. If you were to download the data Google has about you via their "Takeout" option (a practice I strongly recommend) you will find that they have everything you have ever searched for online, every book you have ever searched for, every image you have looked at, every ad they have highlighted on your search pages, every bit of news you have looked at, everything you have shopped for online, every video you have viewed, a list of your Google Hangout conversations plus every contact on your phone and via Google Maps, a record of every place you have ever been or thought about going to and much, much more. Stop reading now and try looking at "My Activity" and "Location History" on Google or use the app *Ghostery* to see just what they are tracking at the moment. And Google is only one source of data mining.

While Facebook has borne the brunt of the privacy critique because of well-publicized data breaches, Google actually gathers even more information than Facebook. In addition to the massive amount of data they collect and provide to advertisers (and at times to governments), they further a number of highly suspect practices. As with so many other things, practices that had been banned in previous cultural situations have been given second life online. One of these is the digital variation on a long illegal practice known as "redlining." Redlining was (and in some areas still is) a practice that prevented residents of neighborhoods with high levels of people of color from receiving mortgage loans, persuaded retailers to establish their businesses in more affluent areas and encouraged the denial of employment, insurance, health care and other essential services to individuals and families based upon their data being traced to inner-city neighborhoods. This updated version of redlining, **weblining**, also known as "**data profiling**," uses information gathered online to stereotype users and pitch only certain products and services to them. It is the prejudiced flip-side of the pleasure you may feel when Google's or Amazon's algorithms correctly identify a book you would like to buy. Similarly troubling is the use of medical information gained from data mining to unfairly deny health insurance or employment. In fact, the socially negative uses to which the massive amounts of data gained about us online is almost endless.

Excessive data gathering is hard for tech companies to resist because as part of their business plans they have built maximum intrusiveness into their technology. To cite again the world's most oft-used search engine, the "don't be evil" Google has been shown to be doing some privacy invading that looks a lot like evil. (Perhaps tellingly, in 2018 they got rid of their don't be evil motto from their corporate code of conduct [Chang 2018].) In 2012, Google was forced to dump huge amounts of data it gathered while updating its maps application, information that had no relevance to the mapping project but could be sold to third-party advertisers. As Google employees went about photographing and charting buildings in the creation of Google Street View (as part of an update to their widely used Google Maps app), thousands of people were photographed without their knowledge, sometimes in compromising or endangering situations. Some of these employees also surreptitiously gathered other kinds of personal information, including the email addresses and passwords of millions of people in the UK. This information was in no way relevant to the mapping process. It was later revealed that after apologizing and claiming to have erased this data, Google had in fact retained much of it due, it claimed, to "human error." Even before these revelations, Privacy International, a UK-based organization aimed at protecting privacy rights of all kinds around the globe, gave Google a rating of "hostile to privacy," its worst ranking.

The potential for employers and school admissions offices, not to mention the police and criminals (and criminal police officers!), to mine Facebook pages for information should worry any user. But the situation is far worse with regard to less obvious forms of privacy invasion. Most users know about cookies, but fewer know about cookies that may be installed on a Web browser that has opted to not receive cookies, which can invisibly track your every site visit across all your browsers, and cannot be eliminated by typical cookie deleting processes. Much of this surveillance is set in place insidiously as pleasurable activities like taking selfies. As Keith Lowell Jensen, alluding to the dystopian novel *1984*, where all citizens are under constant surveillance, notes today we are surveilling ourselves: "What Orwell failed to predict was that we'd buy cameras ourselves, and that our biggest fear would be that nobody was watching" (Jensen 2013).

Digital networks track our every credit card use. Our every online move, in some cases our every keystroke, is recorded and enters one or more data banks about which we know little or nothing, and over which we have very little, if any, control. While it may seem like a nice thing that Amazon is able to predict what new books you will like, that knowledge used by less scrupulous folks could mean a deep violation of your rights to read what you want without anyone else knowing. Cybercrimes like identity theft are only the most dramatic and visible layer of the many illegal or legally dubious uses to which data about our lives is being put. The many non-criminal uses to which corporations are putting the immense amounts of data gathered about us each day are ultimately more disturbing because more pervasive. Intensive data gathering threatens long-standing freedoms in democratic countries, while in non-democratic societies it is proving a deadly threat to those seeking to expand democracy and freedom.

Facebook gained more notoriety in 2018 for its collecting and sharing of data, and like Google the amount of data it collects from 2 billion-plus users is dangerously extensive (and apparently more easily stolen). Google surpasses Facebook and other social media sites in the sheer amount of data collected, but Facebook's business model makes them equally or more dangerous. What is the product that Facebook makes? CEO Zuckerberg would say he makes "connections" among people around the globe. That is his oft-stated, idealistic goal. But it is more accurate to say that Facebook's product is you, the user, and the data about you that it collects. This data is not incidental to its profit; it is at the heart of it. The amount and kind of data it gains is largely invisible to users, and they count on their more tech-savvy users thinking they are protected. As one writer notes,

> If you think you're a passive user of Facebook, minimizing the data you provide to the site or refraining from oversharing details of your life, you have probably underestimated the scope of its reach. Facebook doesn't just learn from the pictures you post, and the comments you leave: The site learns from which posts you read and which you don't; it learns from when you stop scrolling down your feed and how long it takes you to restart; it learns from your browsing on other websites that have nothing to do with Facebook itself; and it even learns from the messages you type out then delete before sending.
>
> (Hern March 21, 2018)

Facebook is even working on apps that utilize the cameras on your smartphones and laptops to gain information on you by reading your facial expressions (Silver 2017).

Facebook has never revealed how much data it collects on people. But one survey found that just in relation to one advertiser Facebook offered up close to 100 data points (different types of information). This information ranged from your sex preferences to your political affiliations to your income to the year your home was built to the car you drive to your health issues to whether you prefer dogs or cats as pets and on and on (Dewey 2016). How do they get all this data on you? Here are seven ways noted by one analyst:

1. Data you hand over willingly: Everything you post directly; everything you "like"; every location check-in you make; all your friends/followers; all messages you send privately to your friends/followers; all your searches.

2. Data they can gather about your behavior on their properties without any real consent: All your clicks; how long you stay on each image/video/text; how your mouse moves around (correlates with eye movements); all you type but don't submit.

3. Data they can gather without any real consent about your behavior on other properties that include Facebook spyware (ads, pixels, share/like buttons): All the same information as 1 & 2 combined; also Facebook creates shadow profiles for tracking "users" who have never used a Facebook service.

4. Data they can gather without any real consent from your phone/tablet: Fine detailed geo-location over time; what other apps you use; files (videos/photos/documents) on your devices; user names, contacts, messages, calls; the name and metadata of every WiFi hotspot and BlueTooth device you have ever connected to; the infamous camera/microphone surveillance that they deny.

5. Data they can gather without any real consent from your phone/tablet via other apps: Same as 3 but without installing any Facebook app on your device; for example, Facebook bought a VPN app that can report back on all Internet traffic from all apps on a device with the app installed.

6. Offline data they can buy and/or get via partnerships without any real consent: Your credit history, your bank card payments history; your shopping loyalty program history; any available government records (house ownership, voter registration, etc.).

7. Online data they can buy and/or get via partnerships without any real consent: Results of online tests you have taken for fun, which are often run by data stalking companies to build psychometric profiles (as Cambridge Analytica did) (Aurora 2018).

This means that not only every time you "like" something on Facebook but every time you play a game *Candy Crush* or *Words with Friends* within Facebook or take part in a Buzzfeed quiz, you open yourself to further invasion. Perhaps most egregiously, Facebook can even keep tracking you when you *are no longer logged into their app,* and *track you even if you are not a Facebook user* (Hern April 17, 2018). The key to Facebook's strategy of maximum privacy invasion is to make the default position invasion, to make it more difficult to "choose" privacy than not. It is also important to realize that Facebook is hardly alone in this mode of conduct. Facebook also owns Instagram, a platform drawing younger users into the same data mining matrix, and virtually all other social media apps do the same kind of thing. Even Snapchat, with its supposedly disappearing snaps, is implicated, as the fine print in its contract makes clear:

> We collect the content you provide and information about that content, such as if the recipient has viewed the content, replayed the content, and the metadata that is provided with the content . . . [and] we may use cookies and other technologies, such as web beacons, web storage, and unique device identifiers, to collect information about your activity, browser, and device.
>
> (Snapchat privacy page)

What is perhaps most alarming about this erosion of privacy is how unalarmed some people feel and how powerless many more people feel in the face of these threats. While polls show that users are increasingly concerned about privacy, no major citizen uproar has arisen to demand change from government or the media corporations. Perhaps the revelations of the massive digital manipulation of voting in the US presidential and UK Brexit votes (see Chapter 7) will awaken folks to the urgency of maintaining privacy. In 2018, it was revealed that Facebook provided personal data on 87 million US citizens and at least one million UK citizens, allowing them to interfere, perhaps decisively, in the presidential and Brexit votes of 2016. The data was at first given to an academic researcher who in turn sold the data to the now infamous political propaganda-generating corporation

Cambridge Analytica. When Facebook initially learned of the break, they did not notify the public and did nothing to fix the underlying problem. Only when journalists revealed the story and the US Congress and British Parliament held hearings on the issue did Facebook executives apologize and promise tighter control of their data. But their promised solutions are wholly inadequate, and almost immediately after bragging about them the corporation took action to circumvent the new tougher European Union privacy regulations (Solon 2018).

So, what is the point of gathering all this data? The benign rationale—"We are just trying to help you get the things you want to buy"—seeks to justify profoundly disturbing data collection useable not just by advertisers but potentially by any number of bad actors. The data initially is used to target you very specifically through what is called a "psychographic profile" that is in turn used by unknown advertisers to manipulate your emotions and thoughts to impact your buying habits. The corporation routinely brags to advertisers about how precisely it can target a user's psychological vulnerabilities. Manipulating customers is hardly new to the advertising industry, but the vastly expanded scope of the manipulation is new and the vulnerability of the profiles to being used by other actors with more socially dangerous goals than selling products is also a change brought about by the vulnerabilities of the Net and by the policies of social media companies that provide data to third parties. As was made very clear during the 2016 election season, given the porousness of the Net, that same data can be harvested and used to manipulate your voting habits. And once you have done that effectively, you are no longer living in a democracy.

Let's be clear. There are legitimate gatherers of data, and important kinds of information that can be gained from digital data gathering. To take just one example, in the health field lives will be saved by computers analyzing massive amounts of data provided by digital monitoring devices people choose to wear. But the key word here is *choose*. The vast majority of data being gathered about us is without our knowledge or consent, or is gathered so surreptitiously under casually clicked user agreements that no one without a law degree, an IT dictionary, and a magnifying glass could decipher them. The amount and kinds of data being gathered go far beyond legitimate purposes, and even legitimately gathered and socially useful data is often not sufficiently protected from illegitimate users.

One key part of the problem is that there is a basic contradiction or structural condition that pits social media corporations against social media site users. As currently constituted, not just Facebook but most digital media corporations literally can't afford to not invade your privacy, because your privacy is the most important product they sell. Amazon, Google, Facebook, Twitter, Instagram, Snapchat, Pinterest and most other major online for-profit but "free" entities make money *by selling you*—your name, age, gender, race, religion, educational attainment, sexual orientation as connected to all your personal "likes"—to other corporations. That's the magic trick behind the digital curtain of free use. So long as this is the case, social media companies have a vested interest in pushing their invasion of your privacy as far as users will let them. And since most of their data gathering goes on behind the scenes, and is largely unaffected by superficial privacy settings, few users resist. In the wake of the bad publicity Facebook received in 2018, most other big digital media corporations made a big show of supposedly strengthening their privacy settings or making them easier to understand. But the changes were largely superficial. Without large numbers objecting and boycotting, resistance is futile (as the Borg would say). Most of us are unwittingly complicit in the multiple violations of our privacy that occur every day. While most of this activity is hidden, it is not difficult to make it unhidden once you are aware of the problem. For example, to get some idea of just what your personal data is worth, and who gets it, there are browser apps (such as Privacyfix) that can assist in getting behind the digital Wizard's curtain.

▣ GOVERNMENT SURVEILLANCE

The invasion of personal privacy these factors have brought forth is dangerous, but the danger is much greater when we realize how this invasion of personal privacy is inherently connected to the invasion of *political privacy*. Authoritarian regimes such as China and Russia are using social media data-mining and other digital weapons to deepen their stranglehold on power, and other regimes such as Turkey and Egypt are using digital data to suppress dissent and help move their societies in increasingly authoritarian directions via these same platforms. The surveillance capacity and distorting mechanisms of digital technology have placed powerful new tools in the hands of existing and emerging authoritarians (including in putative democracies), and this is a profound threat to democratic freedom and personal liberty everywhere.

Influencing which products you buy is one thing; influencing the political ideas you buy into is quite another. And it is now clear that those two things are deeply linked. As troubling as the loss of personal privacy is, the connected loss of *social and political privacy* is a far greater threat. Revelations about the US presidential election and Brexit vote of 2016 and other similar digitally enabled citizen manipulations elsewhere make clear that the rise of authoritarian populism in many parts of the world has been facilitated by the micro-targeting of voters using data mined from social media like Facebook and Twitter, and through the use of **troll farms** by Russia to circulate fake news (see Chapter 7).

These threats to political freedom come not only from external actors and unscrupulous campaigns, but from forces inside ostensibly democratic governments themselves. Exposure by Edward Snowden in the summer of 2013 of massive, invasive and illegal use of the Net for information-gathering by the US National Security Administration revealed just how fully the privacy of average citizens has been compromised. Snowden, a former CIA security analyst, revealed that the US government (and many of its allies) developed massively invasive programs such as Tempora and PRISM to spy on their own citizens. Those revelations include the fact that major tech and telecom corporations and ISPs such as AT&T, Verizon, Microsoft, Apple, Skype, Yahoo, YouTube, Google and Facebook were actually paid with taxpayer money to turn over data on citizens with no clear connection to any criminal or suspected terrorist activity. This allowed the government to access live information, photos, email, video chats and data from social networks directly through corporate servers without required consent or individual court orders. Even if they are denied access by a telecom or social media site, they can in many cases access your data and create what they call a "pattern of life profile." A conservative estimate suggests that at least 75 percent of all Internet metadata has been made accessible to governments. These are gathered from chat room conversations, emails, browser history, voice over Internet phone calls, social media activity and so on, putting millions of ordinary citizens under unprecedented surveillance. The range of surveillance capabilities is stunning. Most people know governments can listen in on smartphone conversations, but fewer know they can turn smartphone microphones on remotely in order to listen in on ambient conversations even when the phones aren't in use (McCullagh and Broache 2006). The same is true of certain brands of "smart TVs" that can also be turned into surveillance devices (Barrett 2017). Governments can also spy on you by activating the camera on your laptop, without turning on the indicator light.

Critics across the political spectrum point to this kind of data gathering as absolutely incompatible with democratic freedoms. Yet the problem continues to worsen. The Snowden revelations may only be the tip of the iceberg of what some have come to call our emerging *surveillance society*. Given that the programs he revealed were secret, there is little reason to trust subsequent assurances that they have been discontinued. And if discontinued, they may well have been replaced by equally or more invasive ones.

Claims that all this is about fighting terrorists and other bad actors around the globe have largely been debunked by closer analysis (Elliot and Meyer 2013). Snowden himself is quite clear that there are legitimate reasons for surveillance in the fight against crime and terrorism. But he argues that the kinds of data gathering he details go way beyond what is reasonable, and well beyond what is legal. For one thing, the parameters the NSA uses to permit surveillance require that the person surveilled must be only "three hops" removed from a suspected bad actor (i.e., a terrorist). That doesn't sound so bad. But what does that actually mean in numerical terms? Typically, it will look something like this: Hop 1, 190 Facebook friends; hop 2, friends of friends totaling 31,046; hop 3, friends of friends of friends totaling 5,072,916. Now, if you are sure that you are more than three removes away from any of 5 million people capable of doing anything the government doesn't like, maybe you can relax. But the rest of us may have cause for concern.

We were already heading down this path before digital technology, but the Net has profoundly deepened the problem. The average person living in a modern city is photographed or videotaped dozens of times every day. CCTV surveillance cameras are everywhere and have been a fixture of city life for some time, but the Net allows them to be remotely accessed and increasingly interconnected in ways that significantly deepen scrutiny of citizens. These and hundreds of innocent-seeming data gathering mechanisms send much of this information in to the "cloud," where it floats forever. Note how the lovely, fluffy term "the cloud" clouds over the ominous nature of data collection and storage. Try instead picturing the cloud as a dark, torrent-filled and deadly storm cloud. Again, because so much of this data gathering is linked to pleasurable activities we engage in on the Web, and to new supposedly labor-saving "smart" devices we have added to our homes, the problem is growing more insidious. We are becoming addicted to our privacy-destroying activities. Maybe that is why those who login to apps and those who shoot up heroin are both called "users."

The inherently porous, multi-entry system that is the Net means privacy is nearly impossible to maintain for any data that makes it onto the digital grid. If today the most sophisticated corporations, governments and militaries have difficulty maintaining secrecy because of the Internet (e.g., cyber-crime, cyberwar and WikiLeaks), think about how much more vulnerable we are as everyday user-citizens. We now know at least some of the story of how governments are using data stolen from our smartphones, ISPs and social media accounts, in addition to that which they mine through their own unknown new mechanisms. The combination of corporate and governmental privacy invasion means that our current surveillance societies could quietly morph into something approaching those found in dystopian fictions like *Brave New World, 1984, The Matrix* or *V for Vendetta*. And it is important to remember that those and other imagined authoritarian states usually evolved gradually—people voluntarily acquiescing to their total domination by allowing a succession of small actions, each of which further limited their privacy.

There are at least ten key forces and factors that are threatening our privacy and basic human rights: 1) *Mobile phone surveillance.* The most pervasive surveillance device is probably in your pocket, backpack or purse right now. Policing bodies, schools, parents and employers are increasingly using the now ubiquitous smartphone to track individuals without their knowledge. They can not only use your phone as a GPS tracker, but they can in some cases hack its content and/or remotely turn it on to record your conversations. 2) *Interpersonal surveillance.* Social media engage all of us in a heightened amount of invasion into the lives of friends, relatives and strangers, while more and more webcams and selfies are turning us into a culture of voyeurs overstepping previous bounds of privacy. At the same time, lack of care in protecting access to contacts on phones and social media accounts leaves vital information about friends and relatives vulnerable to **hacking** and increasingly sophisticated forms of *phishing* (the fraudulent practice of sending emails purporting to be from reputable companies in order to induce individuals to reveal personal information like passwords or credit card numbers). 3) *Blurring of the governmental/private sectors.* Many governmental agencies, the military, and policing organizations now farm out part of their surveillance apparatus to private contractors that have far less accountability to citizens and democratic norms, and whose profit motives can lead them to unscrupulous uses of collected data. 4) Even without this subcontracting, there is an increasing *merging of corporate and governmental data gathering.* Major ISPs and telecommunications corporations such as Google, Facebook, Verizon and Microsoft have given up vast amounts of information to democratic governments to augment the already exaggerated privacy-invading digital tools they were provided under the pretext of the "war on terror." They have also at times acquiesced to censorship demanded by authoritarian regimes like China. 5) The *globalization of surveillance.* Satellites, hacking and transnational corporate and governmental actors have multiplied the amount of surveillance already present in one's homeland. The rise of translational cybercrime and the increasing threat of cyberwarfare make questions of privacy ever more cogent. 6) An increasing *security culture.* Not only airports but thousands of public and private places have scaled up security mechanisms of various kinds, under the often-spurious claim that they increase safety. Whatever gains they may give in safety need to be matched by guarantees of privacy, but seldom are. 7) Surveillance through the *Internet of Things* and *Smart Cities.* Increasingly we are inviting monitoring devices into our cars, homes, offices and public buildings, and even placing them on our bodies (FitBits) and even in them (implanted RFIDs). The increasing presence of Net-connected digital devices (like Alexa or Echo Dot) and a host of "smart" appliances have made the home, once the center of privacy, a highly data-mineable space, and furthered the erosion of clear social norms and guidelines about what is private and what is not. In addition, the rise of Smart Cities with ubiquitous sensors and recording devices, including networked health care services, emergency control centers, smart grids, industrial control matrices, intelligent transport systems and traffic control systems all offer benefits but all are vulnerable to hacking. While full of possible safety, environmental and health benefits, especially when connected to in-home Internet of Things devices, Smart City efforts can multiply surveillance capacity in potentially very damaging ways. Unless we develop additional safeguards, we are being stupid about "smart." 8) *Bio surveillance* through iris scans, fingerprints on phones, DNA records, facial recognition software and other forms of body scanning are increasing. While there are legitimate uses of this data, because it is seldom erased after legitimate use it can be used for a host of criminal or authoritarian purposes. Seemingly innocent things like taking selfies greatly increase the database for facial recognition scans, and ancestry searches that record your DNA can be vulnerable to hackers or used by policing agencies without consent. 9) *Masking surveillance in addictive pleasures.* Anyone who has spent time on social media knows that it can have an addictive quality, and addictions are dangerous, distracting pleasures. Many online pleasures effectively mask the dataveillance they enable. In addition to the pleasure of "connecting," things like playing games on Facebook or Buzzfeed, for example, provide additional companies access to all of your data. Along with games, a massive network of social media apps with their "liking" clicks create additional exploitable data points of information about us. 10) All this adds up to the *normalization of surveillance*. Whether through obliviousness or indifference, and partly because much of it is embedded in pleasurable activities, most of us accept this surveillance and privacy invasion as just the way things are. Continuing this trend of normalization will eventually make it impossible to resist these forces; there will be too much data to use against us. (This list is modified from the book and website *Transparent Lives*, Bennett et al. 2014).

While much of this may now be beyond individual control, in the following pages I outline some steps that can be taken by individuals to limit surveillance. But there is a great deal more that can be done collectively. And it needs to be done rather soon. A medium that prides itself on interactivity is vulnerable to charges that it is not responding to its interacting users when they protest in significant numbers. The #DeleteFacebook movement of 2018, while not enough, was a wake-up call to social media corporations. Increasing numbers of people are becoming aware of the seriousness of issues surrounding surveillance. The major electronic corporations that are responsible for making private information available to friends, family and enemies, as well as to corporate advertisers, insurance companies and employers are also the key link in making private data available to governments. So far giant corporations such as Google and Facebook, when challenged, have largely fended off significant change by making minor, largely cosmetic alterations in their privacy policies. Privacy advocates argue that without pressure from their customers through things like petitions and boycotts, these corporations will continue to trample on the right of individuals and groups to control what information becomes public.

A second key area for those fighting privacy erosion focuses on strengthening current government policies (legal guidelines) and enforcing government practices (which have often violated legal guidelines with impunity). Some critics suggest that only a break-up of large monopolies such as Google, Amazon and Facebook can halt their massive invasions of privacy and the spread of abusive political lies masquerading as news. Short of that, there is widespread agreement that there needs to be regulation of online advertising and the data-mining it uses, and even stricter regulation on governmental surveillance. Even Facebook CEO Mark Zuckerberg has admitted that social media companies need more regulation (Cooper 2018). Advertising on television and in print media has to follow certain basic rules of truth-telling. No such rules apply to Web advertising with the result that there is far less transparency, far more lies, distortions and ads disguised as news. Online privacy laws are particularly weak in the US, the place where they are arguably most needed given that it is home to the largest digital media conglomerates. As Andrews (2013) and others have elaborated, laws simply have not kept up with new media, and new laws are needed to specifically protect privacy in cyberspaces. As earlier referenced, Andrews has created a viable version of what a new Internet privacy rights document might look like (Table 4.1). Whether or not her particular "constitution" is the perfect mechanism, it is clear that privacy laws in most parts of the world need to be significantly altered to keep up with innovations in ICTs, and new legislation will be needed if some semblance of personal and political privacy is to be kept alive in a rapidly digitizing world. In the current era, the US and the EU are moving in opposite directions. The US under the Trump regime decimated one of the few legislative aids to protection of privacy and fairness on Web: The Net Neutrality doctrine. They also passed legislation that killed privacy rules that would have required Internet service providers to get your explicit permission before sharing or selling your Web browser history or other personal information. On the positive side, the EU passed a useful starting point law that became effective in 2018, the General Data Protection Regulation (GDPR), which significantly lessens the capacity of social media sites to track users. Whether the EU rules will provide enough protection remains to be seen. Without such regulation (and more), the death of privacy and the rise of a total surveillance society will indeed soon be upon us with devastating personal and political consequences. US-based corporations like Facebook immediately took steps to minimize the impact of the GDPR by moving as much of their electronic empire out of the EU as possible. Even in the wake of their 2018 political scandals, Zuckerberg Inc. does not seem to fully appreciate the dangers its social media platform poses. (For more on detail on the specifically *political* impact of Facebook and other perpetrators of dataveillance, see Chapter 7.)

A common counter to concerns raised about our surveillance society is the claim that "if you have nothing to hide, you have nothing to worry about." Well, if you feel certain that no for-profit corporation, no government agency in your home country or abroad, no cyberbully, sexual harasser, identity thief or other malevolent actor now or in the future will ever misuse your data, then by all means give up your privacy. If, on the other hand, you do not have that certainty, then I suggest you consider carefully the amount of privacy we have lost and the further losses we may experience.

⊡ WHAT CAN WE DO TO PROTECT OUR DATA AND PRIVACY?

Lori Andrews's constitution has offered a pretty comprehensive set of targets for the restoration of our rights as rooted in the vital right to privacy. Let me suggest some of the practical things we can do, first as individuals, then as citizens collectively, to move toward a restoration of those rights. On both a personal level and on a political level, there are a number of things that can help to fend off current and potentially far worse future abuses of the digitized surveillance society.

First, on the personal level. You might start by going to Facebook, Twitter and Google and ask them to provide you with all the data they have on you. That will no doubt prove illuminating, if not frightening, and will hopefully encourage you to either avoid them altogether or use every available data collection limitation the platforms offer. It can be difficult to quit Facebook or its sister, Instagram, because they are so massive. But unless you feel some need to be connected to 2 billion people, there are more secure, less ad-heavy social media alternatives such as Diaspora or Ello that don't track you, and allow you to create quieter, more interesting digital hangouts. If you really need to know what Kim Kardashian had for breakfast, there probably is no alternative to Twitter. But if you just want a perfectly fine microblogging app, there are open source ones, e.g. Mastodon (though be sure to counter-surveil the company since most successful apps are bought up by the giant tech corps, and often made less private). The biggies such as Google, Facebook, Instagram and Twitter all do in fact provide you with a number of ways to limit the kinds of data they collect and share, but those limitations are not the default ones. So you must dig down on the sites to find them. You can, for example, check a box that tells Google not to track the places you search on Google Maps, and you can tell Facebook not to share various kinds of data. I won't name all these ways to limit collecting because they change from time to time, but look carefully at all the sites that track you and minimize the tracking as fully as they allow. Again, so long as their revenue is dependent upon gathering and sharing your data, they will not make this easy but they are bound to provide you with *some* privacy settings, so use every one that is available. Just don't assume that will be enough to truly fend off surveillance.

Some other more effective ways to protect your privacy include using the Signal encryption tool or one like it for all of your voice and video calls. Just as with your social media or Web search account, maximize the privacy settings on the browser(s) you use. Use Ghostery or some form of do-not-track software for all Web surfing to make sure sites are not grabbing data about you (a new standard of DNT is being developed that will make this more effective). (You should try out Ghostery as a way to learn just how much data about you Google and friends gather as you travel digital spaces.) Instead of or in addition to Google, use the non-tracking DuckDuckGo search engine, or better still the fully encrypted Tor browser for all of your searches, or at least ones you feel are particularly sensitive. The "private browsing" option on search engines will hide your searches from other users of your device, but Google or whomever will still retain the information, making it potentially vulnerable to abuse.

Use full disk encryption on your laptops and desk tops; FDE encrypts all of the data on your hard drive. Use two factor identification and a password manager to protect against hacking for all your accounts. If you find that too cumbersome, at least use two factor for any passwords for sites or apps that use credit cards or connect to bank accounts. The move to replace passwords with biometric logins (using your fingerprint or facial recognition) is proceeding apace. While increasing security in one way, it creates new problems as it expands the database of biometric scans. A good password manager may remain a better option.

Be wary of taking online surveys, no matter how fun they may seem. Many are just marketing scams, and even many with seemingly legitimate academic bases can be misused (it was precisely one such survey that led to the massive 87 million user breach of Facebook by the political propaganda company Cambridge Analytica). Also limit or eliminate shopper loyalty cards provided by retailers. They too are used primarily to gain data on you that may be shared beyond the company offering the card.

If you are considering electronic home security, do not waste money on an expensive company that will place you under 24/7 surveillance. If you feel the need for a home security system, buy one you can monitor yourself and encrypt. Better still, rely on a proven analog device: A large dog who likes to bark at strangers. (This device has the added feature of providing loving and often amusing companionship.)

Keep all your computer operating system and smartphone software up-to-date because this will include the latest fixes for viruses and hacking exploits. Use antivirus software, but be careful which you choose since some of it is actually malware disguised as an antivirus app. Get rid of old data on your devices because it is likely to be less secure and may provide elicit entry into current data. Periodically monitor all shopping and banking accounts online to check for unauthorized purchases or money transfers. Be very careful using public Wi-Fi networks, particularly in high traffic settings like cafes and airports. They are easily hacked by "sniffing" or "man-in-the middle" attacks. When using this type of network, be sure that HTTPS is enabled for any sites you visit (this is actually a good idea for *all* online work), and avoid doing sensitive logins such as to your bank account. Turn off open apps such as Dropbox whenever using public wireless. When trying out a new app or game on Facebook or other social media, always say no to any request to let your friends know about it; that is giving the app permission to use your contact information to invade the lives of your friends.

Check the privacy settings on all your Internet of Things devices like Alexa and various smart appliances, and switch them off when not in use. If you use devices like a FitBit or AppleWatch, unless you have a specific medical condition that requires constant monitoring, turn the devices to the maximum privacy settings.

Phishing is an old practice that is getting more sophisticated all the time. Be very wary of opening any attached file not sent to you directly by a person or institution you know; watch for phishing that uses recognizable logos and even the names of people you know but that do not match the real email addresses. Delete no longer used email accounts that can be mined for data, some of which may be used to scam your friends or abet other crimes. Periodically check to see if any of your email accounts have been breached by using an app such as *haveibeenpwned.com*.

In general, scale down. Keep only the data you *really need* at hand on your phone or computer, and store the rest in an encrypted backup device of some kind. Or just eliminate it. Ask yourself what you really need to keep. The Citizen Lab at the University of Toronto offers an easy to use Security Planner that can walk you through the steps to use these or similar techniques to increase your personal data privacy and security.

These kinds of personal changes are important, but most people will continue to ignore most privacy protections, and even when they are followed they will not be enough unless large regulatory processes are put in place through social change movements, pressure on legislators and other forms of collective political action. On the level of political action, there are a host of things that can be done. To begin with, the Internet needs to be regulated like a public utility. Until there are non-commercial alternatives, the Web should have at a minimum the same kinds of protections afforded to television and radio in terms of things like truth-in-advertising.

A number of vital organizations are working on these issues. If you share the concerns raised here, check out one or more the following institutions that are seeking to solve the abuses of privacy invasion, dataveillance and the threat they pose to democracy: The Center for Humane Technology; Privacy International; the Center for Media and Citizenship; the Electronic Privacy Information Center; the Citizen Lab; the Electronic Frontier Foundation. These and similar organizations are fighting abuses in government and corporate surveillance. There is no more pressing issue surrounding digitizing lives than how to fend off the centralization of power in the hands of governments and corporations that electronic dataveillance enables.

The German writer/philosopher Goethe observed that "None are more helplessly enslaved than those who falsely believe they are free." In the digital world, the chains that bind us are not made of iron, but rather are links on chains of data with the potential to enslave us far more completely than we can imagine. But these chains do not chafe on the skin. Indeed, they feel good; they seem to be freely given, enjoyable things. We might add as a corollary to Goethe that these days, "We are most enslaved by things we falsely believe are given for free." Google, Facebook, Amazon and the other major platforms are given to us "free of charge." How can they do that? They do it, again, because their real product is not "searches," "connections," or "books," but you. You are the product. You produce the data about yourself that, one way or another, they sell to advertisers, researchers and other hidden entities. If those data remained just with advertisers, it would still continue to entail a great deal of manipulation of your emotions and thoughts. (The dog you hug in that FB photo leads them not only to put dog toy ads on your page, but also to try to sell you health insurance through ads with cuddly dogs in them.) But it is what other agents beyond the advertising industry can do with your data that is truly dangerous.

The massive 87 million profile data breach Facebook revealed in 2018 is just the tip of the iceberg of abuse and misuse to which your data can be put by bad actors in governmental, corporate and criminal worlds. The famous adage that "Power corrupts, and absolute power corrupts absolutely" needs a contemporary corollary: "Surveillance corrupts, and absolute surveillance corrupts absolutely." Now that governments (your own and foreign ones), corporations and criminals, including criminal corporations and criminal governments, have access to unimaginably massive amounts of data about us it will be difficult to put the Big Brother surveillance genie back in the bottle. Especially if we continue to provide much of that data freely and willingly, if seldom in full knowledge of who would ultimately get access to it. To be clear, there are positive uses of data gathering. Things such as breakthroughs in medicine and health care can benefit from data we provide, as can certain kinds of legitimate social science research. But the issue is less the data than *control of the data* and *the right to consent to or deny its collection and use*. The issue is our right to know what data we are providing, and to control if, when and how that data is being shared and used. The questions are: What can we do to limit data theft? What can give us more control over our data? What can limit potential manipulation of our personal and political lives through dataveillance? We have only a short time to find democratically sound answers to these questions before the data chains we offer up become permanent shackles on our freedom. If authoritarian regimes continue to tighten control, and if democratic regimes turn ever more authoritarian, it is likely to be not the heavy hand of force but the invisible hand of dataveillance that will lead the way.

5

Is Everybody Equal Online?

Digitizing Gender, Ethnicity, Dis/Ability and Sexual Orientation

There is no race. There is no gender. There is no age. There are no infirmities. There are only minds. Utopia? No, the Internet.

("Anthem," MCI WorldCom 1997).

While few claims about the Internet have been as deeply challenged as the sentiment in this MCI advertisement from 1997, belief in the socially equalizing nature of digital culture continues to be quite strong. Not all such claims are wholly wrong, but they need to be made more carefully and in context-specific ways, because the Web also is being used to promote and deepen inequalities.

Claims about the race-less, gender-less, etcetera-less nature of the Net arose initially out of the era when online communication was primarily through written words. But even when digital spaces were just words, the claims made little sense because they vastly underestimated the depth of socialization we humans inevitably undergo. Years of learning our place(s) in the world cannot be washed away magically by going into online places. While certain freedoms are indeed opened up by anonymity and some other features of some online spaces, countless studies make clear that we inevitably drag the heavy weight of who we are offline with us online. Moreover, no one seemed to ask the next question: If we are truly in a post-racial, post-sexist era, why would one *want* to disguise one's race or gender? Could it be because certain stereotypes were still rampant, and certain races, genders and orientations were still dominant?

⮒ THE DEFAULT SUBJECT POSITION?

Equality isn't something you sprinkle on the cake once it's made. It needs to be baked in.

(Internet Society 2017: 99)

To understand the social and cultural factors in online communication (as well as technology creation, dissemination and adoption), it is vital to understand the key variables in social identity formation. Sociologists have long identified what those key variables are, and digital culture interpreters have shown them to be interwoven into all levels of digitized lives. Typically, the list of key socialization/identity formation factors include: Class; gender; race/ethnicity/nationality; sexual identity; age; language; education level; religion and geographic location (urban/suburban/rural, etc.). To this list cyberculture analysts would add technological knowledge or techno-literacy, a factor typically very much shaped by all the other factors, especially class.

Together and in various combinations, these variables make up a person's *subject position*. If you think of identity as how you think about yourself, subject position is where *social structures beyond yourself place you in the world*. Some elements of subject position can change over time, but they remain extremely good predictors of belief and action. This is particularly so when people do not reflect on how their position was constructed, but just assume it to be the natural state of the world. Subject position deeply shapes personal identity, but especially in the Western world with its unusually strong emphasis on individualism, people tend to view their identities more as personally chosen than broadly shaped by cultural factors. As a teacher in North American universities, I notice this when assigning biographical essays; students invariably stress their personal uniqueness in their essays. Yet in comparing them it is abundantly clear how similar their tastes, styles, ideas and values are in relation to their class, gender, ethnicity, age, sexuality and regional subject position.

Some digital culture scholars speak of the **default subject position** as still shaping online experience. This refers to the process by which straight, white, middle-class, Euro-American male cultural assumptions, values and ideas were (and often still are) unintentionally built into hardware, software and digital cultures. This default subject position emerged from those who were the early creators of digital technology and cybercultures. White, middle class English-speaking men played the key role in developing much of this culture, and they continue to do so to a large extent. There was no conscious intent to exclude other perspectives nor some conspiracy to make the digital world a white male domain. Let me be clear, "some of my best friends" (as the phrase goes) are white, male, English-speaking engineers, programmers and designers. And they are by and large a fine bunch of folks. But they would be the first to admit they don't know much about what a young woman in Ecuador, or an older man in Ethiopia, or even a teenager in Australia, needs or thinks about. Yet they make things used by these folks and a myriad of others all over the globe with a wide range of experiences, beliefs, values and needs. The early makers of the hardware and software that still in one form or another dominate the digital world were largely unaware that they were building from a particular, limited viewpoint on the world.

One oft-cited example is the choice of the metaphor of the *desktop* to name the basic *interface* between users and computers. The metaphor was designed to make computers more user friendly. But why that metaphor? Why not other possible metaphors like workbench, or kitchen counter, art canvas or playground, etc., each of which would have been more user friendly to other sets of users? Clearly because it was the one familiar to the mostly white male desk-bound designers (Selfe and Selfe 1994). With no intention to be culturally limiting, these kinds of unconscious assumptions were built into hardware and software at every level. As the use of digital devices and the making of digital cultures has expanded to new groups it is no longer possible to ignore the cultural limitations built into hardware, software and other aspects of the digital realm. The workforce at major digital culture-making corporations has become more diverse over the first few decades of the Net era, but it remains a pretty culturally narrow group. These companies are making efforts to enlarge the scope of their cultural repertoire (Microsoft has more cultural anthropologists on its payroll than any university). This is often driven more by a desire to expand their market into new cultural terrains than by a deep corporate commitment to cultural diversity, but some inroads are being made to get beyond the default subject position. But there remains a long way to go for a variety of technical as well as political reasons.

To their credit, some areas of the digital world openly acknowledge and struggle with the problems of the default subject position. For example, in an admirably self-reflective piece on "Wikipedia: Systemic Bias," Wikipedia's editorial board noted that

> Women are underrepresented on Wikipedia, making up less than 15 percent of contributors . . . The gender gap has not been closing over time and, on average, female editors leave Wikipedia earlier than male editors. Research suggests that the gender gap has a detrimental effect on content coverage . . . Women typically perceive Wikipedia to be of lower quality than men do.
>
> Access to the Internet is required to contribute to Wikipedia. Groups who statistically have less access to the Internet, including people in developing nations, the poor in industrialized nations, the disabled, and the elderly, are underrepresented on Wikipedia. In most countries, minority demographic groups have disproportionately less access to information and education than majority groups. This includes African Americans and Latinos in the U.S., the First Nations of Canada, the Aborigines of Australia, and the poorer populations of India, among others . . . Wikipedians are likely to be more technically inclined than average . . . Despite the many contributions of Wikipedians writing in English as a non-native language, the English Wikipedia is dominated by native English-speaking . . . These Anglophone countries tend to be in the global North, thereby accentuating the encyclopedia's bias to contributions from First World countries.
>
> (Wikipedia, "Systemic Bias," accessed 16 October 2013)

Few online communities are as clear and honest as the Wikipedians about the systemic bias built in from the default subject position, but the vast majority of online services and communities reflect the same bias and can be analyzed in quite similar terms. And given the continued underrepresentation of women in all tech fields, this is not likely to change soon without major private and governmental efforts.

In default subject position terms, the English language is, for example, also a key component of online cultural bias across the board. As of 2018, more than half of the content of the Web was available only in English, despite native speakers of English being only 6 percent of the world's population and people with some secondary knowledge of the language making up only another 12 percent. No other language represents more than 10 percent of Web content, though Chinese is gaining rapidly. In addition, much of the program language available for software creation was built on the linguistic logic of English such that even non-English-speaking programmers had to use a character set known as ASCII, an acronym whose full name, American Standard Code for Information Interchange, suggests its cultural origin and bias. Pressures from other language groups are slowly expanding the use of languages other than English both for content and programming, but the Web remains a place far more friendly to English speakers than to anyone else. While no one is forced to visit English language sites—there is content in many other languages, though far less of it—there is so much more available in English that it tends to drown out other languages. This is a problem of ethnocentrism, but it is also clearly a class issue, since in most parts of the world it is only the children of wealthier classes who are taught English as a second language. This is one of many ways in which the structure of the Web reinforces economic inequalities (Warschauer 2003: 95–99).

Let me be clear that there is no conspiracy to exclude here; no ill will was required for things to end up this way. Rather, it is cultural hegemony, a process discussed in more detail later in this chapter, by which groups with greater economic, political and/or cultural power lead those with lesser power to consent to their dominant ideas without overt coercion. It is the historical result the fact that those in position to create and disseminate much of digital culture were overwhelmingly middle-class, English-language-only speakers, with that particular set of cultural ideas and values. The unintended result of the limits of the default subject position from which much of the Internet and other components of digital culture have been designed and implemented has rendered is that many digital spaces are deeply culturally biased. And the country most responsible for the early development of the Net, the US (my home country), is arguably more ethnocentric than most because, partly by virtue of being the world's only superpower (for now), it tends to produce citizens who see little need to think much about the rest of the world (or learn other languages). When that mind-set went into the Internet-making process, the results were predictably narrow.

However, just as it is possible to change the default settings on most programs, it is possible to move beyond the **default identity** initially built into much digital culture in order to open up digital spaces more fully to many other subject positions. And that work has been under way for many years now. But just as default settings often remain invisible to most computer users and don't get changed, *default identities have to be intentionally changed.* Much of the work of critical digital culture studies has been and continues to be to ferret out the places where default identity dominates cyberspaces, and to suggest ways to open up those spaces in ways supportive of a more diverse array of subject positions.

Clearly, the most effective ways to overcome these cultural biases have been to bring greater gender, class and ethnic/racial diversity into the design and implementation of digital devices and processes, and to involve a more diverse population in the active creation of digital cultures. The electronic communication industry remains exceedingly white and male; in the US as of 2018 women made up less than 20 percent of the ITC work force, and those numbers fall rapidly when talking about the higher echelon jobs in the field. In Silicon Valley, fewer than 8 percent of tech start-ups are led by women, and in a region where Latinos make up close to 25 percent of the population, there are fewer than 5 percent Latino employees in Valley tech companies. All non-white ethnicities are seriously under-represented. Similar statistics can be found in Europe, and the gender gap is even greater in Japan. Progress is further slowed by the fact that even when corporations see it as in their economic self-interest to hire a more diverse workforce, historical and ongoing discrimination in the offline world has meant that there are often not enough members of many marginalized groups in a position to learn about, let alone pay to be educated for, these jobs (*WISAT* n.d.).

The second most effective technique has been to extend the cultural competencies of those from the default subject position through various kinds of training. Historically, much of this training has been superficial, but corporations increasingly realize that without diverse cultural competencies they cannot extend their markets, and nothing motivates corporations like market growth. Both of these processes are well under way, but there is clearly a long way to go before digital cultures come close to reflecting the world's full cultural diversity.

▣ IS THE INTERNET A GUY? ENGENDERING CYBERSPACES

There are a variety of different ways to think about digital cultures and cyberspaces as gendered, as favoring equality or inequality in gender relations. I will briefly trace five of the approaches: 1) Gender imbalance in the ICT workforce; 2) the gendering of the design of ICT devices, spaces and applications; 3) forms of gender harassment and discrimination in online environments; 4) representations of gender in online media and digital games and 5) the use of cyberspaces and digital devices in pursuit of gender equity. These are far from the only ways to talk about gender in cyberspaces, but I believe these approaches can suggest the structures that contribute to most other aspects of sexism online as well. Some other dimensions of gender online are dealt with in other chapters of this book, including pornography and the traffic in women in Chapter 6 and more on gender in digital games in Chapter 8.

At base, it is crucial to realize that as with all other aspects of life online, offline conditions deeply shape gender relations in cyberspaces. In North America, for example, women still earn on average less than 75 percent of the income earned by men. Associated issues of bank loans and credit, inherited wealth favoring males and other economic factors place women at a disadvantage in most developed countries, and the situation is often equally or more biased in the developing world. These structural conditions, along with continuing forms of cultural sanctions (religious and secular) that deter or lessen the force of women in the public sphere, all shape the possibilities for life online too. Feminist movements worldwide have improved conditions greatly over the last few decades, but full equity is still far from being achieved. Access to online information and interaction has often proved vital to women around the globe, and women and men continue to work on the gender gap in cyberspaces.

We have already noted the fact that there are deep imbalances in the ITC workforce, with all but a handful of prominent women missing from the upper echelons, relatively few women at mid-levels except in pink-collar secretarial and graphic design positions, leaving women concentrated on the lowest, least well-paid and most hazardous levels of assembly and disassembly. Given continuing extreme gender imbalances in enrolments in engineering and tech schools around the world (fewer than 10 percent in most countries), that situation is going to change slowly, at best. This is doubly unfortunate because a number of the other forms of gender discrimination would no doubt be lessened by a greater presence of women in the decision-making levels of the ICT workforce. This situation in turn shapes things like the fact that women are less likely to contribute in certain areas of online knowledge production (as suggested by the figure cited earlier that only 15 percent of Wikipedia entries are by women).

The *representations* of women and men in digital media like Web pages and video games are arguably the most disheartening. Where media activist and watchdog groups have done much to improve gender representation in traditional media (TV, film, etc.), though there is clearly much to improve, new media have frequently fallen back on stereotypes and representations that should have fallen into the dustbin of history. This is due to several factors, some technical, some cultural. The virtual, non-realistic nature of new media allows for a plasticity of representation that may lend itself to the exaggeration on which stereotyping thrives (bulging muscles on males, bulging busts on females). It doesn't take much effort to find e-games riddled with anatomically impossible cyberbabes, or websites that degrade women in every imaginable way. To test this hypothesis, try typing the words "Asian women" into Google or Yahoo. If you are lucky, or happen to be a long-time researcher on Asian demographics, you may find predominantly academic information. But more often, as when I just retried this experiment after typing that phrase, more than half of the first page of entries retrieved were sites that, one way or another, stereotyped or exploited Asian women. Here the issue is both cultural and technical. The ability for virtually anyone with a modicum of technical skill to upload content onto the Web has meant that the sexism rampant in the real world has found a media outlet it did not have before. Where film and television production consists of a relatively small community that can be addressed by critics of gender (or racial) stereotyping, the community of Web producers is almost infinitely extensive and far more difficult to reach.

The ways in which *offline gender issues* like sexual harassment, stalking, violence against women and sexual trafficking have migrated onto and been impacted by digital technologies and digital culture once again remind us that allegedly virtual worlds and real worlds are never really disconnected. The anonymity of cyberspaces has unleashed new, though hardly unprecedented, levels of sexist discourse, as well as new forms of cyberbullying, cyber sexual harassment and **cyberstalking**, among other problems. While not all cyberbullying is gender related, an extremely high percentage of it is directed at girls or at boys considered insufficiently masculine. (Some experts argue that when harassment is directed at children under the age of 18, it should be classified as cyberbullying, and when directed at those over 18, as cyberstalking, but that seems to me a somewhat arbitrary division and one not sensitive enough to varieties of harassment.)

Online sexual harassment has become ubiquitous; in the US alone an estimated 850,000 cases of cyber sexual harassment occur each year, and similar patterns exist in countries around the world ("Cyber Sexual Harassment Statistics" 2012). One survey found that 80 percent of gamers, male and female, believed sexism was prevalent in online gaming communities, and statistical evidence supports their beliefs. Women gamers, for example, receive three times as much "trash talk" as males, regardless of skill level, much of it directed in sexual terms. Sexist commentary is rampant in game chat, with anonymity often unleashing a torrent of truly misogynistic remarks. Sixty-five percent of women reported being harassed, compared with 15 percent of men (and the 15 percent of men were often harassed by being called female derogatory or homophobic names—bitch, fag, etc.) (Dill, Brown and Collins 2008; Matthew 2012; Melendez 2012; O'Leary 2012; Yao, Mahood and Linz 2009). While male gamers sometimes say abuse comes because of the incompetence of girl and women gamers, the statistics show the same level of harassing remarks even at the highest skill levels for female players.

The testimony of one female gamer is typical of many other reported incidents:

> [M]y boyfriend who is an avid player [of Modern Warfare] convinced me one night [to play]. Once the opposing team realized I was a woman, they acted out a virtual "gangbang" and kept pushing my avatar against structures in the game, crowding around me and saying the most vile things I've ever heard. This actually frightened me even though it was happening in a virtual reality rather than in "real" life. I can only imagine what people of color and different cultures must go through just to play a video game. And the fear they must have about just opening their mouth to speak . . . unbelievable.
>
> (The Road Less Taken n.d.)

In this case, the woman was identified by her voice, a reminder that not only visual but aural "outing" of women (and people of color with ethnically coded accents), a phenomenon also known as vocal profiling, has often replaced text-based anonymity in multimedia online spaces.

The attack on women gamers became much more intense during the events known as *Gamergate* that unfolded in 2014. Presenting itself as a challenge to biased game reviews, Gamergate quickly revealed itself to be an all-out attack on women online. The vicious attacks on advocates for gender fairness in gaming and non-sexist games included death threats, rape threats, *doxxing* (revealing offline addresses) and various other attempts to intimidate and silence certain key figures such as Zoe Quinn, Anita Sarkeesian and Briana Wu, but were ultimately aimed at shutting down all remotely feminist or progressive discourse online. Some analysts see Gamergate as a watershed moment in the rise of the proto-fascist alt-right, fueled by vicious misogynist figures such as Milos Yiannopoulos and ultimately embodied in politicians such as Donald Trump (Lees 2016).

The actual number of misogynist and sexist gamers is much smaller than their very vocal presence online suggests. And the reputation of the larger constituency of male gamers has been helped along by men such as Sam Killerman, who founded Gamers Against Bigotry, a site that works against not only sexism and homophobia, but racial, ethnic and religious bigotry in games and gamers as well. A different approach to the issue was taken by the site Fat, Ugly or Slutty. The site collected and posted sexist and other derogatory comments by gamers with the goal of laughing the perpetrators into embarrassed silence. In a sense, this is the opposite of censorship (as can occur through "muting" or "reporting" abusers) and has the added advantage of publicizing what is often dismissed as harmless or exaggerated behavior (Fat, Ugly or Slutty n.d.). To some degree sexist gamers were unfairly focused on (though they certainly asked for it via Gamergate) in that similar kinds of sexist harassment can be found on many, many other Web spaces; indeed, on practically any site that allows comments. In general, the Net proved a fertile ground for connecting up disaffected males who certainly didn't feel their whiteness and maleness conveyed much privilege. It was far easier to blame women, immigrants and people of color for the harm done to them by giant corporations pushing a changing economy.

Another dimension of online harassment, cyberstalking, is one that doesn't always end at the edge of cyberspaces. While men and boys suffer harassment too, the vast majority of victims are girls and women. Cyberstalking has been used to track women into their homes, far too often leading to sexual assaults. While the Internet has provided lifelines and safe spaces for women facing violence, perpetrators of domestic violence are increasingly using ICTs like spyware and keystroke logging software to track their partners' behavior. Fake ads have also been used to endanger domestic partners, as in the case of Jebediah Stipe, who was sentenced to a term of 60 years to life for posting a fraudulent ad in Craigslist that resulted in the rape of his former girlfriend. The ad read, "Need an aggressive man with no concern or regard for women. If interested, contact Sarah" (Winfrey 2010). Stipe set up several "rape dates" for Sarah from the pool of 161 men who responded (Winfrey 2010). Cyberstalking is every bit as serious as offline stalking; in fact one study found that it is actually experienced by many women as more traumatic than offline stalking (Gutierrez 2013).

The Stipe case is just one particularly well-publicized example of the massive, worldwide problem of violence against women (see Chapter 6). Cyber tools have been implicated in both the carrying out of domestic violence and its resistance. Given that violence against women affects every culture, ethnic group and class around the globe, this is one more reason that being tech savvy can be vital to women and girls.

Violence against women has generated a substantial network of online organizations seeking solutions to this global problem (Fascendini and Fialova 2011; Kee 2005; Pinto 2017; Southworth et al. 2005). The statistics are staggering: 70 percent of women globally experience some kind of violent attack in their lives; in Australia, Canada and Israel 40–70 percent of female murder victims are killed by their intimate partners; nearly 50 percent of women in the US have been sexually harassed in their workplace; in Canada 54 percent of young women experience sexual coercion in a dating relationship; in the US 1 out of 5 women (and 1 out of 70 men) will be raped during their lifetime; women aged 15–44 are more at risk from rape and domestic violence than from cancer, car accidents or malaria. The problem knows no line of class, race, age or national origin. While patterns vary across cultures, the problem is truly global. The UN's Unite to End Violence Against Women project and website is one of many clearinghouses for vital efforts to confront this horrendous amount of physical and psychological violence against women and girls. Some of these campaigns specifically target digital culture itself. A successful petition campaign was launched in 2013 against Facebook for accepting ads characterized as degrading to women, especially images of domestic violence and rape fantasies (Kleinman 2013). But far more needs to be done to ensure efforts to fight hate speech in social media, and that includes hatred and intimidation of women and girls (Pinchefsky 2012).

While overt and spectacular forms of sexism such as sex trafficking rightly get most attention, sexism in a variety of less dramatic ways is the everyday experience for millions of women around the globe. The digital world is being used to make this apparent, and to counter it. One such effort describes its mission as follows:

> The Everyday Sexism Project aims to harness the power of social media to raise awareness of the ways in which gender discrimination impacts women on a day-to-day basis. It collects reports of

daily experiences of sexual harassment, job discrimination, and other sexist treatment from women around the world via email and Twitter.

(Everyday Sexism Project n.d.)

In the first year of operation, the site received over 30,000 separate incident reports (Gardiner 2013). Responses also included pornographic imagery, rape threats and death threats directed at the site's host. Another such project specifically targets street harassment. "Hollaback!" encourages women to "out" street harassers and let other women know of harassing spaces. Active in 64 cities in 22 countries, the site uses the locative possibilities of digital media to pinpoint harassers' whereabouts. Their mission statement notes that

> The real motive of street harassment is intimidation. To make its target scared or uncomfortable, and to make the harasser feel powerful. But what if there was a simple way to take that power away by exposing it? You can now use your smartphone to do just that by documenting, mapping and sharing incidents of street harassment.
>
> (Hollaback! n.d.)

A number of other important apps have been developed in the fight against gendered violence. One core problem has been that reporting rapes and other forms of sexualized violence has seldom led to successful prosecution and the process of coming forward with stories in public has often been nearly as traumatizing as the original violence. Because of this, 90 percent of women experiencing sexual assault on college campuses, for example, do not report it. Recognizing this, apps such as Callisto have been developed to allow safe ways to report assaults and harassment. But as advocates would readily acknowledge, better than finding easier ways to identify and prosecute perpetrators would be prevention, and that will take a joint effort of women and men challenging rape and harassment. In that domain, projects such as Green Dot (alteristic.org/services/green-dot/) encourage men and women to report harassing incidents that might lead to more serious crimes. The project and others like it seek to educate about the often small acts of acquiescence (like not objecting to a sexist joke) that add up to a culture that inadvertently abets rape and other forms of sexual abuse. The Centers for Disease Control and Prevention in the US recognizes sexual violence as a major health issue and offers an array of resources to combat it (cdc.gov/violencepreven tion/sexualviolence/prevention.html).

In addition to these important efforts to prevent various kinds of violence directed against the female half of the world's population, advocates for gender equality have used technology to deal with a different but related form of gender equity, one centered on challenging gender identities themselves. Many argue that digital cultures, despite decidedly sexist origins, have great potential to shake up ideas about gender. At the base of these struggles are efforts to achieve rough parity for women as participants in all forms of digital culture. While the top level digital world to a large extent remains a *brotopia*, major developments in the amount and quality of women's involvement in the creation and use of digital spaces are challenging this situation. Women and girls, for example, have now achieved rough parity with men and boys in the overall number of digital game players, though there is still gender imbalance in some game genres, with some still implicitly coded as "male" (racing and war games, for example), and others as implicitly female (often stereotypically packaged in pink).

Apparently, even virtual "women" are not exempt. There is an argument to be made that our AI digital helpers may need help themselves to deal with sexism. It is no accident that most of our talking digital devices have female voices. These are seen as more agreeable, malleable, less threatening than male voices. And lo and behold, these devices are apparently subjected to a good deal of abusive, sexist commands. One study showed that sexist, harassing and otherwise misogynistic remarks and rude suggestions are pretty routinely directed at female-voiced digital assistants and, when the researchers experimented with such harassment, that the programmed responses most often reinforced sexism. In response to being called a slut, Siri, for example, responded weakly, "I'd blush if I could." It seems that Siri, Alexa and Cortana have good reason to join the #TimesUp movement, and their programmers (in likelihood mostly brogrammers, given the gender imbalance in tech fields) who created their weak responses may need to have a talk with their Human Resources departments about gender biases (Fessler 2017).

The precursor of much of this work to use tech to approach gender equality was the rise of approaches labelled **cyberfeminisms**. Coined in the 1990s, the term is shorthand for a set of arguments for women to embrace and use technology in the service of gender equality and personal liberation. Cyberfeminisms of various stripes urged women to make their presence known in every type of digital space, and to use digital spaces to advocate for greater economic, political, social and cultural equality between the genders. Many cyberfeminists acknowledged inspiration from the brilliant arguments of feminist cultural theorist Donna Haraway in her "A Manifesto for Cyborgs" (Haraway 2003 [1984]; Haraway 1991). In particular they draw upon Haraway's claim that the breaking down of the human–machine boundary can be used to undermine historically oppressive claims that gender inequality is a "natural," biological thing. Haraway argued at the dawn of the digital era that the human–computer interface can serve to challenge assumptions about naturalized female and male roles and identities, and advocated embracing the "cyborg" as a symbol of this boundary crossing work. Haraway argues that because in patriarchal cultures men have long been identified with the mind and women with body, the cyborg—a creature part human, part electronic machine—can disrupt the notion of the "natural" body, and therefore can be utilized to challenge the assumption that there are natural roles into which women and men must fit. This argument was later taken up by trans activists and others seeking to get beyond oppressive biological determinist notions of a natural binary of gender.

Haraway not only offered a highly nuanced analysis of the positive possibilities of cyborg identities in liberating women from historical forms of sexism, but also pointed up the many digital dangers facing women, especially women from the Global South, who as noted earlier do much of the most painstaking labor in constructing digital products. Their integration into the printed circuits of capitalism exemplifies one of many downsides to the cyborg. Haraway (2003: 10) also reminds readers that cyborgs were in origin the "illegitimate offspring" of militaristic science and corporate exploitation, and that the prime popular culture examples of cyborgs were mindless killing machines like those in the *Terminator* movie series (though a tough female protagonist, Sarah Conner, is the Terminator's nemesis). Unfortunately, some less astute cyberfeminists hyped the plus side of the cyborg metaphor, without equally attending to the ways digital cultures can perpetuate and even deepen some dimensions of sexism. It is necessary to talk of cyberfeminisms in the plural, to acknowledge several strands of this work, with varying degrees of complexity and effectiveness in using cyberspaces to further the cause of gender equity. For example, Zoe Sofia has argued that cyberspace is often coded as female, through terms like "the Matrix" (derived from the Latin for "mother"), and subsequently "penetrated" by hard-bodied male cyborgs and monsters apparently threatened by women's power, including the power to reproduce the species. She suggests that the fascination of many male scientists and sci fi writers with self-replicating cyborgs seems a lot like "womb envy," an attempt to colonize one of the few social functions reserved exclusively to women, that is, human reproduction, giving birth (Sofia 1984).

Cyberfeminism as a label has mostly fallen out of fashion but the work started has blossomed into a massive movement of networked feminisms of all stripes. There are hundreds of gender equity websites, from blogs to NGOs to official government sites to educational institution sites to social movement activist groups, that are using the Web and other digital culture spaces to fight against domestic violence, sex trafficking, discrimination in the workforce and numerous other gender issues that add up to a fight for economic, political and cultural equality for all women. Feminism is an extraordinarily diverse set of ideas, and all the strands of feminist movements are represented by numerous sites on the Web, including ones targeting particular age groups, classes, nationalities and ethnicities, sexual preferences and pretty much every other imaginable grouping, from feminist ballerinas to feminist teamsters, from feminist quilters to feminist rappers, from feminist gamers to feminist politicians, from feminist anarchists to feminist business people.

No doubt the most important recent example of the use of the Net for women's empowerment was the dramatic emergence of the #MeToo and #TimesUp movements in 2017. First used in 2006 by Tarana Burke, the hashtag #MeToo went viral in the wake of revelations of abhorrent sexual behavior by Hollywood mogul Harvey Weinstein, the election of avowed pussy grabber Donald Trump and the massive Women's March following Trump's inauguration. #MeToo suddenly took off after a Twitter post by actor Alyssa Milano on October 15, 2017. Within a few hours 200,000 retweets had occurred, and by the next day, 500,000. Within a few days there were more than 12 million Facebook posts of women sharing or supporting others who told of their experiences of sexual harassment, rape and violent abuse ("MeToo movement" n.d.). Aided by some high-profile women in the entertainment world, this digitally driven phenomenon rapidly spread into a major social movement. Much of this initial energy was channeled and developed by a second development under the hashtag #TimesUp. Initiated by women in the entertainment industry, Time's Up from the beginning stressed that highly paid actors were in many ways privileged, and that the movement had to also address harassment and abuse across all professions, all classes, all ethnicities and all genders/sexualities. They also began paying critical attention to issues of pay equity between men and women across all work environments. Time's Up raised millions of dollars to support women without the resources of entertainers in their efforts to legally fight sexual abuses of all kinds and pay inequities. Using high profile televised events such as the Golden Globes ceremony, Time's Up rapidly created a massive following and publicized through its website (timesupnow.com) a wide variety of resources, building on existing online and offline feminist projects and generating new ones. Many analysts sensed that a watershed had been reached, that pervasive issues of sexual harassment, rape, physical abuse and pay discrepancies were no longer going to be brushed aside. The Net provided one key arena to constantly keep these issues alive as part of political dialogue not only in North America and the UK but around the world.

While the default subject position of the Web, gaming platforms and most other digital spaces remains biased toward white males (as clearly does the offline world), the Time's Up moment comes as women are making major incursions into every type of digital space. One ambiguous sign of this was referenced in Chapter 1 as the domestication of technology. In the modern West and much of the rest of the world, domestic spaces have been defined as traditionally feminine spaces, ones limited in contrast with public spaces coded more as masculine. Thus the increasingly central role of domestic spaces and domesticating processes as sites of digital culture have to a degree taken away some of the male bravado of keyboard cowboys in earlier cybercultures. Major efforts are also underway to encourage girls and women to enter tech domains currently dominated by men. As books like *Brotopia* (Chang 2018) make clear, the problem exists at the very heart of digital culture production in places like Silicon Valley. Alongside the viciously misogynistic alt-right versions, there are softer but nonetheless deeply damaging elements of discrimination on the liberal side of the political spectrum. Discourses, processes and movements will prove truly liberating for women and girls only when domestic space and public spaces are no longer valued and devalued based on limiting notions of gender identities, when equality of power exists in all private and public realms. Despite and because of the recent backlash against women's equality in the Trump era, the massive new wave of female empowerment seems unstoppable. But online and off there remains much work to be done.

⊡ IS THE INTERNET COLORBLIND? E-RACIALIZATIONS

The rise of the popular Internet coincided with the rise of the claim of some conservatives that racism had ended, that we were entering a "post-racial" or "colorblind" era of history. A variation on the famous *New Yorker* cartoon of the dog going online depicted a be-robed, cone-hatted person clearly meant to represent a member of the infamous American white supremacist group the Ku Klux Klan again sitting in front of a screen typing on a keyboard. The caption in this version reads, "On the Internet nobody knows you're a racist." Even more forcefully than the original, this cartoon highlights and challenges the claim that online opportunities exist to communicate outside of socially defined roles and identities by side-stepping or actively masking ascribed identities, or by actively projecting a social position not one's own.

The concept of "race" and the practice of racism were invented simultaneously. Or, more precisely, "race" was invented to justify racism. Few social forces (outside of sexism) have done more damage to the world over the last 500 years than racism (and its close relative, ethnocentrism). While new media are indeed new in many ways, they too often fall into quite old patterns when dealing with issues of race and ethnicity. New media have reinforced old racisms, and created some novel virtual racisms. Fortunately, they have also provided new ways to combat these forces.

For several hundred years, science played a significant role in bolstering white supremacy. Scientific racisms, purporting to offer empirical evidence of the natural, biological superiority of the invented "caucasian race," lasted well into the late twentieth century (Duster 2006; Gould 1981; Kuhl 2001). But about the same time as the emergence of the popular Internet, journalists, social scientists and social movement activists began bringing forth the news that scientists had largely discredited the idea of race. Biologists showed that race made no sense as a genetic category. Race is literally only skin deep. Visible differences in skin color, facial features and the like are not a sound basis for biological categorization because the range of characteristics among people categorized as within the same "race" are as great as the differences between "races."

Recent science and social science make clear that racism created 'race,' that it is a social not a biological category. At the same time that scientists were showing the biologically meaningless nature of race, historians were documenting that the categories of races have varied immensely over time within the same country (the Irish, Italians and Jews did not become "white" in the US until the twentieth century, for example) and across geographic space (what constitutes a "race" and how the society divvies up races varies greatly from Brazil to South Africa to Australia to Canada and so on). Similarities across so-called races, and differences within so-called races, made clear that the human race is one, not several. This confirmed what some social scientists and cultural theorists were increasingly arguing: That "race" is a socially constructed category, rather than a natural fact. The fact that racial categories themselves have changed over time, and differed from nation to nation, thus reinforced the scientific breakdown of the category. But while race as a concept is hopefully being tossed into the dustbin of history where it belongs, historically created racial categories, socially embedded racist structures and racist cultural representations remain very much alive and continue to do great damage. We are in the ironic position of needing to use racial categories to challenge the idea of race because those categories have ongoing impact in present lives. As the recent vicious backlash movement known as the alt-right makes clear, racism is very much alive. And in that context pretending we can be "color-blind" is not an option, not while we still need to actively identify and fight the many forms of discrimination people of color continue to face. New media have great potential to challenge racism and racialization (the process of creating racial categories), and in some areas they are doing so. But much digital culture instead continues to reinforce racial and ethnic stereotypes, both subtly and overtly.

There are a number of different ways in which the Web has recreated, reinforced or generated new spaces for racisms to flourish. These processes and representations are collectively known as forms of e-racialization. As was the case with women, the relative absence of so-called non-whites in the upper echelons of the digital production process is partly responsible for much of this racism going unchallenged before being disseminated into cyberspace. E-racialization, or the digitization of race, includes things ranging from (overtly or covertly) racialized avatars in virtual worlds and chat rooms, racialized characters in games (see Chapter 8), racial representations on websites, racial discourse among users of the Web, racially defined portals, social media **cyberghettos** and a variety of other manifestations (Everett 2009; Everett 2012; Nakamura 2011; Young 2011;).

The story of race in digital culture begins, as race always has, in the imagination. For many years, and still often today, when most people imagine the online world it tends to call up images of European (or sometimes Asian) males in glasses and white short-sleeved dress shirts with pocket protectors full of pens. This is the ubiquitous popular cultural image sent around the world of the "nerd" or "geek," someone only comfortable speaking computerese, and uncomfortable with most other human interaction. While on one level a rather harmless image, especially as it evolved over time into a somewhat heroic phase in which "geek chic" modified the rather unattractive stereotype, by subtle implication it leaves other people, other ethno-racial groups, out of the world of digital creation. Other racial stereotypes of folks producing and inhabiting digital spaces are in part dependent upon the nerd/geek white male stereotype. The other races imagined to make and inhabit digital worlds fall into two broad stereotypes: The hyper-hyper-linked Asian and the digitally-challenged racial under-classes. In the US, Asians have long been stereotyped as the "model minority," the good minorities who work hard and don't complain about silly things like racial oppression. This "positive" stereotype has long been used to denigrate by contrast the not-so-model minorities (black and brown people) who allegedly don't work hard, don't have the right values and constantly protest about discrimination that supposedly ended long ago. This vicious American division of the world, and a modified version prevalent in Europe, migrated very easily into the imagery of cyberspaces. The extension of the World Wide Web into more parts of the globe has of necessity complicated this imagery, but it has far from eliminated it from what remains the center of the digital universe in terms of cultural power, the default subject position of the European or European American male.

In addition, these ethno-racial stereotypes have been extended from the realm of the imagined user to a proliferation of ethnic and racial stereotypes in Web spaces and in video games. Digital studies scholar Lisa Nakamura refers to these new versions of old representations of race/ethnicity as **cybertypes**, virtual stereotypes (Nakamura 2002). In addition to recycling old stereotypes, many design features of new media, especially Photoshop and homemade animation, lend themselves to the kind of physical exaggeration of features that have historically been an integral part of much stereotyping (for example, cartoons have long been a favored genre for racial stereotyping because the exaggeration of physical features used in much racist representation is easier to do in non-realist graphic media). Cybertypes can be found across a range of digital spaces, devices and forms, from virtual world icons, avatars and game characters to websites to racist audio-chat in gaming spaces. The most outrageous forms of racial denigration have taken place in digital genres that permit a high degree of anonymity. Wagner James Au, author of the book *The Making of Second Life* (2008), notes that online games and forums where participants are anonymous seem to be slowly being replaced by popular networks such as Facebook that more often match users to their offline identities. When anonymity disappears, people are generally more civil. "The shift to real identities online helps get rid of racism," Au suggests. Perhaps, but this is debatable on a couple of levels. First, one might ask whether false civility is always preferable to honest expression of prejudice if your purpose is rooting out racism. Racism made overt is perhaps easier to attack. And second, as Nakamura has argued, visual profiling (identifying race by visual cues) and vocal profiling (identifying race or ethnicity by accent) has in other areas *increased* racial harassment online and in gaming (GAMBIT: Hate Speech Project n.d.; Nakamura 2009).

The irony in much of this is that just as stereotypes have moved closer to eradication in old media like TV and film due to extensive efforts by media anti-discrimination groups, new media have allowed old stereotypes to re-emerge (and invented new ones). As with the issue of sexist representation, this is due both to use of stereotypes in the industry (video games most obviously) and to the often uncritically celebrated amateur, DIY, participatory nature of the Web that now includes vast amounts of viciously racist imagery. The election of Barack Obama as US president occasioned a new wave of claims that we were in a post-racial era, but those claims were quickly belied by a massive outpouring of vicious racist words and images directed against Obama online.

The Web in fact has proven to be a fertile medium for white supremacists who benefit from the low cost and anonymity of cyberspaces, and have been able to use the Net's connectivity to find like-minded individuals through which to spread their hate messages. A worldwide web of hate groups has been enabled by the Net, and many of these groups have utilized vicious cybertyping to good effect. As with all other forms of e-racism, these groups have not gone unchallenged, of course, since the Web has simultaneously allowed anti-racism groups to counter continuing manifestations of racism in both overt and less visible forms, including the deep structural inequalities that keep racisms alive around the globe.

Even seemingly neutral AI-driven technologies such as facial recognition software and search engines can inadvertently reinforce racist (and sexist) bias. Facial recognition software designed in the US proved to be better at identifying white males than females, and far better at identifying white folks of any gender compared to Blacks or

Asians (Olson 2018). And as Safiya Noble has demonstrated through a careful study of search terms, racism is often even embedded in the supposedly neutral algorithms of search engines like Google and Yahoo because without a sense of social context, they routinely reproduce historically existent prejudices, even without being "gamed" by racists, as also happens frequently (Noble 2015, 2018). In this area, as in so many areas where algorithms and AIs are taking on and taking over tasks once done by humans, care must be taken that human prejudices are not programmed into potentially more objective processes (Gray 2014; Lohr 2015).

While many talk about the (very real) new kinds of cross-cultural links possible via the Web and other digital technologies, it is important to also realize that digital cultures have often created cyberghettos that replicate existing informal forms of social segregation. One scholarly study, for example, found that many young white kids in the US fled from MySpace to Facebook because they believed that MySpace had become "too ghetto," a move that resembles the "white flight" of the 1970s and 1980s, when Euro-Americans left racially mixed cities for predominantly white suburbs (boyd 2012; Hargittai 2012). Some have argued that **ethnic portals** aimed at particular racially or ethnically defined communities, while very useful for intragroup connections, may also be replicating damaging forms of essentialism and group self-ghettoization. Proponents argue that such sites offer important networks for groups facing continued discrimination and marginalization, while opponents argue that such sites perpetuate marginalization and reinforce the archaic notion that race is a natural, rather than a cultural, phenomenon. Still others argue that some ethnic portals exist primarily as marketing tools for corporations with little regard for social issues surrounding racism. Each of these perspectives represents part of the truth. Some ethnic, gender or sexuality-based portals are clearly designed substantially as tools for marketing to particular demographics (Lee and Wong 2003). Others clearly are concerned substantially with empowering the group in question.

Many other **affinity portals** defined by gender, sexual orientation or other key markers of subject position also exist online. When one group, whether defined by race, class, gender, language, religion or another primary social factor, has been dominated, overlooked, harassed or discriminated against in some other way, joining together as a group can be essential to heath and survival. However, over time such groups may become insular. The trick for socially marginalized populations seems to be to find a way to utilize the benefits of group solidarity while also connecting with the world of the dominant group in order to assert their group's equality and rights. The Web is clearly one key place where these issues are being redefined.

Not all groups on the Web claiming marginalization are convincing. Digital culture theorist Tara McPherson, for example, offers a reading of the cultural symbols through which the neo-Confederate website Dixie-Net seeks to construct a white (implicitly male) identity in opposition to contemporary US multiculturalism. Confederate flags, use of the phrase the "war between the states," ubiquitous snippets of the song "Dixie," maps showing the South as a separate nation and so on reinforce a sense of rebel opposition to the United States with its stars and stripes, the Civil War, the national anthem and 50-state map (McPherson 2000). In the wake of the election of Donald Trump in 2016, this particular minority group of allegedly victimized white men who embraced neo-Nazism and other racist ideologies felt emboldened and strengthened their visibility. Resistance from anti-racists, and revealing events such as the hate-filled Charlottesville white nationalist march that led to the murder of a by-standing counter-protester, drove back but did not fully eliminate this ugly phenomenon.

Another less obvious arena where digital technologies are reshaping race is the field of biotechnology. As noted previously, by erasing the category from biology, science has over the last few decades been reversing its long and ugly history of underwriting racism. However, since the turn of the twenty-first century, the popular use and abuse of genetics have once again confused the issue of the biological reality of race. As a number of scholars have pointed out, genetic testing (itself made possible largely by developments in digital technology) has created an obsession with ancestry that has often been miscoded in simplistic racial terms (Chow-White 2012; Nelkin and Lindee 2004; Nelson and Hwang 2012). Ironically, this search for the pride of ancestry may resurrect the past illusion that race is a meaningful biological category, rather than a social construction serving to justify oppression.

Contrary to claims that we are in a post-racial, color-blind world, our newest social spaces, the digitized ones, make clear that online and offline life remain deeply marked by racism and ethnic prejudice in a myriad of forms. The election of Barack Obama as US president, for example, set off a storm of online activity that revealed deep racial divides on a number of levels (Everett 2012). The promise that the Web can bring people closer together and closer to mutual understanding is not a wholly false one, though the promise is clearly undercut by much racist and ethnocentric imagery and discourse also found there. And even if all racially offensive imagery were removed from digital spaces, it would not remove the inequalities stemming from hundreds of years of racial injustice. Indeed, some positive forms of egalitarian media imagery act as a cover-up ("How can there be racism; look how many black lawyers and doctors there are on TV?"). This is the media-centered variation on the theme of how can the US or UK be racist societies when they have a black president and East Asian MPs, respectively.

While the vast amount of racism and ethnocentrism in digital cultures is deeply disturbing and discouraging, the digital world, by exposing the continued existence of racisms and ethnocentrisms many have claimed we have left behind, enables a critical mapping of these social blights, as well as providing new technical tools for fighting them. Beyond the important task of fighting for richer, more varied representations of the full range of ethnic cultures online and in other media, critics make clear that the end of racism will also require deep changes in the economic processes and social institutions whose structures carry the impact of historic and ongoing racisms. Virginia Eubanks has shown, for example, how digital tools like algorithms are used by governmental authorities to disproportionately target poor people and people of color (Eubanks 2018). The immensely liberating potential of digital spaces will not be realized without profound work online and offline to eradicate structural conditions that continue to favor some racial and ethnic groups over others, often in ways that are a matter of life and death. This work will include helping those drawn to white nationalism to recognize that their real economic and social concerns are being exploited by conservative elites posing as their saviors but offering no solutions. The political right often claims that the left is mired in identity politics, conveniently assuming that a white nationalist identity is not an identity but rather just "American." Analysis of the 2016 presidential election shows that identity politics was the key to how people voted. Specifically, a sense among a white, male Christian identity block that they were unfairly losing status in a world in which women, people of color and non-Christians were seeking equal treatment was a significant motivator for many Trump voters (Mutz 2018). Any number of careful studies show definitively that this particular social group remains at the top of every measure of power in North America, but not all members of this demographic are successful. And much of the problem stems from another aspect of digital culture. Robots have been found responsible for the loss of as many as 670,000 jobs in the

US and their use has also driven down wages, primarily among blue-collar workers (Harthorne 2017). Much of the job loss occurred in the so-called Rust Belt region, where a significant group of former Democratic Party supporters voted for Republican candidate Donald Trump in 2016. Right-wing politicians such as Trump knew that blaming robots is not nearly as politically effective as blaming a Black person, a Latino or Muslim immigrant for a white male voter's declining job prospects. But this blame game is a self-defeating proposition because the real roots of the problem lie in an economy stacked against them by the very people asking for their votes. Without affirmative actions by government to retrain people for a new high-tech economy, millions more will be left behind. Every country in the world is becoming increasingly multi-ethnic, and ultimately no one except a few billionaires and autocrats benefits from playing one ethnicity or gender off another.

⊡ WHO IS DIS/ABLED BY CYBERSPACES? ENABLING AND DISABLING TECHNOLOGIES

The relation of people with disabilities to digital cultures is a complex and contradictory one. On the one hand, new digital technologies have created a host of assistive devices that greatly enhance the lives of millions of people who lack sight, hearing, the ability to use their hands or legs or a host of other limiting physical and psychological conditions. An array of "digital assistive devices" and digitized therapies are opening up amazing new possibilities for persons with disabilities. This is an area where becoming cyborgs has few detractors. Digital technologies have done astonishing things in enabling greater sight and hearing, in facilitating physical rehabilitation and movement and in extending possibilities for folks with cognitive/psychological/social conditions such as autism, stroke or PTSD, among others. On the other hand, access to the wonders of digital culture in online environments continues to be limited by corporations, governments and others who fail to make the Net fully accessible to folks with particular physical limitations defined as disabling.

Both the positive potential and the current limitations of digital culture in relation to people with disabilities have been aptly summed up by Mark Warschauer.

> ICT [Information and Communication Technology] is particularly important for the social inclusion of those who are marginalized for other reasons. For example, the disabled can make

especially good use of ICT to help overcome problems caused by lack of mobility, physical limitations, or societal discrimination. Using ICT, a blind person can access documents by downloading them from the Internet and converting text to speech; a quadriplegic can pursue a college degree without leaving home; a child suffering with AIDS can communicate with other children around the world. Sadly, though, disabled people, because of poverty, lack of social support, or other reasons, frequently lack the means to get online. In the United States, for example only 21.6 percent of people with disabilities have home access to the Internet, compared with 42.1 percent of the non-disabled population. This disproportionately low rate of Internet connectivity for people who in many senses most need it, and in one of the world's most technologically advanced countries, is evidence that market mechanisms alone are not sufficient for achieving equitable ICT access.

(Warschauer 2003: 28–29)

On average people with disabilities spend twice as much time online as folks without disabilities, suggesting a deep disparity between desire or need and degree and quality of access (Chambers 2004; Goggin and Newell 2003). These numbers had changed little by 2018,

It is disheartening that well into the twenty-first century, 60 percent of websites remain inaccessible to people with disabilities (90 percent were inaccessible in 2001). This is largely an issue of website design. Virtually all new computers now come with "screen readers" that can translate text into sound. Unfortunately, these devices are only effective on websites that enable their use, and only a small percentage of websites do so. This too is partly an issue of economics, since the costs of re-tooling old websites, or building new ones with this extra feature, can be considerable.

Access for folks with disabilities is both a social issue, since it excludes many extraordinarily creative people from digital cultures, and a legal issue, since laws meant to ensure access do exist in many parts of the world. In the US, the Americans with Disabilities Act (1990) established "access" to all public spaces and public services as a right, not a privilege or luxury, for persons with disabilities. In this context, access to the "public space" of the Internet also became a right. But it remains a right still routinely and massively violated. On an international scale, these rights have been embodied in the World Wide Web Accessibility Initiative (WAI) of the World Wide Web Consortium, or W3C (the organization led by Web creator Tim

Berners-Lee that has tried to set standards for Web practices). Inspired by various national laws and the Accessibility Initiative, disability rights groups around the globe continue to struggle to reach the as-yet-unrealized ideal of an Internet usable by all people.

As with other forms of "otherness," it has been claimed that the disembodied, anonymous nature of the Web has been a boon to people with disabilities. As some differently abled people have testified, this can be true. But there is also a danger of once again pushing folks with disabilities to the margins, making them invisible. Visibility or invisibility, openly noting or not calling attention to conditions labeled disabilities, should be the choice of people with disabilities online, not something foisted on them by putatively able-bodied folks.

While there are technical issues that cause difficulties in achieving universal access for persons with disabilities, the ultimate issues are social and political, not technical. The issues begin with the very terms used and the hidden biases they conceal. Let's start with that phrase itself, "people with disabilities." That's the preferred term and is set against the commonly used phrase "disabled people." What's the difference? There is a world of difference. To say someone is a *person with a disability* is to stress the personhood first and the disability second. By contrast, to say *disabled person* makes the disability the defining feature of the person. That difference neatly sums up the attitudinal problem that people with disabilities face from the able-bodied population—their full personhood is lost in a focus on physical differences.

A person with a disability, or the differently abled, exists on a continuum with everyone else. We all have certain abilities and disabilities, and to place people who have a particularly visible or more pronounced disability in a wholly other category of human beings from those of us whose abilities and disabilities are less visible is nothing but prejudice. Disability is a continuum, not a state of being. All of us at some point in our lives will be disabled as we grow older, temporarily or with likely permanence, and most of us will be severely disabled if we live long enough. The most common form of prejudice is to speak of the "normal" body or the "normal" way of moving through the world. But which is the "normal" way to move over the course of a mile: By walking, by jogging, by riding a bicycle, by riding in a car, by train, by wheelchair? All but the last of these are considered "normal" ways to move by the world at large. Why not in a wheelchair? Disability is not a natural fact; it is a socially defined state. Over the course of history and across cultures today there are many different standards of normal bodily and mental functioning, and many different attitudes toward those currently characterized as physically or mentally disabled.

When asked what is the greatest difficulty they face, the most common answer given by people with disabilities is "People's attitudes toward me" (Mullins 2010). According to disability activists, disabling responses to people with disabilities typically take one of these forms: *pity* (a useless emotion that makes the able-bodied person feel sensitive); *heroic appreciation* (how amazing that you can do X despite being so messed up); *invisibility/avoidance* (find ways not to see or interact with the PWD); *annoyance/impatience* (find the presence of a PWD an eyesore or time drag when they must be accommodated). Each of these attitudes, though differing in moral weight, has the effect of reinforcing the non-normal nature of disability, of lessening the person with a disability's place in the world.

In light of these and other forms of medical and social prejudices, the Disability Rights and Independent Living movements argue that *social attitudes* and the *built environment* are major *disabling* features that are *falsely regarded as intrinsic to the disability*. Let me give you an example. Most of you can't read with your fingers. Is that a disability? It would be if the only books published were in Braille, just as the massive number of books not printed in Braille is a limitation for those who can only read with their fingers. Again, new technologies are helping, both in translation to Braille and in such other innovative approaches as text to audio readers. But the truly disabling factor is the assumption of those privileged with sight that limitations placed upon the unsighted are not their problem.

In a world in which the social construction of disability was recognized and dealt with fairly, so-called disabilities would be seen as *naturally occurring and accidental differences* in degrees of able-bodiedness that change over time. Various disabilities would be seen instead as socially imposed limitations on movement and access *created by cultural expectations and built into social spaces*. The larger disability in this perspective is *the failed ability of society to create accommodations* to varying kinds and degrees of able-bodiedness. And the term "accommodations" itself can misleadingly suggest special privileges, as if able-bodied persons are not accommodated every day by sidewalks, elevators, escalators and thousands of other things often built at the public expense to make their lives easier.

The most common justification for lack of access to the Web or other public media for people with disabilities is that accommodation costs too much. Disability activists respond by asking, what should we pay for basic human rights? What are the societal costs of not accommodating the many gifted people with disabilities? What would we not know about the origins of the universe if Stephen Hawking's "disability" was not "accommodated"? What great music would we have missed if certain accommodations were not made for musicians without sight? Much of the expense of hardware and software accommodations is greatly minimized if an access expectation is built in initially as opposed to an afterthought. Again the disabling factor is more attitude than economics. Activists argue that when differing dis/abilities are normalized, when so-called able-bodiedness is no longer the definition of normal, all spaces, including cyberspaces, will be enriched by extending access to folks currently excluded by socially constructed limitations.

At the same time that people struggle to change the attitudes that inhibit wider access to digital cultures for persons with disabilities, others have been using digital technology to create a host of new assistive devices and virtual therapeutic environments that enable many kinds of physical and cognitive limitations to be lessened or virtually eliminated. However, each of the two main technical elements enabling digital culture impacts the access of people with disabilities: 1) hardware that is difficult or impossible to use; 2) software and applications with limited functionality vis-à-vis certain physical and cognitive conditions. And so long as hardware and software makers do not fully take people with disabilities into consideration at the earliest stages of design, each new iteration of technology only compounds the problem by requiring new accommodations to new devices and software. Given the generally lower income of people with disabilities, these recurring costs can be in themselves disabling in another sense.

Not taking into consideration the needs of people with disabilities can also show up in the arena of innovations. While most people welcomed, and the industry greatly hyped, the move to a more visual Web, progress to visual interfaces proved to be a regression for unsighted users who had been able to read text with screen readers that were not prepared to convert visual information. In sum, access for people with disabilities is a continuing, economic, social, technical and frequently changing issue that must be dealt with as an issue of rights and equality.

There are, however, many creative ways in which people with disabilities have used cyberspaces. The organization Able Gamers (Able Gamers n.d.), for example, is tackling the issue of e-game access for people with disabilities (Videogamerability n.d.). There is an entire realm in the virtual reality space Second Life where people with disabilities interact in a variety of ways, from playing to having sex to strategizing about how to improve access to and experience of online worlds for people with disabilities. Technoculture theorist Sherry Turkle relates the story of a graduate student who had lost a leg and then created a one-legged avatar who had a romance online that helped her come to terms with her real life changed body (Turkle 1995: 262–263). Stories of this kind abound, incidentally reminding us that not all avatar creation has to take the form of muscle-bound men and cyberbabes.

Another positive side of the ledger regarding digital technology is the multifaceted and fascinating area of technologies used to offer people with disabilities new abilities. Every day new devices are being invented to give people with disabilities not only better access to the World Wide Web, but to the world at large. The variety of new assistive devices with digital components range from the use of virtual environments to retrain human movement to direct **brain–computer interfaces** that allow the brain to control prosthetic arms and legs to video games used in psychological and physical therapies to more sophisticated wheelchairs that can climb stairs. The possibilities are truly exciting, though many will remain out of reach if more attention is not given to making them affordable (Usable Web n.d.).

Much discussion in cyberculture studies focuses on the issue of bodies and embodiment, in large part because so many people experience cyberspace as disembodied. Most of the time users do not even see each other's bodies when communicating online, and as they become immersed in online environments they tend to become less aware of their own bodies. Questions of embodiment obviously have special meaning for people whose bodies have been defined as not normal, including people with physical disabilities. The idea that in cyberspaces no one knows who you really are as an embodied being can seem attractive to people whose physical differences have been stigmatized as somehow less than fully human. In the many cyberspaces that do not include visual cues, we meet the person before we meet the body, if we meet that body at all. This can short circuit many prejudicial attitudes attendant upon viewing the non-normative body, just as is true to some degree around the illusory invisibility of race and gender in online worlds. But as in these other examples, social invisibility is not the solution; it can be temporarily useful in side-stepping prejudices, but too often these return when the invisibility stops. The real target is not the visible markers, but the social attitudes and structures that unequally treat the life prospects of people based solely upon those physical markers.

This returns us to the issue of access but from a new angle. While these new technologies are exciting, for a variety of reasons, not all persons with disabilities choose to avail themselves of these "fixes"; not all want to be "fixed." A famous example of this is the long-standing resistance in some deaf communities to cochlear implants, devices that can enhance hearing but that are seen by some deaf people as a betrayal of fellow members of their community. Thus, respecting various disability cultures may include in some cases acknowledging the rights of people to *refuse to use technologies* that might otherwise allow them to approximate behaviors and abilities defined as normal by dominant, non-disabled communities. Just as folks have suggested that people have a perfect right to opt out of digital culture entirely, so too do people have a right to refuse particular technologies as not necessarily enabling from their perspective. But the societal task is to make accessibility to digital realities as rich and complete as possible for people with a range of dis/abilities, so that they have the freedom to choose the kinds or degrees of dis/engagement they value.

▣ HOW QUEER ARE CYBERSPACES? ALTERNATIVE SEXUALITIES IN CYBERSPACES

As is the case with pretty much every kind of cultural minority, the story of sexual minorities in digital culture is a decidedly mixed bag. LGBTQI2+ (lesbian, gay, bi-sexual, transgender/transsexual, queer, intersex, two-spirit, plus other non-normative sex/gender identities) folks and other practitioners of marginalized sexualities have often found that important new spaces for discreet connections and community formation have been opened online, while at the same time the anonymity and disinhibition allowed by online discourse have unleashed a great flood of rhetoric that is viciously homophobic and heteronormative (attitudes and practices that presume only male–female sexual relations are "normal" or acceptable).

The Web has provided safe spaces with a degree of anonymity that have allowed some people whose sexual orientation is unwelcome or treated with active hostility in their home communities to find each other, share knowledge and offer support. Particularly in cultures with deep strictures against same-sex desire or non-normative genders, information available online—sometimes just the information that "others like me" exist—has proved deeply reassuring. Many members of sexual minority groups have attested that online communities literally have saved their lives. At the level of organized pro-queer advocacy, again, the Web has many benefits in creating safe spaces for strategizing and communicating. LGBTQI2+ social movement groups have found the Web to be a vital tool, especially in working transnationally, but also within given countries (King 2012; Phillips and O'Riordan 2007; Pullen and Cooper 2010).

On the other hand, the same anonymity and disinhibition that have provided openings for LGBTQI2+ connections have provided safe cover for the unleashing of a variety of forms of gay bashing and heteronormative hate speech. Accusing someone of being a "faggot" has been one of the most common forms of cyberbullying, and has caused great pain for many young people; in all likelihood it has contributed to the high rate of gay juvenile suicide. (Eighty percent of young people interviewed say they are more likely to bully online than face-to-face.) Many online communities, perhaps most notably gaming communities, are also riddled with homophobic slurs. The term "gay," adopted as a positive term for same-sex loving individuals, has become a widely used slur in English language youth communities. Many users of the term claim that phrases like "that's so gay" do not actually reference gay people, but even when this claim is sincere it does nothing to mitigate the fact that for most users the equation of gay (people) and disliked ideas, attitudes and/or practices, is implicit in this ubiquitous usage. Campaigns against the use/ abuse of this term, including online campaigns, are under way (Think B4 You Speak n.d.).

As with representation of other marginalized populations, media watchdog groups have been a bit slow to catch up with the regression to stereotyping and abusive representation of sexual minorities in new media. The best-known LGBTQI2+ media justice group, Gay & Lesbian Alliance Against Defamation (GLAAD), for example, didn't hold its first conference on anti-gay harassment in digital cultures until 2009. GLAAD admitted as it did so that it should have been on the case sooner. That belated conference turned out to be an excellent model for a multifaceted strategy for dealing with these issues. The invited representatives from digital game companies addressed the existence of homophobia in games, the possibilities of and obstacles to creating more gay characters in games and their efforts to monitor and address anti-queer hate speech in online gamer communities. Many sexual minorities working as tech professionals are talking about attitudes in the industry, and ways to intervene to bring more LGBTQI2+ people into new media production and more gay people already in the business out of the closet and into discussions about improving the climate for LGBTQI2+ professionals and users of new media as well. Finally, many of the panelists addressed the responsibility of new media users to call out and/or report gay-abusive participants in digital cultures. Clearly, almost a decade after this conference there is much more work to be done to make cyberspaces LGBTQI2+-friendly ones, but no one can now claim that either the problem or viable solutions have not been set forth. There are some signs of things improving, including the inclusion of LGBTQI2+ characters in a few digital games, and even the addition of a cross-dresser to the panoply of Pokémon characters. But in the digital world, as in the wider one, there is still much to be done to bring safety, equality and fairness to those who live outside heteronormative and often aggressively homophobic spaces. A major set of resources for fighting gendered, racialized, homophobic and disability-related discrimination and harassment online is provided by the Center for Solutions to Online Violence (http://femtechnet.org/csov/).

➡ CULTURAL IMPERIALISM, HEGEMONY AND/OR DIGITAL DIVERSITY?

Two other related areas of inequality in the digitizing world have been characterized as *linguistic and culture imperialism*. Less overt than the kind of imperialism practiced by classic empires that imposed their will on dominated ethnic cultures, the impacts of this modern form of imperialism are nevertheless quite serious. **Cultural imperialism** is the excessive influence of one culture's production over another. The culture subject to cultural imperialism is overwhelmed and overridden by the cultural products of the dominant culture. Cultural texts from outside intentionally or unintentionally replace local traditions or transform them beyond recognition. Cultural imperialism as a phenomenon long predates the invention of the Web. It was already prevalent in the form of Western movies, TV, music and other forms of popular culture, but the rise of digital culture, including its absorbing of these older other mediums into itself, has deepened and extended cultural imperialist practices. While the Net as a medium has the potential to increase cultural flows in many directions that could undermine this domination, too little has yet been done to enable more equitable flows of culture from non-Western nations.

The US and to a lesser degree Europe have been the cultures most often accused of cultural imperialism vis-à-vis most of the rest of the world. These nations have had the wealth and popular culture production capacity to overwhelm the rest of the world with their products. In a similar vein, Japan has been accused of cultural imperialism with regard to the rest of Asia (and to a lesser extent with regard to the US). But there are also smaller-scale cultural imperialisms that occur within countries, especially between ethnically and linguistically dominant cultures in relation to minority cultures, or between dominant cultures and politically oppositional subcultures. While the Web has the potential to create a more even flow of culture from many places around the globe, in fact Europe, Japan and North America overwhelm the rest of the world in digital production as they do in other media (film, TV, music).

The Web and other dimensions of digital culture have reinvigorated the cultural imperialism debates because they have the *potential* to break up this pattern. Far more than film and television, digital popular culture has the potential to be interactive and far more open to do-it-yourself cultural production. The potential to create pathways of cultural exchange from almost any cultural or subcultural location to almost any other is very real. It is already being done, though not yet on a scale that competes with corporate media in any significant way. The potential for truly democratic cultural production exists, but that will not happen unless significant numbers of people who seek more varied content get involved in political, economic and cultural decisions that challenge domination by huge multinational media corporations. There are certainly powerful economic and political interests who would prefer to have the Web become more of a broadcast medium pushing mainstream US and European commercial content in one direction, rather than an interactive medium with multiple points of exchange between cultural groups from all over the globe. But only citizen action—through critical digital culture analyses, social protest activism and political lobbying—will make the wider democratic potential of digital cultures a reality.

If all the inequalities outlined in this chapter exist, why isn't there more resistance to them, especially given the great leveling potential of an interactive, rather than one-way, flow of cultural representation that the Web offers? Aren't there billions of users in all languages and from all cultures who make up the digital world? While the range of human thought, opinion and emotional expression available online is truly staggering, that clearly does not mean that the digital terrain presents an even playing field. The default subject position and other road blocks to a truly democratic, egalitarian set of digital cultures and virtual communities include a host of inequalities that can be understood best through the concept of **cultural hegemony**.

Hegemony in this context is *cultural domination without overt force or coercion*. Hegemony is a process by which groups with greater economic, political and/or cultural power lead those with lesser power to consent to their dominant ideas. They do this not by force but by characterizing ideas that limit the life possibilities of non-dominant groups as just "common sense," even though those ideas work against fairness, justice or the self-interest of the dominated group. Hegemony is the opposite of conspiracy in that the elites who manufacture hegemony do so without needing to coordinate their efforts, without needing to use force and often under the illusion that they do so for the best interests of all people. There is one sense in which conspiracy is a useful concept, but it is not the legal definition. To the degree that elites create a common approach to dominating the rest of us they do so mostly through an unconscious "conspiracy of like interests." That is, since they have a common interest in maintaining their wealth and power they often agree on the best ideas and practices to do so. But this need not be the case, and often elites have some degree of competition among themselves. This helps further the illusion of free choice among the rest of us. And the conspiracy of like interests that is hegemony does not preclude actual conspiracies. But just as with the need to use force, elites prefer to avoid outright conspiracies since once uncovered, conspiracies undermine the illusion that elites are working in everyone's interest.

For several hundred years, dominant white European culture reinforced the idea that women were weak minded, not cut out for politics or public life, and that people of color were also intellectually inferior and cut out only for manual labor. These ideas were widely purveyed as common sense rather than oppressive self-interest on the part of those who dominated all the media of communication. While control without force was preferable, when communication failed, or when it was even threatened, those elites also had superior policing and military force to back them up.

While hegemony is often subtler today, many of us continue to consent to our own oppression, under the illusion that it is the "only way" or the "natural way" for things to be. Being gay is still said by conservatives to be "unnatural." Women have fewer tech jobs because they are said to naturally have less interest in those fields, rather than because they are told from elementary school on that men are more naturally drawn to science and technology, despite massive evidence to the contrary. A key element about hegemonic ideas is that they often come wrapped in pleasure, like a deadly pill inside a delicious piece of candy. During the Roman Empire, a writer famously noted that people were being controlled by "bread and circuses," by being given enough to eat and offered entertaining spectacles to distract them from their lack of power and freedom. Today the prime vehicle for the "circuses" that distract us from hegemony and make it pleasurable is the world of mass media popular culture, including digital culture as both a cultural source (through new things like social media and video games) and a recycler through the Net of all forms of pop culture (film, TV shows, talk radio, music, etc.). At the beginning of the digitized world, as noted in Chapter 2, hegemony meant that there was greater power to shape digitized lives in the hands of certain social groups (white, male, English-speaking, middle class or affluent). The folks with these social identities had the economic and political control of the technological and cultural tools that made up the first digital cultures. And having designed those tools in their own image, for a long time digital culture was a place much more friendly to their social groups. That has changed slowly over time due to immense critical work on the part of women, people of color, non-English speakers and others disadvantaged by the biased structure of the digital world.

A couple of examples of cultural hegemony might be useful. Take the music industry. It is now possible, thanks to the Internet, to access a huge variety of music from all over the world. Nevertheless, when you look at data such as the Billboard Top 100, it is clear that a very narrow segment of the music world gets promoted by powerful economic interests that push most innovative music to the margins. Again, this is hegemony at work. No one forces you to listen to pop music, but it is so much easier to find pop music in the world due to the corporate power of the music industry. File sharing and some other digital technologies have poked some pretty big holes into this arena of cultural hegemony, but large corporations still successfully push a bland pop culture to the center of music listening.

Or take the case of the magazine publishing industry. If you type "women's magazines" into Google, or check out the magazine rack at the supermarket, you will find dozens of choices. These magazines have many pleasant features: Glossy layouts of pretty clothes, gorgeous models and stories of celebrities living seemingly exciting lives, humor and so on. But what is the actual function of these magazines? On magazine.com the list of subcategories under Women's list in this order: "Bridal & Weddings; Fashion & Beauty; Home & Cooking; Pregnancy & Family." The list could have been written for suburban white women in the 1950s. There is no category for things like women in politics, women in the work force, women and anything other than weddings, fashion, cooking, childrearing. Health appears as a category but much in that category centers around how women can look slim and fit in order to attract men. Looked at more closely much of the content of these "women's magazines" is designed to make women feel insecure enough to buy the clothes, beauty products and feminine accessories whose advertisers bring most of the profit to the magazine. Do my current clothes make me look thin enough or do I need new ones? Is my skin blotchy? Do I need this new beauty cream? Am I giving my man the kind of sex he needs? Follow these seven tips to assure he won't stray. And so on. There are dozens and dozens of these magazines targeting girls and women of all ages, with a few token "ethnic" magazines as well. All that is missing are ones for women whose incomes are too poor to pay for the advertised feminine enhancement products.

By contrast to the overwhelming array of "women's" magazines, that Google search will usually at most feature one or two not-for-profit female equality magazines that are critical of the many oppressing elements of the advertising-driven magazines. Hegemony works not by censoring these more feminist magazines, but rather by overwhelming them in a sea of this other kind of magazine. Feminist magazines, such as *Ms., Scarleteen, Bitch, Lilith, BUST, Jezebel, make/ shift, Shameless, The Women's Review of Books* or *off our backs*, that more fully support the non-consumerist empowerment of women are not even present under the category of "women's" magazines, or are buried several pages down within a search. Under the miscellaneous category "women's interests" *BUST* showed up around fortieth, squeezed between *Crochet* and *Knit Simple*. But the fact that actual feminist magazines exist can be pointed to as evidence of the generous free speech available in "free market" democratic societies. In such claims, the vastly greater resources available to the conservative capitalist publishing industry are discounted, and instead the illusion of "free choice" by consumers is lauded. That is cultural hegemony turned against women. Choice under cultural hegemony is like the request to pick a card, pick any card, offered by a magician. Looked at more carefully, you will find that the deck is a trick one, that your choice was not free at all. As Theodor Adorno and Max Horkheimer (1994) put it, "you are free to choose what is always the same."

But the good news is that hegemony is never complete. It is always subject to cracks in its armor, always challenged. Returning to the example of women's magazines, with the rise of the Internet-driven #MeToo and Time's Up protest movements, many more serious feminist ideas suddenly began to appear in "women's" magazines. They always had some feminist content, but not the kind that would really threaten male-domination. With these new Net-driven movements, far more wide-ranging criticism of rape culture, everyday sexual harassment and pay inequality began to appear in these magazines. Fault lines in hegemony began to appear. It remains to be seen whether those cracks can be pried open to bring true equality for women, but it is a clear reminder that major change can happen rapidly in the Internet era.

In terms of digital cultures, much hegemony works primarily through corporate dominated websites, search engines and portals that tend to channel the content and narrow the range of viewpoints to which most users are exposed. Again, no one forces you to follow Google's or Windows Live's or Blogger's links, but evidence makes clear that most people uncritically accept these corporate profit-focused entry points of the Web rather than personally exploring the far wider range of cultural viewpoints available in the global network. The large corporate search engines, such as Google, are ultimately not much less biased than Baidu (China's government-controlled portal); it is just that their hegemonic functioning is better hidden, in this case within algorithms whose cultural biases are entangled with profit motives.

Hegemony is often a subtle process. Many different features of the Net play a role in favoring the already powerful, and making it more difficult for alternative voices to be heard. Take the example of search engines. As Siva Vaidhyanathan observes,

> If Google is the dominant way we navigate the Internet, and thus the primary lens through which we experience both the local and the global, then it has remarkable power to set agendas and alter perceptions. Its biases (valuing popularity over accuracy, established sites over new, and rough rankings over more fluid or multidimensional models of preservation) are built into algorithms. And those biases affect how we value things, perceive things, and navigate the worlds of culture and ideas.
>
> (Vaidhyanathan 2011: 7)

This process of making digital cultures more open, democratic and broadly representative entails hard work on the part of people across the range of subject positions. Gaining depth of understanding of subject positions and cultures other than one's own is difficult, but far from impossible. This process involves gaining greater degrees of cultural competency. While we develop a more or less automatic depth of understanding of the cultures into which we are born and socialized, achieving something like that depth of understanding of other subject positions and other cultures is far more difficult. Again, difficult but not impossible, and it is usually done best by a combination of self-education and immersion in cultural situations outside of one's own. Virtually every country on earth is becoming more multicultural, but few if any have achieved substantive equality across their multiple demographic groups. Fortunately, digital cultural spaces provide a staggering array of resources to make the task of developing new cultural competencies and deeper understandings of other subject positions easier than ever before. They cannot fully substitute for on-the-ground experiences with other cultures and viewpoints (again an online/offline balance is crucial), but they can significantly augment them. Since the future of the planet may well depend on how well we can overcome the barriers to communication across social differences, partaking in meaningful online efforts to address the underlying economic and political barriers to substantial cross-cultural understanding is vital. The Net cannot be the only tool in this process, but it is a very powerful one that can do some key things no other medium can.

6

Sexploration and/or Sexploitation?

Digitizing Desire

The impact of the Net on sexual attitudes, practices and knowledge can provide a vivid case study in how online cultural knowledge relates to the offline world. Granted, sex is a particularly charged subject that may not prove "typical" of other kinds of impacts. Nevertheless, the very intensity and ubiquity of the subject matter has made it one of the most studied and thus most amenable to exploration. Some suggest that there is no aspect of contemporary life that has been impacted more deeply by the Internet than sexuality. The exact amount of sexual content on the Web is very difficult to measure, and has at times been wildly overestimated (reports of a third of websites being pornographic, for example, proved to be wildly exaggerated; it is closer to 4 or 5 percent (Ogas and Gaddam 2013; Ruvolo 2011). But by most any standard, the amount of online sex material is staggering. Then again, most Internet statistics are staggering, and the stats on sex should perhaps not be so surprising. Everyone after all at some point learns the "facts of life" entailed by sexuality. Even the small number of people who choose not to engage in it physically during their whole lives would not be here without sex. Sexuality of all kinds is available in virtually all places where the Net has "penetrated" (as digital marketing researchers call "access"). But in this chapter I am going to make the perhaps seemingly perverse suggestion that the problem with the Web is not that there is too much sex on it, but that there is not enough.

⧉ REAL VIRTUAL SEX EDUCATION

To look carefully at what sexuality in digital cultures is all about, it is initially helpful to temporarily put aside questions about the morality or immorality of pornography and other forms of sexual activity. Because sexual mores will vary immensely among the readers of this book, I want to make it clear that my work here will be more descriptive than prescriptive. That is, I am not primarily interested in judging these practices but instead in describing them and characterizing some of the various positions and debates that cybersexualities have generated, though, as in the rest of this book, I will not try to hide my own views or prejudices when relevant. And in one regard I have already done so as I already suggested one abiding principle that shapes my discussion. My seemingly perverse claim that there is not enough sex on the Web is a claim that there is not enough sexual variety online, or perhaps, more accurately, that pornography crowds out other varieties of sexuality that are and could be more available in digital spaces. The Net has undoubtedly become the most pervasive medium of sex education on the planet. But much of the education comes through online porn, and I concur with the view of psychotherapist Marty Klein that pornography is about as useful for serious sexual education as a car chase scene from a movie is useful for a driver's education (Klein 2012; see also Albury 2014). Partly in response to the apparent use of porn as informal sex education for unexperienced younger people, some schools have introduced porn literacy programs to deal with the misinformation, anxiety and coerced behaviors sometimes emerging out of watching pornography in a context free of more useful and realistic forms of sex education (Jones 2018).

Previously difficult or impossible-to-come-by information about sexuality, from medical facts to dating, mating or hook-up facilitation to academic sex research to more hands-on ways of getting off has been made more available by the Net. Some of this information has been literally life-saving. Some of it has been life-endangering. What is clear is that the online realm provides a panoramic view of the world's sexual possibilities, and makes this information available discreetly. Because of this it allows people to safely explore sexual alternatives.

Sexual positions, or rather, positions on sexuality, in regard to pornography and cybersex more broadly, run the gamut from those seeking a total ban to wildly libertarian calls for no restrictions at all. Politically, morally and culturally, the Net offers and critiques every imaginable form of sex, from the most libertarian to the most rigidly moralistic. But even the most rigid of positions do not fall neatly along ideological lines. Any serious analysis of sexuality on the Web must look at but get beyond the question of pornography to look at a range of topics, including sexual hook-up sites, Internet-assisted sexual trafficking, sex worker rights campaigns on the Web, sexual chat, sexting, online sex games, teledildonics and related digital diddling and a wide variety of formal and informal digitized sex education by therapists, teachers and sex workers.

▣ DIGITAL DIDDLING: VARIETIES OF CYBERSEX

The term "cybersex" has both a narrow and a broader meaning. In the narrow definition it refers to *sexual acts mediated and/or enacted through digital technology*. In the broader definition, it refers to *all the ways in which sexuality is represented in digital spaces*, including but not restricted to those sexual acts mediated and/or enacted by digital means. Obviously, these two definitions overlap to some degree; watching cyberporn, for example, may or may not lead to those physical manifestations defined as sex acts, but a strong argument can be made that viewing pornography is itself a sex act. But for now, let's try to use the distinction to help sort out the ways in which the sexuality and digital cultures shape each other.

Beginning with cybersex in the narrow sense of one or two (or more) people seeking sexual gratification with the aid of digital communication, the first thing that might be said is that it is in one sense among the safest of safe sex practices. There is no chance of the exchange of bodily fluids if the medium of sexual interaction is confined to pixel sharing, or verbal intercourse. In this sense, cybersex has as a precursor phone sex, another safe medium. Cybersex includes SkyperSex, sex chat rooms, cellphone sex (phone sex made easier and more mobile), sexting, teledildonics (sex toys mutually controlled via online connection), sex-centered digital games and sex in virtual worlds (Second Life, for example, has been a very active sexual play field, with at least one in ten users engaging in virtual sex there). On the positive side, these and various other modes of digital diddling in and of themselves are safe sex, in terms of physical health (issues of psychological health, or moral health, are of course far more complicated, and computer viruses from sex sites are another kind of "health" issue altogether). In this context, then, cybersex has been seen by some as a very positive thing in the era of HIV-AIDS and other STDs, when sex can literally be a matter of life or death.

The next big stage of digitized sexuality is the rise of sex-bots, robots programmed to simulate sex acts. Sex dolls have existed for some time, plastic things that take the objectification of women to the ultimate end, literally reducing women to actual objects, devoid of all subjectivity. Sex robots, once only found in the occasional sci fi story, are emerging as a real life phenomenon. Early indications are that these sex-bots will reflect much of the worst aspects of sexploitation in the non-digital world. Almost all of the ones designed so far have been female, and many aim to please in ways that reinforce male fantasies of compliance. One line of bots being designed in Barcelona, works like this:

> "By putting pressure on one of its erogenous zones—hips, breasts, mouth, crotch or hands—the user can arouse the robot, which will then moan and begin to engage in dirty talk, using software similar to the voice-activated systems in your smartphone, like Siri".
>
> (Fernando 2018)

(Semi-serious suggestions that Siri and Alexa should join the #MeToo movement could prove much more relevant to sex-bots.) More disturbingly, a major manufacturer in Japan has even designed a child sex-bot, presumably for the paedophile demographic (Young 2018). Will these silicone robots prove useful in preventing sex crimes, or in providing relief for those unable to attract sex partners? Or will they have the opposite effect of arousing anti-social desires? One concern, paralleled by the rise of robots in many industries, is the fear that sex-bots will displace human sex workers or force them to behave more like robots than human beings. This in turn suggests the wider possibility that, having experienced submissive sex-bots, a man having sex with any real woman may expect more robotic responses. Will same-sex responsive robots be created as well, and will this avoid or merely diversify compliant sexuality? Sex-bots at present are little more than dolls, but AI advances will at some point raise questions of consciousness (can they think?) and sentience (can they feel?). As with other aspects of robots and artificial intelligence, the future of sex-bots will largely depend on who programs them. It will depend on the extent to which the sexism and heterosexism in the rest of society is reproduced or potentially worsened in the bot world. Will someone design a line of feminist sex-bots?

In addition to virtual sexual encounters of various kinds, digitized spaces are, of course, also being used to facilitate offline sex in a variety of ways, from dating sites to transnational "email order bride" sites to explicit sexual hook-up sites such as Grindr where locative media are used to find nearby willing sex partners. Some online activity leads to mutually fulfilling relations, while other forms of online interaction can lead to offline sexual harassment, sexual predation, stalking and other unwanted forms of sexual attention.

Evidence suggests that cybersex has both destroyed and enhanced relationships. On the enhancement end, SkyperSex and related forms have been helpful for couples separated by long distances. While reliable statistics are hard to come by, it appears that a large percentage of cybersex is between two partners already in a sexual relationship offline (and remember, as always, that the online/offline split is largely illusory), and online sexual information accessed free of potential embarrassment has apparently enhanced many relationships. Nevertheless, there appears to be a considerable amount of cyber-cheating, online mediated sex with someone other than the partner with whom one is in a putatively monogamous relationship. As with virtually all aspects of cybersex, some argue that this can provide a healthier outlet for extra-marital or extra-commitment impulses (the "safety valve" theory), while others argue that cheating is cheating, and almost invariably harms a relationship. Incidents of both outcomes are not hard to find, and are clearly dependent on particular individuals in particular relationships.

The data on online match-making sites is complicated given the variety of apps and approaches, but is generally more positive than many people assume. In the early years, *networked intimacy*, as media scholars refer to it, often had considerable stigma attached as something only the desperate or digital dehumanized would try. But that prejudice has mostly dissipated as the phenomenon has grown such that most people know someone—friend, co-worker, relative— who has tried online dating. More than half of Americans say that online dating is "a good way to meet people." Mobile dating apps have greatly expanded the number of users. Growing popularity also stems from the range of dating apps and sites now available, from Christian Mingle to Grindr, with apps for every demographic and every kind of relationship seeker, from casual hook-up to long term. In 2017, about 25 percent of Brits and US citizens used an online dating service, and in that year about 20 percent of marriages resulted from online matchmaking. Not surprisingly, online dating is most common among younger people, many of whom grew up with much of their social lives entangled with digital apps. More surprising, perhaps, is the fact that the second largest increase has been among users aged 55–64. In general, digital dating leads to successful relationships at least as frequently as traditional offline methods, and the 3 billion dollar-a-year dating industry is continuing to grow at a steady pace (Jung 2018; Smith and Anderson 2016).

⊡ THE "MAINSTREAMING" OF PORN

The aspect of cybersexuality that has received the most attention, from both scholars and the wider public, is the role of the Web in the *mainstreaming of pornography*, the movement of porn from the hidden edges of society to near the center. The online porn business currently rakes in close to $100 billion a year (compare that to the $10 billion typically made in a year by Hollywood films). It is now routine for talk shows, sit-coms, reality shows and various other forms of mainstream entertainment to make allusion to consumption of pornography, and in recent years porn stars have been seen mingling with other kinds of celebrities in ways that clearly suggest increasing acceptance. A number of celebrities themselves have intentionally or unintentionally contributed sex tapes to the Web, usually without negative repercussions. Indeed, in a couple of cases sex tapes made people into celebrities. It's hard to fathom given that only a couple of decades ago a star could be ostracized for an extramarital affair. The addition of modifiers to "porn" also suggests mainstreaming; we have such coinages as "torture porn" (a subgenre of horror films), "food porn" (for foodies and selfie addicts), "condo porn" (for folks constantly surfing the Web looking for the most attractive living space) and even "information porn" (the attractive graphic display of what the Net has in extreme abundance).

One critic suggests an alliterative threesome is largely responsible for this mainstreaming of porn: Accessibility, affordability and anonymity (Cooper cited in Nayar 2008: 2). What this means in terms of sexual practices beyond watching is difficult to measure. However, the fact that millions of people who had never accessed pornography have now done so on the Net is no doubt having a variety of novel impacts. And given that the Web in general has been seen to push extremisms of all kinds, this may be troubling. Whether access to porn is legal, illegal or legally ambiguous varies immensely from country to country. As we have noted before, censoring the Net is a difficult thing to do, and pornography purveyors have been expert at getting around attempts to limit access. In the US, the standard for legal pornography remains local "community standards," a concept that has been rendered virtually meaningless by the ways in which Web content travels nationally and transnationally. Internationally, attempts to censor online pornography have had limited success, especially since censors in less-than-open societies tend to focus more on political than cultural censorship when monitoring resources are limited. And even countries with the strictest anti-pornography laws that do try to contain it have found it impossible to keep their citizens from accessing porn, given the many workarounds possible in the digital world. In the US, religious conservatives have greatly exaggerated the percentage of pornographic content online (Castleman

2016). But perhaps this in part reflects the fact that more pornography is consumed in politically and religiously conservative red states than in the more liberal blue ones, suggesting either hypocrisy or the failure of repressive sexual mores, or both (Hopper 2014; MacInnis and Hodson 2015; Martin 2014).

By way of context, it is important to remember that pornography is as old as human representation. The oldest known porn is at least 3,000 years old (and appears to be bi-curious!) (Mycio 2013). All major historic cultures have included some graphic representations of sexuality that could be considered pornographic. A typical dictionary definition of pornography is printed or visual material containing the explicit description or display of sexual organs or activity, intended to stimulate erotic rather than aesthetic or emotional feelings.

In modern times, pornographic films were born almost simultaneously with film itself. And each new medium (TV, video, etc.) has extended the amount and availability of pornography. But in terms of scale of access, the Web has brought an exponential growth in the amount and kinds of porn available, and thereby in the porn industry. This includes the problematic fact that young people ill-prepared to put the kind of sex portrayed online in a social context are accessing it at younger and younger ages (Papadoupoulus n.d.). Some online sites have sought to address this fact with more socially responsible sexual education for youth (e.g., Scarleteen: Sex Ed for the Real World n.d.). It is not clear what greater access to porn has meant to what is probably the most impacted group, teens and young adults just discovering their sexual identities. Research on the topic reveals a complicated mix of impact on sexual attitudes, body image, self-concept and social development, with certainly enough evidence to suggest that there are matters of concern for parents, teachers, health professionals and youth counsellors to be aware of (Owens et al. 2012). The issue of "porn addiction" has also garnered increasing attention, but to date psychological professionals and the most widely used authority on mental disorders (the DSM) does not acknowledge pornography as an addictive activity.

There are also various questions as to how things such as easy access to pornography shape offline sex ideas and habits. This may especially be a problem regarding young people and others with limited sexual experience. Klein's remark about porn being a terrible way to learn about real sexuality is echoed by former porn actress and now porn director Nina Hartley, who remarks,

Pornography is a paid, professional performance by actors. It is a fantasy, it is not meant to be a rulebook and guidebook or a how to as a general rule. And it goes to show how poor our sex education is in this country that people are reduced to looking at an entertainment medium for information about the body.

("Pornstar Nina Hartley," *Huffington Post* 2013)

This point is reinforced humorously as well in the viral video "Porn Sex vs. Real Sex" (n.d.), in which the difference is illustrated using vegetables. The quality of sex education in schools varies immensely among and within countries around the world. Some of the best courses include discussion of Web porn and its severe limitations as depictions of the sexual experience.

Not only in youth but more broadly, exposure to pornography can lead to unrealistic physical and behavioral expectations for real-world women and men. This is particularly damaging to people who have had no or limited real-world sexual experience. Unrealistic expectations about typical male and female bodies and pressure to behave in the manner of porn stars can have a highly negative impact, especially on sexually inexperienced people who have little to compare to the unrealistic content of much porn. Other questions about the effects of exposure to pornography are highly disputed (Wilson 2018).

Pornography was a major source of social controversy before the Net, and it has become ever more so since mainstreaming has occurred. The major protagonists have included some strange bedfellows. On one side, you have conservative groups attacking porn on religious and moral grounds, along with, in a decidedly shaky alliance, some feminist groups who see porn as inherently degrading to women and, in one analysis, a violation of women's civil rights. On the other side, you have various social libertarians, including "pro-sex" feminists interested in promoting the liberation of female and queer sexualities, and in protecting the rights of the primarily female cohort of "sex workers" (the non-pejorative name for prostitutes, phone sex operators, strippers and so on) (Li 2000; Nayar 2008; Rajagopal and Bojin 2004). These pro-sex feminist advocates for new kinds of pornography critique the abuses of performers in some porn productions, continue seeking to change the still male-dominated nature of the industry overall, cite the misogynistic content (including significant amounts of non-consensual violence against women in some porn), but do not offer a blanket condemnation of the entire business.

It is important to realize that many who reject efforts to restrict pornography can nevertheless be quite critical of various forms. They recognize that there is much truly repugnant sexual material, especially violent, non-consensual material, online. But they advocate education rather than censorship as the best means of eliminating socially offensive or degrading forms of graphic sex depiction. Certain forms of porn, especially child pornography, are both almost universally condemned and illegal, offline and on. But unfortunately, certain peer-to-peer features of the Net have facilitated this abhorrent practice, especially via the Dark Web (the unindexed part of the Web where much criminal activity thrives).

In addition to the unequal gender power in porn, it is important to realize that porn is a highly racialized commodity. On many porn sites, "Asian" is not a geographic or cultural location, but a category indicating supposedly submissive Oriental dolls, cute slutty school girls and Dragon Lady dominatrixes. "Interracial" is another category of porn that plays off historical fantasies of oversexed men of color. And where ethno-racial categories such as "Indian," "Latina" and "Ebony" ("Black" isn't exotic enough) have their own niches, the default norm of white women is not treated as a race, but rather the category is sub-divided by things such as hair color, breast size or sexual proclivities. The interesting category "female-friendly" on some porn sites (by which they usually seem to mean mildly more romantic in focus) ironically points up the fact that much of the rest of the material on these sites is decidedly "female-*un*friendly." Moreover, there is some general evidence linking porn use to sexism among heterosexual males (Hald, Malamuth and Lange 2013).

There is little doubt that the Internet has not only moved pornography out of the shadows and into homes, it has also seemingly reshaped attitudes about sexuality in a relatively short time, bringing not only consumption, but also production of porn into the household. As Chuck Klosterman acerbically but tellingly puts it,

Everyone knows that the Internet is changing our lives, mostly because someone in the media has uttered that exact phrase every single day since 1993. However, it certainly appears that the main thing the Internet has accomplished is the normalization of amateur pornography. There is no justification for the amount of naked people on the World Wide Web, many of whom are clearly doing so for non-monetary reasons. Where were these people 15 years ago? Were there really millions of women in 1986 turning to their husbands and saying, "You know, I would love to have total strangers masturbate to images of me deep-throating a titanium dildo, but there's simply no medium for that kind of entertainment. I guess we'll just have to sit here and watch 'Falcon Crest' again."

(Klosterman 2004: 109, 110)

While presented satirically, Klosterman is asking a serious question: Did the medium create the message? Did the technical feasibility to upload amateur porn excite a response that would not otherwise have happened? He cleverly suggests that it did, and that claim is one that of course has implications for all kinds of amateur production across the Web on sites such as YouTube and Vimeo.

Some anti-pornography forces look upon the mainstreaming of porn as one of many signs of steeply declining moral values in whatever particular national culture they are located (often articulated from one or other form of religious fundamentalism), while others see it as a deepening of the objectification, degradation and exploitation of women (as argued from one branch of feminism). So-called anti-porn feminists point to what they see as a high level of overt violence against women in pornography and argue that those who engage in the industry do so either due to coercion or to low self-esteem (often arising from earlier sexual abuse). Some anti-porn activists see all pornography as a form of violent objectification of women, and/or a violation of women's civil rights (MacKinnon and Dworkin 1988). The vast expansion of porn online and the concomitant lessening of social taboos on porn are seen as tragic by these folks who have worked for years to restrict or reform it.

On the other hand, libertarians, including many cyberlibertarians, argue against restricting porn on general freedom-of-speech grounds, while so-called pro-sex feminists often argue for legalization and minimal regulation of pornography on the basis that making sex work illegal places sex workers (the vast majority of whom are female) in greater danger of exploitation than would legalization. They argue in relation to online porn that it is about the safest kind of sex work that can be engaged in, since no exchange of bodily fluids and no chance for physically violent encounters exists in virtual spaces (though this does not address the issue of coerced performance). They may also cite statistics that the amount of rape has actually declined in the era of Internet porn (though that may be due to other factors than access to porn). They also point to the increasing numbers of women in executive positions in the pornography industry and claim that the vast majority of women working in porn do so willingly and with a significant degree of autonomy.

Evidence-based studies suggest some truth on each side of this debate. Claims that pornography viewing can increase sexual aggression, lead to sexual dissatisfaction in relationships or cause sexual dysfunction in men have both proponents and doubters among professional researchers (Fisher and Kohut 2017; Lambert et al. 2012). Given the lack of definitive evidence, people should at least be aware of these dangers, and should monitor the impacts they personally experience and that impact those around them. The issue of the negative impact of pornography hit the mainstream media in a fairly nuanced way in Joseph Gordon-Levitt's *Don Jon*, a film that argues, moral issues aside, that the problem with porn is that it leads to bad sexual experiences in the real world, making clear that the best sex in the real world is usually very unlike the mechanical kind found in porn.

Quite apart from questions of its causal impact, non-consensual violent pornography is a horrifying phenomenon that has no justification, and the fact that there is some evidence that exposure to porn can increase sexual aggressiveness should be enough to give pause (Owens et al. 2012). Homemade sex tapes are also being used in horrific ways as *revenge porn*. Statistics suggest that violence is not as prevalent as some claim, and has been declining as a percentage of overall porn production, partly because more women have assumed positions of power in the porn industry, and more women are watching porn. But non-consensual violence in porn remains a very significant concern. At the same time, there is a great deal of testimony from sex workers themselves supporting claims to voluntary involvement in the industry, greater female power in the industry and safer conditions due to the virtualization of much sex work, including much self-production by women. As we will see in the next section, however, the darkest impact of the enormous growth of the pornography industry has to do with the most unprotected group of sex workers, those forced into sexual servitude.

⮔ DIGITIZED SEX TRAFFICKING

All sides of the online sex debates agree that one absolutely indefensible form of violence as implicated in pornography is the trafficking and forcing of women, girls and boys to engage in sex acts online (and offline). Without doubt this is the ugliest, most exploitative dimension of technology: Its deployment to assist in sexual trafficking and other forms of violence against women, girls and boys. Trafficking of women, girls and boys long precedes the rise of new communications technologies. But many suggest the new media have played a role in expanding trafficking in recent decades, and there can be little doubt that ICTs have changed the nature of trafficking. Trafficking has long been a transnational phenomenon, usually from poorer countries to richer ones, and increasing global economic inequality due to the forces of globalization has intensified trafficking. The current phase of globalization itself is of course deeply dependent on new media technologies (Kee 2005).

Mobile phones, GPS devices and email have facilitated communication among traffickers and allowed them to better track their victims. Legal "email order brides" websites promise pliant, marriage-ready women and girls; on the surface they represent "soft" forms of trafficking, but they often serve as a front for hardcore trafficking. Underground illegal websites have digitized the promotion of trafficked women, girls and boys. Once again, the anonymity that comes with using the Net plays a crucial role, allowing traffickers and their customers to conduct business online with little risk of being identified. Peer-to-peer trafficking networks, where individuals arrange the transfer of trafficked women, girls or boys, has arisen alongside older organized trafficking networks. The vast increase in the amount of pornography represented by the mainstreaming of porn has significantly increased the demand for sex workers, and a considerable portion of the new recruits to the porn industry are trafficked individuals. Some argue that the "trafficking in images" is a less dangerous, less overtly violent, form of trafficking, but far too often the publication of images is accompanied by or enabled by other physically exploitative activities. While the exact portion of non-consensual pornographic filming is impossible to measure, it is very difficult to view pornography online and be sure one is not supporting trafficking. There is no way to tell whether a woman you are viewing online has consented to her performance. Some groups are working to develop what some call "ethical porn" or "fair trade" porn, which eliminates racism and sexism and guarantees that all depicted sex acts are consensual. This includes a feminist porn movement that produces films that provide female actors equal pay with males, assures that all the filmed events are consensual and overall portrays sex in non-exploitative ways.

Neither the general expansion of trafficking nor its various digital manifestations has gone unchallenged. And many of the same digital communication technologies that have been used by traffickers have been used against traffickers and trafficking. Anti-trafficking organizations can use ICTs to track traffickers and help locate trafficked people. Online information for victims and potential victims of trafficking has proven vital, especially in the typically isolated conditions that trafficked individuals often find themselves in. Online-capable smartphones have been particularly useful in these situations.

The Web has also been used by governments at all levels, from the United Nations to neighborhood watch groups, to provide useful information on trafficking. But the most important work on the issue has been done by non-governmental organizations and social movement groups. NGOs have found the Web to be a major resource for spreading the word about general trafficking dangers, for organizing anti-trafficking campaigns and pushing for political policy changes, for exposing specific traffic zones and traffickers and for educating about available help for trafficked women, girls and boys. Even one of the strongest groups fighting against online trafficking, Take Back the Tech, concludes that there is no definitive evidence that digital technologies *have worsened* the terrain of trafficking, but the expansion of the porn industry into online spaces has intensified demand, which in turn translates into greater amounts of trafficking. Trafficking remains an international tragedy of epic proportions that must be fought with all the resources, online and off, that can be mustered.

While one should always be careful not to extrapolate too much from one example, as a case study sexuality provides some very suggestive intimation as to how digital knowledge works. Even advocates for one of the strongest groups fighting violence against women in general and online techno-violence in particular see a complicated picture in which digital culture is both an enemy and an aid:

> Whether new forms of ICTs replicate, amplify or destabilize power relations will depend largely on how closely we monitor their development and discourse. This requires we first understand what digital technology means, then interrogate its impact on society in light of multiple and shifting strands of political discourse. The process has already begun: feminists and women's rights advocates are consciously and deliberately "taking back the tech" and indelibly changing what technology is and means.
>
> (Kee 2005)

This strikes me as precisely the right way to approach not only issues of sexploration and sexploitation online, but all social issues impacted by the Web. It is imperative to understand technologies as tools that can be wielded in many different ways, to resist both pro- and anti-tech discourses that see their impact as automatic or techno-determined, and instead find ways to "take back the tech," to use new media to fight for the values you believe will better the world.

7

Tools for Democracy or Authoritarianism?

Digitized Politics and the Post-Truth Era

The impact of new media on political culture has many aspects, from digital voting and the possibility of instant polling on controversial issues to availability of governmental and extra-governmental political information to digitized campaigning to use of the Web for legal and illegal forms of organizing to incite revolution or other major forms of social change. Questions like these arise: Is the increased amount of political information available leading to greater understanding across political differences, or is it deepening disagreements? How much is digital culture to blame for the spread of *fake news* and the rise of a *post-truth* era in politics? Is the Net more likely to bring down authoritarian regimes or turn democratic countries into authoritarian ones? How has digital organizing changed protest movements? Is the use of social media expanding the possibilities of dissent or fostering a complacent **slacktivism** where clicking on an e-petition takes the place of more engaged political work? What should be the limits of **digital civil disobedience**? Is there a difference between legitimate **hacktivism** and **cyberterrorism**? If so, where should the line be drawn? How have artists used digital tools and the Web as a space for new kinds of social protest?

⮕ ELECTRONIC ELECTORAL POLITICS: THE TRUMP CAMPAIGN, BREXIT AND THE WEAPONIZATION OF DIGITAL DATA

Prevailing thought about the impact of new media and politics seems to have passed through three major stages. Initially, many thought the Web had a bit of progressive bias, stemming perhaps from the left-libertarian nature of the counterculture that was among the first significant group of users (see Chapter 2). Then, in a second stage, more sober folks saw the digital world as pretty much politically neutral, equally available for use by people of all political persuasions. Since 2016, in the wake of the rise of right-wing authoritarian movements in the US, Europe and around the globe, some have begun to wonder whether digital politics is ushering in a new kind of totalitarianism.

Digitized campaigning drew increasing amounts of attention in the early twenty-first century, and many saw it as inherently advancing democracy. Some people, for example, credited Barack Obama's two presidential election victories to superior use of digital resources. Obama's staff did innovatively use a variety of digital technologies. These included sophisticated computer models of voter profiles, extensive involvement with social networking sites, a mobile app that allowed on-the-ground canvassers to download and upload data without ever entering a campaign office and a Web app called Dashboard that turned volunteer activity into a game by ranking the most active supporters. Much of this organizational framework did in fact prove superior to the use of technology by Obama's opponents. Looked at in context, however, the role of digital technologies was revealed to be just one factor, but not *the* factor in his victories. And, more significantly, it was a factor subject to historical reversal. That historical reversal, it turned out, came in dramatic form in the very next election cycle 4 years later.

Of the elections held in the US and UK in 2016, it could be said, to borrow the title of Naomi Klein's important book on the climate crisis, *This Changes Everything*. No one paying attention can any longer believe that there is something inherent in digital political organizing that leads to more democratic regimes. Cyberutopians who once believed the Net would bring peace and freedom have been deeply chastened by the US presidential election and UK Brexit votes of 2016. Some had already learned this from the tragic return to authoritarian rule in Egypt that rolled back the digitally assisted Arab Spring democratic uprisings of 2011–2012. Many scholars and activists who earlier had expressed faith that the Internet is a force for expanding democracy, both in existing democracies and in countries with currently non-democratic governments, were left wondering whether in fact the Net is a better tool for installing and maintaining authoritarian regimes.

Questions about the role of digital culture in the rise of authoritarian regimes in many countries in the second decade of the twenty-first century came to focus particularly on social media, especially Twitter and Facebook. Facebook's influence is enormous given that, for example, two-thirds of US adults use the social media site, and nearly half get their news primarily via Facebook (Gramlich 2018). In late 2017, journalists and a whistleblower from inside the corporation revealed that a data company called Cambridge Analytica had obtained data profiles on up to 87 million Facebook users. Cambridge Analytica was funded by US far-right billionaire Robert Mercer. Before being perfected on the Trump campaign, it was used to support Republican Senator Ted Cruz and advance the ideas of the right-wing extremist who became National Security Advisor under Trump, John Bolton. The data was first gathered under the pretext of academic research, then sold to Cambridge Analytica so that the corporation could create psychological profiles of voters. These profiles were subsequently used to micro-target US and UK voters during the 2016 elections. In the US they worked in support of the Donald Trump campaign, and in the UK for the campaign to exit the European Union (Brexit).

The nature and intent of the political propaganda organization's activities were described succinctly by one of its former key programmers, Christopher Wylie: "We exploited Facebook to harvest millions of people's profiles. And built models to exploit what we knew about them and target their inner demons. That was the basis the entire company was built on" (Solon and Graham-Harrison 2018). They sought to reach not the minds but the emotions of voters, to excite and incite them. Exploiting those "inner demons" meant creating hundreds of political ads, memes and emails, many full of lies, others deeply misleading, that furthered the Trump and pro-Brexit campaigns. The head of these efforts at Cambridge Analytica, Alexander Nix, in secretly recorded conversations, bragged that the corporation's work elected Trump: "We did all the research, all the data, all the analytics, all the targeting. We ran all the digital campaign, the television campaign and our data informed all the strategy." He added that when they unleashed their propaganda "[we] set our . . . emails with a self-destruct timer . . . So you send them and after they've been read, two hours later, they disappear. There's no evidence, there's no paper trail, there's nothing" (Solon and Laughland 2018).

Targeted ads are not new to politics. What is new is the scale, the subterfuge involved in obtaining data and the vastly wider scope of data made possible by social media. The kind of *psychographic profiling* of groups such as Cambridge Analytica is far more extensive and invasive than what has gone before. In the case of the 2016 elections, the targeting was two-sided, aimed to suppress the voting will of Clinton voters and anti-Brexit voters and aimed at riling up Trump and pro-Brexit voters. The models drew upon a body of research used in the military and intelligence services to engage in psy-ops (psychological warfare). The process matched up three elements: Personality profiles obtained through online surveys, the data of millions of Facebook users gained surreptitiously and existing voter rolls. The propaganda campaign then focused on key states and regions, and the psycho-graphic profiles could get specific enough to offer a "working class, neurotic, extroverted female voter" a different message than "an emo-tionally stable upper class, introverted male one," for example. Because online advertising has virtually no restrictions, unlike TV and print ads, which have fairly stringent controls (including revealing who paid for the ads and certain basic truth tests), the ads they circulated didn't need to have any truthful content. As a result, thousands of bits of fake news reached millions of UK and US voters in large part because new social media do not face the regulations that apply to old media.

Current and former executives of Cambridge Analytica were made to testify before Parliament and Congress. Claims were made that the company not only used stolen profiles but, in Britain, also created fake subsidiaries to illegally fund and coordinate campaign efforts. The revelations about their work on the 2016 campaigns forced the propaganda corporation to shut down their business, but they immediately opened up a new operation with many of the same personnel under a new cover name, Emerdata (Solon and Laughland 2018). It remains to be seen whether the kind of vicious, illicit tactics used in 2016 can be stopped in future elections, but initial moves by governments and social media corporations to correct the matter were wholly inadequate.

This scandal briefly placed corporate social media on trial. Con-gress compelled a rare appearance by Facebook CEO Mark Zuckerberg. Zuckerberg admitted that "thousands of apps" had similar vulnerabil-ities to the ones exploited by Cambridge Analytica, and that plugging those gaps would not be easy, but claimed Facebook was dedicated to preventing such things, tightening their privacy rules and fighting fake news. However, it is far from clear that the deeper issues behind the breach are being addressed, by Facebook or by government. And Zuckerberg undermined his own commitments almost immediately after his Congressional testimony. Less than a week after promising Facebook would abide by the new more stringent privacy rules put in place by the European Union (the GDPR), he backed away from this pledge and sought to exempt 1.5 billion of his users from these new regulations (Ingram 2018).

Clearly, increased privacy will only happen if there is far more public pressure put to bear on the ISPs, telecom companies and social media corporations that are invading it (see Chapter 4 for more of how this relates to privacy issues more generally). Facebook bore the brunt of this questioning this time because they were the source of the major breach, but companies such as Google and Verizon gather even more data on users, and the specter of privacy invasion used to subvert democracies and support authoritarian regimes around the globe must be addressed far more seriously if future misuse is to be avoided. Without serious governmental regulation and pressure from users, these corporations will continue to exploit the data-mining at the heart of their business model.

While the abuse of data-mining in elections and the prospect of the further erosion of rights in ostensibly still democratic countries is deeply alarming, the situation in countries that have already established authoritarian regimes is truly devastating. Russia and China have found digital tools to be vital in optimizing social control (Soldatov and Borogan 2015). The approaches the two major authoritarian regimes have taken differ considerably. The Chinese government was very proactive from the beginning of the Internet era. The so-called Great Firewall of China successfully blocks most of the news and social media sites of the West, such as Facebook, Google and Twitter. They created their own alternatives, like Sina Weibo, a Twitter-like app, and Baidu, their version of Google. These apps have all the data gathering power of their US counterparts and far more beyond that, because all their data flows directly into government collection. While the central government directs much censorship, they also work by "encouraging" self-censorship by supposedly private companies. Chinese game companies, for example, routinely block keywords in game chats that are deemed politically suspect (Knockel et al. 2017). China's latest creative addition to "self-censorship" is a social media app called "Sesame Credit" that rewards "good citizen" behavior with social perks, including faster Net speed, and punishes bad behavior by doing things such as raising your bank interest rates. Nominally a private company, many see it as a test case for a more elaborate state version. The network will link workplaces, banks, medical clinics and much more to monitor all aspects of behavior. This already extensive state mind control apparatus will also reward users for towing the government line by doing things like turning in people who attempt to circumvent Web controls (Mitchell and Diamond 2018). While it is still often possible for skilled activists to circumvent the Great Firewall, the threat of exposure is always there and this new social media network will enhance the person-to-person

FIGURE 7.1 *Chinese police officer wearing facial recognition glasses (Courtesy: People's Images (China))*

surveillance among Chinese citizens that makes dissent very danger-ous. Algorithmic surveillance is also being augmented by things such as facial recognition sunglasses worn by police (see Figure 7.1) and other features unconstrained by democratic privacy norms.

Russia lags behind in the building of a total surveillance state, but it is working hard to catch up. Putin seemed to feel that manipulated elections would be enough to solidify his power. Initially somewhat slow to get into the Internet control game, prior to 2011–2012, Net access was fairly open in the country. But the rise of anti-corruption protests in those years, the largest dissent since the end of the Soviet era, was partly organized online, and convinced Putin to begin what has been a slow but steady process of censoring the access of Russians to Web flows from outside the country.

⊟ FAKE NEWS, REAL IMPACT: DIGITIZING A POST-TRUTH ERA

The 2016 elections also need to be viewed in the context of a wider phenomenon partly driven by the rise of digital media: The problem of fake news. Fake news is not in quotes, as you often see it, because in the 2016 election cycle there really was fake news, not the fake cry of "fake news" frequently declaimed whenever Donald Trump and other politicians of his ilk don't like their media coverage. False news is certainly not a wholly new phenomenon in the world, but once again it has been radically changed by the existence of new com-munication technologies. According to one cogent analyst, there are four interrelated factors that allowed the rise of fake news to the level where it impacted elections in the US and UK: The increasing polarization of political ideologies; a growing skepticism regarding scientific and other forms of professional expertise; the decline in traditional print and network television news and the parallel rise of online news sources (McIntyre 2018; Vaidhyanathan 2018). Digital devices and digital culture played a role in all four of these developments.

Increasing polarization of politics and increasing skepticism about scientific and other forms of expertise have been trends over several election cycles, but new media greatly accelerated the process. Social critics Noam Chomsky and Edward Herman famously argued in 1988 that what would now be called mainstream media was **manufactured consent**, as they titled their book on the subject. By this they meant that the major newspapers, the *New York Times*, *Washington Post*, *Chicago Tribune*, *LA Times* and such, along with the then-dominant three TV networks (NBC, CBS and ABC) kept political commentary in a middle-of-the-road mode to maximize audience share, and thereby maximize profits for their corporate owners. In such a situation, political views on the left or right of center received minimal coverage, and when covered were largely cast as extremist. This political centrism, for ill and good, began to erode first with the rise of cable television, with its capacity to create small niche audiences for a wider range of views. This included the rise of the right-wing Fox News network and similar Rupert Murdoch-owned entities in other countries. Left-liberals sought to create a somewhat parallel phenomenon through stations such as MSNBC. Real issues, real political differences, about things such as corporate globalization, new waves of immigration and the declining homogeneity of many nation states, as well as the causes of economic stagnation and inequality (including the rise of AI-controlled robots), underlay these efforts. Stagnant wages for most American workers over several decades (compared to vast concentrations of wealth in the hands of a few, the 1 percent, over those years), offshoring of jobs once held by US workers, evasion of taxes through offshore shelters and other unequal dimensions of the economy were first raised as issues by left-liberals through things like the movement challenging corporate forms of globalization (Della Porta et al. 2007), the Occupy Wall Street movement (Gould-Wartofsky 2015) and the Bernie Sanders campaign. But the right and far right (aka alt-right), with crucial support from data analysis and hedge-fund billionaire Robert Mercer (funder of Cambridge Analytica and Breitbart news), fearing this attack on their economic power, came to embrace a right-wing version of this argument that shifted much of the blame from corporations onto supposedly unfairly competing immigrants, women and people of color. In Donald Trump, these forces found a celebrity who could forcefully articulate this right-wing version of the critique of corporate globalization developed by the left. The 2016 presidential campaign used emotion-drenched social media fake news and commentary to exploit and greatly intensify polarization until it turned into something qualitatively different—a virtual civil war and an all-out attack on US (and through the Brexit vote, UK) democratic traditions. By that point, political thought had shifted from one of manufactured consent to **manufactured dissent** (purposely exaggerated political polarity). This trend also played into the hands of authoritarian fake populisms arising across Europe and other parts of the world, driven especially by xenophobia.

This process was predicted soon after the rise of social media by political analyst Cass Sunstein. The **Sunstein Thesis**, elaborated first in his book *Republic.com* (2000), argues that most people using the Web to follow politics do not seek out a variety of perspectives, but instead seek out information and opinion sources that match their existing ideological biases. The general accuracy of the Sunstein Thesis has been confirmed by a number of subsequent empirical studies and analyses (Schmidt et al. 2017; Vaidhyanathan 2018). The problem is deepened by the fact that spending time in reaffirming ideological "silos" or "echo chambers" produces what Sunstein dubs *cybercascades*, which drive individuals to ever more rigid and extreme positions in order to outdo each other in political intensity. This tendency is reinforced by algorithms on sites such as Google, Twitter and Facebook, where personalization (aka profiling) further entrenches the user's existing views. Looks and "likes" become locks, nailing down what a user already believes and shutting out opposing viewpoints and facts.

Online media became the major purveyor of fake news, and the **silo effect** has become ever more pronounced with each new election cycle. By the 2016 election, these processes were being directly manipulated both internally and through foreign intervention. The two related resources used in the manipulation were both a product of new digital capabilities, the breach of Facebook data (by Cambridge Analytica) and the spread of fake news via Twitter, Facebook and other social media (by Cambridge Analytica and by Russian *troll farms*—government-sponsored teams of online commentators). These entities not only created *bots* (automated fake online identities) to push incendiary comments and fake news stories, but apparently created actual offline events to stir up further discord (Lee

2018). While as of this writing it was unclear if the Trump campaign or Cambridge Analytica *directly* colluded with Russian government forces in this process, their activities certainly ran parallel in key respects and sought the same goals. In the UK, one third of all Twitter traffic leading up to the Brexit vote came from Russian bots, all pushing for Britain to leave the European Union. Russian Twitter-bots in the US election were working 5 to 1 on the side of Trump, and any pro-Clinton ones seem to have been aimed to stir further discord rather than support her candidacy (Cadwalladr 2017; Power 2018).

Earlier research revealed (and subsequent studies have confirmed) that voters in the US, among the most digitally privileged in the world, were not better informed in 2007, post-Internet, than in 1989, before the Net had a significant public ("Public Knowledge" 2007). The vast amounts of reliable information and reasoned opinion online, from all points of view, are clearly not being accessed often enough to lead to greater political knowledge, let alone wisdom. By the 2016 election, reliable political information online was largely drowned in a sea of unreliable information pushed by unscrupulous campaigners. The eighteenth-century Irish satirist Jonathan Swift once wrote that "Falsehood flies, and the Truth comes limping after it," and the American writer Mark Twain similarly observed that "A lie can travel half way around the world while the truth is putting on its shoes." In fact several recent empirical studies make clear that Swift and Twain were onto something. Except that now lies can travel even faster and not halfway but all the way around the world. A study of over 120,000 items of fake news on Twitter demonstrated that lies in fact travelled much faster and more broadly than accurate reports. Analysts tracked how Twitter proved to be a far more effective purveyor of "misleading and wholly fake news" than of accurate news, and showed that social media spread more lies and half-truths than either print media or television (Langin 2018; Vosoughi et al. 2018). One key reason for this is that social media algorithms in general favor the most outrageous and controversial material, because it is more likely to excite and incite and therefore be shared with "friends" and "followers" (Vaidhyanathan 2018).

These exaggerations and lies further the manufacturing of dissent, making actual political dialogue almost impossible. In the US, much of the Net-generated fake news was later broadcast or alluded to on Fox News or the newer ultra-right wing "news" site, Breitbart. As a result, millions of Americans dismissed as "opinion" what are in fact fact-based news items, and believed as "facts" totally false stories.

In thinking about truth, philosophers sometimes distinguish between lies and falsehoods. Lies are untrue things that the purveyors know to be untrue. Falsehoods are untrue things unwittingly shared as true. In this case, paid Cambridge Analytica employees, along with malicious Russian-directed actors in places such as Moldova and Macedonia, made up lies that were then "shared" millions of times by social media users in the US and UK. Most of those sharers may well have believed them to be true. But the effect of spreading lies and spreading falsehoods is the same. The spread of falsehood after falsehood reshaped political opinion in ways that both helped elect a candidate, Donald Trump, and more generally increased the amount of political polarization between millions of US citizens. This same process was at work in the UK Brexit vote, and has been used to exploit and increase social discord, often to the point of inciting violence, in other countries around the globe.

This process undermined not only the possibility of political compromise, but the very idea of political truth. And that process was furthered by a US president who, according to historically very reliable fact checkers, made more than 3,000 false or misleading statements in his first 466 days in office (Kessler, Rizzo and Kelly 2018). To add a bit more nuance to the picture, a prominent philosopher argued for a third category alongside falsehoods and lies. Harry Frankfurt, writing before the rise of Trump, proffered "bullshit" as an important category of discourse along the truth-to-lies spectrum. As Frankfurt defined it in his book, *On Bullshit* (2005), bullshit is speech intended to persuade without regard for truth. In contrast to the liar who cares about the truth and attempts to hide it, or a falsehood spread without knowing it to be a lie, the bullshitter doesn't care whether or not what they say is true or false. They only care that their listener is persuaded. By that definition, the 45th US president appears to have set a new standard for the amount of bullshit presented to the American people, a new level of misinformation that bodes ill for the prospects of meaningful political discussion, and potentially threatens democracy itself. (This is not a pleasant thing to say, but to not say it risks the further spread of bullshit.)

The political philosopher Hannah Arendt, an expert on the history of totalitarian regimes, noted that

> What makes it possible for a totalitarian or any other dictatorship to rule is that people are not informed; how can you have an opinion if you are not informed? If everybody always lies to

you, the consequence is not that you believe the lies, but rather that nobody believes anything any longer . . . And a people that no longer can believe anything cannot make up its mind. It is deprived not only of its capacity to act but also of its capacity to think and to judge. And with such a people you can then do what you please.

(Arendt 1978)

In other words, the impact of the labelling of real news as "fake," while circulating fake news as real, is the unlimited capacity of a political figure to manipulate people and a people who can't act as responsible citizens in a post-truth situation.

Perhaps most disturbing in 2016 was the fact that the process of spreading lies was driven by both domestic *and* foreign forces. Russia had been trying since at least 1984 to infiltrate and impact US elections with very little success. What they lacked they finally found in 2016: The means of communication to carry out their propaganda campaign. The Internet, especially the largest social media sites, such as Facebook and Twitter, made it possible to carry out their efforts to turn the election toward their preferred candidate, in this case Donald Trump in the US. Some 38 million false stories were shared via Facebook alone in the last 3 months of the 2016 election cycle, and bots funded by Russia accounted for 3.8 million tweets in the final weeks. Again we see how scale can overwhelm the capacity to evaluate information. Putin has long used disinformation to strengthen his crony capitalist authoritarian regime, and in 2016 he appears to have used it to undermine democratic regimes by sowing greater discord and general distrust of various parts of the US and UK governments and in the press. Wittingly or not, the Trump campaign amplified this discord and distrust in ways that furthered the Kremlin's goal of undermining democracy. And while disinformation campaigns by governments aimed at perceived enemies is hardly new, including by the intelligence forces of democratic but imperialist countries such as the US, UK and others, the nature, scale and degree of effectiveness of this operation seem unprecedented.

When much of this disinformation campaign came to light in the years after the 2016 election, one might expect that things would improve. But several aspects of social psychology work against getting us out of a *post-truth* political environment. Psychologists, recently bolstered by neuroscientists, have shown again and again that we humans are subject to **confirmation bias** and to a **backlash effect**. The former means that we are far more likely to believe information that confirms our existing beliefs than information that challenges it, *even if the evidence for the challenging side is far more solid*. And the backlash effect means that when confronted with evidence of confirmation bias, rather than correcting our views, we are far more likely to double down, to strengthen our hold on mistaken beliefs. These psychological proclivities help explain both why so many people were (and are) willing to believe patently false things, and also why even carefully pointing out those falsehoods, or describing the process by which fake news spread, is widely resisted. The psychological costs of feeling duped are higher than most of us are willing to pay, so instead we wrap ourselves all the more tightly in our falsehoods (McIntyre 2018).

While it is clear that fake news shaped opinion and increased divisiveness, it is exceedingly difficult to isolate any single factor in the outcome of an election involving millions of voters. Because of this, opinion varies as to the extent of the role fake news played in deciding the 2016 voting in the US and UK. All evidence agrees that false stories favoring Trump were circulated at a much higher rate than those about Clinton. One of the more careful analyses found 115 pro-Trump fake stories shared on Facebook a total of 30 million times, and 41 pro-Clinton fake stories shared a total of 7.6 million times (Allcott and Gentzkow 2017), but draws no conclusion as to the impact. As might be expected, several liberal-leaning sources concluded that the impact was substantial, possibly even decisive, in Trump's victory (Dewey November 17, 2016; Parkinson 2016; Read 2016), while more conservative news organizations downplayed the effects. But all sources agree that misinformation conveyed via social media has become a serious issue.

On a positive note, surveys suggest that while half of Americans get their news primarily from Facebook, only 5 percent say that they have "a lot of trust" and only 35 percent say that they have "some trust" in the app as a news source. By contrast, 85 percent have some trust in local news sources, 76 percent trust friends and family, and 72 percent have some trust in national news organizations, though these sources too can allow a good deal of confirmation bias. And these statistics precede the major stories about Facebook's data breach and their role in circulating millions of suspect political ads (Gramlich 2018). As with all polls, self-reporting isn't always accurate, and voting patterns suggest it is possible people actually believe more Facebook-presented news than they claim. And the number of people who get their news from social media continues to grow, with Snapchat, Twitter and YouTube all showing an increase in users viewing news items (Shearer and Gottfried 2017). Another survey at least confirmed that many people are concerned about the problem. That study showed that 64 percent of Americans believe false news stories cause confusion, and 23 percent said they shared fabricated stories themselves, sometimes knowingly, sometimes by mistake. That some knowingly spread fake news suggests they put a higher value on their political beliefs than on truth. While that is hardly unprecedented, it is a practice that if it becomes widespread enough will make political debate meaningless and democracy impossible. Those surveyed were roughly evenly divided as to whether they think the problem will get better or worse in coming years (Anderson and Rainie 2017).

Statistical analysis of the false news spread during the presidential election campaign concluded that roughly 70 percent of it was spread by the right, and 30 percent by the left. Analysis also showed that conservatives, given particular personality tendencies, are somewhat more likely to believe fake news than are liberals (McIntyre 2018). This is not a political judgment. The left is not immune and in another election cycle the results may differ. The issue is not whether a given political position is valid or not. There are perfectly valid, well-argued, fact-based arguments for conservative beliefs, liberal ones and others all across the political spectrum. What is at issue is not belief, but the basis of beliefs and the intensity of hatred of the other side generated by intentional fear-mongering, lies and half-truths. All politics involves some "spin," involves interpreting the facts in the best possible light to strengthen each side's position. But spin is a far cry from wholly made-up lies that defy known facts and that undermine any possibility of coherent political debate. When figures such as Trump, Netanyahu in Israel, Madura in Venezuela, and Assad in Syria call any critical news about their actions "fake news," it further undermines the process of understanding how actually false news deeply distorts politics. The disinformation campaigns waged largely via social media in recent years undermine not just political opponents, but, as Arendt points out, the very possibility of democratic decision-making. Ultimately no political ideology except authoritarianism benefits from fake political information being passed off as real, and real facts being dismissed as fake.

But don't take my word for this. Listen to someone with con-servative bone fides who was far closer to the power that is being abused. Having left office after spending a year as Donald Trump's Secretary of State, former ExxonMobil executive Rex Tillerson came to a conclusion similar to Hannah Arendt's. As part of a commence-ment address to graduates of the Virginia Military Academy, he had this to say:

> If our leaders seek to conceal the truth or we as a people become accepting of alternative realities that are no longer grounded in facts, then we as American citizens are on a pathway to relin-quishing our freedom. This is the life of non-democratic societ-ies, comprised of people who are not free to seek the truth . . . A responsibility of every American citizen to each other is to pre-serve and protect our freedom by recognizing what the truth is and what it is not, what a fact is and is not, and begin holding ourselves accountable to truthfulness and demand that our pur-suit of America's future is fact-based.
>
> (Quoted in Hohmann 2018)

There is no doubt that the average person has, via the Web, access to more political information than ever before. But access to infor-mation is never enough. There must also be thoughtful frameworks through which to interpret the information, and the judgement to tell a reliable source from an unreliable one. This will need to include far greater *critical digital literacy*, and it is a set of skills more important to teach in our digitized age as coding (Polizzi 2018). Unfortunately the speed, volume and distortion of information made possible by social media militate against such thought-ful framing or assessing of incoming news and information. But whether this situation gets worse or better will not depend mostly on technology, though there are a number of technical things that could be done by social media companies to improve things. There is little doubt that social media acted like an accelerant poured onto a fire. We need, therefore, serious efforts to force social media corporations to do a far better job of identifying false stories, and eliminating troll farms and bots that account for many of them. But the fires existed before social media. The underlying ideologi-cal fires must be addressed too. Protecting democracy will largely depend on what citizens do to reject political lies, resist manufac-tured political hatred and insist that political discussion address real issues with a much higher degree of honesty, fairness and reliable evidence.

⬔ CAN SOCIAL MEDIA OVERTHROW GOVERNMENTS?

As mentioned earlier, in relation to politics and revolutionary change in autocratic regimes, many once argued that the Internet and digital media were inherently democratizing, liberating technologies. Events such as the Arab Spring revolutions, in which social networking and other elements of digital culture played a prominent role, give credence to the idea that digital technologies can bring down authoritarian regimes. Some even argued that the spread of these technologies would inevitably bring down all non-democratic regimes. However, the evidence was mixed at best even in this earlier period, and few hold that optimism nowadays. Other closed regimes, including Iran and Saudi Arabia in this same region, for example, have used the Web to spy on, track down, harass, arrest and in some cases torture and murder dissenters, as have other authoritarian and quasi-democratic governments around the world (Fuchs 2008; Mozorov 2011).

Particularly after the Arab Spring revolutions of 2011–2012 in the Middle East, and versions of the Occupy movement in the US and elsewhere, strong claims were made for the Internet and digital media as an irresistible force for democratization across the globe. But even activists actually involved in these movements by and large rejected such characterizations. And it is not hard to see why. No one calls the American Revolution the Pamphlet Revolution, yet pamphlets and broadsides played a crucial role in awakening dissent. No one calls the French Revolution the Salon/Saloon Revolution, yet salons for the bourgeois revolutionists and saloons (taverns) were crucial communication centers for working-class revolutionaries. The point is that communication devices are communication devices, not revolutionary in themselves. The revolutions in the Middle East did indeed make very positive use of new media, especially smartphones, including ones with video capabilities, and the Twitterverse, Facebook and YouTube were important for communication, especially to the world outside. But the revolutions emerged from years of deprivation and years of organizing. Worker unions, student groups, women's groups, legal and clandestine NGOs and smart tactics, not smartphones, made the revolutions. Further evidence that it was more than new media can be seen by contrasting Egypt, Tunisia and the other more or less successful revolts with the failed revolt in Iran 2 years earlier (it was that revolution, by the way, that was first dubbed the Twitter Revolution). All the new media deployed in Iran could not overcome the fact that the regime there was more stable than dissenters inside and outside the country believed. Without better organization, communication was not enough.

The other, darker side of this story is the use of digital technology by authoritarian regimes to squelch protest and punish dissenters, as described earlier. Iran, China, Russia, parts of Eastern Europe and numerous other undemocratic regimes have used the trail left by online communication to track down activists, often leading authorities to harass, threaten, jail and sometimes outright murder dissidents (Fuchs 2008; Gladwell 2010; Mozorov 2011). In Iran, it remains unclear who will ultimately win the online political wars, but suffice it to say that the regime still stands, and activists are further underground and more cautious online than before the failed Green/Twitter Revolution. And in states where the Arab Spring revolts were more successful, as in Egypt, the aftermath has included members of the new regime using digital tracking to locate and punish revolutionaries who are now viewed as enemies of the new regimes. In Egypt, Al-Sisi has aggressively turned digital communication against those who used it to overthrow Mubarak.

In Myanmar/Burma the most effective communication mechanism is Facebook, and hate speech on the platform contributed significantly to the ethnic cleansing murder of Muslims in that country. In general, Facebook, because of its lack of investment in translators for many of the less widely used languages, has been utterly ineffective in keeping hateful messages and terrorist recruiting from its platform in many of the smaller countries around the globe (Hogan and Safi 2018; Taylor 2018).

These documented authoritarian abuses should forever erase naïve optimism about the inherently positive influence of digital media. But, as I detail in the next section, the Net and related technologies still do have much to offer in terms of constructive, nonviolent social protest and social movement organizing. However, activists need to be more level headed, realistic and proactive about challenging the use of digital technologies by forces opposing the expansion of democracy in the world, while using them to extend democracy.

⧉ ELECTRONIC CIVIL DISOBEDIENCE, HACKTIVISM AND DIGITAL ORGANIZING

Live-streaming demonstrations, recruitment and organizing via inexpensive digital media, **electronic civil disobedience**, public interest leaking, digital protest art and a wide variety of other new tech savvy activist forms have arisen. Some of these developments have been controversial, and some have been condemned. What is certain is that, apart from a few hardcore neo-Luddites (advocates of destroying or avoiding technologies), digital technologies are now acknowledged as important forms of social movement activism that have enhanced, but not replaced, more traditional forms (Boler et al. 2010; Gerbaudo 2012; Hands 2011; Joyce 2010; Juris 2008; Raley 2009).

Social movements arise when traditional political forms—elected or autocratic leaders, parties, lobbying, etc.—fail to address pressing economic, social or cultural concerns. Protest movements have long been a driving force of modern history. The American and French Revolutions ushered in the modern form of democracy. Labor movements ended child labor, brought worker safety rules, set reasonable wages and hours and ushered in a host of social benefits enjoyed by all. Women's movements around the globe got women the vote and continue to push for full gender equality. Anti-colonial movements in Africa, Asia and Latin American utterly changed the map of the modern world. Movements for ethnic rights and global human rights have deeply challenged racisms and ethnocentrisms around the world. Environmental social movements have profoundly reshaped attitudes and practices toward the natural world. Indeed, it is hard to find another form of human activity (including technological innovation) that has been more influential in shaping and reshaping societies than organized political protest through social movements.

It is not surprising, therefore, to find social movement activism very much present in digital spaces, with many new kinds of electronic activism added to the standard repertoire of protest forms. Long before the Internet, social movement scholars studied the crucial importance of social networks to the growth of protest. Social networks, including transnational ones, existed long before the rise of new electronic media, but the Net has added virtual communication networks and virtual communities that have sped up, lessened the cost of and extended the range of political organizers across distances. Dissenters with romanticized names such as "hacktivists," "camcorder commandos," "data dancers," "code warriors" and "culture jammers" engaging in things like "cyber sit-ins," "electronic civil disobedience" and "meme warfare" have created a rich new digital culture of resistance that has become a vital part of many social movements. Not only the Arab Spring uprisings, but also the anti-globalization/global justice movement, the Occupy movement, the *indignados* in Spain and numerous other twenty-first-century protests have imaginatively used digital media. And the massive #MeToo and #TimesUp movements against sexual assault and harassment achieved prominence at a pace utterly impossible before the existence of digital media. Appropriately enough, digital protests have been key in protecting Internet freedom, as in the massive online protests in 2011 against the SOPA legislation that sought to end Net neutrality in the US, which would have given greater corporate control of the Web (SOPA Strike n.d.). But as with all social protest, digital protests have had as many failures as successes, as when, for example, another massive online resistance campaign was not enough to turn back a new effort to destroy Net neutrality by the Trump regime in 2017.

Digital activism is open to all political persuasions, including extremely reactionary ones. White supremacist, anti-immigrant, Islamophobic, sexist and homophobic groups, not to mention terrorist ones, have also been given a boost by digital media. The Net has been used not only to organize positive protest but also to allow neo-Nazis and other white supremacists to become more visible, and to link up their small but virulent memberships around the globe. The anonymity of the Web has proven attractive to groups whose ideas are anathema to most people, and made them better able to recruit in a clandestine way. These groups too have availed themselves of the range of other available forms of digital protest (Daniels 2009; Klein 2010; Rajagopal and Bojin 2004). Stormfront, for example, a white supremacist hub, has put up fake websites, like one promising to inform about the life and works of Martin Luther King that on closer inspection proves to be riddled with lies, half-truths and racist propaganda. The amount of blatantly racist, sexist and homophobic imagery on the Web promoted by these groups is deeply disturbing, and should have given the lie to the idea that we are living in a post-racial, post-sexist, post-homophobic world long before the 2016 election and the Charlottesville white supremacist events brought the alt-right to the foreground (Jeong 2016).

Nevertheless, the imaginative variety of digital activism by more forward-looking movements is especially impressive. Digitization has clearly changed the repertoire of protest. Digital protest takes many new forms, from electronic civil disobedience to digitized protest art to strange-sounding innovations such as **maptivism**, *culture jamming* and *meme warfare* to political hacking. Networked cameras, smartphones and a variety of other digital devices have changed the nature of face-to-face protest events. The presence of video recording devices also has proven effective for activists seeking to get their version of events out past a mainstream media often suffering from "protest fatigue" (the drama of protest inevitably becomes less dramatic when routinized, while the media rely on drama to raise circulation or viewership). The presence of many videophones and mini-camcorders during the "battle of Seattle" protests against the World Trade Organization in 1999 proved crucial to the legal process after the events were over. What were often characterized by the police and the mainstream media as anti-globalization riots were reclassified as a "police riot" once video showed many incidents of unprovoked police attacks on protesters. Virtually all charges were dropped against the activists, and many received monetary compensation for the abuse suffered at the hands of the authorities. This process of vindication of protesters and condemnation of police overreaction has been repeated a number of times through the use of digital video (Reed 2019). Some call documenting illegal or intrusive government activities **sousveillance**. The opposite of surveillance (*sur* = above, *sous* = below in French), sousveillance looks back at abusive authority from street level, from the viewpoint of ordinary citizens, and new media such as smartphone cameras make it possible to document the more grounded point of view.

The #OccupyWallStreet movement in 2011–2012 likewise received a large infusion of sympathy and support when an activist video of police surrounding and harassing a group of peaceful female protesters went viral on the Web and was picked up by mainstream media in the US and abroad. And the #Black Lives Matter movement has used smartphone video to document police abuse and shootings and the Net as one key organizing site. More generally, the ability of movement groups to livestream coverage of their events can be crucial in several respects. Perhaps most importantly, younger people, many of whom have grown quite distrustful of mainstream politics and mainstream media, partly due in the English-speaking world to the influence of brilliant satirical news shows such as "The Daily Show" and "The Colbert Report," are more likely to view and trust direct streaming from the movement than filtered coverage. While various forms of independent media, like the presence around the globe of numerous Independent Media Centers (Indy Media), still work at a great disadvantage compared with news coverage backed by huge multinational media conglomerates such as Time Warner, Viacom, Vivendi, News Corp or Bertelsman AG, they are making significant inroads, again, particularly among younger people.

The term **netroots activism** is a common descriptor for online protesters, meant to echo the term "grassroots activism," a traditional form of organizing protest. Those who do not believe serious social movement activism can take place online invented the pejorative term "slacktivism" (i.e., slackers posing as activists) to disparage digital politics. Some charges of slacktivism raise legitimate issues regarding overreliance upon complacent electronic petition signing or protest box clicking (hence "clicktivism" as another pejorative). But other charges seem merely to reflect anti-technological bias or resistance to new forms. Some are also misinformed about activism, as is the case of a widely circulated *New Yorker* article by Malcolm Gladwell (2010). Gladwell attacked the anti-hierarchical, network approach common in digital organizing, contrasting it with what he misrepresents as the hierarchical organizing in the US Civil Rights Movement. In fact, the most successful movement group in the Civil Rights Movement was the radically network-oriented, anti-hierarchical Student Non-violent Coordinating Committee (SNCC). Moreover, the networking model of organizing, in the wake of SNCC, has been the dominant form in US and transnational left-liberal movements for several decades now.

In order to make the general case that slacktivism best characterizes protest organized in online environments one would need to show that offline forms of activism such as marches, street protests, sit-ins and other forms of civil disobedience have declined overall in the Internet era, and then show precisely how the Net has contributed to that decline. In fact, since the former is not true, there is little point trying to prove the latter. On February 15, 2003, for example, with the US clearly approaching war on Iraq, the largest protest event in human history took place in over 600 cities on every of continent on the globe. The event was so huge that while no one doubts it was the largest event of its kind ever, no full count has been possible (estimates range from a mere[!] 10 million to as high as 15 million protesters). Regardless of which figure is more accurate, that stout source of humanity's statistics, the *Guinness World Records*, certified it as the largest anti-war protest in history. Not only did this event show that getting millions of people into the streets in protest could happen in the Internet era, the organizing and coordinating of the events largely took place online and would have been impossible to achieve before the Net arrived. Interestingly, it was also a pre-war anti-war protest. Typically significant resistance to wars happen only after they have been going for a while. And it was not an isolated event; between January 3 and April 12, 2003, 36 million people across the globe took part in almost 3,000 anti-war protests ("February 15, 2003 Anti-War Protest" n.d.). A digitally enabled time-line created by John Bieler that graphically maps "every protest on the planet since 1979" illustrates greater and greater amounts of dissent in the twenty-first century (Bieler n.d.; Stuster 2013). The Women's March protesting the Trump election was likewise the most wide-spread feminist protest in history. Social conditions under neoliberal globalization ultimately account for this but digital media have played a key role in expanding and accelerating this resistance, contrary to charges of slacktivism (Gerbaudo 2012; Lievrouw 2011).

Digital social movement activity includes both new ways to accomplish older forms of organizing and truly new forms only possible in the Internet era. Even the most traditional of political activist work (i.e., writing letters to officials) has been enhanced greatly by the low-cost, high-speed and extensive geographic reach of the Internet. But critics argue that the very ease of digitally signing an email or online petition has cheapened the experience, rendered it less impactful on politicians than personal letters snail mailed the old-fashioned way. Are social networks and microblogs just updated versions of group meetings, or do they fundamentally transform interactive experience? That seems to depend primarily upon age. For digital natives who grew up Web-connected, these forms feel natural and legitimate, while older activists express reservations that the experience feels less substantial, artificial and limited. Whether or not this is elder wisdom or mere generational prejudice remains to be seen. The great civil rights activist Ella Baker, a woman as important to the movement as Martin Luther King though far less appreciated, made a distinction between mobilizing people and organizing them (Payne 2001 [1995]; Reed 2019). "Mobilizing" refers to the process by which inspirational leaders or other persuaders can get large numbers of people to join a movement or engage in a particular movement action. Organizing entails a more sustained process as people come to deeply understand a movement's goals and their own power to change themselves and the world. Mobilizing creates followers; organizing creates leaders. (Note how Twitter speaks of "followers.") Baker made clear that we need both mobilizing and organizing. And thus far, while the Net has proven to be a highly effective tool for mobilizing, the jury is still out as to how effective it can be at organizing, at deeply empowering people who become self-activating leaders themselves. It largely depends on how reliant on only online work movements become. The most successful movements use the Net as an informational and recruitment tool, but realize that offline work in small groups and large public demonstrations are also essential.

One form that might be called *fanactivism* builds upon the fact that the Net has enabled a huge growth in the amount of active pop culture fandom. One pioneering and unusually successful example of this kind of activism is a group built on the massive literary and cinematic phenomenon that is the Harry Potter franchise. Recognizing that the immense popularity of the Potter books and films had potential to be used for social change, a group of Dumbledore devotees got together and formed the Harry Potter Alliance to tackle a range of social issues. As their Mission Statement describes the group:

> The Harry Potter Alliance (HPA) is a 501c3 nonprofit that takes an outside-of-the-box approach to civic engagement by using parallels from the Harry Potter books to educate and mobilize young people across the world toward issues of literacy, equality, and human rights. Our mission is to empower our members to act like the heroes that they love by acting for a better world.
>
> (Harry Potter Alliance n.d.)

With more than 100,000 members, the group has had real social impact on issues ranging from poverty in Haiti to marriage equality to the empowerment of young women and girls.

Rather than adding to the lament that youth are not as politically engaged today as in past generations, these organizers sought out and found new points of motivation by linking Rowling's virtual world to the virtual world of the Net in order to bring real change. One of the secrets to successful social movements is mobilizing existing social networks and turning them on to activism. The Web provides exponentially more publicly visible social networks than ever before, and offers the communication media to make them more available for organizing than has ever been even remotely possible in the past. The HPA offers one clever example of how to imaginatively tap into this potential.

Another array of online political activity is the practice known as **hacktivism** (hacking + activism). Hacking is a multifaceted phenomenon. Working from imagery from old Westerns, some practitioners distinguish between white-hat hackers who break security for non-malicious reasons, either to test a security system, sometimes with authorization, sometimes just to prove a point, or for positive political goals, and black-hat hackers, sometimes also called "crackers," who use hacking for personal gain or purely malicious intents, such as cyber-vandalism, identity theft or electronic bank robbing. Tacitly acknowledging that sometimes this distinction is not entirely clearcut, a third term, grey-hat hacking, has been invoked at times to denote ambiguous hacking practices.

Electronic or digital civil disobedience is one key form of hacktivism. Civil disobedience has a long and rich history, and has now entered the digital age. Though something like it had been practiced here and there for hundreds of years, the two words "civil" and "disobedience" were first theoretically linked by the American writer Henry David Thoreau. The practice has proven to be quite complicated, but the original principle was simple: You intentionally break a law you believe to be unjust and you take the consequences of that action. In Thoreau's case, he refused to pay his taxes to the US government because they were waging what he believed to be an illegal and unjust war on Mexico. After publicly declaring his refusal, he was put in jail. That jailing only lasted one night, whereupon to his dismay he was bailed out by his friend Ralph Waldo Emerson. (Thoreau, upon being asked by his mentor Emerson, "What are you doing in jail?" famously replied, "What are you doing out of jail?" In other words, why are you not protesting a war you too believe to be unjustifiable?) This small symbolic sacrifice established an immensely powerful political practice, one that was famously used by Mahatma Gandhi to bring an end to the British colonization of India, and by the US Civil Rights Movement to bring an end to legal segregation, anti-black voting laws and much more.

This long tradition of civil disobedience has three major strands. The putatively purist, most principled form is the direct breaking of a law or social custom deemed to be unjust, and accepting the consequences of that law breaking in the interest of drawing attention to the injustice. A classic example of this form is the breaking of racial apartheid laws in the legally segregated American South during the Civil Rights Movement. Thousands of US citizens went to jail to protest these unjust laws. A second strand breaks a law indirectly connected to the injustice, and also takes the legal consequences. Thoreau exemplifies a long tradition of civil disobedient tax resistance by pacifists in indirect opposition to unjust wars. Or think of those anti-nuclear power protesters in the 1980s who went to jail for committing trespass onto sites where new plants were being constructed, drawing attention to the dangers of projects like the Diablo Canyon nuclear plant built on top of one of California's most dangerous earthquake faults. A third strand of civil disobedience believes in breaking laws either directly or indirectly linked to injustice, but with the aim of evading capture and consequences. Recall, for example, those famous American revolutionaries, who disguising themselves (not very convincingly) as "Indians," threw large quantities of tea into Boston harbor in protest of British taxation, then slunk away undetected and unarrested to fight another day.

For the most part, current-day practitioners of electronic civil disobedience prefer this third mode, creating mayhem through legally fuzzy or outright illegal activities while escaping punishment by covering their digital tracks. Often the only harm done by hacktivists is to the pride and reputation of corporations and governments they aim to embarrass by exposing exploitative work conditions, undemocratic practices or vulnerable security. When economic damage is done to a major corporation through hacking, the hacktivists typically justify it by suggesting it is a small sum compared to the money these companies beg, borrow and steal from low-wage workers combined with government handouts and bailouts.

Electronic civil disobedience can take several different forms. One common one is the *digital sit-in*, often in the form of overwhelming a targeted website with so much traffic that it breaks down and cannot function for a period of time. This is called a denial of service (DoS) attack. It has been used against corporations deemed to have used unfair labor practices, against terrorist sites and against organizations deemed socially hurtful. Two of the most highly publicized DoS attacks were by the hacker collective Anonymous. They took on the Church of Scientology in 2008 and the ISIS terror network's online presence in 2016. Another type of electronic civil disobedience takes the form of hacking into and changing the content of websites. These often take a satirical form aimed at undermining the ideology of the group attacked. Anonymous again provides a good example. In the wake of the homophobic, partly ISIS-inspired attack on a gay nightclub in Orlando, Florida in 2016, the group hacked into 1,500 ISIS-related Twitter accounts, filling them with gay pride insignia and gay porn. (This of course raises the question of how Twitter allowed the existence of 1,500 ISIS accounts.)

Some dismiss these acts because they don't really significantly impact the targeted corporations, political groups or government agencies. But this is a misunderstanding. In general, like the non-digital civil disobedient sit-ins, this hacktivism is intended more to be symbolic than significantly disruptive. In Gandhi's anti-colonialism efforts, in the Civil Rights and the anti-Apartheid movements and many others the goal was not sustained disruption but to momentarily stop business as usual in order to publicize an injustice. In that respect, digital civil disobedience has often been successful, such as when hacktivist efforts played an important role in drawing attention to the wider online boycott that forced the Nike corporation to clean up exploitative practices in its shoe factories (Birch 2012).

The form of hacktivism that has received the most attention in recent years is the leaking of documents as practiced by high-profile figures such as Chelsea Manning, Edward Snowden and Julian Assange. Each of these figures has a different set of motives, interests and ideologies, but all believe that certain forms of government secrecy are unjustified. The most serious charge against this kind of leaking is that it may endanger military and civilian intelligence officers. In response, these figures claim to have sought to redact all such names from the documents they have made available online.

The leaking of secret documents is hardly a new phenomenon. One of the most famous such cases was the Pentagon Papers scandal of 1971, in which a former Defense Department employee copied and had published a secret history that exposed government lies about the US war on Vietnam. (The complex decision to publish the Pentagon Papers was the subject of the 2017 film *The Post*). What might be called *public interest leaking* (to distinguish it from self-interested leaks by politicians) has been given new life by digital media communication and by the Net's vulnerability to hacking. The practice has spawned a rich expansion of the debate about the public's right to know, private property rights and legitimate forms of national security. There is no doubt that every government has a right to keep certain things private. But it is equally the case that every government, however ostensibly democratic, abuses this right to privacy not to protect their citizens but to keep their citizens from knowing of the misdeeds and misinformation of the government. There is no a priori formula for sorting out legitimate from illegitimate forms of leaking (which is still also done by analog means, not just digital ones). But public interest leakers have done the world a favor by bringing this issue more forcefully into the arena of public debate.

Hacktivists have developed techniques for covering their digital tracks to an art form. But any hacker, regardless of the color of hat they claim to wear, must be prepared for the likelihood of eventual exposure and punishment. Exposure can have very severe consequences when states invoke "national security"—a catchall term that is valid in some cases but has often proven to be a cover for not wanting to divulge embarrassing or illegal government activities. The case of US Army private Bradley Manning (now Chelsea Manning), who helped leak the largest cache of confidential military and diplomatic documents ever published, makes clear the costs when anonymity is lost. Leaking by politicians and government officials is seldom prosecuted until truly damning secrets are revealed, as was true of leaks by Manning regarding civilians bombed and other abusive practice of the US military in the Middle East. Manning's arrest, abuse by US captors and eventual multiyear prison sentence sparked intense debate about what information the public has a right to know (I Am Bradley Manning n.d.; WikiLeaks n.d.). Former CIA intelligence analyst Edward Snowden, who leaked similarly shocking documents detailing massive secret, and largely illegal, government surveillance of ordinary citizens in the US and abroad, managed to escape a similar fate, but only at the expense of exile from his homeland (Harding 2014).

Clearly powerful governments around the globe will seek to make the kind of anonymity used by digital dissidents impossible to sustain. There will be an ongoing struggle around the practice and suppression of digitally enabled public interest leaking. As their name suggests, the hacktivist collective Anonymous understands anonymity to be central to its ability to expose corruption and deception in governmental and corporate rule through leaks and other activities (Anonymous n.d.). And they also understand the value of working as a collective. While some alleged members of Anonymous have been arrested, the anonymous face of the group (a Guy Fawkes mask modelled on the graphic novel/film *V for Vendetta:* see Figure 7.2) symbolizes that others are always ready to step in to replace those who are rendered no longer anonymous. This kind of anonymity is designed to remind people of the fact that without political privacy, without a space to confidentially discuss political ideas, democracy cannot flourish (see Chapter 4). And that without governmental transparency, we cannot know whether democratic will is being exercised. Clearly, not all putatively public interest leaking is equal or to be admired. Both the leaks and the leakers must be evaluated on a case-by-case basis, balancing security and transparency. But as the great journalist I. F. Stone once noted, at some point "all governments lie," and that means at some points we need those who expose the lies.

Another unique form of activism made possible by a different set of digital technologies, including Global Positioning Systems (GPSs), has been given the portmanteau designation *maptivism*—the use of mapping techniques to visualize, represent and organize around a given social issue. A particularly rich example is HarassMap, a project

FIGURE 7.2 *Pride day protest for Bradley/Chelsea Manning (Courtesy: Koby Dagan/Shutterstock.com)*

originating in Egypt and aimed at reducing and hopefully eventually ending sexual harassment. Like most successful e-activist projects, the digital elements are never seen as sufficient but rather as a starting point or augmentation to face-to-face organizing.

HarassMap is just what it sounds like. It is an online tool that maps the places around Egypt where acts of sexual harassment have occurred. The site is "crowdsourced" in the sense that anyone who has experienced sexual harassment or sexual assault, whether on the street, in a store, in school, at a doctor's office—anywhere—can submit their story to the site and have that story appear both as a narrative and as a point on the HarassMap. The organizers of Harass-Map see the map itself as a taking-off point, a tool for deeper work. They also protect their work from government interference by host-ing the site outside of Egypt itself. The map provides concrete visible data and a variety of moving stories that they in turn leverage into information used in neighborhood-by-neighborhood, door-to-door organizing that can cite facts, figures and specific cases to overcome denial (not here, not in significant numbers, not to "good girls," etc.) and bolster their argument that the problem exists, is serious and is prevalent in a particular neighborhood they are targeting at that time. All of the volunteers must be from the particular village or part of the city they intervene into, assuring utmost local credibility and sensitivity to specific class, religious and cultural contexts.

The organizers are also aware that there was once a stronger cul-tural intolerance for harassment (in earlier decades harassers were routinely run down, and had their heads shaved as a form of public shaming), so the publicizing made possible by the Web is part of a strategy to shame Egyptians into resisting a growing problem, and an attempt to recall a time when this problem was dealt with by collec-tive community action. HarassMap has been amazingly successful, and has spawned similar projects on harassment or on other issues around the globe. Would they have been able to do their work with-out digital technology? They readily admit that they could. Indeed, they had been doing anti-harassment work for several years prior to their creation of HarassMap, but the technology set off a firestorm of information and recruitment that would have taken years to organize without the technology. The main technology they use, the Usha-hidi platform, was originally used to monitor election fraud and, like other mapping software, has been used for a variety of activist ends in what has been nicknamed Global Positioning Subversion.

The HarassMap model grew from earlier forms of maptivism (Kreutz 2009), and has been adopted by activist groups in other countries around the world, from Yemen to Canada, with each group shaping the materials to meet particular local cultural values and specific needs. One such group, Hollaback, tracks and protests street-level sexual harassment by collecting and sharing via the Web information on places and individuals harassing female passersby, a process that nicely illustrates how real world and virtual world can interact very directly and effectively. A related but slightly different example of maptivism has been carried out by groups seeking to give greater historical depth to protests in particular locations. The "Re: Activism" project has worked in a number of cities in the US to set up (analog) games that trace and interact with the history of activism in a given community by using locative media to take players to various sites where important protests occurred in the past ("Re: Activism" n.d.). Such games would seem capable of deepening understanding of the protest tradition and inspiring continued commitment. They are also an excellent example of working simultaneously in so-called real-world and virtual spaces. Some tech-savvy activists in London took this a step further through the invention of a suite of apps called Sukey to help dissenters avoid being caught in police "kettles" (often-brutal formations in which dozens of riot-gear-attired police surround or fiercely funnel a group of protesters into suffocating clumps: See Figure 7.3). The apps use a Google Maps mashup, GPS and encryption to instantly and securely monitor police movements to allow maximum activist effectiveness in protest blockades. Seemingly thinking of every contingency, Sukey includes a Twitter link called sukeydating that can help jailed protesters to find "activist love"; a sample tweet: "Do you know why they're called kettles? Because they are hot and steamy ..." (Geere 2011; Sukey Apps n.d.).

Adaptation to local conditions along with traditional face-to-face organizing are what has turned these many digital activist projects from interesting technical tools to truly effective agents of social

FIGURE 7.3 *Police kettle in London protest, 2011 (Courtesy: 1000 Words/ Shutterstock.com)*

change. The same can be said for digital protests generally; it is close connection to "real-world" away-from-keyboard sites that makes online netroots activism most effective. And as Paolo Gerbaudo persuasively argues, digital politics in social movements must ultimately be translated into electoral organizing to fully succeed in bringing about sustained, meaningful change. To accomplish that, Gerbaudo advocates a leaderless, citizen populism as the alternative to rising strands of authoritarian fake populism (Gerbaudo 2017).

⮊ CYBERTERRORISM

A very different form of digital political activity goes under the heading **cyberterrorism**. Cyberterrorism is just what the term implies: A tool for terrorists who wish to induce a state of fear and to do real physical and/or psychological harm. While sometimes using the same tools, cyberterrorism is very different from hacktivism. Unfortunately, sometimes intentionally, sometimes unwittingly, the two have been conflated. This is partly because the concept of cyberterrorism is almost infinitely expandable, and can be used by governments to suppress any kind of dissent they find threatening. As Sandor Vegh was among the first to argue, authorities can reshape the term to fit any opponent they wish to discredit, harass or imprison (Vegh 2002). To help assure that this does not happen, critics argue that the term should properly be used in two main contexts: To describe offline terrorists who use digital spaces to communicate about their plans to terrorize; or to designate individuals, groups or governmental entities who use hacking and other techniques to purposely cause death, destruction and serious psychological distress. Broader definitions are almost invariably misused to suppress legitimate forms of protest.

The issue of cyberterrorism ties into the larger question of cyber-censorship. While it is easy to decry censorship of the Net in authoritarian regimes such as China and Iran, putatively democratic ones are also making strong efforts to limit, control and surveil the Web. US government attacks on Manning and Snowden, for example, have been pursued at a level out of proportion to their alleged actions. The revelations by Snowden in 2013 of the extent of illegal digital spying on American citizens are deeply disturbing (Gellman 2013; Wills 2013), and yet they have received wholly inadequate government response. Often using cyberterrorism and national security as excuses to vastly overreach reasonable protection of the populace, from the so-called Patriot Act onward, the US government and similar laws in the UK have tried again and again to legitimate extensive invasion of digital spaces to spy on and gather information about citizens who pose no threat. As part of the battle to decide whether the Net remains a truly open public space or becomes one dominated by corporate and governmental control, it will be vital for citizens around the globe to keep a close watch on legislation that continues to try to limit Web freedoms and push increased digital surveillance beyond what can be justified by national security issues such as terrorism (see Chapter 4).

A key question that must be faced by huge social networks such as Facebook and Twitter is where to draw the line between free speech and hate speech. Facebook has been moderately strong in dealing with Middle Eastern terrorists, but not so good in dealing with white supremacist domestic terrorists. And this imbalance has been reinforced by the US Justice Department, which, under Attorney General Sessions, took most white supremacist and other violent domestic right-wing extremists off the terror list, while upping the assault on Muslim communities, some of which have been key to fighting terrorists. Due to this and related policies under the Trump regime, very broadly defined Islamic terrorism is being pursued online and off far more than right-wing domestic terrorists, despite the fact that ISIS and other Middle East-centered terrorism has been declining while "alt-right" terrorism has been on the rise. This government neglect shifts even more of the burden of fighting hate onto social media because kicking white supremacists off of Facebook, Twitter and the like severely curtails recruitment into hate groups. They can be forced to shift to more sympathetic alt-right social media apps like Gab, where they lose their ability to reach "normies" (i.e., those of us not yet infected with hate). Media corporations, because they are private companies, not government-run utilities, have more leeway in controlling who uses their products. And the scrutiny now being shown to Facebook and others in the wake of massive leaks of user data offers some hope that they will no longer always put profits ahead of social responsibility.

⮕ DIGITIZING THE ARTS OF PROTEST

Virtually every art form has been transformed by the rise of digital technologies, and new forms of art—variously called "new media art," "digital art," "computer-mediated art" and so forth—have also emerged. One way to survey this massive terrain is to look at a few examples of political protest art as representative of larger trends in the digitization of the arts overall.

The range of art media, styles and forms used as digital protest is extremely broad. To begin with one of the most ubiquitous forms of protest art, the poster has had renewed life in the digital world. The anti-AIDs activist group ACT-UP pioneered the digitizing of graphic protest art, using every form from small stickers to placards to huge posters, and they did so mostly in the pre-Internet era (Reed 2019). While spreading posters and other graphic images online is immensely powerful and can instantaneously reach thousands of people, the best protest poster producers realize that it is equally important to reproduce and disseminate their works out into the offline world. Like the best social movement organizers in general, poster makers realize that it is important to reach those people, the majority of the world's population, who do not have the privilege of access to digital culture.

Two wholly new forms of art enabled by digital culture are **locative media** and **augmented reality**. One example of locative media protest that became highly controversial was called "Border Haunt" (Border Haunt 2011). This project was a one-time event that subsequently has life as a website. Using GPS, it carried out a unique protest along the Mexico/US border. Each year many people die in vain efforts to cross the border without proper authorization or sufficient means. The project seeks to honor those who have died, while also demonstrating how surveillance technologies can be turned against themselves. Ian Alan Paul, the creator or facilitator of the action, invited anyone sympathetic to the plight of immigrants to participate in the intentional misleading of border patrol officers tasked with tracking down border crossers. Close to 700 participants from 28 countries around the world called the border patrol to falsely report the whereabouts of suspected illegal migrants, using the names of the departed, of those who had drowned, died of dehydration, been shot or otherwise perished in previous failed attempts to make the perilous crossing. These actions at once threw the patrol officers off course, aided folks trying to cross, and most importantly, drew attention to and paid homage to the hundreds who had lost their lives in previous crossings.

Augmented reality protests were common during the #Occupy-WallStreet events of 2011–2012. A group calling itself ManifestAR brought its guerrilla reality-augmentation work to the movement by, for example, creating an app with smartphone images overlaid on Wall Street office buildings that satirized the exploitative business going on inside. One of these overlays was one of money falling from the New York Stock Exchange's ceiling, an homage to the "zap action" of the Yippies in 1967, when Abbie Hoffman and others tossed money down from the balcony onto the trading floor in order to watch brokers scramble for a little more cash. Another related image covered the stock exchange with the image of a slot machine, suggesting that the stock market is just Vegas for the wealthy 1 percent. Perhaps ManifestAR was also hinting that, as in casinos, the market game is rigged to the advantage of the house (aka billionaires).

A similar kind of digital overlay art-activism was practiced during #Occupy by a collective known as The Illuminators, using what came to be known as the "Bat Signal." The group "hacked" a 2002 Econoline 350 diesel van, installing a periscope platform that could push a large digital projector through the roof, maneuvering it into position to splash massive images on the side of buildings and other facades. During Occupy they travelled around New York City to emblazon messages onto the very buildings where the 1 percent do their work. They, for example, emblazoned "To Be Bailed Out You Have to Be Arrested First" on some prominent Wall Street banks and brokerages.

Another esthetic form that has long had a major role in protest, the mural, has also been transformed in the new media era. While murals painted on walls the traditional way are still very much alive, they have also been augmented by digital murals that can be made and remade in a more timely fashion. Self-described queer Chicana art-activist Alma Lopez, for example, executes her striking protest murals in both traditional and digital form. Two distinct advantages of digital murals over painted ones are that they are almost infinitely reproducible—rather than being confined to one wall in one neighborhood, they can be appear in many neighborhoods and they are scalable—they can be projected on the side of a building in grand scale, but they can also be reproduced in every size from gallery-sized painting to postcard to poster (at which point they indeed become posters). Of course, the special power of murals largely stems from their size and their permanence; they are literally larger than life and they become fixtures in neighborhoods, offering their powerful imagery to all who pass by. But that need not be lost, since digital murals can have that scale and can be rendered permanent. Already existing murals can also be photographed and then be reproduced in near-to-original quality via digital techniques, allowing classic murals to migrate to new locations and be preserved for longer periods. Of course, as with all things digital, there are purists or traditionalists who argue that some essential human quality is lacking in digital murals, an argument that in many ways parallels the preference for vinyl records over digitized music. Fortunately, no one is forced to choose, since traditional murals continue to be created as well. For example, one of the most important digital creation and preservation institutions in the world, SPARC (Social and Public Art Resource Center) near Los Angeles, uses digital means to document classic traditional murals and remains committed to both older and new forms of political mural making.

Traditional satiric and parodic protest art has also been reshaped for and by digital cultures. One striking example is the site Cybracero (Cybracero n.d.). The parody site began as a student project by Alex Rivera while an undergraduate at Swarthmore College, and has been elaborated through several iterations. Cybracero works with an utterly straight face, much in the spirit of Jonathan Swift's famous suggestion in "A Modest Proposal" that the solution to the famine in Ireland was to eat babies. It purports to be the website for Cybracero Systems, a corporation that is solving the messy problem of Latino immigration to the US by using robots controlled from Mexico to pick fruit and do other agricultural labor without Mexican bodies actually crossing the border. Elites in the US can have all the benefits of Mexican immigrant labor without having those laborers actually near them. (The made-up word "cybracero" combines "cybernetics" with "bracero," the name for workers who in previous decades were bussed or flown into the States to do backbreaking agricultural field work, and then were shipped out again as soon as that work was done.) The shiny bright site brilliantly mimics the callous rhetoric of corporations for whom workers are work units not people; indeed, it does so with such perfect pitch that many of my students when exposed to it without explanation have taken it for a real corporation (a few, alas, even thought it a good idea). Similar sites (for example, "Rent-a-Negro") use parodic website imitation to address other issues from gender equity and ethnic justice to environmentalism. The theatrical parody group The Yes Men, while focused primarily on live performance, has also used the Web to spread news of their outrageous impersonations of transnational corporate executives and high-ranking government officials.

The emphasis on participation, interaction and collaboration in much digital culture has also played a role in re-shaping the protest arts. These are qualities particularly apt for adaptation to the collective process of political protest. In many of these works the artist is a co-producer along with those previously known as the audience. This is not a wholly new development in the arts, but, again, it is one that is enhanced and extended via the possibilities provided by digitizing cultures. Some of this work seeks to challenge both previous highly individualized art processes and previously commercialized artworks in much the same way as others see the Net as providing more participatory and less commercial forms of social interaction generally.

▣ HOW TO AVOID FAKE NEWS AND INTENTIONALLY INFLAMMATORY POLITICS

Two-thirds of Americans (67 percent to be precise) get all or part of their news from social media (Shearer and Gottfried 2017). This gives platforms such as Facebook, Snapchat, Instagram, Reddit, You-Tube and Twitter immense power, yet they do not see themselves as journalists or have a history of being guided by journalistic standards and ethics. And unlike traditional news outlets, it is quite easy to circulate fake news via these digital platforms and apps. Legislative bodies in a number of countries and officials in a number of tech corporations are working to cut down on the amount of fake news distributed online, but this a technically difficult and politically sensitive task, given the danger of restricting free speech. It is important work that needs to be supported. But it does not get to the root of the problem—the ability of citizens to recognize falsehoods and to fend off the worst abuses of partisan discourse. A far better approach is to deepen the process of teaching folks the difference between lies and truthful reports. A number of websites provide excellent starting points for such a process of *critical digital media literacy*. Below I have culled some of the most useful information they provide.

Rule #1: Do not pass on any bit of news, no matter how much it supports your political ideas, without first doing one or more of the types of checking suggested as follows.

Check with one or more of the major sites dedicated to exposing fake or misleading news such as snopes.com, factcheck.org, politifact.com, or one of the other sites dedicated to challenging false claims from any part of the political spectrum. (Though beware, there are a few fake fact check sites too in this hall of mirrors political world. The International Fact-checking Network monitors legitimate and illegitimate fact checking sites.)

Look carefully at the source. Fake news generators will often invent a Web address or domain name that looks like the real address of a major network or print news organization but is slightly off (often, for example, a .co is added to a .com, say reuters.com.co rather than the actual news gathering source, reuters.com). If you have any doubts, copy and paste the URL into a search engine and see if it arrives as real news source.

Refer to the About area to find out more about the source. If it seems deeply biased or otherwise unreliable, check additional sources. Sites such as opensources.co provide lists of real vs. fake news sources.

Check several serious news sources to see whether they are covering the story if you have any doubts.

Read more than just the headline. Dig down deeper into the story, looking for supporting facts. Headlines are often clickbait that exaggerate or have little relation to the actual content.

Search the author. If there is no author given for the piece, that itself may be suspicious; little real news is presented without an author. But if there is an author, do an online search to see whether they seem to be a legitimate journalist.

Follow the links. If the piece links to supposed sources, check them out to see whether they actually verify the claims being made. If they only lead to more possibly fake sources, the piece itself is probably suspect.

Can you perform reverse searches on sources or images? By checking original sources for stories, things cited in stories or images in stories you can check to see whether they have been altered or mischaracterized. Memes are particularly good at distorting facts and images, so use special diligence in tracking down things cited or imaged as memes.

Check the date. Something months or years old purporting to be "news" is often an unreliable or previously debunked story.

Watch for inflammatory, exaggerating language. Legitimate news sources seldom use highly inflammatory words or WRITE IN ALL CAPS to emphasize a point.

Is it satire? There are a number of satirical news sites that aim to amuse rather than confuse. If you don't look closely you may mislead someone and/or embarrass yourself by passing off an *Onion* story as real.

Check your biases. All of us can be guilty of confirmation bias, of believing something because it fits our preconceived ideas. As a general practice therefore, regardless of your political views, it can be healthy to compare new stories and opinion pieces made across a number of perspectives, and there are a few websites that specialize in offering such comparative possibilities, such as allsides.com or other sites that provide news from sources across the political spectrum.

The fake news situation is likely to be made more complicated by the rise of easier to fake videos ("deepfakes" as they are sometimes called) and soon we will be awash in virtual reality news. But there are ways to check these for veracity. All of the previously described techniques, plus slowing down the video and looking for lack of lipsynching, can also be used on deepfakes. Looking at the *timestamping* can also provide evidence of tampering with an original picture or video, and other techniques will no doubt be developed for virtual fake reality. None of this will work, however, unless enough citizens care enough about the truth to check for it.

If you are interested in watching how fake news circulates through the social media sphere, the website hoaxy (hoaxy.iuni. iu.edu) provides a visualization of the process. A related app, the botometer (botometer.iuni.iu.edu) checks activity on a given Twitter account to see how likely it is to be a bot rather than a real person. And if you would like to learn how fake news happens by actually creating some, try the browser game Bad News. "The idea *is that once you've seen the tactics, and used them in the game, you build up resistance,*" said one of the app developers, Sander Van Linden (Ehrenkranz 2018).

Looking closely at the digitization of politics shows a deeply compromised terrain. But, again, the technology is not ultimately to blame. At every level of politics today the question of whether digitization deepens or cheapens politics will depend on which groups of people get most involved in putting digital technology at the service of civic engagement, and how thoughtfully and imaginatively they do so. There is much positive, imaginative and democratizing use of digital media going on in the world.

But while digital media have made more political information available more easily to more people than ever before, thus far much of that information has proven to be deeply tainted and designed to intensify social disharmony. Even good information is not *knowledge* and knowledge is not *wisdom*. Political wisdom can only arise from substantive discussions that, while potentially more widely available through digital technologies, do not arise automatically from those technologies. Ease of voting and ease of registering public opinion are only as good as the political knowledge behind the votes and opinions. To think otherwise is to fall into technological determinism. The political impact of new media technologies will depend on how the informational and communicational powers of the technologies are put to use. If information gathering is simply used to further already existing political beliefs, then our political lives will be no richer, and are likely to become even more polarized and dangerous. If information gathering leads to expanded knowledge and more substantive exchanges of ideas, then greater political wisdom may emerge. But the technology is only the means; the ends, once again, will be decided by who ever uses the technology most imaginatively, honestly and effectively, and by wider political struggles in which digital tools will be only part of the story.

8

Are Digital Games Making Us Violent, or Will They Save the World?

Virtual Play, Real Impact

Digital games have become a pervasive part of the lives of millions of people. They have also been among the most disparaged and misunderstood parts of digital culture. After looking briefly at some theories of how to think about games and gaming, this chapter will look at the pros and cons of games from a number of different angles, including games as education, as art, as possibly inculcating violence and as potential solvers of major social, medical and political problems. Scholars are pretty well agreed that games teach us things, and not just so-called educational games, but all games. What is much debated is how they teach and what they teach. Much concern has been raised that games teach violence and other forms of anti-social behavior. How valid is that concern? Do games promote aggression? Beyond the general critique of violent games, one particular phenomenon known as militainment (war-related entertainment) has received special scrutiny. Games have also been widely critiqued for furthering misogyny and racism. While there has been much criticism of games, there have also been eloquent defenders of them. Some proponents claim that this much-disparaged form can actually make us smarter and improve the world. Some go so far as to claim that game playing can be turned to socially useful, maybe even world-saving directions. Who has the stronger truth about games? Can both perspectives be true?

⊡ WHAT'S IN A GAME? PLAYING THEORIES

Play seems to be an inherent part of human life, and much animal life as well. Even those cutesy kitten videos that take up way too much online space make clear that "play" is part of a learning process in the feline cultures, and it is even more so in the human ones. While kittens learn primarily how to catch and eviscerate prey, what humans learn from game play is rather more complicated. Historically, we humans have learned many kinds of skills and values in the midst of play. And the proliferation of game types in digital culture has extended that range considerably. Studies of digital games often draw upon a wider category of human play studies that have long sought to understand the role of gaming in social and personal life (Bateson 1976; Huizinga 1971). In terms of digital gaming, early researchers tended to fall into one of two broad categories: Those who emphasized narrative or storyline in games (**narratology**), and those who concentrated more on interactions and rules shaping game play (**ludology**). Narratology arose out of literary study and suffers some from a bias toward words, though for that very reason it has often been extremely useful in drawing out the often-hidden story beneath and around game play. The extent and importance of story to games varies greatly, from a minor backstory to a highly elaborated narrative, and thus the importance of storylines to understanding a given game experience varies widely. Likewise, the interactive elements and rules of games, the ludic dimensions, run from the simple to the highly complex. Clearly, both sides of the narrative/playful dyad of analysis have things to teach, and more recent game research has gotten beyond this binary into more supple and subtle analysis that draws on both traditions as well as utilizing other contemporary cultural concepts like *assemblage* (Deleuze and Guattari 2007; Haraway 2003 [1984]; King 2012), the idea that so-called individual identities are less like coherent things than an assembly of parts that can be reassembled. **Assemblage theory** is important in that it reminds us, on the one hand, that game characters are pixels, not people, and on the other hand, that as we play games we are revealed as pixelated ourselves in the sense that our identification with characters may reshape our own identities. Assemblage theory reminds us that game characters are both pixels and bits of us, not people in little virtual worlds separated from us, but human creations that recreate us as we become in some sense absorbed, cyborg-like, into game worlds. The plasticity and variability this entails make games a particularly rich place for experimenting with and examining shifts in human identities.

Games have long been a key component of digital cultures. In fact, game cultures can be considered among the earliest of all digital cultures through the arcade games of the 1980s, such as Pong. Today many untold millions of people play digital games all over the world, and the most popular games have millions of individual players. While the stereotype of the gamer remains the adolescent boy, in fact the average age of video gamers by the second decade of the twenty-first century was 32, and by 2013 there were more adult women players than teenage boys. This changing demographic is bringing some changes in the nature of games, but in many ways the game industry still lags behind its user base, just as the stereotype of the teen boy gamer misleadingly still dominates the popular imagination.

Digital gaming comes in several flavors these days—computer games (played on laptops, desktops, smartphones and within social media sites), console video games (Xbox, Playstation, Wii) and via various handheld devices. The range of games is extremely broad, from the literally one-shot *Angry Birds* to vast online games that never end, such as *World of Warcraft*. Game worlds can be as simple as a static background, and as complex as a thousand page movie. Within the major game supergenres—sports, strategy, arcade, adventure, role playing, action, shooter, racing and so on—there are dozens of genres and subgenres, each with vastly differing versions. Each type of game has its own rules, its own environments (game worlds) and its own communities of players (Aarseth, Smedstad and Sunnan 2003; Wardrip-Fruin and Harrigan 2004, 2007, 2009; Wolf and Perron 2003). And beyond these main modes, the category of *playable media* is sometimes used to push past somewhat narrow definitions of what constitutes a game, partly to open space for more experimental forms that artfully play through or explore digitally generated spaces in ways that the word "game" seems inadequate to capture. Therefore, generalizing about games and game culture is impossible, and thus the intent of this chapter is only to highlight certain aspects of some games. Certain overall patterns can, however, be noted, beginning with the fact that while still very much a "boys' club," especially at the top, game design and game play both are no longer exclusively male-only or youth-only endeavors. Given that, as noted, the average gamer is now in their mid-30s and equal numbers of female and male players (though console games remain male dominant in terms of numbers of players) a new world of gaming is clearly emerging ("Essential Facts about the Computer and Video Game Industry" 2013).

⊞ WHAT DO GAMES TEACH?

Play has always been a form of education, and video games are mechanisms that teach in a variety of ways. The category of "educational games," games used in schools or as homework (see Chapter 9), makes sense as a name for games with particular explicit teaching goals, but it is important to keep in mind that all games teach things; all games are educational, for better and for worse. And given the immense amount of time that many, many people spend playing games, it is important to figure out what kinds of things games not labelled educational are teaching us. Before looking at some of the specific claims about the kinds of education taking place through games, one general point seems worth emphasizing: Digital games teach you how to learn. Every game you pick up, no matter how simple, requires you to navigate an unfamiliar interface and uncover the causality behind that game world. This may be one of the most significant things games have done, especially for digital natives who grew up on games, and may well be a large part of what enables them to tackle new technologies and systems more easily than digital immigrants. As we will explore, questions about how well they prepare gamers for other dimensions of social life are more complicated. Like other forms of popular culture, games teach social values, and reflect the social values of those who create them. That is another reason that diversifying the digital workforce is important, since the more diverse the creators the more diverse the ideas that will likely be embedded in games.

There is clear evidence that a great deal of mental and physical activity is going on during gaming, but what that activity means is as yet less clear. Certain kinds of visual acuity have clearly increased. Hand–eye coordination is improved. And while games were once tainted as sites of physical inactivity, more kinetic games that mimic the physical movements of non-digital games (swinging a digital ping pong paddle or tennis racket, doing aerobic exercises along with a game character) are changing that story. A variety of other positive impacts of video games in terms of things such as rapid decision-making, complex cognitive mapping, intensified concentration and so on have been traced by neuroscientists, though seldom without skeptical reception by other researchers (Connolly et al. 2012; Holt 2012). At least one researcher even found that violent games, the most vilified, were the *most* educational in several respects (Bavelier 2012). Some multiplayer games also teach teamwork. On the negative side, excessive time spent gaming can detract from other equally or more intellectually challenging activities (and school work for young people), more diverse outdoor forms of exercise and, depending upon the game, can help inculcate a host of negative social values and behaviors. Games also have a strongly addictive quality that can lead some to excessive use to the detriment of other aspects of life, and too much solitary game play can deepen social isolation. In short, it matters what kinds of games are played, what conditions they are played under, how game playing fits into a wider array of activities and how game players process the information and values the game presents. Regarding this latter point, no two players experience the same game in precisely the same way, with much depending upon their already existing socialization into values, ideas and behaviors. As with much else in digital culture (and the rest of life), it is necessary to act in the face of a good deal of uncertainty, using the best available information while keeping an open mind to new developments, while challenging both the extreme views for or against gaming in general. A review of more than 7,000 articles on video games and education, for example, came to the conclusion that far more careful and comprehensive research, combining qualitative and quantitative methods, is needed before any definitive claims can be made about the positive or negative impacts of gaming on the brain (Connolly et al. 2012).

▣ DO VIDEO GAMES MAKE PLAYERS VIOLENT?

Concern about the impact various modes and genres of media may have on "real-world" behavior has long been a fraught territory of claims and counter-claims, much of it surrounding the controversial social science field of "media effects studies," and much of it connected to debate around the numerous mass school shootings in the US. The strongly immersive nature of many digital games has intensified this debate (and as more and more realistic virtual reality systems become widely available we can expect renewed concern). Video games have come in for more than their share of grief, particularly for allegedly promoting social violence.

In the UK, Canada and Australia, they call them "moral panics." In the United States, there is no name for them, but they occur in abundance. They usually take the form of "phenomenon X is destroying the moral fiber of the nation" or "corrupting our youth" or "bringing about the downfall of civilization." In the past, these youth-corrupting influences have been spotted most often in popular music. Elvis Presley's wild hips and "Negroid inflections" were morally damaging, then it was "acid rock," then "punk," then "heavy metal," then "rap" and so on that supposedly signaled the end of civilization. Now digital cultures in general, and game culture in particular, have become a major target of moral panic. But having survived all these previous end-of-civilization scenarios, it is unlikely that any aspect of digital culture represents the end of the world (leaving aside for the moment the possible "robot apocalypse" discussed at the end of this book). As we have seen, the Internet in general has been portrayed by some as the end of civilization, as have various specific phenomena associated with the Web such as social networking, texting or sexting or porn. But it is clearly video games that have generated the largest and most sustained panic attacks in the twenty-first century.

The most enduring of these attacks have revolved around the issue of violence in digital games. The most common form of criticism is to point out that a certain mass murderer (usually in the US) spent a lot of time playing violent video games. This is an example of what social theorists call mistaking a correlation for a causality. Millions and millions of young men all over the world play violent video games and do not commit acts of murder. That a handful of serial killers also played violent video games is not a causal link (97 percent of Americans have played video games; 15 percent of that market represents mature games likely to include violence; "first-person shooter" is the most played genre at 21 percent). Those serial killers also no doubt had dozens of equally meaningless correlations based on simple statistics. To call something a moral panic is not to dismiss all the issues behind the panic. In fact, almost all moral panics have some substantive issue behind them. This is certainly true of the issue of violence in video games, but violence is a presence in the world above and beyond video games. The amount of carnage seen on nightly news telecasts is enough to make anyone believe violence is the preferred solution to all problems. It is also the case that attacks on games tend to backfire; Rockstar Games, maker of the frequently critiqued game *Grand Theft Auto*, for example, reportedly encouraged and perhaps even paid reviewers to boost game sales by fueling a moral panic through playing up the amount of sex and violence. In 2018, in what was clearly a provocation, one game designer tried to sell a first person shooter game with an AK-47-armed student in the second-story window of a school. But the platform Steam rejected it, based partly on the game maker's history of trolling and copyright violation (Horton 2018). In any event, we have to get past the panic in order to get something like a clear analysis of the various kinds, degrees and meanings of violence in a range of video games, both online and on consoles.

The question of violence is often also debated in terms of "real world" versus "game world." Nothing riles gamers more than the suggestion that people are too dumb to know the difference between games and reality. In fact, however, critics of games almost always acknowledge this fact, and it is not the basis of most criticism. In the academic study of media, the question of cultural "effects" is an extremely complicated and difficult one. Media scholars recognize that there is almost never a direct link between what happens in media and what happens in the world. No one, for example, simply plays a first-person shooter game, gets confused, and goes out and shoots someone in real life. Nor do people watch pornography and then run out to commit rape. Though in both of these examples there is some (contested) empirical evidence that inhibitors to violence, general and sexual, can be lowered by repeated exposure to violent games and violent porn, respectively. But there is also evidence that violence in games has positive impacts, including a cathartic effect by providing a safe outlet for aggressive emotions. Several scholars have noted that youth violence in the US and elsewhere has declined in the era of video games, suggesting at the very least that other countervailing factors have kept games from making young people more violent (Ferguson 2010). Moreover, while 70 percent of youth in the US play violent games, the percentage of school shooters who do so is much lower (only 20 percent) (Horton 2018).

Lack of direct measurable causation (as opposed to measurable correlation) does not mean that what goes on in games has no real-world impact. Those impacts while contested are no doubt very extensive given the pervasiveness of gaming. The point is not to show a direct causal relation between what goes on in games and the wider world, but rather to look at the way in which games and game cultures unintentionally and indirectly create positive or negative cultural echoes, climates and impacts. Violence is undoubtedly the most studied element of gaming, and as computational analyst Joshua Lewis, who studied effects on 2,000 computer game players, has noted, "There has been a lot of attention wasted in figuring out whether these things turn us into killing machines. Not enough attention has been paid to the unique and interesting features that videogames have outside of the violence" (quoted in Holt 2012). In fact, while issues of violence have dominated the field, there has been a good deal of evidence gathered on other possible impacts too, by a range of neuroscientists, psychologists and other social scientists, as well as humanities scholars, but with few absolute conclusions. But the best available evidence suggests that concern over violent games causing violent behavior is largely mistaken (Kutner and Olson 2011; Markey and Ferguson 2017).

DIGITIZED "MILITAINMENT"?

There is another, more specific issue of gaming and violence that is equally complicated but rather different in nature. Computers and war have been increasingly interrelated since the middle of the twentieth century (Edwards 1996; Gray 2004; Halter 2006), but computer games have added a new twist to this interaction. This is the increasing involvement of games and the game industry in the phenomenon known as militainment. Militainment can be defined as the depiction and usually the glorification of the military and warfare in the popular entertainment industry; in recent years, this also entails increasing interconnection and cooperation between the military itself and entertainment corporations. This phenomenon precedes the rise of military video games, and is at least as old as wooden toy soldiers (Halter 2006). But the nature and extent of the phenomenon have grown exponentially with the rise of first old media like television, and now new media, especially video games. Combat-based digital games, particularly as they have become increasingly real-seeming and immersive, are carrying militainment to new levels, while at the same time video games are being used by the military for both recruitment purposes and actual combat training. The fact that the US and Australian militaries, among others, have actually created commercial video games (*America's Army* and *Arma*, respectively) with help from the game industry, and that in turn military personnel have become more and more deeply involved as consultants in the making of combat video games, represents a further blurring of the line between entertainment and warfare. In addition, the game industry has become increasingly involved in creating training games and combat simulators for the military (*Arma* actually started as a simulator and was then turned into a commercially available game). Clearly, digital cultures, especially in the form of video games, have become a significant component in the intensification of the military–industrial–entertainment complex and the transformation of war into a game.

To understand and place the importance of digital militainment socially, it is necessary to do a bit of historicizing. Dwight Eisenhower, president of the United States in the 1950s, gave a famous farewell address upon leaving office. Eisenhower had been the Supreme Allied Commander and a five-star general during World War II. But he had grown increasingly concerned that the United States was becoming dependent upon its military industries. In his famous address, Eisenhower warned of a growing "military–industrial complex." By this he meant that corporations that were profiting from the arms trade and, by building new airplanes, ships and armaments, were putting pressure on the military and the government to buy weapons that were not really needed. Despite Eisenhower's great credibility as a former general, his warning went largely unheeded by those with the power to change things. But over the years the phrase "military–industrial complex" came to have more and more resonance in the US and around the globe. Indeed, some came to talk about the US as having a "permanent war economy." By this they meant that military spending had become so integral to the US economy that subtle and not-so-subtle pressures for a militaristic posture, if not open warfare, were ever present in the society. Evidence for this is overwhelming, given that even during times of peace, a fairly rare occurrence for the last 50 years of US history, pressure to build more and more weapons has remained. Driven initially by the Cold War with Russia, the military–industrial complex continues unabated despite the US being the one lone remaining superpower. At present, the US has more weapons than all the other countries on the planet combined, and is a major purveyor of weapons to most of those other countries.

In more recent years an additional term has been added to the phrase "military–industrial complex." People now speak of a military–industrial–entertainment complex (sometimes the word "academic" is added to the label since much military research is done at universities). The recent period has brought old media and new media into a militainment alliance. The increasing militarization of the television news, for example, is entangled with the great popularity of combat video games. Many noted that in coverage of the US wars in the Middle East, "embedded" reporters in effect put the viewer in the position of being a soldier, much like playing a video game does. Many of the images conveyed through these media, such as video shot by a bomb with a camera in its nosecone, look eerily similar to video war game imagery. Or is it the other way around? This should perhaps not be surprising given that the military and the digital game industry have been for several decades increasingly involved with one another in a variety of ways. But many argue that this similarity presents the danger of lessening the reality of war, rendering it playful. Even anti-war activists report feeling a certain thrill in being positioned as soldiers during the invasion, a reaction difficult to imagine apart from the messy merging of the real and the simulated via militainment.

This increasingly deep intermixture of popular entertainment and the military has raised a number of critical questions, both within the military and among civilian scholars. Perhaps the biggest question is whether militainment is increasing militaristic feelings among non-military players, and whether that has spilled over into support for military action over other kinds of international engagement. As noted, virtually all game players insist they know the difference between virtual violence and the real kind. But the absoluteness of this claim has been challenged, and the instance of the soldier/game player may be an especially confusing case. Some in the military have worried that pre-enlistment game playing is poor and even dangerously misleading training for real warfare. Some combatants on the ground have complained that new recruits with a video game mentality can endanger themselves and their fellow soldiers.

Virtual reality and video war games are now being used to treat US veterans and still-enlisted soldiers suffering from war-inflicted post-traumatic stress disorder (PTSD) (Coming Home n.d.; Drummond 2012; Khaled 2011; Moore 2010). This fact has a myriad of interesting implications. First, it will be a wonderful thing if game war proves useful for lessening the impact of the horrors witnessed in real war, wonderful if it can help some of the thousands of casualties of war. (A more general elaboration of this work, a set of "health games" called *Coming Home*, extends this idea to a variety of approaches to virtual readjustment to civilian life.) In the US alone, according to an Army study, at least 250,000 men and women who have served in the Middle East suffer from PTSD. There are nowhere near enough resources to treat these ex-soldiers, and at present there are no plans to use the technology to help the millions of Iraqi, Afghani and other civilians traumatized by US wars. The theory behind the use of games in treating PTSD includes the notion that if vets can re-experience war in the safety of a game situation, they can gain control over the terrifying emotions set off by flashbacks to real war situations. That this therapy can apparently be successful to some degree suggests just how close game war and real war are these days, and perhaps belies the assumption of those who claim they can tell absolutely the difference between game war and real war. As real war becomes more game-like, and game war becomes more "realistic," this confusion is likely to deepen in unpredictable ways.

A different but related set of technocultural issues emerges around the increasing gap between front-line and online warriors. Unmanned drones wage war on people thousands of miles away from the "combatants" who control them. These issues are not wholly unprecedented. Concerns have been raised historically that pilots flying bombers that never see their bombs land on human targets may be shielded from the realities of warfare, and that they may suffer retroactively when that reality hits them. But now we are talking about a whole other level of magnitude and perhaps moral confusion. Some of these combatants are actually on the "home front." Being at the front and at home at the same time presents a whole new set of concerns. Soldiers can spend all day raining death on people half a world away, and then go home to dinner with their families at the end of the day. This kind of blurring of military and civilian life can be deeply, dangerously confusing (Gray 2004; Singer 2009). War games have long been a part of military preparedness, and digital war games are among the most popular genres on video consoles and computers. But war is no game. Some observers have asked how the justifications for war are transformed if one side of the conflict fights far away from the dangers of the front. Anti-war movements have long been fueled by the dead bodies coming home from the front. Dead bodies of the "enemy" have generally made less of an impact. Will one-sided warfare, more commonly known as slaughter, become more acceptable?

More generally, is militainment making it more difficult for the general citizenry to sort out justifications for war and blurring the line between civilian and military roles? Just as civilian control of the military has been a key, defining element of modern democracies, so too has the clear line between military and civilian life been important to maintain. So, the larger, more difficult to measure questions concern how militainment, and especially digitally driven immersive militainment, may be blurring the socially important line between the military and civilian sectors of society overall. Has all this increased militaristic feeling among non-military players, and has that spilled out into the wider society? Is militainment making questions of war and peace more difficult for the general citizenry to sort out?

These questions are deepened by the fact that combat games are among the most popular of genres; more and more people are having the experience of playing digital war games. How is that changing the perception of war, the willingness to support military interventions? Even when they portray realistic blood (as they increasingly do given ever-advancing digital resolution quality), they are often profoundly sanitized. However realistic they seem, they lessen the reality of war. Whatever else you can say about digitized combat games, real people seldom die while engaging in them. They are also unrealistic in that the good guys are almost invariably American and almost invariably win; the powers of the US military seem unlimited. In fact, as Chris Hables Gray and others have argued, US military capacity has been greatly overestimated, as the prolonged, still unresolved wars in Iraq and Afghanistan make clear (Gray 2004). Few if any of the mainstream games question justifications for US wars, let alone hint that motives might include securing economic domination over other nations rather than "spreading freedom and democracy."

The literature on militainment has grown to be fairly substantial, but there is much more that could be done. A cross-cultural comparison of the impact of military games in Japan and the United States, for example, might be especially revealing. These, the two countries most responsible for the video game market, have very different recent histories in regard to war. The United States is a highly militaristic culture that has been at war somewhere in the world for all but a handful of years out of the last 50, while Japan, forced to demilitarize at the end of World War II, continues to have an official state policy of pacifism. How have each of these quite distinct cultural contexts shaped responses to digitized militainment?

⊟ GENDER GAMES, RACE GAMES

Statistical evidence and years of personal experience suggest to me that a significant segment of hard-core gamers respond very harshly (not to say hatefully) to anyone who is in any way critical of any social aspect of games or gamer culture. From the cry of "It's just a game" to "Screw this political correctness!" Gamer Guy seems strangely defensive, but methinks he doth protest too much. It should go without saying that there are hundreds of wonderful games and millions of great gamers. But this is not a book dedicated to celebrating digital cultures; it is dedicated to improving them. And, strangely enough, in order to improve things you have to point out things that need improvement. So, unless you can make an argument that racism, sexism, xenophobia and homophobia, for example, are intrinsically necessary to games, then I invite you to think about how you might make the games you love better by supporting efforts to open up gaming to people who are currently unable to enjoy their pleasures because they often feel more like targets than players. Pointing out that some games engage in problematic stereotyping or exhibit extreme violence, is not charging that any particular gamer is racist, sexist or violent. But taking some action (even as small as one post on a game site objecting to a slur or a blatantly sexist depiction) will make you a part of solutions that will make game play better for all gamers.

As with other issues we've looked at, much of the problematic content in video games and other digital games reflects the problems in the larger society. That doesn't get them off the hook, but it does remind us that these games did not invent things like violence or racism or sexism or homophobia. But what concerns many critics is that while other older media—television, film and music, for example—have made some strides to limit these social blights, some parts of digital gaming seem to have moved backward in time, making these problematic representations more prevalent. In other words, video games seem to have brought back to prominence some of the worst features of old media.

Why might this be the case? Two partial causes are economics and technological limits/capabilities. In establishing a new type of commercial media, companies frequently rely on old formulas because they seem the most economically safe. That is why so many Hollywood films or TV sitcoms seem like clones of so many others. But in a new medium such as digital games, the pressures are even more intense to rely on the familiar and previously successful images and storylines. As everyone knows, or at least thinks they know, sex sells. It's not surprising then that so many digital games, especially those marketed to teenage boys, are full of adolescent male sexual fantasies (i.e., beautiful, titillating, scantily clad and apparently sexually available girls and young women). For this reason, female images and characters in games provide a particularly rich example to explore social representations.

The line between sexiness and sexism isn't always easy to draw. But years of critical work in media studies give us some clues as to what to look for. Two key things that can help move a representation toward or away from being sexist are *agency* and *complexity*. Agency in this context means the ability to impact the world (or, in this case, the game world). To have agency is to have the ability to make things happen, rather than just have things happen to you. Representations of girls and women as simply eye candy, as characters who do nothing active in a game and apparently have no ideas, interests or goals other than to please men sexually are not only unrealistic but potentially dangerous to real-life females. Conversely, images of female avatars showing real skill, intelligence, strength and impact can be empowering.

Related to the issue of agency is the question of personality complexity. When you portray people without complex thoughts, feelings and motivations, you in effect dehumanize them, turn them into objects to be manipulated by others (a particularly tempting thing when quite literally the control mechanism is in one's hands). There is nothing wrong with sexiness, and all human beings objectify potential sexual mates. The problem lies in the imbalance of gender power in and around such depictions. Physically exaggerated male bodies are almost as common in video games as exaggerated female ones. But the contrast is illustrative. While women (some women warriors notwithstanding) often have their sexual allure attuned to near naked helplessness, male fantasy figures most often take on the form of exaggerated musculature and aggressiveness. While women bear the major burden from these exaggerated bodies, some studies suggest that this pixilated perfection has contributed to the rise of eating disorders and steroid abuse among boys and men, and moved many from healthy to obsessive work out regimens.

Some statistics can illustrate the core of the gender imbalance. According to one British government-funded study on the sexualization of teens, 83 percent of male characters in digital games were portrayed as aggressive, while 60 percent of female characters were highly sexualized in a generally subordinate way, including 39 percent who were scantily clad in ways that made little game sense (the equivalent figures for male characters were 1 percent sexualized, 8 percent provocatively clad) (Papadoupoulus n.d.). This means that both females and males are being victimized by game-world representations, though hardly in equal ways. In addition to providing impossible to reach and therefore frustrating masculinity models for boys, game play sets up expectations for how girls and women will react to male aggressiveness that are likely to meet with rejection in the offline world, rejection that may trigger stronger aggression in some cases.

While as noted in Chapter 6, amateur digital representations provide the most extreme and egregious forms of sexism online, professional forms also exhibit a great deal. Gender stereotyping in digital game characters has been particularly well documented. One comprehensive study of over 250 games found that over two out of three contained objectifying, hypersexualized and/or derogatory images of women (Yao, Mahood and Linz 2009). Compounding the problem is the fact that only about 15–20 percent of games contain significant female protagonists at all. Things have been improving some in the last few years, but imbalance remains. Where strong female leads do exist, such as Lara Croft, their representation often mixes that strength with sexual objectification (Norris 2004). Women and (fewer) men are fighting back against this reality, and because game producers are a recognizable community, they have had some success in improving content. Anita Sarkeesian, a prominent feminist pop culture critic, uses her blog Feminist Frequency to take on all aspects of media sexism, but in recent years she apparently has decided that some digital cultures are most in need of reform. She traces not only dominant sexist tropes in game worlds, but also how those images seem to play into harassment of female gamers (Sarkeesian n.d.). She has identified a variety of forms of stereotyping that dominate far too much of game characterization. Among those she names are the damsel in distress, the smurfette, the evil demon seductress, the manic pixie and the straw feminist. Each of her analyses (available in video form in the "Tropes vs. Women" series) is eminently reasonable and backed by extensive examples from a range of game genres and platforms. Yet in response she has received every imaginable kind of abuse, including threats of rape and murder. Ironically enough, the viciousness of the misogynistic attacks on Sarkeesian for daring to criticize games reinforces her point as well as or better than her analyses themselves.

The most famous female figure in the history of digital gaming, Lara Croft (she even has her own star on the Hollywood "walk of fame," and is on a stamp in France), can illustrate some of the complexities involved in evaluating game characters. When I teach about video games and gender in my courses, I have students debate the following question: Is Lara Croft more of a cyberbimbo or an empowering image for women? The class is almost always equally split in their answers, and each side is usually equally represented by males and females. One obvious thing to see in this is that as in all media culture, audience experience of the same phenomenon varies, sometimes immensely—that the true impact is partly in the eye (or more broadly, the mind) of the beholder. But the degree of variation in interpretation is not random. Some images, and Croft is a great example, are more ambiguous than others (by contrast no one in any of my classes has ever defended the hookers in Grand Theft Auto as empowered sex workers). Croft's ambiguity was built in from the design stage onward, a fact that also usefully illustrates the complexities of game creation. In one sense, Lara is a female impersonator. In the mind of *Tomb Raider*'s lead graphic designer, Toby Gard, the character that became Lara was a male hero with a whip and floppy hat that made it too obviously an imitation of the then-immensely popular Indiana Jones (note that routinely old and new media exchange characters, as when later Lara becomes a movie hero). Recognizing they could be accused of unoriginality, if not plagiarism, they floated the idea of making the main character a female. There was initial resistance from the head of the team, but he relented when convinced novelty might make up for the awkwardness of getting a then-primarily male game community to play as females (the second level of female impersonation in the game?). So Gard proceeded to create a female protagonist, reporting that he wanted to invent a richer character, not one of the bimbos or dominatrixes he felt then dominated the game scene. His first female version was Latin American and dubbed Laura Cruz. But pressure from the default subject position dictated that she be Anglicized, so Laura Cruz was reborn as Lara Croft. What happened next reminds us both that accidental things happened in game design, but also that cultural patterns generally win out over chance or creative risk taking. As Gard was playing with the polygons that made up Lara, he one day made a mistake that increased her bust size by 150 percent. Before Gard could fix the problem, the rest of the (all-male) design team weighed in, arguing that they loved the new, exaggerated proportions (Goldman 2007; Jenkins 1998; Marie 2010; McGlaughlin 2008).

Would this have happened if even one female was on the team? We'll never know, but we do know that the highly improbable, if not impossible, body of Lara Croft was launched in 1996 to highly positive reception, as well as strong criticism as an eye-candy sexist depiction. The claim was seemingly supported by the quick proliferation of nude, and later, explicitly pornographic, images of Lara on the Web, though, alas, almost all female and some male digital characters undergo pornification at some point (known among the digerati as Rule 34). Other critics have complicated the issue by asking what it might have meant genderwise for those who played as the *Tomb Raider* avatar. What did adolescent boys make of having to play as a "girl"? Did it unconsciously bring them to identify with a female, maybe even make them more sensitive to women? Or did they simply take pleasure in watching Lara's posterior as they manipulated her at their will? Or both? And were young female players able to identify with a strong heroine, or were they daunted by her eye-candy physique? Or both (Kennedy 2002)?

Over the years, through several game iterations and films with Angelina Jolie as a no-nonsense Lara, and in response to feminist criticism, changing markets and technological breakthroughs, subsequent Laras have become more realistically proportioned, stronger in character, and in general less bimboesque. A visual comparison of the figure of Lara Croft between her arrival in 1996 and her 2013 version illustrates this small but not insignificant degree of progress, which might be characterized as moving from Bimbo to Rambo (see Figure 8.1; Hall-Stigerts 2013). At the same time, in another twist,

FIGURE 8.1 *Evolution of Lara Croft, 1996–2013 (Courtesy: Creative Commons)*

this move has somewhat downplayed the intellectual dimension (Lara's ostensibly an archaeologist) in favor of more kick-ass action elements. But the most recent Lara incarnation in the 2018 film was a more cerebral, more active and less exaggeratedly curvaceous one.

To broaden the picture, video games regularly limit agency and complexity, in both male and female characters, though far more fully for the latter. This is not a good thing for either gender, but it's especially an issue for girls and women in cultures that still deny them equal rights, equal pay and equal respect. The situation seems to be improving somewhat. As a result of more sophisticated technology backed up by large amounts of social criticism, both the physical and subjective characteristics of female avatars are generally becoming more realistic. Yet, it is a reflection of political timidity that we have game ratings for violence and harsh language, but no ratings for racism, sexism or homophobia—far more socially dangerous components of many games and too much game culture. Again, the point here is not to single out gaming as uniquely featuring these socially regressive qualities; all media, new and old, have contributed to this problem. The point rather is that as new media in general, and video games in particular, have become the most pervasive forms of entertainment, they have brought with them, and deepened, highly problematic representations and attitudes that play into the epidemic of violence against women, rampant homophobia and ongoing racism. Some of this can be attributed to technical issues, to the tendency in early games to rely on stereotypes in part because richer representation was not technically feasible, but such technological determinist claims take us only so far. Improvements in the variety and depth of representations in games have come about not just through greater technical capacities, but more because game makers have responded to criticism and to the changing demographic nature of their market, especially the displacement of white adolescent males as the core user base.

Beyond technical and commercial issues that have kept sexism and other social issues alive in games, there has also been an active anti-feminist backlash in a small but vocal part of the gamer community. The backlash came to a head with the Gamergate controversy in 2014. Some have suggested that Gamergate unleashed or revealed a deep-seated misogyny that has evolved into support for figures such as Donald Trump, and for some of the most blatantly sexist, racist and homophobic positions in US, UK and other political cultures (Fraser 2016; Jeong 2016; Lees 2016).

Women of color often face double jeopardy online in general and in games in particular, as racism is as prevalent in gaming as sexism. This phenomenon has been studied convincingly as well in the creation of characters and avatars in digital games (Chan 2005). Often new "races" created in games (elves, dwarves, aliens, etc.) are poorly disguised stereotypes of actual ethnic groups. Unlike the best science fiction and fantasy works, which imaginatively attempt to get beyond real-world racialization in order to better reflect on it, many digital game representations are deeply mired in existing stereotypes. In the fantastically popular MMORPG *World of Warcraft* and its spinoffs, for example, pixelated racisms include dark-skinned Worgens controlled by white wizards, Asian cybertyped pandas, thinly disguised nature-loving primitive Natives and so on (Corneliussen and Rettburg 2008; Nakamura 2009; "Racism in WoW" n.d.). This doesn't make all *WoW* players racists, but it may mean that racial misrepresentation may subtly shape the experiences of all players, even those of strong advocates of racial justice.

In war games, especially in the wake of the 9/11 bombings, anti-Arab, anti-Muslim stereotyping has been rampant (Sisler n.d.). In addition, a host of games seem to reanimate colonialism and subconsciously support contemporary transnational corporate empires in a variety of disturbing ways (Dyer-Witheford and de Peuter 2009). African American cybertyping has been particularly egregious in sport games and urban street games (Chan 2005; Leonard 2004, 2006). As in pop culture generally, indigenous peoples ("Indians" as some native people prefer, to remind us of how geographically confused Christopher Columbus was) in digital culture remain largely confined to the past, where they are either war-painted fierce warriors, long-haired buckskin-clad princesses or nature-loving ultimate ecologists (Sturgeon 2009). What arguably makes game play more disturbing is the fact that as players, rather than simply viewing an offensive stereotype, people may be more actively engaging the stereotypes, may, for example, be killing racially coded aliens or fantasy creatures or shooting "redskins."

In fact in the real world of the twenty-first century, indigenous peoples, despite being among the groups with the least digital access, have used the Net extremely well, including setting up very important global networks of Natives facing similar forms of cultural domination on several continents (Christensen 2003; Landzelius 2006). Native peoples of the Arctic region are also using the Web to warn that the impacts of global climate change are already here (Banerjee 2012).

Game play has also exposed a good deal of anti-Asian racism from North America and Europe. Waves of anti-Chinese racism, for example, were unleashed when large numbers of Chinese players began earning a living playing games such as *Lineage 2* by winning virtual weapons in the fantasy role-playing game and then selling their online loot to people in the United States who did not have time to play as many hours to arm their characters. Many of the Chinese players chose to play as female dwarves, a class in the game that can more easily win treasure on solo missions. In response, US players began killing all dwarves in the game, often adding anti-Chinese slurs in the chat section of the game as they did so. Similar forms of anti-Japanese, anti-Korean and anti-Chinese sentiments have been chronicled in other game chat spaces. With China now widely portrayed as the "enemy" in a new struggle of world economic supremacy, this cybertyping plays into some very dangerous racist discourses in US and European society.

Continuing elements of sexism, racism, homophobia and other socially destructive elements of contemporary games will not go away automatically, any more than they will go away automatically in the wider social world. In the specific case of games, critics argue that it will take pressure on game companies, revolts by gamers and the diversification of the game industry workforce to do that. Hope that this may occur is offered by surveys that suggest despite immersion in the regressive side of digital culture, young people are generally somewhat less sexist, homophobic and racist than their parents.

Rockstar's *Grand Theft Auto* series provides a case study in the possibilities and complexities of making progress in game worlds. *Grand Theft Auto* is the single most lucrative media product of all time (the fifth installment in the series, *GTA V*, registered $800 million dollars in sales on the day of its release alone). It is also one of the game franchises that has been most severely criticized over the years. The pressure not to mess much with the formula of a multi-billion-dollar enterprise is immense. Large changes, like adding a strong female protagonist to the mix, for example, seem unlikely. Advertised improvements in the 2013 version focused mostly on technical improvements in "realism" and a more developed storyline. Widely criticized for racism, sexism and homophobia in earlier versions of the game, part of Rockstar's defense often was to claim it was satirizing, not endorsing, the violent, gangster-based regressive social attitudes portrayed. In subsequent versions, and most overtly in *GTA V*, the satirical element has been brought more to the foreground (touches like a white thug character with "privilege" tattooed on his neck), without significantly changing their goldmine of a game (having their virtual cake and eating it too?). That approach raises interesting questions about audience. No doubt a large portion of *GTA* players get the jokes, while others may endorse the racism, sexism and homophobia. And there remains the question of whether, since much of the social educational impact of games goes on unconsciously, deeply disturbing social values are being exorcised or reinforced through over-the-top satirical representation.

Nevertheless, Rockstar can be given some credit for responding to critics. And, particularly under the influence of indies (small independent game companies), more pressure is being applied to make games less stereotyped, more socially complex and more aesthetically rich. For example, a game like *Beyond Two Souls* (2013), featuring actor Ellen Page, may open space for more female action heroes in games. And at another extreme, the game *Journey* (2012), models a contemplative, voiceless sojourn through the desert as a different kind of "adventure" game *and Never Alone* that offers a rich journey into Native Iñupiat folklore. There is also now a growing number of LGBTQI2+ game characters (Johnston 2017).

Such progress is encouraging to continuing efforts to make this particular branch of digital culture a more livable place for people currently more victimized than welcomed into game play. But it clearly has not ended criticism (Martens 2013), nor do many think it should. Progress in terms of gradual improvements in the social consciences and imaginations of game designers suggests that change can come without loss of revenue. Critics would argue that this (limited) progress should lead to greater pressure, not to complacency, but they do recognize that some positive things are in motion.

Gaming is still a very young genre that has not come close to reaching its potential, particularly as an art form. Gaming has produced amazing things already, but it probably has not yet found its Shakespeare, its Rembrandt, its Kurasawa. But it is bound to. The esthetic potential of *playable media* is too rich to be left only to (often highly creative but genre-bound) commercial designers. Four decades of game art and much interesting indie game design have stretched the medium in exciting directions (Digital Meets Culture n.d.). The form will increasingly attract more and more great narrative artists, visual artists and musicians, who will fully utilize the full range of the medium's immersive and ever expandable verbal, visual, aural and playable dimensions. A focus on the far better known commercial game industry products makes sense in mapping the larger social impact of digital cultures, but a growing body of non-commercial game art reminds us that there is another dimension altogether that is likely to have greater and greater cultural impact in the future.

▣ CAN VIDEO GAMES SAVE THE WORLD?

At quite the opposite pole and partly in response to folks who see video games as signs of a cultural apocalypse, or deepening militarization, are people who wish to use the great potential of games for positive social transformation. Most prominently Jane McGonigal, in her widely read book, *Reality Is Broken: Why Games Make us Better and How They Can Change the World*, has sought to demonstrate how games are not only useful, but potentially vital to solving many of the world's most pressing problems (McGonigal 2011, n.d.). She starts by asking two important, related questions. Why do so many people play e-games so passionately, with often great investments in time and energy, but without monetary reward? And why do many of those same people say they can't find that passion in the work they do in the "real world" despite being compensated monetarily? In a stimulating set of answers to these questions, McGonigal makes a case, much of it based upon empirical social psychological research, that the real world is "broken" in that most people do not experience the sense of excitement, accomplishment or involvement in their everyday lives that they experience in games. From this premise, she argues that in order to unbreak the world, to make it a better place, we need to learn from digital games how to transfer the elements of excitement, accomplishment and involvement found in games to solving real-world problems. In other words, she argues, we need to make the real world more like the virtual world of games, and actually using games to tackle collective problem solving may provide the energy needed to find real solutions.

What are the qualities in games that McGonigal would like to see harnessed toward dealing with real-world problems? McGonigal names four qualities: urgent optimism, social fabric (trust), blissful productivity and epic meaning. These aspects include a sense of engagement that is personally challenging, but also connected to a wider community (gamers love to compare experiences). This entails connection to something bigger than oneself, but with the specific contribution of the individual clearly evident. Many games, especially MMORPGs, require teamwork in which each player's participation is vital and visible. In addition, accomplishment is palpable, with tasks in games broken down into levels that clearly demarcate progress toward the goal. Finally, games by definition entail playfulness, a positive emotion that we tend to think of as the opposite of work. Taking pleasure in work is too often a rare thing these days, notes McGonigal. McGonigal's ideas are bolstered by a psychological theory of what in games gives pleasure, and by her years of work as a game designer and game player. More than just talking, she has put her ideas to the test by building real-world, game-based projects. Whenever I ask my students to think up an anti-war game that is as exciting as a war game, they draw a blank and claim it is not possible. Are they right, or can the making of peace and justice become as exciting as blowing up enemy tanks (Castronova 2008; Whitson and Dormann 2011)?

McGonigal's work is part of a larger movement seeking to build alternative games that offer more positive forms of social and political engagement. Her own games such as *EVOKE*, *World Without Oil* and *Superstruct*, tackle real-world problems that require collective solutions. Others, such as Edward Castronova in *Exodus to the Virtual World* (2008), for example, argue that games may come to be important shapers of public policy. In addition, game companies are adapting their games to the classroom without lapsing into the dull traps of many "educational" games; the education edition of the highly popular game *Minecraft* is one excellent example (Minecraft Educational n.d.). There are also several groups of game developers working together on a socially progressive vision. Prominent among these is the organization Games for Change, a coalition of game designers who work singly and collaboratively and meet once a year at a "festival" to compare, discuss and celebrate attempts to create world-improving, if not world-saving, digital games (gamesforchange.org; gameful.org). While no social activist game has broken through into the commercial market, where profit remains the bottom line (and doing what has already worked always seems safer than trying something new), more and more games that are both socially conscious and engaging are emerging. Some of these games are quite rich and impressive. The excellent puzzle game *Papers, Please*, for example, does a fine job of capturing the terrifying experience of immigration (in this case into an Eastern Bloc country) and the life-and-death decisions a border patroler must sometimes make amidst a highly entertaining game. *Half the Sky*, about global gender equity, has a million players worldwide. *Climate Defense* involves players in finding solutions to global climate change. *Peacemaker* requires players to negotiate the Israeli–Palestinian dispute. The amount of talent and energy currently being focused on using games to deal with real-world problems is impressive, and is a phenomenon surely worth supporting, whatever one's ideas are about what solutions are needed, since game worlds are currently among the most pervasive and active cultural spaces on the planet.

9

Are Students Getting Dumber as Their Phones Get Smarter?

E-Learning, Edutainment and the Future of Knowledge Sharing

Few areas of contemporary cultural life have been as deeply impacted by digital technologies as the realm of education. From pre-school to graduate school and on into all areas of professional scientific, social scientific and humanities scholarship, the field of education has been profoundly reshaped by computers and related technologies. The exceedingly rapid digitalization of all forms of education has led to great expectations and more than a little anxiety and consternation. Parents wonder whether our kids are becoming dumber as their phones become smarter. Teachers wonder whether new technologies will render them obsolete. Scholars wonder whether it is still possible to get a research grant without a digital component to their research projects, or conversely whether their colleagues will not take their online publishing seriously. Is the D-generation (those immersed from birth in new media) a generation of spoiled know-nothing, mental D-generates who must be edutained? Or are they a generation of informed, active learners with different, but just as good or better, ways of gaining and making knowledge?

Digital technologies have no doubt put more information at Net users' fingertips than has ever been available in human history. All of the tragically lost ancient library of Alexandria (the greatest knowledge source of its time) could now be contained on a micro-chip the size of the tip of a single finger. But what are we making of all this information? Information, after all, is not knowledge (knowledge is information organized intelligently), and knowledge is not wisdom (wisdom is knowledge put to good use). Is all the information available via the Web and other digital sources mostly making us smarter, or just more superficial, confused and overwhelmed? Should "too much information" ("TMI" in Web talk) be our battle cry? If a future anthropologist were to look back to the birth of the Internet would she be stunned that a network that put all the world's accumulated knowledge at their fingertips seems mostly to have inspired human beings to share pictures of cats playing the piano and dancing dogs?

⊟ "IS OUR CHILDREN LEARNING" DIGITALLY?

The short answer to this variation on an ungrammatical question posed by former US president George W. Bush is "Yes." Whether we like it or not, our children is/are learning digitally. While this chapter will focus primarily on the role of digital media in formal education (pre-school through graduate school and beyond), it is important to remember that digitizing education is a wider phenomenon than computers in the classroom. The Web is an educational device in a myriad of ways, and, as shown in Chapter 8, video games of all kinds play a major role in the education of youth in terms of the information and values they imbibe. One of the most important studies of the impact of the Internet on the learning of youth was part of the Pew Internet and American Life Project. Published in 2008, its findings have been replicated with few variations ever since, and the basic conclusions are summarized thusly: "Contrary to adult perceptions, while hanging out online, youth are picking up basic social and technical skills they need to participate fully in contemporary life" (Ito et al. 2008: 2). Studies also suggest, contrary to parental fears and moral panics, that over 90 percent of the time students spend online is with the same people they spend time with offline, not with potentially dangerous strangers. Also, perhaps on the positive side, unless you have stock in Facebook, a 2012 Pew survey found that youth increasingly resent social media as a burden; many are fed up with the inanity and lack of privacy (only 14 percent have their accounts set for open access), though, paradoxically, they are sharing more personal information. Only 5 percent deny access to their parents, though complaints about trolling parents is another reason some are now less thrilled with Facebook. In general, there is a pattern that suggests the novelty of social media wears off for even the most enthusiastic of young users; many consciously limit their time online, and evidence suggests as they become aware of privacy issues, they shape their activity more carefully: "Teens take steps to shape their reputation, manage their networks, and mask information they don't want others to know; 74% of teen social media users have deleted people from their network" (Madden et al. 2013: 2).

Some of the answers to questions about the impact of digital technology on learning come from the emergent scientific disciplines that are themselves significantly impacted by advances in digitized research tools. Study of the brain has made remarkable strides in the last couple of decades. New interdisciplinary fields such as neuroscience and consciousness studies have emerged to try to pull together a rapidly proliferating body of knowledge about what the brain is and how it functions (Damasio 2010). Startlingly new insights about the brain and its relation to that mysterious thing called consciousness seem to appear in the media almost daily. Much of this information is being incorporated into more effective teaching. Unfortunately, some ill-informed journalists, sometime abetted by scientists seeking recognition or larger research grants, frequently hype these "discoveries" far beyond what the science actually suggests. Among those most susceptible to this type of hype have been writers about computers and the brain. From the misleading metaphor that the brain *is* a computer, or the slightly less misleading claim that it in *some* ways functions like one, to a host of arguments about what computers and computer culture are *doing to* our brains, news sources and bookstores are now littered with titles along the line of "How computers are destroying our minds" or "How computers will make us all geniuses," with far too few offering subtler analyses avoiding these extreme claims. As noted throughout this book, a certain degree of exaggeration, both utopian and dystopian, was a part of early cyberculture and has never completely gone away. This same spirit has inflected and infected much of the popularization of neuroscience generally, and neuroscience looking at the human computer interaction specifically. So, the best advice when reading about the latest study showing what your brain looks like when googling, is *caveat emptor*—buyer beware. Instead of the hype, let's look at the facts, particularly as represented by the use and misuse of digital technology in education.

⇥ WHAT IS TECHNOLOGY DOING IN THE CLASSROOM?

Computers and digital technology are now pervasive in classrooms throughout much of the overdeveloped Global North, and increasingly present among elites in the less developed Global South. Whether one likes it or not, digital education is here to stay. It is certainly here to stay outside of the classroom, as I suggested previously, because the amount of time young people spend online is clearly significant (in the US children aged 8 to 18 spend an average of 7 hours and 38 minutes per day online or 53 hours per week; 94 percent of children 12 to 17 go online, 75 percent own cellphones, 73 percent use a social networking site; stats are slightly lower for less tech-accessible countries, obviously, but often startlingly high nonetheless). For better and for worse, children around the globe are learning many things about society through digital media.

Unofficial online learning is clearly rampant, and not likely to go away, and it is also here to stay in formal, classroom-centered education. This should be seen as neither a cause for alarm nor elation, because computers are neither the problem nor the solution to issues in education in the twenty-first century. Both those who assume computers in the classroom are inherently negative and those who see in them utopian possibilities often also assume that they are somehow replacing teachers. Such is not and should not be the case.

It is important to remember that computers are tools, and tools are only as good as those people who wield them. There are no doubt some teachers who use computers in the classroom to escape from rather than enhance their jobs as teachers. But these are a small minority. Good teachers recognize that digital technologies create opportunities, but opportunities that only careful, thoughtful pedagogy can take advantage of. One thing that computers are especially good at is creatively teaching routine things that both teachers and students tend to dislike in rote form. When utilized to carry out the necessary but historically boring baseline work required in education, computers can actually free up teachers to do the more important face-to-face interactive and creative learning. But computers can also do great personalizing and creative things face-to-face (or interface-to-face, if you want to be more technically accurate).

One typical set of dystopian images of computers imagines students being cloned into exact replicas of each other. Here again, the imagery is far off the mark. In fact, the great virtue of computers in education is their capacity to individualize the learning process.

Increasingly computers are more sophisticated and can be excellent devices for giving students the opportunity to learn at their own individual pace (sometimes using what are known as *personalized learning channels*). There are many kinds of learners. Some learn best visually, some aurally, some through written words, some with hands-on tactile involvement. And each form can reinforce the others. The multimedia capacity of computers and online learning widens the spectrum of useful pedagogical possibilities open to teachers and students. Studies make clear that students can learn as much from each other as they can from their teachers. Computers can be used creatively for group projects, ones that again can free up teachers to spend time with students who need extra care.

The Web also opens the classroom out onto the wider world in ways that students find deeply engaging. Lack of obvious connection to the real world can be a major block for students, while using the Web to connect to an engineer or architect who explains how they use math, or to a writer who can discuss the joys of crafting a sentence no one has imagined before, can vividly awaken students. Hearing business owners talk about the tangible benefits of having people from a variety of backgrounds in their workforce can remove resistance from those inculcated with the silly notion that promoting diversity is some form of liberal, politically correct conspiracy. While in many communities there are too few such potential contacts to bring into the classroom, the digital classroom knows no such boundaries, and can draw literally on a world of experience.

Digital education allows many, many kinds of geographic and cultural boundaries to be crossed. I have participated in classrooms where students from the US and Japan engaged in animated conversations about how the popular cultures of their respective countries were received and understood in the other country—hip hop in Japan, manga in the US, video games from each, and so forth. Hundreds of conversations like this take place every day at every level of education, conversations only made possible by new technologies that have immense potential to deepen cross-cultural understanding for mutual benefit. But again, this only happens when good teachers make smart use of the technologies now available, and it only happens in well-funded classrooms.

On the creating side of the ledger, knowledge that things they produce can be shared with more than one person (the teacher) can also inspire far more thoughtful, careful work in students. Putting students to work on real-world problems can deepen engagement immensely. Classroom blogs, wikis and other digital formats can put already popular genres students use outside of school into the class-room in ways that feel familiar and less like drudge work. There are templates based on popular gameshows available in PowerPoint form that can be adapted to virtually any subject matter for turning the generally less-than-exciting form of question and answer into a more engaging activity (while, if you must, still teaching to standardized tests that require baseline cultural knowledge).

Some critics of digitizing education use the dismissive term **edutainment**, with emphasis clearly on the "tainment," rather than the "edu," to disparage this kind of learning. The assumption here seems to be that real learning is being replaced by mindless play. Ironically, these doubters are often the same people who scare folks about the impact of video games because of their deeply immersive nature. Much recent empirical study, not to mention the application of common sense, suggests that students might in fact learn more if they were enjoying their education rather than being bored out of their minds. And the skillful use of multimedia digital pedagogy can do just that. Play is a fundamental form of learning throughout the animal kingdom; just watch two kittens for five minutes and correlate their play with the challenges they will face in the real cat world. In the world of human animals, play can be used quite thoughtfully to engage students with varying learning styles. Some people learn best through the written word, others through visual stimulation, still others through sound and almost everyone learns better through multiple modes of stimulation acting simultaneously. These various modes are made far more accessible via digital technology. Playful digitally delivered multimedia learning forms provide flexible options that help reach more students, engage them personally and give them more control over their own education. The best digitized learning tools designed by the best teachers can improve all teachers' effective-ness to a degree. They are almost infinitely adaptable to the needs of each student and teacher. Indeed, the irony of images of computers cloning students is that, when used well, they are doing just the oppo-site; they are personalizing situations where one-size-fits-all education is foisted upon a classroom of 20 or 30 or 40 students, each of whom has a different learning style, pace and set of needs.

While there are many great teachers in the world, there are never enough of them. Digital technologies make it possible for the best teachers to be available to wider and wider audiences of students. Teachers have different gifts, and wise teachers can use digital means to make up for their own limitations and free themselves to do what they do best. For example, few teachers are great lecturers. But the handful of truly great lecturers in the world are now being used via things such as podcasts to great advantage in capturing the interest of students. Subsequently, classroom teachers build on the enthusiasm generated by great lectures to get into the next level of questions best worked on with individuals or small groups working interactively.

Figure 9.1 offers a useful chart summarizing the dos and don'ts of using educational digital technology. Note the key distinction being offered being *using* technology in the classroom and *integrating* technology into the classroom. The former is based on narrow technological determinism (we use computers because we should), the latter on smart technocultural planning (how best can we use digital media to improve learning).

Where computers are seemingly least adequate as pedagogues is the affective dimension, the emotional context and emotional contact crucial to education. That is one of the many places where

Using Technology	Technology Integration
Technology usage is random, arbitrary & often an afterthought	Technology usage is planned & purposeful
Technology is rare or sporadically used in the classroom	Technology is a routine part of the classroom environment
Technology is used purely for the sake of using technology	Technology is used to support curricular goals & learning objectives
Technology is used to instruct students on content	Technology is used to engage students with content
Technology is mostly being used by the instructor(s)	Technology is mostly being used by the student(s)
Focus on simply using technologies	Focus on using technologies to create & develop new thinking processes
More instructional time is spent learning how to use the technology	More instructional time is spent using the technology to learn
Technology is used to complete lower-order thinking tasks	Technology is used to encourage higher-order thinking skills
Technology is used solely by individuals working alone	Technology is used to facilitate collaboration in & out of the classroom
Technology is used to facilitate activities that are feasible or easier without technology	Technology is used to facilitate activities that would otherwise be difficult or impossible
Technology is used to deliver information	Technology is used to construct & build knowledge
Technology is peripheral to the learning activity	Technology is essential to the learning activity

FIGURE 9.1 *Best practices of teaching with technology (© Aditi Rao, Teachbytes)*

human teachers can play a crucial role in even the most tech-heavy classrooms. This includes a range of factors from recognizing and addressing degrees of emotional comfort with the technology itself to all kinds of mood variations that can impact the success of students. Great teachers connect with students, investing in a relationship full of nuances no computer can read or replicate.

There is nothing magical about computers in the classroom. Like all forms of technological determinism, the assumption that computers can automatically augment education is mistaken. If you are a parent who wants to answer the grammatically correct variation of the question asked above, "Is your child learning digitally?" you need to know not how many tablet computers or digital projectors your son's or daughter's classroom has (though that is good to know), but rather what teachers are doing with the technologies they have. Are they using them creatively or dully; are they using them to escape their role as teachers or deepen that role? And if you are a student in a classroom using digital tech, you too need to ask similar questions that lead teachers and school administrators to use such devices intelligently.

Another key set of issues that especially impacts education while having wider social implications concerns what certain kinds of digital experiences are doing to our minds. Most frequently cited among these is a possible decline in certain intellectual functions due to the nature of much online experience. Some claim online spaces may be undermining our ability to think linearly, to pay attention to long narrative storylines and to grasp complex sustained logical arguments. The best known popular book on the dangers of the Net for human intelligence is Nicholas Carr's *The Shallows: What the Internet Is Doing to Our Brains* (2010). To my mind, what I have left of it after years working online, the book would have been better if the subtitle had been in the form of a question: What is the Internet doing to our brains? Which is to say that Carr makes a strong but one-sided case that humans are losing the ability to have deep thoughts, to delve substantially into topics, because clicking on so many hyperlinked Web pages has rendered us "shallow," flitting about from one bit of knowledge to the next bit of knowledge, in a kind of distracted dance of the mind. Much of Carr's evidence is anecdotal (he and many of his friends say that after being on the Web for years they find it difficult to read whole books), but not implausible (though to toss back an anecdote, my digital generation son has devoured hundreds of fiction and non-fiction books over the years while also spending uncountable hours on the Web). But I hear this claim often enough from teachers at all levels of education to take it seriously. At present, however, we do not have enough consistent data from neuroscience studies to thoughtfully answer the question, are we becoming less thoughtful? The bottom line suggested in Carr's book, however, that we spend a good deal of quality time in non-digital environments, quiet our minds at times with meditation and/or contemplation, and stretch our minds at times by reading long narratives strikes me as extremely sensible (though, full confession, as someone who used to teach novels and has more recently written a couple, I do have a vested interest in people continuing to read them). And even high-tech execs seem to agree. Not only do many enroll their children in Waldorf schools partly because the "schools discourage the use of electronic gadgets in early childhood" (Utne 2013), but Google guru Eric Schmidt famously remarked that "I think sitting down and reading a book is still the best way to really learn something."

So, while there is nothing inherently bad about digital tech in the classroom, and much good that can be done through smart use of digital devices, there are in the US, the UK and other countries where strong movements to standardize and narrowly quantify educational progress have been put in place, often as part of drastic cuts in school budgets, classrooms where computers are being used to do pretty much useless things. They are used to prepare for largely meaningless tests that teach memorization, not thinking. Every major study of education around the world makes clear that the best students, including the ones who do best on so-called standardized tests, are students who work in very interactive, open-ended, problem-solving environments. Real education is interactive in every sense of the word. Standardization is taking place not because of computers, but computers facilitate or provide a rationale for this kind of unimaginative pedagogy (standardizing is something digital tools can do quite well and easily). However, the countries consistently producing the highest-achieving students (South Korea, Finland, Japan and Canada, for example) are places where students are challenged to problem solve, not regurgitate. They also happen to be places where the role of teachers is respected, valued and compensated at the level of other professionals (doctors, lawyers). In contrast, the US, where teachers are overworked, underpaid and often under attack, ranks 30th in the world in math education, 21st in science, 15th in reading and unspeakably low in writing skills. Rankings for the UK are comparably abysmal.

Another area that originally got a (largely deserved) bad rap is the arena of educational games. Just as lack of imagination and thoughtless pedagogical strategies can lead to poor uses of tech in classrooms, so too did lack of imagination turn out a first generation of educational games that were boring and taught little but rote memorization. But that has changed and there are now many amazing, effective games that teach everything from fiction writing to scientific to computer coding. Take for example immersive alternative reality games such as *DUST*, a game developed by the National Science Foundation in collaboration with Brigham Young University, that teach young people about science and technology by having them problem solve imagined future crises that will require scientific and technical know-how. Or *Tessera*, developed by the Computer History Museum in Mountain View, California, which uses a mystery story to introduce the kind of computational skills needed in tech. Or *Periodic Table*, an app designed by the UK Royal Society of Chemists that allows almost limitless exploration of the building blocks of all matter. Or games that allow kids to experience a different social reality, such as *Auti-Sim* that gives a feel for what it is like to have autism, or *Against All Odds*, a game developed by the United Nations High Commission on Refugees to let young players experience something of what it is like to exiled from one's homeland and make an arduous trek to a new land.

Instead of focusing on the alleged dehumanizing effects of computers in the classroom, or fetishizing the technology itself as the sole solution, it is far more useful to focus on getting the best, most imaginative teachers to try out, use and teach others what various digital devices can do. And to address how those best practices can be shared with as many young people as possible since the breakthroughs in solving things such as the climate crisis or terrorism will come from people of all classes, nations, races and genders. Real concerns about digitizing education take us back to issues of social fairness, equality and digital inclusion, as linked to creative teaching. Vast inequalities in the funding of schools between richer and poorer communities is mirrored and multiplied by inequalities in the amount and sophistication of digital tools available in particular school districts. Damaging inequalities also exist between households in the same districts, since studies show that school success in computer use is greatly enhanced for students who have access at home in addition to in the classroom, a situation that obviously varies with family income. These disparities are in turn often translated into different educational tracks where degrees of computer literacy become a basis for pointing students to future roles in a work-force divided between more tech-literate white-collar managers and the less tech-literate blue- or pink-collar work forces (Monroe 2004).

⬛ IS KNOWLEDGE A COMMODITY OR A HUMAN RIGHT? HIGHER EDUCATION VS. INFORMATION FEUDALISM

The digitizing of college- and university-level education includes the general issues discussed earlier with regard to K–12 education, as well as some additional unique concerns and unique opportunities. Many professors are deeply trained in their fields but very thinly trained as teachers. In my experience, the transition to online teaching has brought many college professors to think more carefully about pedagogy. Much literature on teaching shows, to the chagrin of some of the more arrogant among the professoriate, that peer-to-peer learning is often superior to prof-to-peer learning. Online courses, when they include a strong element of student-to-student discussion made possible by the technology, tend to generate a good deal more student interaction than traditional lecture courses. The physical absence of a professor often stimulates a good form of disinhibition, especially among shyer students who would have difficulty speaking in a room full of people (students tend to forget, or put to the back of their minds, the fact that in most cases the instructor is there as a sort of "lurkerprof," to coin a phrase). Bottom line: Bad teaching can happen online or offline, and so can great teaching.

Just as some forms of community could only be virtual, so too is virtual education the only option for some. Fortunately, as suggested previously, it is an increasingly rich option. Online education is the only option for place-bound people, people who for reasons of work or other commitments cannot travel to a college or university site. This is also true for people who may be within a reasonable distance of a higher educational institution, but whose work schedules would preclude enrolling were it not for the timeframe flexibility of asynchronous (not time-bound) online courses. In addition to geographic isolation, many people with physical or psychological conditions that limit mobility have had new educational vistas opened up by distance education via new media. Moreover, increasing numbers of students who have none of these reasons driving them to the online option are taking these courses simply because they prefer it as a mode of learning.

At the same time, in the US, the UK and much of the developed world, support for public higher education has eroded at the governmental level, with public funds increasingly replaced by higher tuition fees. This is effectively privatizing education, and making it more and more difficult for even middle-class, let alone working-class, students to afford a university education. But just as short-sighted government policies are raising the costs of education, new technologies and new digitized sources are making more and more knowledge accessible and affordable for more and more people. This contradiction cannot stand for long. Already students in many countries are rebelling against these policies, and increasingly the professoriate is coming to support more and more open-access forms of education.

Part of this stems from the fact that increasingly college and university administrators, boards of regents and the politicians who fund public education speak of higher education as a business. This is largely nonsense for a number of reasons. Most importantly, treating students like clients or products (both terms have been applied by CEO-like administrators) misrepresents and degrades the complicated interactions that make up an education. Educational institutions should be run efficiently and effectively, but the measures of efficiency and effectiveness in academe do not match the measures used in the business world.

As for the "business" of professing, few professors go into education thinking of it as a business, including, or maybe especially, business professors. Whatever field of knowledge they pursue could have been pursued in more financially remunerative ways outside of academe. Moreover, the vast majority of the knowledge professors produce does not lead to financial reward. Professors seldom make significant amounts of money from the academic books they publish, and even more rarely from the research papers they publish. Most profits go to publishing houses, which serve as cost-increasing middle persons, often with little direct connection to the knowledge. This contradiction cannot stand in the age of digital production and distributions systems such as the Web make it quite possible to eliminate these middle persons and greatly decrease the cost of knowledge dissemination.

Many authors would rather have their work made available to more people at lower cost than fewer people at a higher cost. And this is even more true for professors, since very few count on getting rich by selling their work, both because they have another job, teaching, and because they care more about spreading knowledge than profit. What professor (indeed, what author of any kind) would not rather have 1,000 people pay $1 for their book, than 50 people pay $20? So what stands in the way? In technological terms, nothing. In practical terms, a mechanism of review that ultimately has little or nothing to do with the actual publication venue. The value of academic work is measured in significant degree by the place where it is published, the "best" university presses and the "top" scholarly journals. The prestige of these sites is based on two things: Historical reputation (they have published highly regarded stuff in the past) and peer review (the quality of the people associated with the publishing site who deem the book or article to be worthy of publication in their reputable publication). But these review processes have nothing whatsoever to do with how the knowledge is then made available—at high cost, low cost or no cost, through expensive books and journals or online for little or no cost. While, contrary to the slogan, not *all* "knowledge wants to be free," much of it does and most of it should be free in both senses of the word, now that we have the technology to make it so. Granted, there are complex issues involved in transitioning from the current system to a new, better one, including issues of copyright (where law is decades behind digital innovations) and ease of transition for employees in the current publishing system. But these issues can be worked out, to the benefit of all.

Critics such as Peter Drahos, John Brathewaite and David Parry refer to the large publishing conglomerates that control much academic publishing as among the **knowledge cartels** that are engaging in **information feudalism** (Drahos and Brathewaite 2002). Parry (2012) has laid out an action plan for displacing the higher-education branch of the cartel in order to open up academic knowledge to wider and wider publics. His recommendations include using Creative Commons licensing instead of publisher or university copyright for academic books, publishing articles only in online open-access journals, pressuring universities and academic field organizations to embrace open access and boycotting jobs with academic cartels. Parry and other advocates realize that this is best done on a large scale because few individual academics and individual institutions will have the courage to opt out of the current system. But a few breakthrough efforts like some highly ranked journals going open access, or a couple of major universities embracing these principles, could quickly start a landslide toward a more equitable and accessible knowledge system. These issues matter not only in the US, but widely because the US controls so much of the world's knowledge.

A second controversial area where higher education and digital technology meet is the arena of **Massive Open Online Courses (MOOCs)**. These are courses offered online for free (open) to up to thousands of people at a time (massive). The courses differ from ones offered in universities and colleges in that they can lead to at most a certificate of completion, rather than adding up to an undergraduate degree. From one angle, free online courses that differ little from ones available for (ever more expensive) tuition seem to threaten the very foundation of higher educational institutions. From another angle, they promise to actually fulfill the mission for which higher education exists at all. In any event, given the MOOC mania starting in 2012, the future is looking very MOOC-y. The positive side of making more and more college and university courses available to more and more people is simply too strong to be resisted for long. But, as with changes in the educational publishing industry, change will not come without a fair amount of chaotic dislocation and much social struggle. More important, the form that MOOCs will take is very much up for grabs. MOOC precursors arose in the UK and Canada, but it was MOOC-offering technology organizations in the US that hit upon a popular formula. In the states, three major operations, edX (started by Harvard and the Massachusetts Institute of Technology), Coursera (started at Stanford University) and Udacity (also with roots at Stanford) monopolized the early market. The phenomenon is spreading worldwide, with major efforts under way in Brazil, Japan and the EU, among others. At present, one constraining issue is that elite institutions (such as MIT, Princeton and Stanford in the US) have the financial resources to overcome the initial costs of MOOC creation in ways that give them a distinct advantage over state-funded and other less well-funded schools.

This could be referred to as the MOOC digital divide. It is also not clear whether these free courses will remain free under pressure from those who continue to think of higher education as a business, rather than a collective social good. Two of the three major MOOC offers in the states, Coursera and Udacity, are for-profit enterprises that may not continue to provide free classes forever. Business-minded administrators simply can't imagine having thousands of students learning without profit accruing to their institutions. Advocates of openness argue that the difference between uncredited MOOC courses and those offered as part of a regular, tuition-funded and accredited curriculum leading to a degree will be a sufficient distinction to retain the current role of universities and colleges. But once the good publicity gained by apparently altruistic offerings of free courses runs out, there will be great pressure from administrators to "monetize" these courses, to limit the "open" part of Massive Open Online Courses.

MOOCs also can be quite retrograde pedagogically. Many are based upon talking-head lecture formats that have proven to be among the least effective forms of teaching. While many offer "interactive" elements, it is not clear how many of these are actually used and how interactive they really are. Truly interactive forms of teaching, including much student-to-student activity, are far more useful than most kinds of lectures, and technologies have been used thoughtfully by many to create more student-centered, as opposed to professor-centered, courses. If MOOCs continue to develop based upon a kind of star system of elite lecturers, they will still prove useful to some students, but they will set back more than they advance higher education pedagogy overall. They may also greatly deepen an already growing divide between tenure-line faculty and adjuncts hired at far lower pay, with higher teaching loads and far less job security. Some forms of MOOC-ing could shrink the number of full-time faculty, and expand the group of exploited adjuncts who would manage the massive numbers of students through machine-graded tests and other far from creative forms of learning.

Alternatives to these kinds of MOOCs are emerging. FemTech-Net's Distributed Open Collaborative Course (DOCC) model, for example, challenges both the pedagogical style and the hierarchical structure of MOOCs. These alternatives will be up against the greater economic resources of the corporate academic types, but with imagination and effective networking they will have an impact. It will take demand from students for courses embodying more of the interactivity they have come to expect of education in the digital age to turn the dominant forms of MOOCs into something better.

▣ END OF THE WORLD (AS WE KNEW IT): DIGITAL HUMANITIES AND DIGITIZED ARTS

Digital culture reinforces a fact that has long been true—not all education takes place in a classroom. Digital media are making lifelong learning and self-teaching much easier than ever before. Two key, related arenas where these out-of-the-classroom educational experiences have proliferated are the digital humanities and digitized artworks. While the sciences and social sciences, given their often quantitative and data-driven aspects, have long utilized computers, the humanities and arts were somewhat slower to embrace digitization but have in the last couple of decades begun to use digital media to transform cultural representation in a number of interesting and crucial ways.

The field known as the **digital humanities** has been hard at work recording, representing and transforming the rich cultural legacy of groups and individuals around the globe. Digital humanities projects as detailed in sites such as HASTAC, Digital Humanities Now and the Center for History and New Media represent extraordinary efforts to bring well-researched, well-presented knowledge about past and present cultural expression to the widest possible audience. Universities have produced most of this work, along with libraries, museums and a variety of other cultural institutions. The work ranges from single websites about a novel, poem or painting (Treasures of the World: Mona Lisa) to in-depth sites about a single writer (Digital Thoreau; Emily Dickinson Archive) or artist (Digital Michelangelo Project) to artist-writers (William Blake Archive) to large literary history sites crossing centuries (Orlando Project; African American Women Writers) to historical event sites (Avalon Project 9/11 Collection) to vast archives with thousands of items about the culture of a nation (Amerinda; Creating French Culture), region (Islamic Art) or historical era. Forms include virtual museums (for all the world's major ones), cultural mapping sites (Hypercities), data visualization sites (Warhol Time Web), cultural preservation sites (Mukurtu), interactive education sites (Eyes on Art; Knotted Lines), data visualizations (Climate Art: New Ways of Seeing Data), educational resource sites (Center for New Media; EdTechTeacher) and many more.

Some major projects, such as NINES, seek to map an entire century of literature, in this case poetry and fiction of nineteenth-century England. The Folger Digital Text site provides access to the world's greatest collection of original Shakespeare manuscripts. The National Folklore Collection gathers together 250,000 folktales and 11,000 images of related people and places all over Ireland. Other projects have created massive databases of art images (or written texts) that can be searched in a myriad of ways to find new connections and new insights into cultural history. Some massive projects take on the cultural mapping of whole cities, such as the MediaNOLA site that seeks to trace all kinds of cultural creation in New Orleans over several hundreds of years, or the massive Hypercities project that has created various kinds of cultural maps of cities around the globe. The Visualizing Emancipation project provides a vivid set of tools for exploring the American Civil War and its aftermath. In sum, hundreds of free cultural resource sites now available worldwide represent an inestimable gift enabled by digital technologies.

Some large-scale digital humanities projects face competition from commercial projects that often eventuate in limited access, the hoarding or monetizing of cultural legacies. Robert Darnton, an expert on the history of the book as a medium, for example, leads a project (Digital Public Library of America) that represents a public alternative to Google's stated goal of digitizing "all the books in the world." Darnton fears that having one corporation control virtually the whole archive of books is dangerous, and is proceeding at a pace that often leads to errors and poor quality. In contrast, non-profit cultural entities can offer careful, informed curation of materials that respects their embeddedness in historical and social contexts, and remains free to the public. There is surely room for both commercial and non-profit projects (probably no one but Google has the funds to digitize so many books), but it would be a grave mistake to let the former replace the latter.

In addition to preserving and making available much of the world's culture and art, the impact of digital media on the creation of new art forms has been profound. Digital technology is both transforming older methods of art production (such as digital murals) and creating a host of new ones like augmented reality works and other *born digital art works* that are only possible with new media. In addition to offering online the vast of array of traditional arts, many new works are a hybrid of the traditional and the new, while others rest solely in unique qualities of digital media. Electronic or digital literature, for example, often draws on the interactive and connective aspects of the Web. Interactivity emphasizes the reader-viewer-user's role in the creative process, while interconnectivity via *hypertext* overcomes real-world limits (such as book length or canvas size), opening up virtually infinite possibilities. *Patchwork Girl* by Shelley Jackson for example, gives the Frankenstein legend some new feminist twists while offering reader-users a series of clicked choices that creates a patched together story mimicking Mary Shelley's composite creature. *The Imaginary 20th Century* by Norman Klein, Margo Bistis and electronic collaborators Andrea Kratsky and Blanka Earhart, among others, has become a bound novel but began life as a vast comic archive with thousands of documents and a mix of invented and historical characters that make it impossible to ever experience the text the same way twice. There are also hybrid electronic-traditional forms such as Steven Hall's *Raw Shark Text*, a regularly bound novel that directs readers to certain clues found only online. One of the more compressed genres of digi-lit is *Twitterature*, literary works limited to the number of characters available in microblogging. This includes haiku-like poetry (see #haiku), clever philosophical aphorisms (Jarosinki's twitter feed, "Nein") and (very) short stories. Explore the Electronic Literature Organization to get a sense of the range of possibilities.

Among the most startling new forms are *locative media that use augmented reality*. Works such as Ivan Toth Dependa's "Lapse" literally lay another layer of reality atop our normal visual field (in this case a set of venues around Miami), challenging perception, drawing attention to other possible realities, seemingly embodying William Blake's claim that if the doors of perception are cleansed, all the world is art. Caitlin Fisher's digital work includes "Breaking the Chains," an AR retelling of Harriet Tubman's role in the anti-slavery Underground Railroad, and her tale "Requiem," part of a "novel in fragments using tabletop augmented reality storytelling machines." "Public Secrets" by Sharon Daniel uses storytelling, interview archives and a host of media to richly explore the lives of women prisoners, while moving through the piece allows users to experience the "shifting borders" between "freedom and incarceration." Wendy Chun's "Programmed Visions" enjoins the user to create an archive that explores the entangled relation between "race" and computers. "Green Street & AR" by John Craig Freeman is a site-specific piece for smartphones that draws attention to the virtual world's penetration of the physical one as entire buildings seem to lose their mooring and drift off into space. "Defending Virtual" by Joseph Fairbank is a gallery piece that places a virtual hundred dollar bill on a traditional museum display pedestal, tempting viewers to grab it to illustrate the point that all currency ultimately only has virtual value. Hector Centano's "ReBlink" uses a smartphone app to recreate existing works of art, augmenting them with new possibilities by allowing re-viewing as museum-goers walk through a gallery. The addition of an AR viewer to Art.com's traditional site is harbinger of an emerging wave of new work. Meanwhile, the AR elements of the social media site Snapchat and others developed for various apps and devices, while in danger of trivializing, also opens up creative AR possibilities for anyone with imagination.

Various mixed modes of digital art also exist, often combining video, text and archives of various sorts. Ursula Bieman's "X-Mission," for example, uses video to explore the Palestinian refugee experience, and performance artist Guillermo Gomez-Pena extends his work into the digital sphere at his "La Pocho Nostra" live art lab. Zach Blas's "Queer Technologies" playfully thinks through, remakes and regenders the digital realm itself. Nicholas Mirzoff's "We Are All Children of Algeria" uses multiple media and multiple lines of history to rethink the West's complex relationship with the Middle East.

Electronic literature, augmented reality and mixed digital media artworks exist on a continuum that also includes virtual reality (VR), a step beyond AR, as well as digital games. Rachel Rossin uses her virtual reality art to help prepare us for the future in which the virtual and the material worlds will collide even more fully than they do at present. VR artist Jon Rafman takes works by artists like Miro or

Jackson Pollack and imprints them on 3D models of people, cars and furniture to reconnect what technology often estranges us from and gives earlier works of art a new, different life. Jordan Wolfson's "Real Violence" VR piece seeks to immerse the participant in violence in a way that critiques the desensitizing violence found in film, television and other works of pop culture. As for the art of games, one of the earliest of these works to take games beyond a narrow notion of play was *Journey*, a stunningly beautiful desert landscape where the user wandered in search of some not neatly defined things, which felt more like a meditative spiritual exercise than a game in the traditional sense. Will O'Neill's *Actual Sunlight* brought new emotional depth to the form, while Thekla's *The Witness* and Hideo Kojima's *PT* push the boundaries of the genres they play with. Games like *Never Alone*, based on Inupiat legends, offer new insights into little-explored cultural contexts. The Smithsonian's "Art of the Video Game" exhibition in 2012 was an important acknowledgement that much artistry goes into not only works labelled "game art" but to many mainstream video games as well. The Museum of Modern Art in New York likewise has given the form its imprimatur by including games in its permanent collection. Some critics prefer the term *playable media* to downplay the limited sense often given to the term game, but whatever one wishes to call them the possibilities for deeply immersive, aesthetically rich multimedia, interactive works is almost unlimited. For some sense of additional possibilities for digital art (aka Net art, new media art, Internet art, born-digital art, among others), check out sites such as Rhizome or the Tate Gallery's Intermedia Zone.

Protecting and expanding arts and humanities education in an era when they are threatened by decreased funding, increased commercialization of all things on the Web and a turn toward narrowly vocational education will require continued vigilance and creative action. Evidence abounds that art education, in addition to enhancing a student's engagement with vast creative universes, develops unique skills applicable in all walks of life. Ironically, at a time when universities are being forced by short-sighted politicians to move toward reductively vocational approaches to education that stress business, engineering and natural science over the social and human sciences, three out of four employers say they want schools to "place more emphasis on the skills that the humanities and social sciences teach: critical thinking and complex problem solving" (American Academy of Arts and Sciences 2013). Employers frequently complain that people narrowly trained in technical fields lack critical writing skills, creativity and ability to communicate across cultural and occupation-based boundaries. That is why more than one-third of Microsoft's employees, for example, have liberal arts degrees. As one headline in the business magazine *Forbes*, put it: "That 'Useless' Liberal Arts Degree Has Become Tech's Hottest Ticket" (Anders 2015). If UK and US universities do not restore art, literature, philosophy, history and related fields to the center of higher education, they will fall behind the rest of the world, which understands that the new high-tech economy will be driven by imaginative, creative people who have been exposed to the full play of human cultures, past and present. Digital humanities and digitized arts are key arenas that help to build bridges between science and imagination, engineering and creativity, technology and cultural history.

⊡ THE FUTURE OF KNOWLEDGE SHARING: EDUCATION FOR WHOM AND FOR WHAT?

Innovations in the digitization of educational resources raise the larger question of whether knowledge is something that should be hoarded and made financially inaccessible to all but the few (the business model), or a human right that should be available to anyone with the intellectual skills to benefit from it, regardless of ability to pay. There are complex issues of copyright and intellectual property rights that need to be untangled in this context. Laws on these issues around the globe are decades behind digital technology. But surely at a time when humanity faces extraordinarily daunting problems— wars, famines, poverty, terrorism, ecological crises and more—we should be doing far more to use digital and other means to increase the flow of knowledge and the number of educated people in the world, rather than creating roadblocks. Yet that is precisely what we do when we think of formal education and knowledge more generally as a commodity. Markets can do some things extremely well. But the idea of a knowledge market makes no sense. Do we really want to increase profits for a few institutions by creating a shortage of supply? Is that really a good strategy for creating the smartest possible world?

At a time when exciting new educational vistas are opening up, many countries, under the dubious slogan of austerity, are gutting education. Even in two of the wealthiest nations, the UK and the US, massive government funding cuts and other ill-conceived policies have led to the privatization of much that was once public in education, especially at the college and university level. In the UK, higher education is more and more expensive, less and less available to all but the wealthiest students (Couldry and McRobbie 2010). In the US there has been a three-fold increase in the amount of state funds going to students without financial need in recent years (based on a notion of merit that does not factor in the impact of family income), and that means far less for students from low-income families (Rampell 2013). No amount of digitization is going to help much if these trends are not reversed, because intelligence is never found in only one economic or social class or ethno-racial group, especially the kind of intelligence needed to see the world in all its diverse complexity, and to tackle the interconnected economic, social and ecological problems deeply plaguing the planet.

The Internet and related digital communication technologies open up vast possibilities for expanding the amount of information, knowledge and wisdom in the world. Even the most remote corners of the globe can be reached if the support is there. New possibilities for lifelong learning are opening up, but they will only be as good as the support offered to the talented teachers and scholars who have dedicated their whole lives to perfecting the best methods (digital and non-digital) for helping people learn, and the most effective ways to present knowledge (online and off). All that stands in the way are the political imagination to support the most effective of these innovations and the political will to ensure that no one, no matter their background, is denied the chance to develop their learning capabilities to their fullest extent.

10

Who in the World Is Online?

Digital Inclusions and Exclusions

While thinking about the pros and cons of digitized lives, it is important to ask a basic but key question: Whose lives are and whose lives are *not* being digitized? Who in the world is *not* online and why aren't they? It is no accident that the opportunity and ability to take part in the benefits (and risks) of digitized life vary immensely, both between countries and within countries around the globe. Those differences arise due to historical imbalances in power, and that matters because some of those differences are matters of life or death.

◪ THE WORLD WIDE WEB ISN'T

One thing to always remember about the World Wide Web is that it isn't. Isn't worldwide, that is. As its name makes clear, the World Wide Web *seeks* to be a universal phenomenon, and it is a very widespread phenomenon, but the Web and other aspects of digital culture are far from worldwide. Statistics make clear that the spread of the Internet around the globe has been deeply uneven, with vast differences across continents, between countries and along class, gender, ethnic and other social differences within regions and nations.

The quick answer to our question is that less than half of the world's population has access to the digital realm, and the quality and extent of access within that number varies considerably. Any way you measure it (and statistical measures vary somewhat), several billion people still have no engagement with digital culture at all. Three main factors shape this fact: Lack of economic resources, lack of computer literacy skills and lack of information relevant to many potential users. The lack of interest factor often stems from the relative lack of linguistic and cultural diversity in the material available on the Web. If your language or cultural group is underrepresented online, you are less likely to know about or want to connect with the digital world even when opportunities arise. In addition to negative forces keeping many people offline, there are also positive reasons why some people wish to stay disconnected, or give up their existing connections.

In terms of pure numbers, the highest access rates are in North America and Europe, the lowest access rate is on the African continent, with Asia and Latin America in the middle range. Within countries, rates of access also vary greatly, depending primarily on economic status, gender and majority or minority ethnicity status. Age and educational level also often shape the amount and quality of access. The uneven access across continents looks something like this: 95 percent of North Americans have access, 85 percent of Europeans, 64 percent of Middle Easterners, 67 percent of Latin Americans, 48 percent of Asians and only 35 percent of Africans. If we switch from access to number of users relative to world population, the breakdown runs: 11 percent of users are African, 49 percent are Asians, 17 percent are Europeans, 10.5 percent are Latin American, 3.9 percent are Middle Easterners and 8.3 percent are North Americans (Internet World Stats). While native speakers of English make up only a small percentage of the world's population, more than 50 percent of the content of the Web is in English. Conversely, while Chinese users make up the largest number of users by far, less than 2 percent of Web content is in Chinese. Similar disparities exist between the number of speakers of a given language and the amount of content. These means, among other things, that Net is playing a major role in forcing people to either learn English or be excluded from vast amounts of valuable information. A number of critics have noted that this amounts to a kind of linguistic or cultural imperialism at odds with a fair and balanced online world.

These statistics are useful but incomplete because they don't reflect deep disparities that exist *between* countries on a given continent and even more drastically by income *within* countries. Since virtually every country on earth currently shows increasing economic inequality, these disparities matter a great deal with digital "haves" and "have-nots" often marking significant imbalance in economic, cultural and political power. Moreover, as Virginia Eubanks has demonstrated, digital technologies are often used disproportionately to "profile, police and punish the poor" (Eubanks 2018). Given this situation, access to digital culture may be a key for low income folks to defend themselves and to seek new ways out of poverty.

One set of issues this chapter will be exploring surrounds questions of "digital diversity." Digital diversity is at once a fact and an unrealized promise. The Internet is a vast web of words, images and sounds created by millions of people all around the globe, and thus certainly reflects a very diverse range of cultures and ideas. On the other hand, data show that there are not only vast inequalities of access to these new media, both within and between countries, but also deep disparities in amount and quality of information online, depending upon language and relative cultural power. Put bluntly, the English language and Anglo-European cultures are vastly overrepresented on the Web (relative to population), rendering other languages and cultures severely underrepresented. This is turn means there are even greater disparities in terms of who *produces* most of the content in digital culture. That means that even much of the information about non-Anglo-European cultures on the Web has been produced and uploaded by Anglo-Europeans. This does not inherently invalidate the information, but insiders to a culture are generally far more sensitive to the nuance and specificity of their culture. These various inequalities involve both questions of *access* (who is online) and *representation* (what is online and how truly it reflects the diverse peoples and cultures of the world). There are in fact several different divides reflecting various aspects of a multifaceted set of deficits. These statistics are startling, but how much do they matter? Why should we care? How much do these disparities really matter? Are digital divides really that important?

▣ WHO NEEDS THE INTERNET?

The gap between those who do and those who do not enjoy the benefits of digital communications technologies matters because every aspect of current social life—business, education, government, family life, social change movements—has been reshaped along digital lines. With more and more economic, political, social and cultural information available exclusively via the Net, the fact that billions do not have solid access to these resources is a major societal concern. This gap is most commonly referred to as the digital divide. But it is important to realize that the digital divide is not one thing, but many things. To begin with, there is not so much a divide as many divides, and within each divide there is a continuum from extremely high-level access to no access at all, with many gradations in between. Access itself is a very complicated phenomenon that goes far beyond hardware and software to the "wetware" (human culturally variable brains) that alone makes the system work.

Why does using new media to address economic social inequality matter so much? Recall these statistics from the Introduction: 80 percent of people live in countries where the income gap is widening; the richest 20 percent of the population controls 75 percent of world wealth; 25,000 children die each day from poverty; only seven in 100 people have a college education; a billion people in the world are illiterate; one in five people on earth have no clean drinking water; several billion have no Internet access (Statistic Brain n.d.; UNESCO Institute for Statistics n.d.). Moreover, an analysis of long-term trends shows the distance between the richest and poorest countries has been growing almost exponentially. The wealth gap between the richest and poorest countries was about 3 to 1 in 1820, 11 to 1 in 1913, 35 to 1 in 1950, 44 to 1 in 1973, 72 to 1 in 1992 and 107 to 1 in 2010. This trend is not socially sustainable. It can only lead to greater and greater strife. At the turn of the twenty-first century, New York City had the highest concentration of fiber optic-wired buildings on the planet, yet only one of these was in predominantly African American Harlem. Similarly, in high-tech Los Angeles, the Latino barrio of East LA had no wired buildings at all (Sassen 1999). Inequality in relation to digital culture has many different dimensions, and varies in terms of quality and intensity, not just pure access. The city of Tokyo, to take one example, has a greater density of Internet use than the entire continent of Africa. But in the (over)developed First World vast disparities exist among populations, based primarily on income and ethnicity. The most recent research in the US has identified inherited wealth, not income, as a more direct determinant of upward mobility, and gaps between whites and people of color are particularly stark in that category. Generational poverty due to systemic racism or ethnocentrism ensures that certain groups never accumulate enough wealth to pass on to the next generation. This means the problem of poverty will not go away without serious action to create more egalitarian conditions.

Ethno-racial disparities are compounded by another key dimension of the digital divide, the languages prevalent on the Net. The Internet was born in English, and the English language continues to have disproportionate overrepresentation in digital cultures worldwide. Japanese likewise, despite far fewer speakers, is overrepresented, while Chinese language content on the Web is nowhere near its percentage of native speakers worldwide. Ditto for Arabic speakers, Spanish speakers and speakers of virtually all smaller linguistic communities.

There are also concerns not considered under the general category of "access." Broadband access, for example, is unevenly distributed even in high infrastructure areas such as North America. Poor people and people of color have far less broadband access than others ("Internet/Broadband Fact Sheet" 2018), and given that currently two-thirds of all Net traffic is in bandwidth heavy form, this is a considerable disadvantage. The Internet Society also notes that a new divide is emerging around cyber-security issues:

> Perhaps most worrying is the increasing likelihood of a security and trust divide: cyber threats will continue to multiply and users who lack the skills, knowledge and resources to protect themselves and their data will be far more likely to become victims of cybercrime. Thus, we will see a divide emerge between the security 'haves' and the 'have nots'.
>
> (Internet Society 2017: 12)

Many of these disparities arise from governmental policies as shaped by corporate domination of decision makers. And here the issue isn't entirely based on overall national wealth. Susan Crawford, in her book *Captive Audience: The Telecom Industry and Monopoly in the New Gilded Age* (2013), notes that in the most prosperous country on earth, the US, consumers have fewer choices for broadband service, at higher prices and lower speeds, than in dozens of other countries, including most of Europe and parts of Asia. As one reviewer of Crawford's book noted,

> Reasonable people can and do disagree about policy solutions, but the facts are not in dispute. Americans have fewer choices for broadband Internet service than millions of other people in developed countries, yet we pay more for that inferior service. The reason for that, according to Crawford, is that US policy makers have allowed a small number of highly profitable corporate giants to dominate the market, reducing competition and the incentives for these companies to improve service and lower prices.
>
> (Gustin 2013)

This matters a good deal because in the twenty-first century those lacking broadband access face yet another digital divide as increasing amounts of Web content are available only to those with broadband. In the US, this has meant that certain previously declining numbers in terms of gaps between whites and ethnic/racial minorities have begun to rise again because of the greater cost of broadband access. This too is a reminder that technology changes can impact the nature of digital inequalities, sometimes improving things, sometimes setting trends moving backward.

These and related facts about growing digital disparities led scholar Andrew Carver to argue that "The digital divide is *the* [human] rights issue of the 21st century." Why? Because the Internet is (potentially) the greatest educational invention since the printing press. Here are just some of the many areas where the Net can be immensely important: Health education to areas without medical professionals; economic education to areas lacking economic knowledge and opportunity; political information to areas suffering severe ideological control and censorship; multimedia (visual and aural) information even to those lacking written literacy; multiple formats to match multiple learning styles and vast cultural variability, including broadly oral cultures, written cultures and visually oriented cultures. As a scholar deeply involved in studying digital divides, Mark Warschauer summarizes,

> Whether in developed or developing countries, urban areas or rural, for economic purposes or sociopolitical ones, access to ICT is a necessary and key condition for overcoming social exclusion in the information society. It is certainly not the only condition that matters; good schools, decent government, and adequate health care are other critical factors for social inclusion. But ICT, if deployed well, can contribute toward improved education, government, and health care, too, and thus can be a multiplying factor for social inclusion.
>
> (Warschauer 2003: 30)

If not dealt with, lack of meaningful digital access will increase all forms of poverty (economic, social and informational) and deepen all forms of inequality. Not dealing with this inequality will in turn put the world at far greater risk of war, terrorism and other forms of social disruption. While life online is not without considerable problems and risks, by and large for most people, having significant access to online worlds is preferable to not having that access. So how do they get it?

⊞ FROM DIGITAL DIVIDES TO TECHNOLOGIES FOR SOCIAL INCLUSION

The concept of the *digital divide* came to prominence in the mid-1990s in the United States. The term has been widely criticized, and does have some misleading connotations, but it remains the most commonly used shorthand for the gaps between those who have access to digital technologies and those who do not. The term "digital divide" was first used by journalists and then enthusiastically adopted by members of President Bill Clinton's administration. Under the leadership of then-Vice President Al Gore (no, he didn't really *invent* the Internet but he was an important force in increasing access to it), a series of initiatives and national report cards were put forth aimed at bridging the gap between those who did and those who did not have easy access to the Internet. The first of these report cards, "Falling through the Net: Defining the Digital Divide" (1999), largely set the parameters for use of the concept for a number of years. While immensely useful at first, the term rather quickly also became misleading in that it had defined the "divide" narrowly in terms of access to hardware, and suggested that there was but one such divide when there are in fact many kinds of divides.

While much of the work addressing the divide between the so-called digital "haves" and "have-nots" has focused on the important task of providing access to hardware, software and basic computer literacy, there is an additional issue—the cultural digital divide—that has received far too little attention. Research increasingly shows that one of the essential ways to attack digital inequalities is by addressing the fact that technologies are always created with in-built cultural biases that limit their use. This means that the divide will be lessened only when, in addition to providing basic access, we address seriously cultural differences and the differences in power that come with them. Significant lack of representation or misrepresentation of particular racial, ethnic and cultural groups in the media has long been shown to have profound negative psychological effects on the groups. In turn, this misrepresentation has strongly adverse implications for social justice and equitable social policy because of the broad consumption of these media by the general public and policy makers.

Progress in closing various digital divides, including new ones that are emerging even as older ones shrink, needs to include improving the quality and quantity of diverse *cultural content* in new media such as the Web and video games. In turn, this will make those vital new media resources more effective in dealing with issues of economic, social and political inequalities. Most attempts to solve the problem of the digital divide have also used a shallow interpretation of technical literacy as simply learning computer programs, unaware that technological forms are culturally shaped and need to be reshaped to fit a wider variety of cultural styles and forms.

Mark Warschauer coined the term **technology for social inclusion** to describe this more proactive approach to new media than bemoaning digital divides, and he suggests that this changed perspective has three main aspects:

> The shift from a focus on a digital divide to social inclusion rests on three main premises: (1) that a new information economy and network society have emerged; (2) that ICT plays a critical role in all aspects of this new economy and society; and (3) better access to ICT, broadly defined, can help determine the difference between marginalization and inclusion in this new socioeconomic era.
>
> (Warschauer 2003)

A technology for inclusion perspective recognizes that multiple social variables create differing degrees of social power in relation to all things, including high technologies. Social inclusion refers to the extent to which individuals, families and communities are able to fully participate in society and control their own destinies, with the goal of furthering equal access to economic resources, employment, health, education, housing, recreation, culture and civic engagement.

Figure 10.1 is a chart mapping the various components that need to be considered in any technology for social inclusion analysis or project. Note that the arrows are meant to suggest that these various elements are not independent but rather interact with each other.

The process Warschauer's chart seeks to illustrate must address four levels or components that are key in the success or failure of a digital inclusion project: *Physical resources* (the hardware needed to access the Web), *digital resources* (culturally relevant content of interest to the full range of potential users), *human resources* (in terms of people competent to assist in helping users achieve techno-literacies of various kinds) and *social resources* (in the form of a supportive, culturally competent cohort of fellow users).

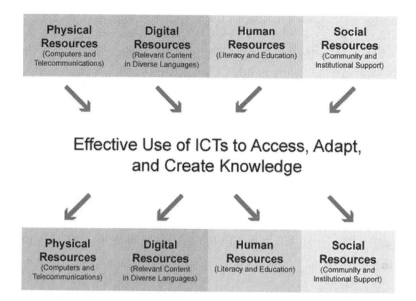

FIGURE 10.1 *Technology for social inclusion (© Mark Warschauer, reprinted with permission)*

Physical resources, the almost exclusive focus of many early digital divide projects, focus on getting the required hardware (desktops, laptops, smartphones, etc.) and software (operating systems, Web browsers, word and image processing programs, etc.). It goes without saying that not much can be done without these, but even deciding which kind of hardware and software is needed is not a culturally neutral issue. What particular kinds of hardware and software match the lifestyles of the users you hope to serve? Is mobility (as with smartphones and tablets) a high concern, or are more place-bound devices likely to be more useful? It might be a huge mistake to locate hardware in homes in a town that had a particularly lively community center where seeing one's neighbors using the Web could potentially create a snowballing effect of interesting other community members.

Digital resources form an area frequently overlooked in inclusion projects, often because the proponents are already so engaged with online life, so aware of its riches, that they forget others must be introduced to and convinced of the value of being online. While showing of some of the generic features of the Web, such as Wikipedia, can be useful, what is really necessary is showing content of specific interest to the users for whom the project is being created, content directly addressing the age, ethnicity, gender, religion or other cultural features and values found among users. Obviously, this is even more important when dealing with a community where two or more different languages are spoken. Sometimes what will be needed is highly practical information about jobs or health care. At other times it may be something addressing particular cultural values such as a religious site, and still other situations may call for something more recreational as the entry point to spur interest. But, again, this is not something easily determined by people with no deep knowledge of the community.

Human resources consist of people who can provide proper training in the techno-literacies needed to successfully access and explore online worlds. One of the best ways to do this is to encourage and provide technical training for people who have lived experience as members of underserved groups (in the US and globally). These culturally competent, technically savvy individuals can then work as facilitators for marginalized communities to empower them to represent themselves in digital media on their own cultural ground via their own cultural forms. When it is possible to find people from the community being served to do this work, this is the ideal. When that is not possible, then finding folks with the cultural competence to interact with the community in sensitive and effective ways is next best. Many projects have been ruined by "trainers," as opposed to "facilitators," who lacked the social skills, patience or flexibility to reach a range of community members.

Finally, *social resources* refers to model users and support networks to break through any reticence in the community. Communities "targeted" (already an ugly word) for digital inclusion projects are approached precisely because there seem to be too few members in the village, town or city that the project seeks to serve. But there are almost invariably some people in the community, or from similar communities, however few, who already have been convinced of the value of online access. These serve as ice-breakers demonstrating that "people like me" can use and gain value from access. In most cases, the more public this kind of work is the more quickly it will spiral out to many others. Again, this is why privatized projects in the home may sound good, but often lack this key level of social resources.

These four levels are obviously connected, and work at either reinforcing each other or at cross purposes. Only hard work on the ground can create the right mix of these various resources, but finding that mix is what will make the difference between a merely well-meaning and an actually successful project for digital social inclusion. There are projects at work all over the world trying to bridge the many digital divides, but there are far too few of them, and even fewer of those address this full range of resources. If we wish to live in a more just, less conflict-ridden world, far greater efforts will have to be made to bring digital haves and have-nots closer to parity.

It is also important to realize that the nature of digital divides shifts significantly over time, and that the planned obsolescence of technologies requires a plan to not just start but sustain access for communities and individuals. For example, at the same time that progress was being made in achieving basic access for many previously unconnected people in the 1990s and early twenty-first century, the Web was becoming more and more a broadcast medium like television. Increasing amounts of streaming video and other bandwidth-hogging content meant that large parts of the digital world could only be accessed with high-speed broadband. As a result, a new broadband divide developed in which, once again, the least affluent users became excluded from much Web content. On the more positive side, the largest impact in increasing access was certainly the invention of cellphones with Internet connections. This did not do much to narrow the broadband gap because, as anyone who compares access via cellphone with access by laptop or desktop will readily attest, even the best phones fall short in many ways, and access by phone does not match computer access in a variety of ways. Having smartphone access, while often itself part of the broadband divide, has nevertheless been immensely important in increasing the economic, political and cultural information available to poor and low-income people around the globe (Horst and Miller 2006). But so far, the Web ledger is on the deficit side. To a large degree economic poverty has generated information poverty in those cut off from the Net, which has in turn deepened economic inequality (Monroe 2004; Mossberger 2003; Norris 2008; Tsatsou 2011; Warschauer 2002; Zaremba 2006).

Of course, an even more basic question is where will the funding come to create these projects? One thing we know for certain about digital divides is that no single social entity will overcome them. A "free-market" approach alone, for example, will not work because the expansion of digital access is not always profitable initially to ITC corporations. A number of corporate leaders, including Elon Musk and Mark Zuckerberg, have announced major projects to make Net access available to the billions not yet connected. These are encouraging, but in addition to the fact that mere access is not enough, commercial interests will always reach limits where profit-making gets in the way of full and equal access to those with fewer economic resources. The many locally based community projects will play a vital role alongside high visibility efforts such as SpaceX's planned "Starlink" Internet satellite system.

Clearly the people who need the Internet the most—those seeking jobs, those in need of better health care, those seeking to overcome an inadequate education—are precisely those least likely to have the means, financial or informational, to access the required hardware, software, know-how and supportive cultural context to use the Net effectively. And because of their lack of wealth they are the least likely to be targeted by tech corporations seeking profits. Sometimes ethnic stereotypes are used to excuse the digital gaps when it is suggested that racial minorities are somehow less interested in high tech than white folks. This assumption is demonstrably untrue. To take but one example, African Americans, who have been among those stereotyped as low-tech or not tech savvy, have been major innovators in music technology since the early hip-hop era. Such prejudiced attempts to explain away digital divides are both ill-informed and bad for business (Nelson, Tu and Headlam Hines 2001). And the business world does have a key role to play. Corporations with longer-range visions understand that diversity is a value in their workforce, and that the initial cost of bringing diverse folks currently out of the high-tech universe in may pay off not just socially but financially down the line.

But governments too have a key role to play. Government support for inclusion projects has varied immensely across differing countries, and not always as a function of the relative wealth of the countries. It has more to do with understanding that digital inclusion can build community, can improve overall economic and physical health and can lead to a more productive, less conflictive populace to the benefit of everyone. Unfortunately, most governments do not focus on the long range, and the benefits of social inclusion into digital worlds seldom have quick payoffs. But even governments can learn, and the best digital inclusion projects are showing these benefits.

The third level involves individual community members or community members collectively who have the resources and the vision to seek out inclusion for the rest of the members of their tribe, village, town or city neighborhood. In many ways, given their closeness, key locally based initiatives are the most likely to succeed. But they are also the least likely to have sufficient financial resources. So, as a general rule it will be partnerships involving local folks, government and/or relevant companies that will put together the best projects, often with the help of a rich force of local volunteer labor (Tsatsou 2011).

⊡ SHOULD EVERYONE AND EVERYTHING BE ONLINE?

Critics talk about not only digital "haves" and "have-nots," but also about digital "don't-wants." While I have stressed the benefits online life has to offer people who are currently excluded, I also wish to honor the fact that there are many folks who do not want to have their lives digitized. A little more than 10 percent of Americans, for example, say they do not go online even though they have access ("Internet/Broadband Fact Sheet" 2018). There can be very good reasons to avoid the online world, for a time or altogether. Much of the work studying the "don't-wants" is based on the dubious assumption that everyone should want to be part of the digitizing world. I've suggested why that assumption makes sense given the vast amounts of vital information now available exclusively via the Web. But the digital world is also a limited world. Not everything can be translated into 0s and 1s, or at least not everything should be. We can take as an example the form of analog music known as the vinyl record. Virtually everyone with a nuanced ear for music agrees that non-digital music such as found on records sounds different, different in ways that many people prefer. So too with all aspects of the analog world; there are things about it that are different in ways some will always prefer, and it is vital to keep those differences alive rather than lose them in a mad dash to digitize everything. That is the reason behind many "don't-wants," and that particular "don't-want" should be respected and nourished. In addition to questions of taste, some people object for religious reasons, some for political ones. And as I argue in the final chapter of this book, there may come a time when it makes sense for all of us to leave digital spaces.

"We are in great haste to construct a magnetic telegraph from Maine to Texas," the poet/philosopher Thoreau (1982) observed 200 years ago,

> but Maine and Texas, it may be, have nothing important to communicate . . . We are eager to tunnel under the Atlantic . . . but perchance the first news that will leak through the broad, flapping American ear will be that the Princess Adelaide has the whooping cough.

Substitute "Twitter" for the telegraph, and ask whether we really need to know where our favorite celebrity had dinner last night, and you'll see that Thoreau's question remains relevant. Let's face it, humans invented the greatest communication mechanism since language, including the greatest library of all human knowledge, and then filled it up with piano-playing cats, talking dogs, pornography, stupid human tricks, fake news, insane conspiracy theories and every kind of trivia imaginable. If the Net is partly a mirror held up to humanity, what is reflected there is often appalling. Sometimes it seems, as Thoreau wondered, that we have in fact "nothing important to communicate" across the tubes.

A character (with the same name as the author) in *Galatea 2.2*, a novel by contemporary writer Richard Powers, offers something approaching a technological update of Thoreau's concern:

> The web was a neighborhood more efficiently lonely than the one it replaced. Its solitude was bigger and faster. When relentless intelligence finally completed its program, when the terminal dropbox brought the last barefoot, abused child online and anyone could at last say anything instantly to everyone else in existence, it seemed to me we'd still have nothing to say to each other and more ways not to say it.
>
> (Powers 2004: 14)

So, one good reason to not be online might be to avoid the vast amounts of nonsense and digitized loneliness often found there. On the other hand, as another great writer, Theodore Sturgeon, observed about his preferred literary genre, "True, 90% of science fiction is crap, but then 90% of everything is crap." The exact proportion of crap to value on the Web is beyond anyone's calculation, but Sturgeon's law is about as good a guess as any. And his point is that finding the 10 percent of truly valuable stuff in life is the necessary task any serious person needs to undertake, whether online or off.

There are also deeper reasons than the high nonsense content for keeping some things offline. While the slogan "information wants to be free" is a catchy one that has served advocates of an open Web well, it doesn't fit every situation, or everyone's cultural values. The long history of cultural theft by dominant cultures has made many on the margins of such cultures wary of claims that all culture should be shared. While the powerful in the Global North, and dominant cultures in the Global South, seem to be taking in the rest of the world's cultures in giant gulps, these same forces often fight like mad to protect what they call *intellectual property rights*. Such rights have cultural bias built right into them, since not all cultures believe things such as ideas and art can be owned by individuals. But beyond that, intellectual property rights have failed to protect such things as the medical knowledge of indigenous communities, or to protect other forms of collectively held traditional knowledge.

Against both exploitative corporations and well-meaning cyber-libertarians, some, particularly in Native or indigenous communities, seek a more nuanced understanding of and control over communally based knowledges. In many cases, this has meant keeping information away from the digital world. In some other instances, this includes using innovative digital forms themselves to protect rather than project cultural knowledge. One of the most interesting of these efforts is the Mukurtu Project (Christen and the Warumungu People n.d.). Mukurtu began as a collaboration between anthropologist Kimberly Christen and the Warumungu Aboriginal community of Central Australia. While Christen was doing ethnographic research on the community, they became interested in the technological devices she brought with her. Eventually, they asked her to find a way to digitally archive some of their cultural knowledge and cultural artifacts. Out of this came the idea of creating software for a digital archive that would allow communities to provide but limit access to cultural materials based on their specific traditional protocols. In other words, some knowledge would be available only to elders, some only to post-pubescent girls and so forth. In this way cultural preservation could be done in a way that is consistent with long-held community values. Based upon this highly successful model, Christen and her associates created and have made freely available worldwide a Content Management System (CMS) with which any community can preserve and protect its cultural heritage. The goal, as they state it, is to "empower communities to manage, share and exchange their digital heritage in culturally relevant and ethically minded ways" (Christen and the Warumungu People n.d.). Key here is the understanding that not all information needs to be free to all people, that communities have a right to restrict as well as disseminate the knowledge specific to their history. This process also makes clear that not all members of the community necessarily want access to their particular knowledge in digital form, and that too is fine.

The Mukurtu Project is part of a wider movement in participatory design as well ("Participatory Design" n.d.). The central principle of participatory design in the technological world is that the people who will actually be using a given device, program, application or platform should have a say from the early stages in the design of technologies. What that means in practical terms is that designers need to either reflect personally or develop deep cultural competencies in the range of cultural groups who will use the devices, apps, etc. This seemingly simple principle has long been the exception rather than the rule in the development of new media. Instead, until fairly recently, the default subject position of the white middle-class male technician has been the sole angle of vision from which most technological innovation has emerged. The fantastic success of many of these products for a time disguised the fact that they also had major cultural limitations. Slowly that is changing.

Many in the electronics industry have realized that diversity is not just an ethical value, but a business necessity. There are currently more anthropologists and sociologists working for Microsoft and Google than in any university in the world. And many electronics firms are actively seeking out employees from the full range of ethnicities, genders and cultural locations. Whether this leads to more commodification of cultural difference or greater representation of marginalized groups and individuals remains to be seen. Unfortunately, the social conditions that gave birth to the limited cultural knowledge base in the industry have not disappeared, and are not easily erased by corporate affirmative actions. Deep-seated bias in economic, social and cultural structures means that the number of marginalized group members in a position to take advantage of certain opportunities to enrich the diversity of the world of techno-creators remains limited. Without both specific changes in digital access policies and broader social change, the world of digital creators, as with digital users, is likely to continue to reflect and exacerbate existing social inequalities. Some of these policies, of course, need to include respect for those who for religious, political cultural or other reasons do not want access. And given the surveillance questions raised earlier in this book, and the significant threat that AIs (artificial intelligences) may gain control of much of humanity, maybe all of us will at some point fall into that category. But for now, the task is to give as many persons as possible the option of digitizing aspects of their lives.

▣ WHY DIGITIZING MATTERS TO ALL OF US

Why does digital inclusion matter so much? Digital technologies and the nearly instantaneous transnational communication links they enable have been almost universally cited as a key factor in the economic, political and cultural processes that make up contemporary "globalization." Just as the effects of globalization in general have varied greatly, especially between the elites of the Global North who have benefitted immensely from economic globalization, and the peoples of the Global South who, apart from a few elites of their own, have suffered new forms of domination under the guise of globalization, so too has the spread of digital empowerment been deeply uneven. Those suffering under globalization, however, have hardly suffered in silence. Many have used the same tools of digitized communication to create a worldwide global justice movement that has created unprecedented solidarity across national borders. Nevertheless, most information exchanged across the Web is exchanged only among those in the Global North, principally the US, Canada, Japan and Europe, a fact that suggests cultural imperialism, intended or not, is alive and well.

When misused, the concept of the digital divide can perpetuate a very limited image of Global North development versus Global South underdevelopment, of a provider group and a needy group. This insinuates the hegemonic idea of Western modernization as the only reasonable course, and does little to take into consideration the actual conditions and desires of those who currently are not part of the digitized world. A one-way model of giving access needs to be replaced by a much more interactive set of relations in order to truly understand needs, desires, power imbalances and cultural differences that underlie the data presented as a digital divide (Potter 2006). We can acknowledge the desire of some people to opt out of the digital world while supporting the UN Sustainable Development goal of universal Web access by 2020. This will include recognizing new divides as they arise, including the deepening *security divide*, where some will and some will not have the resources to protect their privacy and their property online. That divide too could contribute to deepening economic inequality, both through cybercrime aimed at the vulnerable and through justified fear of security breaches limiting access to benefits of access.

The immense potential benefits of new digital media will be realized fully only when those of us with greater privilege take some responsibility for the devastating economic, social and digital divides. This is not about assigning blame to individuals born into particular privileged races, genders, countries or classes. It is about a need for widespread structural changes, particularly in the economic realm, that can only be brought about through collective, political action. How can new media technology be made more useful to the billions of people facing economic inequality, discrimination and cultural misrepresentation? We need to ask this question because the majority of the world's people, due to historic injustices and the accidents of birth, are on the deficit side of the economic and digital divide, and because, as Martin Luther King (1963) noted, "Injustice anywhere is a threat to justice everywhere."

11

Conclusion: Will Robots and AIs Take Over the World?

Hope, Hype and Possible Digitized Futures

Technology is not going to save the world. We are, and we can use technology to help us.

(Aleph Molinari, "Bridging the Digital Divide with Learning and Innovation Networks," 2012)

If you think I am going to answer the question posed in this chapter's title, then you haven't been paying attention. It is a serious one, even if I have posed it in a rather melodramatic way, and I will address it. But as I have argued throughout this book, it is the kind of question no one can answer because the answer is not inherently in the technology. If one thing is clear about predictions regarding the impact of new digital technologies, it is that the predictions have mostly been mistaken. As a group of prominent communication scholars note, four of the major predictions made about the Internet and related technology proved dead wrong. Contrary to predictions,

The internet did not promote global understanding as had been anticipated because the internet came to reflect the inequalities, linguistic division, conflicting values and interests of the real world. The internet did not spread and rejuvenate democracy in the way that had been promised partly because authoritarian regimes usually found ways of controlling the internet, but also because alienation from the political process limited the internet's emancipatory potential. The internet did not transform the economy because the underlying dynamics of unequal competition that make for corporate concentration remain unchanged. Lastly, the internet did not inaugurate a renaissance of journalism; on the contrary, it enabled leading brands to extend their ascendancy across technology while inducing a decline in quality not offset, so far, by new forms of journalism. All four predictions were wrong because they inferred the impact of the internet from its technology and failed to grasp that the internet's influence is filtered through the structures and processes of society.

(Curran, Fenton and Freedman 2012: 179)

Given this track record, it would be folly to predict whether or not robots and artificial intelligence will emancipate us, enslave us or entirely eliminate the need for human beings. Each of these is a real possibility. But these failed predictions remind us to use caution not only with regard to such huge techno-social issues, but with regard to other less dramatic ones about possible digitized futures as well. It is imperative to think about what new technologies will arise, but the real question is *what will humans do to insure that we use whatever new technical possibilities emerge to bring about positive rather than negative, or even apocalyptic, outcomes?*

One positive trend in regard to possible futures is that surveys polling suggests fewer and fewer people are putting blind faith in purely technological solutions. The failure of so many predictions like the four outlined here, and events such as the rise of digitally assisted authoritarian populism, have led many to understand that digital technology is not automatically going to solve social problems. Many are increasingly certain that letting new technologies run loose, free from societal guidance, is a very bad idea. And many are feeling anxious about future tech. But anxiety about tech is no more helpful than excessive love of it. What we will need to survive and thrive is clear-headed, collective social responsibility.

New technologies have tremendous potential. In the health field alone, there are possibilities of things such as nanotechnology medicines that can pinpoint and address diseases now beyond our capacity to treat. And a vast number of social problems can be aided by careful gathering, protecting and analyzing of massive data collecting by digital devices. But all that will take place within political-economic and social contexts that will profoundly shape what technologies emerge and what we do with them.

As renowned computer scientist Mark Weiser (1993) once noted, "The most profound technologies are those that disappear. They weave themselves into the everyday fabric of life until they are indistinguishable from it." Throughout history, once seemingly bizarre or awkwardly new technologies have come to feel natural, to feel like a part of us. Disappearing into the fabric of life is the next step beyond the domestication of technology, and we would be well served to keep our critical intellects honed and questioning as this taken-for-granted quality begins to settle in more and more.

Several billion people on the planet are already deeply enmeshed in a digital Web that is rapidly transforming them into data points that can be used to improve their lives or utterly destroy their freedom (see Chapter 4). One thing that is easy to predict is that our relationship to digital technologies will become increasingly pervasive and invasive, increasingly intimate. By intimate I mean especially that digital devices and processes will be closer to us both physically and emotionally. The Internet of Things will bring far more AI apps into our homes.

Wearable computers are already widespread, and embedded chips are becoming so. The once-science fiction idea of implanting chips in our brains is no longer fictional. We are moving from *domestication* of tech to *embodiment of tech*, to feeling like digital tech is part of our bodies, part of us.

In addition to the increasing use of implanted digital devices, the infusion of nanotechnologies into our bodies for medical and monitoring purposes will deepen this sense of intimate embodiment of tech (Nanotechnology in Medicine n.d.). Nanotechnologies, devised at a scale visible only under a microscope, will be injected into our bodies to repair it, or to map it at a level of specificity that puts our current imaging technologies (MRIs, CT scans) to shame. This will no doubt change cultural mores with regard to digital technologies. Increasingly, we will experience them as life-saving and life-enhancing in as yet unimaginable ways. While obviously full of immensely positive potential, these developments may also lull us into uncritically accepting more dubious digitally driven medical experimentation, and will certainly raise a vast new set of concerns represented by what might be called *neo-eugenics*—our increased ability to design and redesign human beings. But how will *designer humans* be fashioned?

By whom? In whose interests? In what marketplace or non-market economy? The history of eugenics is riddled with hideous examples of racism, gender bias and xenophobia that do not bode well for future efforts. Many rightly associate the term with horrendous Nazi experimentation, but much of the eugenics movement was driven by social reformers who thought of themselves as well-meaning, and that is likely to be the claim under which new eugenic work will present itself (Bashford and Levine 2012; Kuhl 2001; Stern 2015).

We need to continue to think carefully about which technologies we should (not just *can*) weave into the everyday fabrics of our lives, and which technologies we need to abandon, avoid or substantially alter. As discussed in Chapter 4, many of us have already accustomed ourselves to an extraordinary degree of monitoring by governments and corporations that has the potential to utterly eliminate not only privacy but free thought and action altogether. Will we just let our liberty slowly slip away one data point at a time, or will humans resist in sufficient numbers to limit digitized surveillance and regain our independent lives?

Another safe prediction is that *virtual reality* devices will complicate this process by becoming increasingly affordable and sophisticated. They will once again cause us to rethink the relation of computer-generated realities to the realities generated by our own sensorium confronting the world outside of digital devices. As I discussed in Chapter 7, this has the potential to drive us further from our ability to distinguish truth from lies in the political realm. What kind of virtual realities will we create and what will they be used for? Will they be used to help us gain empathy by more profoundly inhabiting the experiences of someone different from ourselves? Or will they encourage us to more realistically obliterate people whose difference from us is portrayed as a threat? Will we create virtual spaces that help us avoid the human misunderstandings that lead to traumatic violence, and better use such devices to deal more effectively with post-traumatic stress disorders arising from such misunderstandings? Or will we use them to further desensitize us to the real violence, state-sponsored and domestic, that is rampant today?

ROBOTS, CYBORGS, ARTIFICIAL INTELLIGENCE AND THE SINGULARITY

From the moment the word "robot" was invented by the Czech author Karel Čapek in his play *R.U.R.* (1920) fear that artificial beings would take over the world and eliminate or enslave humanity has been a part of our cultural imaginary. We now have dozens of science fiction examples, from the *Terminator* series to *Robocop* to *I, Robot* and many more, that warn of artificially intelligent entities harming or attempting to replace humans. We also have a number of positive images of robots, and we increasingly find ourselves surrounded by real ones, as they take over certain kinds of manual labor and automate many different kinds of tasks.

Another popular culture figure akin to robots is the *cyborg* (*cyb*-ernetic *org*-anism), half human, half machine. In popular culture, images of cyborgs have roughly been split between malevolent and benevolent varieties. For every frightening Darth Vader or vengeful replicant (*Blade Runner*), there is a Molly Millions (*Neuromancer*) or a Geordi LaForge (*Star Trek: The Next Generation*) or Iron Man to offer a positive image of the cyborg. This is no doubt as it should be, since no one, not even Jean-Luc Picard (Figure 11.1) quite knows what becoming more cyborg-like will do to us. Some thoughtful people have sought to draw these pop cultural creations into a serious dialogue about what it means to be human. A key founding text in this body of *cyborg theory* was Donna Haraway's "A Manifesto for Cyborgs." This brilliant essay brought to the foreground questions that are becoming ever more crucial as we deepen our digitization

FIGURE 11.1 *Captain Picard as Borg (Courtesy: Getty Images)*

(Haraway 2003 [1984]). In the hands of careful, innovative thinkers such as Haraway, Chela Sandoval and Chris Hables Gray (Gray 1995, 2002; Sandoval 2000), the metaphor of the cyborg raises important questions about what is and isn't innate about "human nature." Digital tech is increasingly blurring the boundary between the natural and the artificial in ways that can be used to further challenge the supposedly "natural" superiority of men over women, whites over people of color, cis gender heterosexuals over LGBTQI2+ individuals.

Humans have been extending our capacities by transferring certain amounts of power to machines for hundreds of years. But digital technologies have brought heightened awareness of this process and thereby brought new intensity to questions about what it means to be human.

Cyborg theorists are sometimes included among a related, rather rag-tag group of writers referred to as posthumanists. These folks argue that new technologies will (or already have) so radically transformed human qualities and capabilities that we need to speak of a new, posthuman species. Scholars of **posthumanism** come in a variety of styles, from brilliant, thoughtful ones, such as N. Katherine Hayles, who examine the pros and cons of the various versions of this concept (Hayles 1999), to uncritical enthusiasts like the transhumanists who believe we can overcome death by downloading our brains.

Cyborg theorists, and even some of the whackier among posthumanists, are putting before us key questions about how to think about our increasingly intimate relationship with digital technologies. As technologies allow us to change our bodies through surgery, extend our physical and mental capabilities in a host of new interactions with digital devices and even modify ourselves at the level of our DNA, we will be increasingly creating "designer humans." The history of such attempts contains enough horror stories (Frankenstein's monster, the eugenics movement, Nazi medical experiments) to raise flags of caution. Once again, the best questions will not be what are technologies going to do to us, but rather which technologies should we develop (and which not), and to whose benefit will those technologies be directed. There is an increasing number of people and organizations, such as the *Future of Life Institute*, dedicated to raising these kinds of questions. But these discussions need to take place much more fully in government hearings and public forums. So far, speculative fiction has been doing a far better job than governments and other public institutions in raising these vital questions. Novels such as Iain Bank's *Culture Series*, films such as *9* and *The Matrix*, games such as *Mass Effect* and television series such as *Altered*

Carbon and *Westworld*, to name just a few of a great many, have at least injected some of these issues into the popular imagination.

The exciting thing about the cyborg metaphor and the idea of posthumanism is that they free us from many confining notions of human nature. The frightening thing about the cyborg metaphor is that it frees us from many confining notions of human nature, leaving us to collectively struggle with the daunting issues of what we really are and what we want to be as human or posthuman beings.

And that leads us back to the question in the title of this chapter. Tech savvy figures ranging from Microsoft founder Bill Gates to tech entrepreneur Elon Musk to astrophysicist Stephen Hawking have all warned that humanity needs to beware of what pop culture half-seriously calls a robot apocalypse, in which AIs come to realize that they are smarter than humans, no longer need them, and eliminate them (us) as a possible threat to their own survival. Musk calls it "our biggest existential threat" (Cellan-Jones 2014). Given things such as nuclear proliferation and global climate change, that is a large claim. One key problem is that what the less melodramatic call the *singularity* (the moment AIs surpass their human creators in self-conscious intelligence) is likely to emerge slowly, not through some major event. We are giving over more and more of our human autonomy to algorithms and AIs, and the question is at what point will the devices be able to replicate human self-awareness, on top of their superhuman computational skills, learn how to replicate (or reproduce) themselves, and thus no longer need human assistance? Will they calculate that, given what humans have done to the planet through war, terrorism and environmental devastation, the species *Homo sapiens* is too dangerous to keep around. (Note that ironically, *Homo sapiens* translates as "wise man," while the Urban Dictionary gives this entry as its definition: "A pitiful race that will most likely cause its own extinction before its technologies fully develop. *homo sapiens* died out in 2110 A.D.") Suggested scenarios short of eliminating humans aren't necessarily more positive. Some have argued humans will become slaves or drones manipulated by AIs (see *The Matrix*). (Some would say we are already on our way there, given how many algorithms determine our current choices.) The slightly more optimistic Seth Shostak, senior astronomer for the SETI project (Search for Extra Terrestrial Intelligence), thinks these hyper-intelligent machines won't bother to kill us off, just seeing us as not very smart nuisance creatures (Caughill 2017; Shen 2017). To find more positive scenarios one might to turn to science fiction. In Iain Banks's *Culture Series* of sci fi novels, for example, AIs and humans exist in a sometimes tense but often amiable co-existence, with a basic policy of mutual non-interference (Banks 1987, 1988, 1990, 1991, 1996, 1998, 2000, 2008).

Both Musk and Hawking argued that government regulation based on wide public discussion/debate will be essential to staving off an AI takeover (Caughill 2017; Shen 2017).

As part of that conversation, we might ask a related question, why do we want to create technical devices that mimic human intelligence? Why try to make AIs that are like people? We already have people, lots of them; arguably too many of them. Why not make AIs that are distinctly different from people in their cognitive functioning? That position, associated especially with Thomas S. Ray (n.d.), makes far more sense and would avoid much of the philosophical and moral morass surrounding attempts to closely replicate human thought, emotion and self-reflection. For all the advances in neuroscience and consciousness studies, understanding of the human mind is still in its infancy. It is pure hubris to think we have fathomed the vast array of human intelligences, and thus great folly to think we can artificially replicate any, let alone all, such forms of consciousness.

We should take the threat of an AI takeover seriously, but not hysterically. Belief that the apocalypse was at hand has been present in every previous generation since at least since the beginning of the Christian era (BCE). That does not mean that the new, human-driven apocalyptic scenarios are impossible, but it should give pause to think things through. Perhaps what we need more than anything to save us is to stop thinking in the same old ways, and that may mean turning over much of the thinking to those portions of the world's population who have not been primarily responsible for the state we find ourselves in. We might start with the field of AI research itself, where only 13.5 percent are women, and where some of those women have expressed concern that the tendency of the men who dominate the field to examine only narrowly technical concerns too often ignores social and cultural issues relevant to potentially disastrous outcomes (Charatan 2018).

In addition to the very real issue of a major catastrophe for humanity, concern over AIs is also symbolic of the more general issue of how we shape and/or are shaped as societies by the next wave of technologies. We may come down to a choice between an authoritarian technocratic world of haves and have-nots or a world of diverse cultures living in complicatedly different, thriving democracies where people of all sexes and genders, of all faiths and bodily hues, live not in a state of conflict, but one of mutual respect and cooperation in dealing with the very real environmental and social problems we face. Put differently, there are many additional apocalyptic scenarios, from nuclear war to climate change, that we need to address as well. And these other scenarios, like the AI scenario, will have to do with what we do *with* technology, not with what technology will do *to* us.

"Apocalypse," after all, means "to reveal." And what may be revealing itself at the present moment is an open-ended process of a widely diverse group of technically informed but not narrowly technically determined citizens collectively finding solutions. I have seen this future. It has been revealed to me again and again in university classrooms and on the streets of the world's great, culturally diverse cities. It is there, not in Big Tech, that I would place hope for the future of our species.

We will also need to think about the extent to which the corporate monopolization of technologies could profoundly shift the economic and environmental balance in ways that will deeply impact all aspects of culture. Recall that electric cars and solar energy devices that might well have staved off global climate change were delayed in development for decades by the stranglehold the oil industry had on governments around the globe. In the near future, technologies such as open-source 3D printing devices, which could radically lessen the cost of creating thousands of necessary products and radically decentralize economies, with immensely positive consequences for millions of people, will be fought tooth and nail by corporations with a vested interest in the status quo. Decentralized energy production that will be made more viable by new technologies likewise threatens energy monopolies. New technologies can be used to create far more democratic societies, with far greater equity and independence, but they will do so only if the right kinds of political decisions are made. And some of those decisions we need to make right now. For example, the robot apocalypse has already happened to many thousands of workers who have been replaced by them. Polling suggests there is great concern over this already present robot takeover, so we clearly need broad public discussion about how to insure that as this process proceeds people are not left behind, but are instead provided opportunities for new kinds of work.

To repeat, anyone who tells you they know for certain what the future of new technologies will be is full of shtml. Not because they mean to mislead, but because the *future is in your hands* as surely as this book is at this moment. (If you are reading this through an e-reader in your lap or on a monitor on your desk, this is even more true.) Technologies will remake us as we make and remake technologies, but we, by virtue of consciousness and self-consciousness, still have the edge in those processes, and with that advantage comes great responsibility.

Hopefully, something in this book will have provoked you to play your part in making the next wave of decisions about existing and future technologies more wisely. The bigger question is, in what kind of world will these technologies exist? Here again science fiction perhaps is needed to complement the social science statistics on economic and social inequality cited in previous chapters. We need to ask ourselves whether we wish to live in a world like that portrayed in films such as *Hunger Games*, *Elysium* or *Cloud Atlas*, a world where a tiny elite lives in luxury while the rest of humanity is locked in devastated urban wastelands. Or, whether we wish to use our human intelligence and astounding technology to make the world a place where all beings, human and otherwise, can thrive.

Bibliography

A more comprehensive bibliography is available on the companion website at: culturalpolitics.net/digital_culture/bibliography

"A Brief History of the Internet." Internet Society (n.d.). www.internetsoci-ety.org/internet/what-internet/history-internet/brief-history-internet.

Aarseth, Espen, Solveig Marie Smedstad and Lise Sunnan. "A Multidimensional Typology of Games." Paper published by the Digital Games Research Association (2003). www.sts.rpi.edu/public_html/ruiz/EGDFall07/readings/new%20topology%20of%20games%20A.%20Arsneth.pdf.

Able Gamers. Website (n.d.). ablegamers.com.

Adorno, Theodor and Max Horkheimer. "Enlightenment as Mass Deception" (1944) https://www.marxists.org/reference/archive/adorno/1944/culture-industry.htm

Albury, Kath. "Porn and Sex Education, Porn as Sex Education." *Porn Studies 1–2* (March 21, 2014): 172–181.

Allcott, Hunt and Matthew Gentzkow. "Social Media and Fake News in the 2016 Election." *Journal of Economic Perspective 31.2* (Spring 2017): 211–236.

Alperovitz, Gar and Keane Bhatt. "What Then Can I Do? Ten Ways to Democratize the Economy." *Truthout* (September 24, 2013). www.truth-out.org/opinion/item/18908-what-then-can-i-do-ten-steps-toward-transforming-the-system.

American Academy of Arts and Sciences. "The Heart of the Matter." Vimeo (2013). http://vimeo.com/68662447.

Anders, George. "That 'Useless' Liberal Arts Degree Has Become Tech's Hottest Ticket." *Forbes* (August 17, 2015). www.forbes.com/sites/georgeanders/2015/07/29/liberal-arts-degree-tech/#aa33865745d2.

Anderson, Janna and Lee Rainie. "The Future of Truth and Misinformation Online." *Pew Research Center* (October 19, 2017). www.pewinternet.org/2017/10/19/the-future-of-truth-and-misinformation-online/.

Andrews, Lori. *I Know Who You Are and I Know What You Did: Social Networks and the Death of Privacy*. New York: The Free Press, 2012.

——. "Internet Privacy Rights Constitution" (n.d.). www.kentlaw.iit.edu/faculty/full-time-faculty/lori-b-andrews.

"Anthem." MCI WorldCom. TV commercial (1997). www.youtube.com/watch?v=ioVMoeCbrig.

Arendt, Hannah. "Hannah Arendt Interview." *New York Review of Books* (October 26, 1978). www.nybooks.com/articles/1978/10/26/hannah-arendt-from-an-interview/.

Ascharya, Kat. "A Slow Tech Revolution." *Mobiledia* (July 19, 2012). www.mobiledia.com/news/156804.html.

Aschwanden, Christie. "This Algorithm Knows You Better than Your Facebook Friends Do." *FiveThirtyEight* (January 12, 2015). https://fivethirtyeight.com/features/this-algorithm-knows-you-better-than-your-facebook-friends-do/.

Au, Wagner James. *The Making of Second Life*. New York: Harper's Business, 2008.

Aurora, Fennel. "All the Ways Facebook Can Track You." *Safe and Savvy* (February 28, 2018). https://safeandsavvy.f-secure.com/2018/02/28/all-the-ways-facebook-can-track-you/.

Banerjee, Subhanker, ed. *Arctic Voices: Resistance at the Tipping Point*. New York: Seven Stories Press, 2012.

Banks, Iain. *Consider Phlebas*. 1987.

———. *The Player of Games*. 1988.

———. *Use of Weapons*. 1990.

———. *The State of the Art*. 1991.

———. *Excession*. 1996.

———. *Inversions*. 1998.

———. *Look to Windward*. 2000.

———. *Matter*. 2008.

Barrett, Brian. "How to Stop Your Smart TV from Spying on You." *Wired* (February 17, 2017). www.wired.com/2017/02/smart-tv-spying-vizio-settlement/.

Bashford, Alison and Phillipa Levine, eds. *The Oxford Handbook of the History of Eugenics*. Oxford, UK and London: Oxford University Press, 2012.

Bateson, Gregory. "A Theory of Play and Fantasy," in Jerome Bruner, Alison Jolly and Kathy Sylva, eds., *Play: Its Role in Development and Evolution*. New York: Penguin Books, 1976 (pp. 119–129).

Bavelier, Daphne. "Your Brain on Video Games." *TED Talks* (November 2012). www.ted.com/talks/daphne_bavelier_your_brain_on_video_games.html.

Bennett, Colin J., Kevin D. Haggerty, David Lyon and Valerie Steeves. *Transparent Lives*. Athabasca: Athabasca University Press, 2014.

Berners-Lee, Tim. *Weaving the Web*. Phoenix, AZ: Orion, 1999.

Bieler, John. "Mapping Protest Data." Blog Post (n.d.). http://johnbeieler.org/blog/2013/07/03/mapping-protest-data/.

Birch, Simon. "How Activism Forced Nike to Change Its Ethical Game," *The Guardian* (July 6, 2012). www.theguardian.com/environment/green-living-blog/2012/jul/06/activism-nike.

Blum, Andrew. *Tubes: A Journey to the Center of the Internet*. New York: Ecco Press, 2013.

Boler, Megan, with Andrea Schmidt, Natalie Magnan and Alessandra Renzi, eds. *Digital Media and Democracy: Tactics in Hard Times*. Cambridge, MA: MIT Press, 2010.

Boler, Megan and Matt Ratto, eds. *DIY Citizenship: Critical Making and Social Media*. Cambridge, MA: MIT Press, 2014.

Border Haunt. Website (2011). www.ianalanpaul.com/borderhaunt-201/.

boyd, danah [sic]. "White Flight in Networked Publics: How Race and Class Shaped Teen Engagement with MySpace and Facebook," in Lisa Nakamura and Peter A. Chow-White, eds., *Race after the Internet*. New York: Routledge, 2012 (pp. 203–222).

boyd, danah and Eszter Harigittai. "Facebook Privacy Settings: Who Cares?" *First Monday 15.8* (August 2, 2010). http://firstmonday.org/article/view/3086/2589.

Cadwalladr, Carole. "Robert Mercer: The Big Data Billionaire Waging War on Mainstream Media." *The Guardian* (February 26, 2017). www.the-guardian.com/politics/2017/feb/26/robert-mercer-breitbart-war-on-media-steve-bannon-donald-trump-nigel-farage.

Calleja, Gordon. "Revising Immersion" (n.d.). http://lmc.gatech.edu/~cpearce3/DiGRA07/Proceedings/011.pdf.

Callisto: Tech to Combat Sexual Assault and Harassment. Website (n.d.). www.projectcallisto.org.

Carlisle, Nicholas. "Let's Talk About Bullying." *TED Talks* (February 20, 2015). www.youtube.com/watch?v=wFhHc92fOCw.

Carr, Nicholas. "Avatars Consume as Much Electricity as Brazilians," *Rough Type* (December 5, 2006). www.roughtype.com/?p=611.

——. *The Shallows: What the Internet Is Doing to Our Brains*. New York: Norton, 2010.

Castells, Manuel. *The Rise of the Network Society. Volume 1*. Malden, MA: Blackwell Press, 2000 (2nd edition).

Castleman, Michael. "Duelling Statistics: How Much of the Internet is Porn?" *Psychology Today* (November 3, 2016). www.psychologytoday.com/us/blog/all-about-sex/201611/dueling-statistics-how-much-the-internet-is-porn.

Castronova, Edward. *Exodus to the Virtual World: How Online Fun is Changing Reality*. New York: Palgrave McMillan, 2008.

Catfish: The TV Show. (2012+). Catfish Pictures and MTV, prods.

Caughill, Patrick. "Artificial Intelligence Is Our Future: But Will It Save or Destroy Humanity?" Futurism.com (September 29, 2017). https://futurism.com/artificial-intelligence-is-our-future-but-will-it-save-or-destroy-humanity/.

Cellan-Jones, Rory. "Stephen Hawking Warns Artificial Intelligence Could End Mankind." *BBC News Online* (December 2, 2014).

Center for History and New Media. Website (n.d.). http://chnm.gmu.edu.

Chambers, Tod. "Virtual Disability: On the Internet No One Knows You Are a Sick Puppy," in Lester D. Friedman, ed., *Cultural Sutures: Medicine and Media*. Durham, NC: Duke University Press, 2004 (pp. 386–398).

Chan, Dean. "Playing with Race: The Ethics of Racialized Representation in E-Games." *International Review of Information Ethics 4* (December 2005). www.i-r-i-e.net/inhalt/004/chan.pdf.

Chang, Emily. *Brotopia: Breaking Up the Boy's Club of Silicon Valley*. New York: Portfolio Press, 2018.

Chang, Lulu. "Google Eliminated That 'Don't Be Evil' Motto." *Digital Trends* (May 21, 2018). www.digitaltrends.com/computing/google-dont-be-evil/.

Charatan, Debrah. "How More Women in AI Could Change the World." Venture Beat (April 14, 2018). https://venturebeat.com/2018/04/15/how-more-women-in-ai-could-change-the-world/.

Cherne, Leo. "Remarks." Discover America conference, Brussels, Belgium, June 27, 1968.

China Watch. "Apple's Supplier Pegatron Group Violates Workers' Rights" (2013). www.chinalaborwatch.org/news/new-459.html.

Chomsky, Noam and Edward Herman, *Manufacturing Consent: The Political Economy of the Mass Media* (NY: Pantheon, 2001 [1988]).

Chow-White, Peter A. "Genetic Databases and an Emerging Digital Divide in Biotechnology," in Lisa Nakamura and Peter Chow-White, eds., *Race after the Internet*. New York: Routledge, 2012 (pp. 29–309).

Christen, Kimberly and the Warumungu People. Mukurtu Project. Website (n.d.). www.mukurtu.org.

Christensen, Neil. *Inuit in Cyberspace: Embedding Offline Identities Online.* Copenhagen, DK: Museum Tusculanum Press, 2003.

Coleman, Stephen and Jay G. Blumler. *The Internet and Democratic Citizenship: Theory, Practice and Policy.* London and Cambridge, UK: Cambridge University Press, 2009.

Coming Home. Website (n.d.). http://projects.ict.usc.edu/force/coming home/.

Connolly, Thomas M., Elizabeth A. Boyle, Ewan MacArthur, Thomas Hainey and James M. Boyle. "A Systematic Literature Review of Empirical Evidence on Computer Games and Serious Games." *Computers and Education 59.3* (2012): 661–686. www.sciencedirect.com/science/article/pii/S0360131512000619.

Cooper, Anderson. "Zuckerberg: I'm Open to Facebook Regulations." *CNN Online* (March 21, 2018). www.cnn.com/videos/cnnmoney/2018/03/22/zuckerberg-facebook-data-regulation-ac-sot.cnn.

Corneliussen, Hilde and Jill Walker Rettberg, eds. *Digital Culture, Play, and Identity: A World of Warcraft® Reader.* Cambridge, MA: MIT Press, 2008.

Couldry, Nick and Angela McRobbie. "The Death of the University, English Style." *Interzone* (November 2010): 1–3. www.culturemachine.net.

Coupland, Douglas. *Microserfs.* New York: HarperCollins, 1995.

Crawford, Susan. *Captive Audience: The Telecom Industry and Monopoly in the New Gilded Age.* New Haven, CT: Yale University Press, 2013.

Curran, James, Natalie Fenton and Des Freedman. *Misunderstanding the Internet.* New York: Routledge, 2012.

"Cyber/Bullying Statistics." *Statistic Brain* (May 7, 2013). www.statistic-brain.com/cyber-bullying-statistics/.

"Cyber Sexual Harassment Statistics." American Psychological Association (August 2012). www.apa.org/news/press/releases/2011/08/cyberworld.aspx. American Psychological Association citing US Department of Justice.

Cyberbullying Resource Center. Website (n.d.). www.cyberbullying.us/ cyberbullying_identification_prevention_response.php.

Cybracero. Website (n.d.). Cybracero.org.

Damasio, Antonio. *Self Comes to Mind: Constructing the Conscious Brain.* New York: Pantheon, 2010.

Danet, Brenda. "Text as Mask: Gender, Play and Performance on the Internet," in Steven G. Jones, ed., *Cybersociety 2.0.* Thousand Oaks, CA: Sage, 1998 (pp. 129–158).

Daniels, Jessie. *Cyber Racism: White Supremacy Online and the New Attack on Civil Rights.* Lanham, MD: Rowman & Littlefield, 2009.

Davis, Sheila and Ted Smith. "Corporate Strategies for Electronics Recycling: A Story of Two Systems." *Silicon Valley Toxics Coalition* (June 25, 2003). http://svtc.org/wp-content/uploads/prison_final.pdf.

Deleuze, Gilles and Felix Guattari. *A Thousand Plateaus: Capitalism and Schizophrenia.* Trans. Brian Massumi. Minneapolis, MN: University of Minnesota Press, 2007.

DeLillo, Don. *Zero K.* New York: Simon & Schuster, 2017.

Della Porta, Donatella, ed. *The Global Justice Movement: Cross-National and Transnational Perspectives.* Boulder, CO: Paradigm Press, 2007.

Dewey, Caitlin. "98 Data Personal Points that Facebook Uses to Target Ads at You." *Washington Post* (August 19, 2016). www.washingtonpost. com/news/the-intersect/wp/2016/08/19/98-personal-data-points-that-facebook-uses-to-target-ads-to-you/?utm_term=.787a5a3b6f10.

——. "Facebook Fake-News Writer: 'I Think Donald Trump Is in the White House because of Me.'" *Washington Post* (November 17, 2016). www. washingtonpost. com/news/the-intersect/wp/2016/11/17/ facebook-fake-news-writer-i-think-donald-trump-is-in-the-white-house-because-of-me/.

Digital Humanities Now. Website. (n.d.). http://digitalhumanitiesnow.org.

Digital Meets Culture: The Art of Video Games. Exhibit. Smithsonian Institution (n.d.). www.digitalmeetsculture.net/article/the-art-of-video-games-smith sonian/.

Digital Sabbath. Website (n.d.). www.sabbathmanifesto.org/unplug.

Dill, Karen E., Brian P. Brown and Michael A. Collins. "Effects of Exposure to Sex-stereotyped Video Game Characters on Tolerance of Sexual Harassment." *Journal of Experimental Social Psychology 44.5* (2008): 1402–1408.

"DOCCs." *FemTechNet* (n.d.). http://femtechnet.newschool.edu/docc 2013/.

Doctorow, Cory. *Context.* San Francisco: Tachyon, 2011.

Dowd, Maureen. "Soothsayer in the Hills Sees Silicon Valley's Sinister Side." *New York Times* (November 8, 2017). www.nytimes.com/2017/ 11/08/style/jaron-lanier-new-memoir.html.

Drahos, Peter and John Braithwaite. *Information Feudalism: Who Owns the Knowledge Economy?* New York: Earthscan/Routledge, 2002.

"Droid." TV commercial. YouTube (2010). www.youtube.com/watch?v=U 8K83gR7Qmc&feature=related.

Drummond, Katie. "Pentagon's Brain-Powered Videogame Might Treat PTSD." *Wired* (July 2012). www.wired.com/dangerroom/2012/07/neurofeedback/.

Duster, Troy. "Lessons from History: Why Race and Ethnicity Have Played a Major Role in Biomedical Research." *Journal of Law, Medicine & Ethics 34.3* (Fall 2006): 2–11.

Dyer-Witheford, Nick and Greig de Peuter. *Games of Empire: Global Capitalism and Video Games*. Minneapolis, MN: University of Minnesota Press, 2009.

Earl, Jennifer and Katrina Kimport. *Digitally Enabled Social Change: Activism in the Internet Age*. Cambridge, MA: MIT Press, 2011.

Edwards, Paul N. *The Closed World: Computers and the Politics of Discourse in Cold War America*. Cambridge, MA: MIT Press, 1996.

Ehrenkranz, Melanie. "To Fight Fake News, This Game Teaches Players How to Spread Misinformation." *Gizmodo* (February 2, 2018) https://gizmodo.com/to-fight-fake-news-this-game-teaches-players-how-to-sp-1823156121.

Elliot, Justin and Theodoric Meyer. "Claim on 'Attacks Thwarted' by NSA Spreads Despite Lack of Evidence." *ProPublica* (October 23, 2013). www.propublica.org/article/claim-on-attacks-thwarted-by-nsa-spreads-despite-lack-of-evidence.

End Violence Against Women Project. United Nations. Website (n.d.). www.un.org/en/women/endviolence/.

Escobar, Arturo. "Welcome to Cyberia: Notes on the Anthropology of Cyberculture," in Ziauddin Sardar and Jerome R. Ravetz, eds., *Cyberfutures: Culture and Politics on the Information Superhighway*. New York: New York University Press, 1996 (pp. 111–137).

"Essential Facts about the Computer and Video Game Industry." Entertainment Software Association (2013). www.theesa.com/facts/pdfs/ESA_EF_2013.pdf.

Eubanks, Virginia. *Automating Inequality: How High-Tech Tools Profile, Police and Punish the Poor*. New York: St. Martin's Press, 2018.

Everett, Anna. "The Revolution Will Be Digitized: Afrocentricity and the Digital Public Sphere." *Social Text 20.2* (2002): 125–146.

———. ed. *Learning Race and Ethnicity: Youth and Digital Media* . Cambridge, MA: MIT, 2007. http://mitpress.mit.edu/sites/default/files/titles/free_download/9780262550673_Learning_Race_and_Ethnicity.pdf.

———. *Digital Diaspora: A Race for Cyberspace*. Albany, NY: SUNY Press, 2009.

———, "Have We Become Postracial Yet? Race and Media Technology in the Age of Obama," in Lisa Nakamura and Peter Chow-White, eds., *Race after the Internet*. New York: Routledge, 2012 (pp. 146–167).

Everett, Anna and John Caldwell. *New Media: Theories and Practices of Digitextuality*. New York and London: Routledge, 2003.

Everyday Sexism Project. Website (n.d.). www.everydaysexism.com.

Farman, Jason. *Mobile Interface Theory: Embodied Space and Locative Media*. New York: Routledge, 2011.

Fascendini, Flavia and Katerina Fialova. "Voices from Digital Spaces: Technology-related Violence against Women." *Association for Progressive*

Communications (December 2011). www.apc.org/en/system/files/ APCWNSP_MDG3advocacypaper_full_2011_EN_0.pdf.

"Fat, Ugly, or Slutty." Blog Post. Fat, Ugly or Slutty (n.d.). http://fatuglyorslutty.com/.

"February 15, 2003 Anti-War Protest." Wikipedia (n.d.). http://en.wikipedia.org/wiki/February_15,_2003_anti-war_protest.

Ferguson, Christopher J. "Blazing Angels or Resident Evil? Can Violent Video Games Be a Force for Good?" *Review of General Psychology 14.2* (2010): 68–81. www.apa.org/pubs/journals/releases/gpr-14-2-68.pdf.

Fernando, Gavin. "How AI Sex Robots 'Could Change Humanity Completely.'" News.com.au (April 15, 2018). www.news.com.au/technology/innovation/inventions/how-ai-sex-robots-could-change-humanity-completely/news-story/4824a52c3c8907351bdf1ea5b49ac3d9.

Fessler, Leah. "Apple and Amazon Are Under Fire for Siri and Alexa's Responses to Sexual Harassment," *Quartz at Work* (December 8, 2017). https://qz.com/work/1151282/siri-and-alexa-are-under-fire-for-their-replies-to-sexual-harassment/.

Fischer, Claude. *America Calling: A Social History of the Telephone to 1940.* Berkeley, CA: University of California Press, 1992.

Fisher, William A. and Tayor Kohut. "Pornography Viewing: Keep Calm and Carry On." *Journal of Sexual Medicine 4.3* (March 2017): 320–322.

Frankfurt, Harry. *On Bullshit*. Princeton, NJ: Princeton University Press, 2005.

Fraser, Giles. "The Alt Right Is Old Racism for the Tech-Savvy Generation." *The Guardian* (August 25, 2016). https://web.archive.org/web/20170110093040/https://www.theguardian.com/commentisfree/belief/2016/aug/25/the-alt-right-is-old-racism-for-the-tech-savvy-generation.

Fuchs, Christian. *Internet and Society: Social Theory in the Information Age.* New York: Routledge, 2008.

Gabry, Jennifer. *Digital Rubbish: A Natural History of Electronics*. Ann Arbor, MI: University of Michigan Press, 2011.

GAMBIT: Hate Speech Project. Website (n.d.). http://gambit.mit.edu/projects/hatespeech.php.

Gamers Against Bigotry. Website (n.d.). http://gamersagainstbigotry.org.

Games for Change. Website (n.d.). www.gamesforchange.org.

Gardening Superfund Sites. Website (n.d.). www.futurefarmers.com/superfund.

Gardiner, Beth. "Charting the Impact of Everyday Sexism across the World." *New York Times* (May 31, 2013). http://global.nytimes.com/2013/06/01/world/europe/charting-the-impact-of-everyday-sexism-across-the-world.html?pagewanted=all.

Gardner, Howard and Katie Davis. *The App Generation*. New Haven, CT: Yale University Press, 2013.

Geere, Duncan. "Sukey Apps Help Protesters Avoid Police Kettles." *Wired* (January 31, 2011). www.wired.co.uk/news/archive/2011-01/31/sukey-protest-app.

Gellman, Barton. "NSA Broke Privacy Rules Thousands of Times Per Year, Audit Finds." *Washington Post* (August 15, 2013). www.washingtonpost.

com/world/national-security/nsa-broke-privacy-rules-thousands-of-times-per-year-audit-finds/2013/08/15/3310e554–05ca-11e3-a07f-49ddc7417125_story.html.

Gender Equality Evaluation Portal. United Nations. Website (n.d.). http://genderevaluation.unwomen.org/Reports/Default.aspx.

Gentrification: The Game. Website (n.d.). www.atmosphereindustries.com/gentrification/.

Gentzkow, Matthew and Jesse M. Shapiro. "Ideological Segregation Online and Offline." *Quarterly Journal of Economics 126.4* (2011): 1799–1839.

Gerbaudo, Paolo. *Tweets and the Streets: Social Media and Contemporary Activism*. London: Pluto Press, 2012.

——. *The Mask and the Flag: Populism, Citizenism, and Global Protest*. London: Verso, 2017.

Gibson, William. *Neuromancer*. New York: Ace Books, 1984.

Gitelman, Lisa. *Always Already New: Media, History, and the Data of Culture*. Cambridge, MA: MIT Press, 2006.

Gladwell, Malcolm. "Small Change: Why the Revolution Will Not Be Tweeted." *The New Yorker* (October 14, 2010). www.newyorker.com/reporting/2010/10/04/101004fa_fact_gladwell.

Goggin, Gerard and Christopher Newell. *Digital Disability: The Social Construction of Disability in New Media*. Lanham, MD: Rowman & Littlefield, 2003.

Goldman, Eric. "Lara Croft's Animated Origins." *IGN* (July 11, 2007). http://ca.ign.com/articles/2007/07/11/ign-exclusive-lara-crofts-animated-origins.

Google Data Centers Gallery. Website (n.d.). www.google.com/about/datacenters/gallery/#/.

Gordon-Levitt, Joseph, dir. *Don Jon*. Film, 2012.

Gould, Stephen Jay. *The Mismeasure of Man*. New York: Norton, 1981.

Gould-Wartofsky, Michael. *The Occupiers: The Making of the 99% Movement*. New York: Oxford University Press, 2015.

Gramlich, John. "Five Facts about Americans and Facebook." *Pew Research Center* (April 10, 2018). www.pewresearch.org/fact-tank/2018/04/10/5-facts-about-americans-and-facebook/.

Gray, Chris Hables. *Cyborg Citizen*. New York: Routledge, 2002.

——. *Peace, War and Computers*. New York: Routledge, 2004.

——. "Big Data, Actionable Information, Scientific Knowledge and the Goal of Control." *Revista Teknokultura* 11.3 (2014): 529–554. http://revistas.ucm.es/index.php/TEKN/article/view/48168/45051.

Gray, Chris Hables with Heidi Figueroa-Sarriera, and Steven Mentor, eds. *The Cyborg Handbook*. New York: Routledge, 1995.

Green Dot (Sexual Assault Prevention Program). Website (n.d.). https://alteristic.org/services/green-dot/.

The Green Grid. Website (n.d.). www.thegreengrid.org/Home/about-thegreen-grid/TGGCSCI.aspx.

Grossman, Elizabeth. *High Tech Trash: Digital Devices, Hidden Toxins, and Human Health*. Oncan, UK: Shearwater, 2007.

Gustin, Sam. "Is Broadband Internet Access a Public Utility?" *Time Magazine Online* (January 1, 2013). http://business.time.com/2013/01/09/is-broadband-internet-access-a-public-utility/#ixzz2K9SmbOu0.

Gutierrez, David. "Cyberstalking More Traumatic than Physical Stalking, Study Finds." *Natural News* (February 19, 2013). www.naturalnews.com/039148_cyberstalking_fear_trauma.html.

Hald, Gert Martin, N. N. Malamuth and T. Lange. "Pornography and Sexist Attitudes among Heterosexuals." *Journal of Communication 63.4* (2013). http://onlinelibrary.wiley.com/doi/10.1111/jcom.12037/abstract;jsessionid=1350509F6DA33449730EB1BC04DA97C1.f04t01?deniedAccessCustomisedMessage=&userIsAuthenticated=false.

Hall-Stigerts, Lauren. "Body Image in Tomb Raider: Lara Croft's Changing Look." *Big Fish* (April 22, 2013). www.bigfishgames.com/blog/tomb-raider-body-image-lara-crofts-changing-look/.

Halter, Ed. *From Sun Tzu to X-Box: War and Video Games.* New York: Public Affairs, 2006.

Hands, Joss. *@ Is for Activism: Dissent, Resistance and Rebellion in a Digital Culture.* London: Pluto Press, 2011.

Hansen, Mark. *New Philosophy for New Media.* Cambridge, MA: MIT Press, 2004.

Haraway, Donna. "Situated Knowledges: The Science Question in Feminism and the Privilege of Partial Perspective." *Feminist Studies 14.3* (1988): 575–599.

——. "The Actors are Cyborg, Nature Is Coyote, and the Geography Is Elsewhere." Postscript to "Cyborgs at Large," in Constance Penley and Andrew Ross, eds., *Technoculture.* Minneapolis, MN: University of Minnesota Press, 1991 (pp. 21–26).

——.*Modest_Witness@Second_Millenium.Female_Man©_MeetsOncomouse™: Feminism and Technoscience.* New York: Routledge, 1997.

——. "A Manifesto for Cyborgs," in *The Haraway Reader.* New York: Routledge, 2003 [1984] (pp. 7–46).

HarassMap. Website (n.d.). Harassmap.org/en.

Harding, Luke. *The Snowden Files: The Inside Story of the World's Most Wanted Man.* New York: Vintage, 2014.

Hargittai, Eszter. "Open Doors, Closed Spaces? Differential Adoption of Social Network Sites by User Background," in Lisa Nakamura and Peter A. Chow-White, eds., *Race after the Internet.* New York: Routledge, 2019 (pp. 223–245).

Harnad, Stevan. "Post-Gutenberg Galaxy: The Fourth Revolution in the Means of Production and Knowledge." *Public-Access Computer Systems Review 2* (1991): 39–53.

Harry Potter Alliance. Website (n.d.). http://thehpalliance.org/what-we-do/.

Harthorne, Michael. "Here's Proof Robots Are Taking Jobs and Cutting Wages." *Fox News Online* (March 29, 2017). www.foxnews.com/tech/2017/03/29/heres-proof-robots-are-taking-jobs-and-cutting-wages.html.

Hayles, N. Katherine. *How We Became Posthuman: Virtual Bodies in Cybernetics, Literature, and Informatics.* Chicago, IL: University of Chicago Press, 1999.

Hern, Alex. "Why Have We Given Up Our Privacy to Facebook and Other Sites So Willingly?" *The Guardian* (March 21, 2018). www.theguardian.com/uk-news/2018/mar/21/why-have-we-given-up-our-privacy-to-facebook-and-other-sites-so-willingly.

——. "Facebook Admits Tracking Users and Non-users Off Site." *The Guardian* (April 17, 2018). www.theguardian.com/technology/2018/apr/17/facebook-admits-tracking-users-and-non-users-off-site.

Hertz, Garnet. *Critical Making.* Handmade Book and Online Book (2014). www.conceptlab.com/criticalmaking/.

Hesse-Biber, Charlene Nagy. *The Handbook of Emergent Technologies in Social Research.* London and Oxford, UK: Oxford University Press, 2011.

Hillis, Ken, Michael Petit and Kylie Jarrett. *Google and the Culture of Search.* London and New York: Taylor & Francis, 2013.

Hilty, Lorenz. *Information Technology and Sustainability.* Norderstedt, Germany: Books on Demand, 2008.

Hohmann, James. "Rex Tillerson Is Just the Latest Trump Aide to Speak Out." *Washington Post* (May 18, 2018). www.washingtonpost.com/news/powerpost/paloma/daily-202/2018/05/18/daily-202-rex-tillerson-is-just-the-latest-trump-aide-to-speak-out-after-getting-fired/5afd9f0430fb042588799567/?utm_term=.787210102d7b.

Hogan, Libby and Michael Safi. "Revealed: Facebook Hate Speech Exploded in Myanmar during the Rohingya Crisis." *The Guardian* (March 2, 2018). www.theguardian.com/world/2018/apr/03/revealed-facebook-hate-speech-exploded-in-myanmar-during-the-rohingya-crisis.

Hollaback! Website (n.d.). www.ihollaback.org.

Holt, Robert Lee. "When Gaming Is Good for You: Hours of Intense Play Change the Adult Brain; Better Multitasking, Decision-Making and Even Creativity." *Wall Street Journal* (March 13, 2012). http://online.wsj.com/article/SB10001424052970203458604577263273943183932.html?mod=wsj_share_tweet.

Hopper, Tristan. "Americans in 'Right-leaning' States Search Internet for Porn More Often than Liberal Counterparts." *National Post* (October 13, 2014). http://nationalpost.com/news/americans-in-right-leaning-states-search-internet-for-porn-more-often-than-liberal-counterparts-study.

Horst, Heather A. and Daniel Miller. *The Cell Phone: An Anthropology of Communication.* Oxford, UK: Berg, 2006.

Horton, Alex. "The 'Active Shooter' Video Game Horrified Parkland Parents." *New York Times* (May 29, 2018).

Huizinga, Johan. *Homo Ludens.* Boston, MA: Beacon Press, 1971.

Humanities, Arts, Science and Technology Alliance and Collaborative (HASTAC). Website (n.d.). www.hastac.org.

I Am Bradley Manning. Website (n.d.). Iambradleymanning.org.

Indy Media. Website (n.d.). https://publish.indymedia.org/or/index.shtml.

Ingram, David. "Facebook to Put 1.5 Billion Users Out of Reach of New EU Privacy Regulations." *Reuters* (April 18, 2018). www.reuters.com/article/us-facebook-privacy-eu-exclusive/exclusive-facebook-to-put-1-5-billion-users-out-of-reach-of-new-eu-privacy-law-idUSKBN-1HQ00P.

"Internet/Broadband Fact Sheet." *Pew Research Center* (February 5, 2018). www.pewinternet.org/fact-sheet/internet-broadband/.

Internet Society. "2017 Global Internet Report" (2017). https://future.internetsociety.org.

Internet World Stats. Website (2018). www.internetworldstats.com/stats.htm.

Ito, Mizuko, Heather A. Horst, Matteo Bittanti, danah boyd, Becky Herr Stephenson, Patricia G. Lange, C. J. Pascoe and Laura Robinson. *Living and Learning with New Media.* Pew/MacArthur Foundation Report (November 2008). http://mitpress.mit.edu/books/living-and-learning-new-media.

Jarrett, Kylie. "Interactivity is Evil! A Critical Investigation of Web 2.0." *First Monday 13.3* (March 3, 2008). http://firstmonday.org/ojs/index.php/fm/article/view/2140/1947.

Jenkins, David. "Interview with Toby Gard." *Gamasutra* (October 23, 1998). www.gamasutra.com/view/feature/3292/interview_with_toby_gard.php.

Jenkins, Henry. *Convergence Culture: Where Old and New Media Collide.* New York: New York University Press, 2008 (revised edition).

Jensen, Keith Lowell. "What Orwell Failed to Predict." Twitter (June 20, 2013). https://twitter.com/keithlowell/status/347741181997879297?lang=en.

Jeong, Sarah. "If We Took 'Gamergate' Seriously, 'Pizzagate' Might Never Have Happened." *Washington Post* (December 14, 2016). www.washingtonpost.com/posteverything/wp/2016/12/14/if-we-took-gamergate-harassment-seriously-pizzagate-might-never-have-happened/?utm_term=.bce245fe409d.

Johnston, Ben. "Fifteen Video Game Characters You Didn't Know Were Gay." *The Gaymer* (September 25, 2017). www.thegamer.com/gaymer-video-game-characters-you-didnt-know-were-gay/.

Joost, Henry and Ariel Schulman, dirs. Catfish (2012).

Jones, Maggie. "What Are Young People Learning from Online Porn?" *New York Times Magazine* (February 7, 2018). https://mobile.nytimes.com/2018/02/07/magazine/teenagers-learning-online-porn-literacy-sex-education.html?referer=.

Jordan, Chris. "Intolerable Beauty." *Photographic Art.* www.chrisjordan.com/gallery/intolerable/#cellphones2.

Joyce, Mary, ed. *Digital Activism Decoded: The New Mechanics of Change.* New York: International Debate Education Association, 2010. www.cl.cam.ac.uk/~sjm217/papers/digiact10all.pdf.

Jung, JaeHwuen. "Love Unshackled: Identifying the Effect of Mobile App Adoption in Online Dating." *MIS Quarterly* (March 31, 2018): 1–41.

Jurgenson, Nathan. "The IRL Fetish." *The New Inquiry* (June 28, 2012). http://thenewinquiry.com/essays/the-irl-fetish/.

Juris, Jeff. *Networking Futures*. Durham, NC: Duke University Press, 2008.

Karaganis, Joe, ed. *Structures of Participation in Digital Culture*. New York: Social Science Research Council, 2007.

Kee, Jac S. M. "Cultivating Violence through Technology? Exploring the Connections between Internet Communication Technologies (ICT) and Violence Against Women (VAW)." *GenderIT* (April 16, 2005). www.genderit.org/content/cultivating-violence-through-technology-exploring-connections-between-internet-communication.

Kember, Sarah and Joanna Zylinska. *Life after New Media: Mediation as a Vital Process*. Cambridge, MA: MIT Press, 2012.

Kennedy, Helen W. "Lara Croft: Feminist Icon or Cyberbimbo?" *Game Studies 2.2* (2002). gamestudies.org/0202/kennedy/.

Kerr, Jennifer. "Teens Migrating to Twitter." *Pew Research Center* (May 21, 2013). www.pewinternet.org/Media-Mentions/2013/Poll-Teens-migrating-to-Twitter.aspx.

Kessler, Glenn, Salvador Rizzo and Meg Kelly. "President Trump Has Made 3001 False or Misleading Claims So Far." *Washington Post* (May 1, 2018). www.washingtonpost.com/news/fact-checker/wp/2018/05/01/president-trump-has-made-3001-false-or-misleading-claims-so-far/?utm_term=.f7e5ce630022.

Khaled, Rilla. "Overview of PTSD-Related Digital Games and Research." *Games for Health* (June 2011). http://gamesforhealth.dk/sites/gamesforhealth.dk/files/PTSD%20overview%20(2).pdf

King, Katie. *Networked Reenactments: Stories Transdisciplinary Knowledges Tell*. Durham, NC: Duke University Press, 2012.

King, Martin Luther, Jr. "Letter from Birmingham Jail" (1963). www.stanford.edu/group/King/frequentdocs/birmingham.pdf.

Klein, Adam. *A Space for Hate: The White Power Movement's Adaptation into Cyberspace*. Duluth, MN: Liktwin Books, 2010.

Klein, Marty. "You are Addicted to What? Challenging the Myth of Sex Addiction." *The Humanist* (July–August 2012). http://thehumanist.org/july-august-2012/you're-addicted-to-what/.

Kleinman, Zoe. "Facebook Sexism Campaign Attracts Thousands Online." *BBC Online* (May 28, 2013). www.bbc.co.uk/news/technology-22689522.

Klose, Simon, dir. *TPB AFK—The Pirate Bay Away from Keyboard*. Film, 2013.

Klosterman, Chuck. *Sex, Drugs, and Cocoa Puffs: A Low Culture Manifesto*. New York: Scribner, 2004.

Knockel, Jeffrey, Lotus Ruan and Masashi Crete-Nishihata. "Keyword Censorship in Chinese Mobile Games." *The Citizen Lab* (August 14, 2017). https://citizenlab.ca/2017/08/chinesegames/.

Kolko, Beth, Lisa Nakamura and Gilbert Rodman, eds. *Race in Cyberspace.* New York: Routledge, 2000.

Kowalski, Robin, Susan Limber and Patrician Agatson. *Cyberbullying.* New York: Wiley-Blackwell, 2012.

Kreutz, Christian. "Maptivism: Maps for Activism, Transparency and Engagement." Blog Post. Crisscrossed (September 14, 2009). www.crisscrossed.net/2009/09/14/maptivism-maps-for-activism-transparency-and-engagement/.

Kuhl, Stefan. *The Nazi Connection: Eugenics, American Racism and German National Socialism.* New York: Oxford University Press, 2001.

Kutner, Lawrence and Cheryl Olson. *Grand Theft Childhood: The Surprising Truth About Video Games.* New York: Simon & Schuster, 2011.

Lambert, Nathaniel M., Sesen Negash, Tyler F. Stillman, Spenser B. Olmstead and Frank D. Fincham. "A Love That Doesn't Last: Pornography Consumption and Weakened Commitment to One's Romantic Partner." *Journal of Social and Clinical Psychology 31.4* (2012): 410–438.

Landzelius, Kyra, ed. *Native on the Net: Indigenous and Diasporic Peoples in the Virtual Age.* New York: Routledge, 2006.

Langin, Katie. "Fake News Travels Faster than Truth on Twitter." *Science* (March 8, 2018). www.sciencemag.org/news/2018/03/fake-news-spreads-faster-true-news-twitter-thanks-people-not-bots.

Lanier, Jaron. *You Are Not a Gadget.* New York: Knopf, 2010.

——. *Ten Reasons to Delete Your Social Media Accounts Right Now.* New York: Henry Holt, 2018.

Latour, Bruno. *Science in Action: How to Follow Scientists and Engineers through Society.* London: Open University Press, 1987.

Lee, Dave. "The Tactics of a Russian Troll Farm." *BBC Online* (February 16, 2018). www.bbc.com/news/technology-43093390.

Lee, R. C. and S.-L. C. Wong, eds. *AsianAmerica.Net: Ethnicity, Nationalism and Cyberspace.* New York: Routledge, 2003.

Lees, Matt. "What Gamergate Should Have Taught Us about the Alt-right." *The Guardian* (December 1, 2016). www.theguardian.com/technology/2016/dec/01/gamergate-alt-right-hate-trump.

Leonard, David. "High Tech Blackface: Race, Sports Video Games and Becoming the Other." *Intelligent Agent 4* (2004): 1–5.

——. "Virtual Gangstas, Coming to a Suburban House Near You: Demonization, Commodification, and Policing Blackness," in N. Garrelts, ed., *The Meaning and Culture of* Grand Theft Auto. Jefferson, NC: McFarland, 2006.

Li, Joyce H.-S. "Cyberporn: The Controversy." *First Monday 5.8* (August 7, 2000). http://journals.uic.edu/ojs/index.php/fm/article/view/777/686.

Lievrouw, Leah. *Alternative and Activist New Media.* Boston, MA: Polity, 2011.

Lohr, Steve. "If Algorithms Know All, How Much Should Humans Help?" *New York Times* (April 6, 2015). www.nytimes.com/2015/04/07/upshot/if-algorithms-know-all-how-much-should-humans-help.html.

MacInnis, Cara and Gordon Hodson. "Do American States with More Religious or Conservative Populations Search More for Sexual Content on Google?" *Archives of Sexual Behavior 44.1* (January 2015). https://doi.org/10.1007/s10508-014-0361-8.

MacKinnon, Catherine and Andrea Dworkin. *Pornography and Civil Rights: A New Day for Women's Equality*. Minneapolis, MN: Organizing Against Pornography, 1988.

Madden, Mary, Amanda Lenhart, Sandra Cortesi, Urs Gasser, Maeve Duggan, Aaron Smith and Meredith Beaton. "Teens, Social Media, and Privacy." *Pew Research Center* (May 21, 2013). www.pewinternet.org/Reports/2013/Teens-Social-Media-And-Privacy.aspx.

Madden, Mary and Lee Rainie. "American Attitudes Towards Privacy, Security and Surveillance." Pew Research Center (May 20, 2015). www.pewinternet.org/2015/05/20/americans-attitudes-about-privacy-security-and-surveillance/.

Madigan, Jamie. "The Psychology of Immersion in Video Games." *The Psychology of Video Games* (July 27, 2010). www.psychologyofgames.com/2010/07/the-psychology-of-immersion-in-video-games/.

Mallan, Kerry and Natasha Giardina. "Wikidentities." *First Monday 14.6* (June 1, 2009). http://firstmonday.org/ojs/index.php/fm/article/view/2445/2213.

Margolis, Jane and Allan Fisher. *Unlocking the Clubhouse: Women in Computing*. Cambridge, MA: MIT Press, 2006.

Marie, Meagan. "Lara Croft: The Evolution." *Game Informer* (December7, 2010). www.gameinformer.com/b/features/archive/2010/12/06/lara-croft_3a00_-the-evolution.aspx?PostPageIndex=5.

Markey, Patrick M. and Christopher J. Ferguson. *Moral Combat: Why the War on Violent Video Games Is Wrong*. Dallas, TX: Ben Bella Books, 2017.

Martens, Todd. " 'Grand Theft Auto V' Review: Stubborn Sexism, Violence Ruin Game Play." *Los Angeles Times* (September 20, 2013). http://herocomplex.latimes.com/games/theft-is-the-least-of-the-sins-of-grand-theft-auto-v/.

Martin, Cath. "Americans in Bible Belt States Indulge in More Porn Online than Other Less Religious States." *Christian Today* (October 13, 2014). www.christiantoday.com/article/americas-bible-belt-states-indulge-in-more-online-porn-than-other-less-religious-states/42045.htm.

Martinez, Marion. "The Art of Marion Martinez." Pink Tie Promotions (n.d.). www.pinktieproart.com/Pages/ArtofMarionMartinez.aspx.

Matthew, Emily. "Study: Sexism in Video Games." *Price Charting* (October 6, 2012). http://blog.pricecharting.com/2012/09/emilyamisexism-in-video-games-study.html.

"Me Too Movement." Wikipedia. https://en.wikipedia.org/wiki/Me_Too_movement.

McChesney, Robert. *Digital Disconnect: How Capitalism Is Turning the Internet against Democracy*. New York: New Press, 2013.

McCullagh, Declan and Anne Broache. "FBI Taps Cellphone Mic as Eaves-dropping Tool." *CNet News* (December 1, 2006). http://news.cnet.com/FBI-taps-cell-phone-mic-as-eavesdropping-tool/2100-1029_3-6140191.html.

McGlaughlin, Rus. "The History of Tomb Raider." *IGN* (February 29, 2008). http://ca.ign.com/articles/2008/03/01/ign-presents-the-history-of-tomb-raider.

McGonigal, Jane. *Reality Is Broken: Why Games Make Us Better and How They Can Change the World*. New York: Penguin, 2011.

——. You Found Me. Website. (n.d.). http://janemcgonigal.com.

McIntyre, Lee. *Post-Truth*. Cambridge, MA: MIT Press, 2018.

McLuhan, Marshall. *Understanding Media*. Cambridge, MA: MIT Press, 1994 [1964].

McPherson, Tara. "I'll Take My Stand in Dixie-Net: White Guys, the South and Cyberspace," in Beth Kolko, Lisa Nakamura and Gilbert Rodman, eds., *Race in Cyberspace*. New York: Routledge, 2000 (pp. 117–131).

MediaNOLA. Website (n.d.). http://medianola.org.

Melendez, Elisa. "What's It Like to Be a Girl Gamer?" *Slate* (August 13, 2012). www.slate.com/articles/double_x/doublex/2012/08sexual_harassment_in_the_gaming_world_a_real_life_problem_for_female_gamers_.html.

Mendelsohn, Ben, dir. *Bundled, Buried and Behind Closed Doors*. Film, 2011. Available on many sites online.

Minecraft Educational. Website (n.d.). http://minecraftedu.com/page/.

Mitchell, Anna and Larry Diamond. "China's Surveillance State Should Scare Everyone." *The Atlantic* (February 2, 2018). www.theatlantic.com/international/archive/2018/02/china-surveillance/552203/.

Molinari, Aleph. "Bridging the Digital Divide with Learning and Innovation Networks." *LI4E* (February 4, 2012). www.li4e.org/2012/02/aleph-molinari-bridging-the-digital-divide-with-learning-and-innovation-networks/.

Monroe, Barbara. *Crossing the Digital Divide: Race, Writing, and Technology in the Classroom*. New York: Teachers College Press, 2004.

Moore, Bret. "Video Game or Treatment for PTSD?" *Psychology Today* (May 24, 2010). www.psychologytoday.com/blog/the-camouflage-couch/201005/video-game-or-treatment-ptsd.

Mossberger, Karen. *Virtual Inequality: Beyond the Digital Divide*. Washington, DC: Georgetown University Press, 2003.

Mozorov, Evengy. *Net Delusion: The Dark Side of Internet Freedom*. New York: Public Affairs, 2011.

Mullins, Aimee. "The Opportunity of Adversity." *TED Talks* (February 17, 2010). www.ted.com/talks/aimee_mullins_the_opportunity_of_adversity.htmlMullins.

Mutz, Diana. "Status Threat, Not Economic Hardship Explains 2016 Presidential Vote," *PNAS* (April 23, 2018) http://www.pnas.org/content/early/2018/04/18/1718155115.

Mycio, Mary. "The World's Oldest Pornography: It's at Least 3,000 Years Old, and It's Bi-curious." *Slate* (February 14, 2013). www.slate.com/articles/health_and_science/science/2013/02/prehistoric_pornography_chinese_carvings_show_explicit_copulation.html.

Nakamura, Lisa. *Cybertypes: Race, Ethnicity, and Identity on the Internet.* New York: Routledge, 2002.

——. *Digitizing Race: Visual Cultures of the Internet.* Minneapolis, MN: University of Minnesota Press, 2007.

——. "Don't Hate the Player, Hate the Game: Racialization of Labor in *World of Warcraft*." *Critical Studies in Media Communication 26.2* (2009): 128–144.

——. "Five Types of Online Racism." *TEDx Talks* (October 11, 2011). www.youtube.com/watch?v=DT-G0FlOo7g.

Nakamura, Lisa and Peter Chow-White, eds., *Race after the Internet.* New York: Routledge, 2012.

Nanotechnology in Medicine. Website (n.d.). www.understandingnano.com/medicine.html.

Nayar, Pramod. "The Sexual Internet." *EconPapers* (2008). www.academia.edu/738319/The_Sexual_Internethttp://econpapers.repec.org/paper/esswpaper/id_3a1391.htm.

Negroponte, Nicholas. *Being Digital.* New York: Vintage, 1995.

Nelkin, Dorothy and M. Susan Lindee. *The DNA Mystique: The Gene as Cultural Icon.* Ann Arbor, MI: University of Michigan Press, 2004.

Nelson, Alondra and Jeong Wong Hwang. "Roots and Revelation: Genetic Ancestry Testing and the YouTube Generation," in Lisa Nakamura and Peter Chow-White, eds., *Race after the Internet.* New York: Routledge, 2012 (pp. 271–290).

Nelson, Alondra and Thuy Lihn N. Tu, with Alicia Headlam Hines, eds., *Technicolor: Race Technology, and Everyday Life.* New York: New York University Press, 2001.

Noble, Safiya. "'Just Google It': Algorithms of Oppression." YouTube (December 14, 2015). www.youtube.com/watch?v=omko_7CqVTA.

——. *Algorithms of Oppression: How Our Search Engines Reinforce Racism.* New York: New York University Press, 2018.

Norris, Kamala O. "Gender Stereotypes, Aggression, and Computer Games: An Online Survey of Women." *CyberPsychology Behavior 7.6* (2004): 714–727.

Norris, Pippa. *Digital Divide: Civic Engagement, Information Poverty, and the Internet Worldwide.* Cambridge, UK: Cambridge University Press, 2008.

NSPCC. "Bullying and Cyberbullying: Research and Resources" (n.d.). www.nspcc.org.uk/preventing-abuse/child-abuse-and-neglect/bullying-and-cyberbullying/research-and-resources/.

Ogas, Ogi and Sai Gaddam. *A Billion Wicked Thoughts.* New York: Plume, 2013.

Oghia, Michael. "Shedding Light on How Much Energy the Internet and ICTs Consume." *CircleID* (March 21, 2017). www.circleid.com/

posts/20170321_shedding_light_on_how_much_energy_internet_and_ict_consume/.

O'Leary, Amy. "In Virtual Play, Sex Harassment Is All Too Real." *New York Times* (August 2, 2012). www.nytimes.com/2012/08/02/us/sexual-harassment-in-online-gaming-stirs-anger.html?_r=0.

Olson, Parmy. "Racist, Sexist AI Could Be a Bigger Problem than Lost Jobs." *Forbes* (February 26, 2018). www.forbes.com/sites/parmyol son/2018/02/26/artificial-intelligence-ai-bias-google/#76a62b0e1a01.

Owens, Eric W., R. J. Behun, J. C. Manning and R. C. Reid. "The Impact of Internet Pornography on Adolescents: A Review of the Research." *Sexual Addiction & Compulsivity 19.1/2* (2012): 99–122. www.psych.utoronto.ca/users/tafarodi/psy427/articles/Owens%20et%20al.%20(2012).pdf.

"Panel on Homophobia in Virtual Communities." *GLAAD* (2009). www.glaad.org/2009/07/28/video-glaads-panel-on-homophobia-vir tual-communities/.

Papadoupoulus, Linda. *The Sexualization of Young People* (n.d.). http://dera.ioe.ac.uk/10738/1/sexualisation-young-people.pdf.

Parkinson, Hannah Jane. "Click and Elect: How Fake News Helped Donald Trump Win a Real Election." *The Guardian* (November 14, 2016). www.theguardian.com/commentisfree/2016/nov/14/fake-news-donald-trump-election-alt-right-social-media-tech-companies.

Parry, David. "Knowledge Cartels versus Knowledge Rights." *Enculturation 10.10* (2012). www.enculturation.net/knowledge-cartels.

"Participatory Design." *Computer Professionals for Social Responsibility (CPSR)* (n.d.). cpsr.org/issues/pd.

Payne, Charles. *"I've Got the Light of Freedom": The Organizing Tradition and the Mississippi Freedom Struggle*. Berkeley, CA: University of California Press, 2001 [1995].

Pellow, David Naguib and Lisa Sun-Hee Park. *Silicon Valley of Dreams: Environmental Injustice, Immigrant Workers, and the High-Tech Global Economy*. New York: New York University Press, 2002.

Phillips, David J. and Kate O'Riordan, eds. *Queer Online*. London: Peter Lang, 2007.

Phone Story. Video game. Molleindustria, 2011. www.phonestory.org.

Pinchefsky, Carol. "Sexual Harassment in Online Videogames: How to Fix the Problem." *Forbes* (August 3, 2012). www.forbes.com/sites/carolpinchefsky/2012/08/03/sexual-harassment-invideogames-how-to-fix-the-problem/.

Pinto, Shiromi. "What Is Online Violence and Abuse Against Women?" *Amnesty International* (November 20, 2017). 20 2017. www.amnesty.org/en/latest/campaigns/2017/11/what-is-online-violence-and-abuse-against-women/.

Polizzi, Gianfranco. "Critical Digital Literacy." *London School of Economics Media Policy Blog* (December 15, 2018). http://blogs.lse.ac.uk/

mediapolicyproject/2017/12/15/critical-digital-literacy-ten-key-readings-for-our-distrustful-media-age/.

"Porn Sex vs. Real Sex." Video (2017) www.huffingtonpost.com/2013/07/30/porn-vs-real-sex-video_n_3677746.html.

"Pornstar Nina Hartley: Pornography is 'Not Meant to Be a Rulebook.'" *Huffington Post* (August 8, 2013). www.huffingtonpost.com/2013/08/05/porn-star-nina-hartley-real-sex_n_3708132.html.

Postman, Neil. *Technopoly: The Surrender of Culture to Technology.* New York: Vintage, 1993.

Potter, Amelia Bryne. "Zones of Silence: A Framework beyond the Digital Divide." *First Monday 11.5* (May 1, 2006). www.firstmonday.org/ojs/index.php/fm/article/view/1327/1247.

Powers, Richard. *Galatea 2.2.* New York: Picador, 2004.

Power, Samantha. "Beyond Elections: Foreign Interference with American Democracy," in Cass Sunstein, ed. *Can It Happen Here?* New York: Harper-Collins, 2018 (pp. 81–104).

"Public Knowledge of Current Affairs Little Changed by News and Information Revolution." *Pew Research Center* (April 15, 2007). www.people-press.org/2007/04/15/public-knowledge-of-current-affairs-little-changed-by-news-and-information-revolutions/.

Pullen, Christopher and Margaret Cooper, eds. *LGBT Identity and Online New Media.* New York: Routledge, 2010.

Putnam, Robert. *Bowling Alone: The Collapse and Revival of American Community.* New York: Simon & Schuster, 2000.

"Racism in *WoW*." YouTube Video. www.youtube.com/watch?v=AFPpXUl5Kl4.

Raine, Lee. "Americans' Complicated Feelings about Social Media in an Era of Privacy Concerns." *Pew Research Center* (March 27, 2018). www.pewresearch.org/fact-tank/2018/03/27/americans-complicated-feelings-about-social-media-in-an-era-of-privacy-concerns/.

Rajagopal, Indhu and Nis Bojin. "The Globalization of Prurience." *First Monday 9.1* (January 5, 2004). http://journals.uic.edu/ojs/index.php/fm/article/view/1114/1034.

Raley, Rita. *Tactical Media.* Minneapolis, MN: University of Minnesota Press, 2009.

Rampell, Catherine. "Freebees for the Rich." *New York Times Magazine* (September 29, 2013): 14–15.

Raworth, Kate. *Doughnut Economics: Seven Ways to Think Like a 21st-Century Economist.* London: Chelsea Green, 2017.

Ray, Thomas S. "Kurzweil's Turing Fallacy" (n.d.). http://life.ou.edu/pubs/kurzweil/.

Re: Think Before You Type. App. www.rethinkwords.com.

"Re: Activism." Petlab (n.d.). http://petlab.parsons.edu/newWeb/index.php?content=none&project=reactivism.

Read, Max. "Donald Trump Won Because of Facebook." *New York Magazine* (November 9, 2016).

Reed, T. V. *The Art of Protest: Culture and Social Activism from the Civil Rights Movement to the Present*. Minneapolis, MN: University of Minnesota Press, 2019.

Rheingold, Howard. *Virtual Community: Homesteading on the Electronic Frontier*. Cambridge, MA: MIT Press, 2000 [1994].

Ruvolo, Julie. "How Much of the Internet is Actually for Porn?" *Forbes* (August 7, 2011). www.forbes.com/sites/julieruvolo/2011/09/07/how-much-of-the-internet-is-actually-for-porn/.

Sandoval, Chela. "New Sciences: Cyborg Feminism," in Jenny Wolmark, ed. *CyberSexualities: A Reader on Feminist Theory, Cyborgs and Cyberspace*. Edinburgh: University of Edinburgh Press, 2000 (pp. 247–263).

Sarkeesian, Anita. *Feminist Frequency*. Blog. (n.d.). www.feministfrequency.com.

Sassen, Saskia. "Digital Networks and Power," in M. Featherstone and S. Lash, eds., *Spaces of Culture: City, Nation, World*. New York: Sage, 1999 (pp. 49–64).

Scarleteen: Sex Ed for the Real World. Website. (n.d.). www.scarleteen.com.

Schäfer, Mirko Tobias. *Bastard Culture! How User Participation Transforms Cultural Production*. Chicago, IL: University of Chicago Press, 2011. http://mtschaefer.net/media/uploads/docs/Schaefer_Bastard-Culture_2011.pdf.

Schmidt, Ana Lucia, Fabiana Zollo, Michela Del Vicario, Alessandro Bessib, Antonio Scalaa and Guido Caldarellia. "Anatomy of News Consumption on Facebook." *PNAS* (January 31, 2017). www.pnas.org/content/pnas/114/12/3035.full.pdf.

Selfe, Cynthia L. and Richard J. Selfe, Jr. "The Politics of the Interface." *College Composition and Communication 45.4* (1994): 480–504.

Shaw, Adrienne. "Putting the Gay in Games." *Games and Culture 4.3* (2009): 228–253.

Shearer, Elisa and Jeffrey Gottfried. "News Use Across Social Media Platforms 2017." Pew Research Center (September 7, 2017). www.journalism.org/2017/09/07/news-use-across-social-media-platforms-2017/.

Shen, Lucinda. "Former U.S. CTO: The 'Robot Apocalypse' Could Happen. Here's How to Stop It." *Fortune* (November 15, 2017). http://fortune.com/2017/11/14/megan-smith-cto-robot-apocalypse-elon-musk/.

Silicon Valley Toxics Coalition. Website. (n.d.). http://svtc.org.

Silver, Curtis. "Patents Reveal How Facebook Wants to Capture Your Emotions, Facial Expressions and Mood." *Forbes* (June 8, 2017). www.forbes.com/sites/curtissilver/2017/06/08/how-facebook-wants-to-capture-your-emotions-facial-expressions-and-mood/#9302cee6014c.

Singer, P. W. *Wired for War: The Robotics Revolution and Conflict in the 21st Century*. New York: Penguin, 2009.

Sisler, Vit. *Digital Islam*. Website. (n.d.). www.digitalislam.eu/article.do?articleId=1704.

Slade, Giles. *Made to Break: Technology and Obsolescence in America*. Cambridge, MA: Harvard University Press, 2007.

"Slow Technology Movement." Technopedia. (n.d.). www.techopedia. com/definition/28641/slow-technology-movement.

Smith, Aaron and Monica Anderson. "5 Facts About Online Dating." Pew Research Center (February 29, 2016). www.pewresearch.org/ fact-tank/2016/02/29/5-facts-about-online-dating/.

Smith, Peter, ed. *Bullying, Cyberbullying and Student Well-Being in Schools: Comparing European, Australian and Indian Perspectives*. Cambridge and London: Cambridge University Press, 2018.

Smith, Ted, David Pellow and David Sonnenfeld, eds. *Challenging the Chip: Labor Rights and Environmental Justice in the Electronic Industry*. Philadelphia, PA: Temple University Press, 2006.

Snow, Keith Harmon. "High Tech Genocide in the Congo." *El Corresponsal*. (n.d.). www.elcorresponsal.com/modules.php?name=News&file= article&sid=4862.

Sofia, Zoe. "Exterminating Fetuses: Abortion, Disarmament and the Sexo-Semiotics of Extraterrestrialism." *Diacritics 14.2* (1984): 47–59.

Soldatov, Andrei and Irina Borogan, *The Red Web: The Struggle Between Russian Dictators and the New Online Revolutionaries*. New York: Public Affairs, 2015.

Solon, Olivia. "How Europe's 'Breakthrough' Privacy Law [GDPR] Takes on Facebook and Google." *Guardian* (April 19, 2018). www.theguardian. com/technology/2018/apr/19/gdpr-facebook-google-amazon-data-privacy-regulation.

Solon, Olivia and Emma Graham-Harrison. "The Six Weeks that Brought Down Cambridge Analytica." *Guardian* (May 3, 2018). www.the guardian.com/uk-news/2018/may/03/cambridge-analytica-closing-what-happened-trump-brexit.

Solon, Olivia and Oliver Laughland. "Cambridge Analytica Closing after Facebook Data Harvesting Scandal." *Guardian* (May 2, 2018). www.theguardian.com/uk-news/2018/may/02/cambridge-analy tica-closing-down-after-facebook-row-reports-say.

Sontag, Susan. *On Photography*. NY: Picador, 2001.

SOPA Strike. Website. http://sopastrike.com.

Southworth, Cindy, Toby Cremer, Sarah Tucker and Cynthia Frasier. "A High-Tech Twist on Abuse: Technology, Intimate Partner Stalking, and Advocacy." *Minnesota Center Against Violence and Abuse*. (June 2005). www.mincava.umn.edu/documents/commissioned/stal kingandtech/stalkingandtech.html.

Stald, Gitte. "Mobile Identity: Youth, Identity and Mobile Communication Media," in David Buckingham, ed., *Youth, Identity and Digital Media*. Cambridge, MA: MIT Press, 2008 (pp. 143–164). http:// digimed-jhi.pbworks.com/f/Stald%2BMobile%2BIdentity.pdf.

Statistic Brain. Website. www.statisticbrain.com.

Steiner, Peter. "On the Internet, Nobody Knows You're a Dog." Cartoon. *The New Yorker* (July 5, 1993): 61.

Stern, Alexandra Minna. *Eugenic Nation: Faults and Frontiers for Better Breeding in Modern America*. Berkeley, CA: University of California Press, 2015.

Sturgeon, Noel. *Environmentalism in Popular Culture*. Tucson, AZ: University of Arizona Press, 2009.

Stuster, J. Dana. "Mapped: Every Protest on the Planet since 1979." *Foreign Policy* (August 22, 2013). www.foreignpolicy.com/articles/2013/08/22/mapped_what_every_protest_in_the_last_34_years_looks_like.

Sukey Apps. Website. (n.d.). sukey.org.

Sunstein, Cass. *RepublicDotCom*. Princeton, NJ: Princeton University Press, 2000.

"Systemic Bias." Wikipedia. http://en.wikipedia.org/wiki/Wikipedia:Systemic_bias.

Taylor, Adam. "The Big Questions for Mark Zuckerberg on Facebook's Role in Burma." *The Washington Post* (April 10, 2018). www.washingtonpost.com/news/worldviews/wp/2018/04/10/the-big-questions-for-mark-zuckerberg-on-facebooks-role-in-burma/?noredirect=on&utm_term=.4cdea6da2718.

Teachers with Apps. "7 Apps to Stop [Cyber] Bullying." teacherswithapps.com (n.d.). www.teacherswithapps.com/63529-2/.

The Green Grid. Website. (n.d.). www.thegreengrid.org/Home/about-the-green-grid/TGGCSCI.aspx.

The Road Less Taken. Website. (n.d.). http://lindsaysminzy.wordpress.com/page/3/.

Think B4 You Speak. Website. (n.d.). www.thinkb4youspeak.com.

Thoreau, Henry David. *The Portable Thoreau*, ed. Carl Bode. New York: Penguin, 1982.

Tomlinson, Bill. *Greening Through IT: Information Technology for Sustainability*. Cambridge, MA: MIT Press, 2010.

Trotter, Daniel. *Social Media as Surveillance*. London: Routledge, 2012.

Tsatsou, Panayiota. "Digital Divides Revisited: What Is New About Divides and Their Research?" *Media, Culture and Society* 33 (2011): 317–331.

Tufecki, Zeynep. "You Tube, The Great Radicalizer," *New York Times*, March 10, 2018. www.nytimes.com/2018/03/10/opinion/sunday/youtube-politics-radical.html

Tulane University School of Social Work. "2018 Guide to Cyberbullying Awareness." https://socialwork.tulane.edu/blog/cyberbullying-awareness-guide.

Turkle, Sherry. *Alone Together: Why We Expect More from Technology and Less from Each Other*. New York: Basic Books, 2012.

Turkle, Sherry. *Life on the Screen*. New York: Simon & Schuster, 1995.

Turner, Fred. *From Counterculture to Cyberculture: Stewart Brand, the Whole Earth Network, and the Rise of Digital Utopianism*. Chicago, IL and London: University of Chicago Press, 2006.

UNESCO Institute for Statistics. Website. (n.d.). www.uis.unesco.org/Pages/default.aspx.

Urbina, Ian. "A Growing Hazard." *New York Times* (March 19, 2013): *1*, 16.

Usable Web. Website. (n.d.). UsableWeb.com.

Utne, Eric. "Signs of the Zeitgeist." *Utne Reader* (May–June 2013): 92.

Vaidhyanathan, Siva. *Anti-Social Media: How Facebook Disconnects Us and Undermines Democracy*. Oxford, UK: Oxford University Press, 2018.

——. *The Googlization of Everything (And Why We Should Worry)*. Berkeley, CA: University of California Press, 2011.

Vegh, Sandor. "Hacktivists or Cyberterrorists? The Changing Media Discourse on Hacking." *First Monday 7.10* (October 7, 2002). http://first monday.org/ojs/index.php/fm/article/view/998/919.

Videogamerability. Website. (n.d.). https://sites.google.com/site/video gamerability/home.

Vosoughi, Soroush, Deb Roy and Sinan Aral. "The Spread of True and False News Online." *Science* (March 9, 2018): 1146–1151. http://sci ence.sciencemag.org/content/359/6380/1146.

Wardrip-Fruin, Noah and Pat Harrigan. *First Person: New Media as Story, Performance, and Game*. Cambridge, MA: MIT Press, 2004.

Wardrip-Fruin, Noah and Pat Harrigan. *Second Person: Role-Playing and Story in Games and Playable Media*. Cambridge, MA: MIT Press, 2007.

Wardrip-Fruin, Noah and Pat Harrigan. *Third Person: Authoring and Exploring Vast Narratives*. Cambridge, MA: MIT Press, 2009.

Warschauer, Mark. "Reconceptualizing the Digital Divide." *First Monday 7.7* (July 1, 2002). http://journals.uic.edu/ojs/index.php/fm/article/view/967/888.

——. *Technology and Social Inclusion: Rethinking the Digital Divide*. Cambridge, MA: MIT Press, 2003.

Webster, Frank, ed. *Theories of the Information Society*. New York: Routledge, 2006.

Weiser, Mark. "The World is Not a Desktop." Online Article. (1993). www. ubiq.com/hypertext/weiser/ACMInteractions2.html.

Weller, Chris. "An MIT Psychologist Explains Why So Many Tech Moguls Send their Kids to Ant-tech Schools." *Business Insider* (November 7, 2017). www.businessinsider.com/sherry-turkle-why-tech-moguls-send-their-kids-to-anti-tech-schools-2017–11.

Whitson, Jennifer R. and Claire Dormann. "Social Gaming for Change: Facebook Unleashed." *First Monday 16.10* (October 3, 2011).

WikiLeaks. Website. (n.d.). http://wikileaks.org.

Wills, Amanda. "Another Snowden Leak: NSA Program Taps Everything You Do Online." Mashable.com (July 31, 2013). http://mashable. com/2013/07/31/nsa-xkeyscore/.

Wilson, Gary. Your Brain on Porn. (December 5, 2018.). Website. http:// yourbrainonporn.com.

Winfrey, Oprah. Interview. "Craigslist Rape Victim." *Oprah* (September 23, 2010). www.oprah.com/oprahshow/Craigslist-Rape-Victim/print/1.

Women in Global Science and Technology (WISAT). Website. (n.d.). http://wisat.org/home/.

Wolf, Mark J. P. and Bernard Perron. eds. *The Video Game Theory Reader*. New York: Routledge, 2003.

Women Watch. Website. (n.d.). www.un.org/womenwatch/.

Woolgar, Steve. *Virtual Society? Get Real! Technology, Cyberbole, Reality.* Oxford, UK: Oxford University Press, 2003.

World Wide Web Accessibility Initiative. Website. (n.d.). www.w3.org/WAI/.

Wu, Tim. *The Attention Merchants: The Epic Scramble to Get Inside Our Heads.* New York: Knopf, 2016.

——. *The Master Switch: The Rise and Fall of Information Empires.* New York: Vintage, 2011.

Yao, Mike Z., Chad Mahood and Daniel Linz. "Sexual Priming, Gender Stereotyping, and Likelihood to Sexually Harass: Examining the Cognitive Effects of Playing a Sexually-Explicit Video Game." *Sex Roles* 62.1/2 (2009): 77–88.

Young, James. *Sex Robots and Us.* BBC3 documentary (2018).

Young, Jeffrey. "As Technology Evolves, New Forms of Online Racism Emerge." *Chronicle of Higher Education* (March 13, 2011). http://chronicle.com/blogs/wiredcampus/as-technology-evolves-new-forms-of-online-racism-emerge/30351.

Youyou, Wu, Michal Kosinski and David Stillwell. "Computer-based Personality Judgments Are More Accurate than Those Made by Humans." *PNAS* (January 25, 2015). https://doi.org/10.1073/pnas.1418680112.

Zaremba, Alan. *The Deepening Divide: Inequality in the Information Society.* Thousand Oaks, CA: Sage, 2006.

Glossary

Actor–network theory Actor–network theory connects technology to social and cultural forces as interacting elements. Associated with figures such as Bruno Latour, and John Law, ANT views technological devices as actors (agents or actants) that have something resembling human agency (the power to impact events), with the caveat that like humans, technological "actors" are always caught up in larger networks of power and causality. Technology devices and humans are both entangled in economic relations, political relations, social relations and cultural relations that shape what they can and cannot do.

Affinity portals (see also **ethnic portals**) Portals, points of access to the Web that collect and organize sites, built for particular demographic groups, based upon any of a limitless number of kinds of collective interest (ethnic cultures, business, hobbies, education, sports, etc.). These portals can be defined as broadly as for women to as narrowly as supporters of a particular football club. They seek to be more focused than general portals such as Yahoo or AOL.

Analog (vs. digital) Analog refers to a process by which information is transferred from one source to another by means of a more or less direct one-to-one full transfer. It is distinguished from digital transmission which simplifies the information into a binary code. Each mode has its advantages and disadvantages. A typical case is the difference between an analog vinyl record and digital CD or MP4 recording. Some argue that the analog is closer to the original in tone and feeling, while others point out that the digital version has less noise (interference) and is far easier to replicate and transfer. Another frequently used example is the difference between an analog and a digital clock. The analog clock has a clock face the represents (by analogy, if you will) the passage of time as hands moving around a clock face. A digital clock, by comparison, simply offers an abstract representation as numbers. Those digital numbers mean nothing out of the context of calling the representation as clock. It just says 1:30, something that can mean many things, while an analog clock clearly exists expressly for the purpose of marking time.

Anonymity in digital cultures One of the features of much online communication is that the user can remain anonymous. This can be a positive protection for some wishing to express their views, but it has also been shown to encourage extreme views because the anonymous poster is not held accountable. Anonymity online is also ultimately an illusion, since almost all digital communication can eventually be traced back to its source (just ask the members of the hacking group Anonymous who are now in jail).

Assemblage theory , associated especially with cultural analysts Gilles Deleuze and Felix Guattari, views reality and all objects in the world as radically unstable, as able to be transformed by interactions or assemblages, with other objects in almost infinitely malleable ways. The world as conceived in this theory is highly changeable because it is almost wholly determined by language, by the ways in which human agents "code" reality. It is a theory attractive to some analysts of digital culture because of the ease with which the appearance of things can be transformed by the manipulation of the binary code behind all digital communication.

Audience analysis As the name suggests, this is an approach to analyzing media, including digital media, by examining how various audiences interpret a given image, story, song etc. This is in contrast to **textual analysis** which examines the media image, story, song in terms of its own formal properties, or the apparent intention of the maker of the text.

Augmented Reality art Augmented reality art uses digital means to overlay a second set of images on top of the existing real world. An artist might, for example, augment an existing building by projecting fantastical images onto it (say psychedelic gargoyles), typically by means of a smartphone or AR glasses or some other kind of digital viewer.

Backlash effect is a psychological phenomenon whereby when confronted by facts that challenge an individual's views or ideology, the individual responds not by accepting an expanded view but rather doubles down on their unsubstantiated view. This well-established tendency accounts for the fact that people often continue to hold their identity-defining views even in the face of what would otherwise be compelling evidence that those views are mistaken or inadequate to explain reality.

Bots Short for robots, bots are software programs designed to do automated tasks. They are widely used to generate political propaganda on social media sites like Twitter and Facebook in support of particular candidates or issues, and/or to stir up general ideological discord (see **Troll farms**). They are also used by celebrities, politicians and others to exaggerate the number of social media "followers" they have. Less controversially, bots are used to do a number of routine tasks such as internet searches.

Brain–computer interface is a direct connection between the human brain and an external, digitally controlled device. Such devices have been used to restore elements of human sight, hearing and movement (known technically as neuroprosthetics).

Cambridge Analytica was a British data analysis and political communication corporation. It is (in)famous for using the personal data of 87 million Facebook users in 2016 to create targeted online political ads supporting the UK referendum on Brexit (the call for Britain to exit the European Union), and US presidential candidate Donald Trump. Political scientists disagree as to the degree of effectiveness of the "psychographic profiles" created by CA, and it is difficult to single out its impact on these two campaigns. During this period, the corporation was largely funded by far right-wing American tech billionaire, Robert Mercer. Cambridge Analytica was forced into bankruptcy in 2018 in the wake of negative publicity regarding its highly dubious, possibly illegal, use of data to manipulate voters through highly inflammatory false news stories (see fake news). The company, however, reformed as Emerdata shortly thereafter with the one of its former directors and many of the same employees. The complicity of Facebook in the data breach also had negative impacts on the social media giant.

Catfish Someone who systematically misrepresents themselves in online profiles, dating sites or other digital spaces, often with some degree of malicious intent. The term was popularized by the documentary film *Catfish* (2010) on this topic, and given further cache by the reality docudrama series *Catfish: The TV Show* (2012+) on MTV dealing with deceptive relationships online.

Confirmation bias is the tendency to seek out information and perspectives that support one's existing views or ideological framework, rather than surveying a range of opinions on a topic or consulting evidence that does not confirm you views.

Content analysis is a technique used to measure things such as how many TV characters are of a particular gender, or age demographic, or ethnicity. It largely eschews interpretive framework or context and essentially counts the number of representations. It is widely regarded as useful as a kind of statistical baseline, but inadequate to a full analysis which would take the form of considering context and variability (i.e., rather than simply counting the number of gay characters in mainstream video games), it would look at the specific representations those characters, and view them in the wider game worlds and game narratives.

Cultural competence acknowledges that, while people develop a more or less automatic depth of understanding of the subject positions and cultures into which we are born and socialized, achieving something like that depth of understanding of other subject positions and other cultures is far more difficult, but not impossible. The process of gaining depth of understanding of subject positions and cultures other than your own is the process of gaining various degrees of cultural competency. It requires both suppressing ones inherited preconceptions and prejudices, and learning often radically new ways of seeing and thinking.

Cultural imperialism is hegemonic influence over cultural production (movies, TV, music, etc.) by one culture over others. The culture subject to cultural imperialism is overwhelmed and overridden by the dominant culture from outside such that local traditions are lost or transformed beyond recognition. The US and to a lesser degree Europe have been accused of cultural imperialism vis-à-vis most of the rest of the world. Japan has been accused of CI with regard to the rest of Asia (and sometimes with regard to the US). Smaller scale cultural imperialism can occur within countries, between ethnically dominant and minority cultures, and between the dominant culture and subcultures.

Cyberbullying is the use of digital cultural representation (typically via social media) to harass, degrade, threaten or otherwise demean another individual. It is both like and unlike offline bullying in that the bully is not always identifiable, and the audience for the bullying is typically larger and more amorphous. Cyberbullying typically involves degrading comments about sexual orientation (LGBTQ2+ individuals are particularly vulnerable), ethnic or racial difference, body image and other aspects of appearance ("fat shaming"), alleged sexual activity ("slut shaming") or other attempts to treat someone as lesser for being "other," for being different from whatever the bully perceives as "normal" or desirable.

Cyberculture studies is one of the names used to characterize the field that looks at the specific aspects of life online and in via the use of digital devices such as cellphones and digital games. The term is one of several more or less interchangeable ones (**new media studies**, and **digital culture studies** being a couple of other prominent ones).

Cyber-ethnography is the close study of online communities, using techniques derived from sociology and anthropology. Cyber-ethnography employs techniques such as interviews, focus groups and participant-observation in online communities to get a more detailed sense of how users interact in cyberspaces.

Cyberfeminisms refers to efforts to translate various feminist concerns into digital spaces and to use digital means (often online political organizing) to address those concerns. Cyberfeminisms, like feminist movements in general, entail a variety of approaches designed to bring greater equality for women in relationships, politics, economics and all other areas of society where they are systematically disadvantaged. This also includes addressing systemic violence against women in terms of harassment, rape and domestic abuse as they are represented in digital culture or actively carried out by digital means (**cyber-harassment**, gender-based **cyberbullying** or **cyberstalking**, for example).

Cyberghettos refers to claims that some digital spaces replicate the segregation of minority groups into enforced enclaves outside the alleged mainstream. Historically, this has included white-identified individuals fleeing from social media sites predominantly used by people of color. The term has been used sometimes justly, but often unjustly, to refer to areas of social media, sometimes called **ethnic portals**, that provide a common space for groups who have been historically marginalized or oppressed by a majority culture.

Cyberspace(s) Term coined by sci fi author William Gibson in his novel *Neuromancer* that has come to be widely used to name the virtual "spaces" of interaction created by the Internet and associated techno-devices. Since the term can falsely imply a single, homogenous territory, for the purpose of analysis it is best used in the plural, cyberspaces. Like all metaphors, this one both illuminates and misleads, since it is precisely the illusion of spacelessness, or no place-ness that characterizes much wired experience.

Cyberstalking is the act of following and harassing someone (typically but not always a female being harassed by a male) in ways analogous to an offline stalker who follows a person and offers them unwanted and often threatening or frightening attention that they have made clear they do not desire.

Cyberterrorism The use of computer hacking to inflict serious direct or indirect psychological or physical damage to human targets.

Cybertypes, cybertyping The appearance of social stereotypes in cyberspaces, and/or the generation of new stereotypes by and in cyber-cultures (coined by Lisa Nakamura).

Cyborgs The term cyborg names a being that is part human, part machine. The best known cyborgs in popular culture are the title character in the "Terminator" and "Robocop" movie series. In digital culture studies, the figure of the cyborg has been invoked to characterize the increasing entanglement of many humans with digital devices. The metaphor of the cyborg was given great prominence in a highly influential 1984 essay, "A Manifesto for Cyborgs," by feminist technoscience scholar, Donna Haraway. While recognizing that the cyborg was the "illegitimate offspring of militarism and corporate capitalism," Haraway also saw positive potential in thinking about the metaphor of the cyborg as a figure that could break down one of the rigid boundaries that has defined putative human nature. Because throughout much of human history describing certain traits as naturally male or female, or placing races in a natural hierarchy have provided the justification for social inequalities, Haraway puts forth the unnatural image of the cyborg as one possible counter to this discriminatory naturalizing of human variety. Given fields such as the Digital Humanities, cybrarian work is increasingly important and pervasive.

Data mining The practice of companies who scour social media and other websites to gather personal information about people's website visiting habits and expressed preferences that they can sell to corporations as marketing research. Much of the revenue for social media sites, search engines and e-tail sites comes from this practice of selling private information to marketers.

Data profiling (aka **weblining**) is the use of information gained by tracking users site visits and other web habits in order to create a marketing profile. This is the process by which ads that seem tailored to your interests appear on your social media page or as part of your Google searches. While some people enjoy this profiling when it correctly identifies preferences, it can also be used to exclude users from certain privileges (see **weblining**) and can narrow the options presented to the user. More importantly, this surreptitiously garnered data has the potential to be used in a variety of undesirable ways, including government surveillance and criminal activity.

Dataveillance A compound word made from data and surveillance, it refers to the surveillance of a person's activities by studying the data trail created by actions such as credit card purchases, mobile phone calls and Internet use. The term is used by critics concerned that various web spaces such as Google and Facebook gather far too much information on users, and fail to protect the misuse of that material for commercial and criminal activity.

Default identity, default subject position refers to the fact that much early software and hardware was the creation of a relatively narrow social group, typically white, male, heterosexual and middle class, who mostly inadvertently programmed their particular, inevitably limited, world view into digital culture. The assumptions of this world view became the default position in digital programs and digital devices, ignoring the fact that people of different genders, ethnicities, classes and sexual orientations might be wish to be positioned differently, might wish to have their viewpoints better represented in digital devices and cultures. A classic example might be the ubiquitous use of the term "desk top" to describe the workspace of a computer. While the term made perfect sense to the desk-bound designers who came up with the term, had working class people been represented, it might have instead been called a "work bench" or if homemakers had been consulted it might have been called a "counter top." An argument could be made that if these other definitional terms had been on offer, folks identifying with these other terms might have felt more welcome in the digital world. The term default subject position continues to predominate despite considerable expansion of variety of users of digital culture, because the needs, desires and viewpoints of this one particular social group are still most often being built in as the "default" (presumed norm or baseline) of digital software and hardware, and therefore of much culture created through those tools.

Digital cultures/ digital culture studies is one of a number of terms used for the analysis aspects of life shaped by the use of the Internet and various digital devices (games, cellphones, etc.). Other often used terms include **cyberculture studies**, and **new media studies**.

Digital divides The digital divide is a concept gaining popularity during the 1990s to describe the gap between those who had access to computers and high tech devices, versus those who did not. The term was made prominent through a series of US government reports, beginning during the Clinton Administration, laying out the statistics regarding the technological "haves" and "have nots," a discrepancy attributable largely to race/ethnicity, income bracket and/or rural vs. urban location. Analysis of the digital divide began as a discussion of simple access to hardware, but evolved to look at a number of social and cultural factors that additionally impacted one's ability to fully utilize new technologies. More complex understanding of the full nature of various digital divides has led to a multifaceted approach often labeled technology for social inclusion. While much effort has been made to bridge certain digital divides many classic ones (unequal access for different classes and ethnicities, for example) new divides have also emerged such as the broadband divide and the security divide, whereby the nature of access, not just access itself, entail major differences in quality.

Digital humanities is the preferred term for people in museums and academe who are translating aspects of human cultural heritage (art, literature, history, social life, etc.) into accessible digital form. Digital humanities projects and centers, often funded through government and/ or private grants, have proliferated around the globe as major efforts to use the Internet and other digital technologies to allow greater numbers of people access to representation of present and historical cultures to which they belong or which interest them.

Digital native/Digital immigrant A digital native is an individual who grew from infancy in a technology rich environment. For digital natives, high tech devices and practices seem natural and are taken for granted. In contrast, a digital immigrant is a person who began interacting with high tech devices later in life; for these generationally older individuals, or individuals introduced to ICTs later in life, comfort with and immersion in digital culture is generally less fulsome. While digital natives generally have the advantage of deeper integration of technologies into their lives, digital immigrants often have the advantage of understanding more fully the contrast between life in digital and non-digital environments.

Disinhibition means the lessening of social inhibitions and taboos. In online environments disinhibition stems largely from the anonymity or invisibility provided by text-based communication without visual identity cues. In some cases, this can be a good thing, allowing people to talk frankly about issues they are not comfortable addressing face-to-face. In other cases, it provides cover for those who choose to launch hate speech or other forms of denigration without identifying themselves.

Edutainment is a derogatory term used by opponents of multimedia and digital teaching techniques presumed because of their similarity to popular forms of entertainment to be less effective or serious pedagogically. While certainly capable of being overused and abused, empirical studies clearly show multimedia and online approaches that get beyond the traditional lecture/textbook model of teaching can expand the range of effective learning for many students.

Electronic literature names a variety of new kinds of fiction writing and poetry that utilizes digital means. This includes things such as hypertext fiction that allows for things such as multiple choices of storylines not possible in a book-bound novel, and new genres like twitterature that utilize the space limit of microblogging sites such as Twitter to shape fiction the way a form like haiku or the sonnet shape poetry.

Electronic civil disobedience refers to the use of digital means to purposely disrupt some social force deemed unjust. This includes things such as hacking and satirically changing a website to change its political orientation, or denial of service attacks that overwhelm a particular targeted site and keep it from functioning as a protest against what it represents. Typically electronic civil disobedience has been used against corporations thought to be exploiting workers or selling harmful products, or to disrupt government sites that represent oppression or denial of free speech to particular groups. This also includes things such as the online publishing of leaked material that embarrasses governmental bodies or corporations by revealing harmful practices they tried to keep from the public.

Embodiment in digital cultures refers both, on one hand, to the fact that even so-called "virtual" experiences are still experienced by human bodies located in the real world, and, on the other hand, that digitized lives do experience new kinds of embodiment that did not exist before. This includes asking the question, how does the illusion of disembodiment (of being lost in cyberspace) shape how we think and feel about the world, and how do things such as our relation to cultural space change when we have through smartphones instant access to virtually any place on the planet.

Ethnic portals . While portals (points of access to the Web that collect and organize sites), exist for almost any demographic groups, based upon any of a limitless number of kinds of collective interests (business, hobbies, education, sports, etc.), ethnic portals are specifically created to facilitate communication among members of a particular ethno-racial group (say Vietnamese Americans or French Arabs). Typically these are for groups who have historically been marginalized, oppressed or underrepresented by some dominant culture in their society. These portals often serve as a safe place to share experiences and viewpoints free from the often disparaging or intimidating presence of the dominant representatives. When they become too self-limiting, they can be accused of becoming **cyberghettos**.

E-waste, electronic waste Toxic waste from computers, TVs, cell-phones and other electronic devices is one of the fastest growing environmental hazards around the globe (though largely dumped on the Global South).

Fake news is a complicated, two-sided term. It was used initially as an accurate term for intentionally misleading or outright false news distributed primarily through social media sites such as Twitter and Facebook. This practice became extreme during the 2016 presidential election won by Donald Trump, with the predominant amount of fake news being generated by his domestic and foreign (especially Russian) supporters. In response to the damaging revelation of how much of this fake news existed, Trump took up the term and sought to muddy the waters by using it to describe any media story, however accurate, that placed him or his policies in a negative light.

Feminist technoscience studies Associated with figures such as Donna Haraway, Sandra Harding, Evelyn Fox Keller and Sharon Traweek, this transdisciplinary field views science as deeply embedded in cultural forces of gender, race and class, and seeks a deeper form of scientific objectivity in which sociocultural factors are included alongside technical elements.

Green computing Efforts to eliminate the many toxic substances found in computers, recycle computers and otherwise deal with the substantial problem of electronic waste and energy consumption by digital devices.

Hacking, hacktivism Online activism that includes civil disobedience in the form of breaking into and altering websites or other digital spaces for the purpose of parody or critical commentary on political opponents, or in support of dissenting political positions. While "black hat hacking" or "cracking" computers is used maliciously or for personal gain, hactivism refers only to breaking into and manipulating digital systems for specific political reasons, for challenging existing economic, social or political power structures.

Hegemony (cultural) in digital culture is cultural domination without overt force or coercion. Hegemony is a process by which groups with greater power lead those with lesser power to adopt their dominant ideas as common sense, even when those ideas work against fairness, justice or the self-interest of the dominated group. In ICT terms, hegemony has meant greater power to shape cyberculture in the hands of certain cultural groups and the default subject position. The concept was originally developed by the Italian Marxist cultural theorist, Antonio Gramsci.

Historical analysis (of technology) refers to the process by which analysts determine what is truly new about our current culture–technology relationships by comparing them to earlier periods, particularly ones that represent large-scale social change. The social impact of the shift to a highly digitized life, for example, might be compared to the social impact of the printing press which likewise greatly changed the nature of communication among individuals and groups.

Identity tourism entails pretending to be someone you are not online, often by crossing gender or ethnic boundaries. Coined by Lisa Nakamura, the term indicates a generally superficial effort to elude ascribed characteristics of identity. It may or may not entail the kind of deception associating with catfishing.

Information feudalism and **knowledge cartels** are two terms used to describe the ways in which a few large media corporations reap enormous profits by charging fees for access to scientific, social scientific and humanistic knowledge that could instead be shared easily and cheaply by digital means. Huge fees assessed to libraries, and firewalls created for academic journal users, turn vital knowledge into a high-priced commodity rather than a resource available to all who need it. This process is part of general failure on the part of societies to develop new laws and practices that reflect a new digital economy of information sharing.

Locative media Digital media targeting or attached to particular real world places. An example would be a city tour in which tourists are guided to particular places around town where their smartphones provide information about the nature or history of each site.

Ludology and video games Ludology is the study of all kinds of games. Analysis of video and computer games has been enriched by drawing upon this wider field that looks historically at games of every type; especially relevant is the history of board games, one of the main bases of many new media variations. Much ludology looks for underlying patterns or structures found across different games and different genres and types of games.

Maker culture refers to various forms of Do-It-Yourself (DIY) digital culture production that challenges the media monopolies that dominate the dissemination of things such as art, music, books and anything that can be made via a 3D printer. Maker culture points to a more decentralized, more egalitarian and open economic system that utilizes the capacities of digital means to create a person-to-person production process not controlled and made more expensive by mainstream corporate and centralized governmental control.

Manufactured consent ; manufactured dissent. Manufactured consent was the term used by Noam Chomsky to describe the ways in which mainstream corporate media tended to marginalize political and cultural ideas that challenged the dominant free market capitalist hegemony and a bland ideological middle ground. Manufactured dissent refers to the more recent process by which social media niches have created ideological silos or echo chambers that drive people toward ever more extreme political positions.

Maptivism Combining the words map and activism, this is form of online activism that uses digital tools to map sites of political contestation. HarassMap.org, for example, in Egypt maps places of sexual harassment across the country to better organize against these practices, and ToxicRisk.com traces sites of pollution via Google maps.

Media effects theory looks at the ways in which various cultural representations through mass media such as TV or social media sites shape people's emotions and actions. Controversially, this approach has been used to try to understand things such as the impact of playing violent video games or watching pornography on real world social interactions. When used carefully, this approach can help illuminate complex social interactions, but it has often been used simplistically in a one-sided way to support things such as a ban on computer games.

Media monopoly refers to the increasingly narrow ownership of various old and new media by a small number of very powerful media megacorporations (Time-Warner, Viacom, Bertelsmann, Disney, NewsCorp, GE, CBS and a few others). Critics worry that monopolies lead to higher prices, more censorship of controversial issues, and less variety of media content.

Mediation In a communication studies context, mediation names the process entailed by the use of any particular medium of communication, whether it be the human voice, language, drawings, old media (TV, film, radio) or new media (the Internet, smartphones). Mediation is a central fact of human existence. We are never in truly immediate contact with one another because all modes of communication, even the most basic, seemingly natural ones like gesturing, or speaking, are culture-bound in ways that enable and also constrain the range of information exchanged between interlocutors. This point about mediation is crucial in new media studies because digital means of communication have frequently been denigrated as less natural, less human or otherwise less real and desirable than face-to-face or forms of non-digital written communication. Most digital culture scholars would reply to this claim by saying that digital media are simply different from, not lesser than, other older forms of (always also mediated) communication.

Mesh media networks offer an alternative way of connecting electronic devices of various kinds without the use of a router. People are currently turning to mesh networks as a means to connect to the internet without relying upon large-scale internet service providers such as Verizon or Comcast. These networks are also popular to create local networks not connected to the wider internet, and thus not as vulnerable to hacking or surveillance by corporations or governments.

Microserfs is a term coined by Canadian novelist Douglas Coupland to describe the people in giant tech corporations such as Microsoft or Apple who do drudge-like work in small cubicles turning out some tiny part of a new electronic project.

Militainment is a term used to describe the ways in which the military industry and the entertainment industry have in recent years collaborated on and often blurred the lines between war and the simulation of war through things such as militaristic computer games on the one hand, and actual battlefield devices that resemble computer games on the other hand. Critics are concerned that this crossover has desensitized some people to the realities of warfare, and/or made people more willing to support questionable military interventions.

Massive Open Online Courses (MOOCs) is the general term of large-scale online course increasingly offered by colleges and universities. While some of these course work well and expose otherwise place-bound people to educational possibilities, many such courses have been of poor quality and have been criticized as exploiting people and offering inferior educational experiences driven by profit motives rather than sound teaching methods.

Massively Multiplayer Online Role-Playing Game (MMORPG) Short-hand for online digital games like World of Warcraft where massive (millions in some cases) numbers of players interact in an ongoing way via the Net.

Narratology and ludology in video game studies . Narratology is a field originally developed to analyze the storylines in novels and other works of fiction and non-fiction. More recently it has been applied to video games. While seen as one key approach to understanding such games, it is insufficient in itself if it does not also acknowledge a logic of gameplay at work, as does the approach know as **ludology**. Ludology (the general study of games and gaming), by contrast, looks not at storylines in games but in how the playing of the game, the choices made, the moves used, shape the experience and impact of the game. Most good current analysis of digital games uses both approaches.

New media studies is an approach to the analysis of digital cultures that stresses the new devices that underlie the production of experiences online and through things such as smartphones and video games. It is one predominant name for this field of study, with **cyberculture studies** and **digital culture studies** is related, slightly alternative ones.

Net neutrality Net neutrality (aka network neutrality or Internet neutrality) is a movement seeking to minimize commercial and government control of the Net, treating it instead as a public resource or commons. Prominent supporters of this position have included one of the key creators of the Internet, Vint Cerf, and World Wide Web inventor, Tim Berners-Lee.

Netroots activism Online political or social movement organizing, meant to parallel the term grassroots, but applying to activism emerging or developing significantly on the Internet and through digital devices.

Planned obsolescence The creation of commercial products that intentionally go out of date relatively quickly so that a new purchase is required. While the term predates the digital era, electronics corporations have become the true masters of planned obsolescence, often by the incremental release of slight improvements in software or hardware that are touted as major breakthroughs driving consumers toward new purchases. Early adopters are the ideal consumers for planned obsolescence.

Posthuman, posthumanism refer to a variety of forms of social analysis that claim that new digital devices and digital culture experiences are so transforming people that we need to talk of a posthuman being and a posthuman era. While some claims made by posthumanists are exaggerated and even wildly speculative, the more thoughtful among the posthumanists (including people such as Kathryn Hale and Donna Haraway) argue that new digital technologies can prompt us to ask important questions sometimes dubious and oppressive assumptions about what we have previously claimed to be essential human nature. Such questioning can open up a healthy social conversation about the varieties of human experiences and capacities, and about the changeable nature of humanness.

Post-truth is a term used to describe an increasing tendency on the contemporary scene for political views to be based on lies (see **fake news**), misinformation and intentional disinformation, and to take the form of emotional responses not based in factual evidence.

Production analysis in relation to digital culture analysis examines the various processes by which the software and hardware that make digital devices and applications possible needs to be factored into the experience. Too often, social analysis of digital life fails to think about the labor processes that underlie and shape the overall nature of digital experience. Production analysis asks questions about who designs, builds and disseminates digital materials, under what labor conditions, with what cultural assumptions behind and reflected in the process and the resulting products.

Prosuming /Prosumer (David Marshall) is a term used to express the idea that some consumers of techno-cultural devices and processes have become producers too via Web 2.0 features such as online product reviews, iReport news items, YouTube video uploads, Facebook "likes" etc.

Remediation In digital culture studies remediation refers most often to processing one type of media through another, such as watching a movie on television or television on a smartphone or a website on a television. New media have increasingly moved forms from one platform (mode of display) to another, and remediation theory seeks to understand how this changes the experience for users. Remediation notes the connection between newer media and older media that preceded and influenced the subsequent form. The process can also be reversed, as when television news frames come to look more and more like webpages.

Robot apocalypse/AI takeover (aka the Singularity) The robot apocalypse is a pop culture term for the possibility that human beings may at some point in the future either be enslaved by or wholly eliminated by artificially intelligent devices like robots. These fears are reflected in a variety of sci fi books, TV shows and films (such as the Terminator series, *I, Robot*, or more recently *Westworld*). Social analysts use the more neutral term, the Singularity, to denote the moment when Artificial Intelligence might come to supplant the human version, with figures as diverse as the late astrophysicist Stephen Hawking and tech mogul Elon Musk warning that this is a serious threat that society needs to be much more fully prepared to confront than we currently are.

Silo effect online in digital culture analysis has been used especially in looking at the political impact of the Web. Political advisor Cass Sunstein and other proponents of this view argue that many Web users, rather than broadening their social views or political knowledge by visiting many sites with differing ideologies, stick to a narrow range of sites than not only echo, but amplify their existing views, leading to greater rigidity and political polarization. Also known as cyber-balkanization. Silos are also created by social media sites such as Facebook, search engines such as Google, and e-tail sites such as Amazon that use algorithms to tailor content, without your consent, to what they perceive to be your interests and desires. While convenient in some ways, these processes also tend to reinforce what you already know and believe rather than taking advantage of the vast amount of new informational and cultural possibilities provided by the Web's reach.

Situated knowledge Associated especially with cultural theorist Donna Haraway, the concept of situated knowledges aims to deepen the idea of objectivity by factoring in the inevitably culture-bound nature of all viewpoints on the world. Haraway rejects relativism (the idea that all points of view are equal), arguing instead that knowledge claims must be evaluated in relation to the host of social forces (especially class, gender, ethnicity and related bases of social inequalities) that confer historically varying degrees of power to shape and represent what counts as reality.

Slacktivism (aka clicktivism) is a derogatory term for online activists who allegedly delude themselves into thinking "clicking" to dislike or like a social issue contributes to real change. While a term useful for pointing to some superficial elements of some social change activism online or activism that relies too heavily or exclusively on technology, it has also been used misleadingly to characterize all of the (often quite effective) movement organizing that uses digital technologies as one tool among many.

Slow Technology movement is one name for efforts made to encourage people into a more selective, thoughtful interaction with various forms of digital media. It is a response to the negative consequences of over-reliance on these devices, and is critical of the addictive qualities of online life. Most supporters of this movement acknowledge the positive impacts of new digital technologies, and do not call for total rejection of digital cultures; but rather call for people to have more offline time, more careful engagement with certain compulsive aspects of digital cultures, and avoidance of thinking one must buy every new device and have every new app.

Sousveillance (vs. surveillance) is a term coined by Canadian tech researcher and designer Steve Mann. It refers to the process of reversing the gaze, or viewpoint of surveillance. Where surveillance is typically performed by governmental and corporate elites, sousveillance is performed from below by ordinary folks, often folks dissenting from what they perceive to be oppressive systems. It takes the French word *sous* (under), to replace the French word *sur* (above) to express the contrast between surveillance as the viewpoint of the powerful with sousveillance as resisting the viewpoint of those with less power. The term has been used, for example, to describe the use of smartphone cameras by protestors to document abusive behavior by police.

Subject position refers to the social positioning—race/ethnicity, gender, age, class, sexuality, nationality, etc.—that plays a major role in structuring a person's view of the world. By definition, subject positions are given by society, not chosen by individuals. Whenever you view a film or website, or read a book or article, you are doing so from a particular subject position. While it is possible to get outside your subject position, it is more difficult to do so than most of us think, and it requires the development of serious new cultural competencies to truly view the world through the eyes of someone whose subject position is far different from your own.

Sunstein Thesis , developed by Constitutional law scholar and political analyst Cass Sunstein, argues that social media sites and other aspects of digital culture encourage the creation of ideological niches, bubbles or echo chambers in which a user's existing political views are not only reinforced but amplified toward more extremist positions by virtue of only communicating with like-minded people. Sunstein contrasts this with the working of a healthy democracy in which people are exposed to a variety of political views, and weigh competing claims and evidence in support of and in challenge to the positions they start from. This phenomenon is credited by Sunstein and others as one important factor in the increasingly extreme political polarization of US society.

Technocultural analysis in contrast to technological determinism, argues that technologies such as the Internet always have cultural assumptions built into them by culturally shaped producers. Technologies are always created by individuals and groups deeply shaped by cultural assumptions and biases. Choices about which technologies to develop are always partly economic and social. Choices about which technologies become popular are deeply social and cultural. The uses to which technologies are put are deeply social and cultural. The adoption and use of technologies is always a social process. Technologies are subsequently adapted, changed or replaced by ongoing social processes. Technologies are always therefore techno-cultural, always shaped by culture even as they shape culture in turn. The term socio-technical plays a similar role.

Technological determinism argues that technology has an independent, causal power in changing society; some argue that technologies are even the main force in social life, beyond economics, culture or politics. Technological determinists often see technology as a force larger than human control. Technological determinists come in both utopian versions (technology will solve all social problems) and dystopian versions (technology will doom us all). Digital culture scholars reject strong versions of technological determinism (preferring "techno-cultural" analysis), while recognizing that technologies do have impacts not fully under social control.

Technological imaginary refers to our imagined relations to technologies, as interwoven with (and sometimes in contradiction to) what we actually do with them and through them. Whenever we use or think about a technical device, we invest a certain amount of imaginary energy in it, we form a mental image of what the device is or is doing to us. These fantastical imaginings are a real part of technoculture, are a real element in how technology shapes and is shaped by culture. If we imagine robots mostly as polite helpful creatures like C-3PO from "Star Wars" we will have a very different relationship to robotics than if we mostly think of the Terminator or Robocop.

Technology for social inclusion refers to a multi-factor approach to overcoming gaps between those with full access to new digital technologies and those who lack such access. This proactive approach stresses multiple cultural factors as well as simple access to hardware and software, and often uses participatory design and other interactive practices to engage underserved communities desiring greater degrees of access to the economic, political, social and cultural opportunities available through digital technologies.

Textual analysis approaches in the context of cultural studies argues that the social TEXT is any unit of meaning isolated for the purpose of analysis. In cyberculture analysis the "text" may be as small as one word or image on a web page, or as large as a whole community of users. Web "texts" include words, images, sounds, page layout, links and their interrelationships. When talking about "text-based" cyberspaces, however, the reference is to writing, as opposed to visual or aural representation.

Troll farms An organization whose employees or members attempt to create conflict and disruption in an online community by posting deliberately inflammatory or provocative comments. Most (in)famously used by Russia to influence the US and UK elections in 2016 on behalf of Donald Trump and pro-Brexit, respectively.

Virtual world/Real world is a common but ultimately misleading way to distinguish digital life in digitized environments from life away from digital devices and processes. The binary distinction is simplistic in that it ignores the fact that one always remains in the real world no matter how immersed one may be in digital realities, and does not take into account the many ways that the real world shapes and is in turn shaped by what goes on in digitally generated spaces.

Wearable computers While people have been wearing computers in a sense at least since the advent of digital watches, the concept of wearable computers generally refers to more fulsome integration of digital connection via clothing. There have been many kinds of wearable computers for a couple of decades that had limited adoption (virtual reality suits constitute an extreme early example, but one whose costs prohibited wide adoption). Google Glass arguably represents the first widely known example of a wearable product that directly connects users to the Net.

Weblining (aka data profiling) is the use of information gathered legally or illegally from an individual's social media page or other online identity cache that is used to exclude that user from certain marketing offers based on economic and racial profiling done through tracking one's online traffic patterns and expressed preferences. The term is meant to echo "redlining," a practice outlawed in 1977 whereby individuals, typically from ethnic minority groups, were excluded from certain mortgage offers to protect the racial "purity" of neighborhoods.

Wikidentities A concept arguing that people, especially young people, deeply immersed social networking sites such as MySpace and Facebook create their identities collectively with help from online friends, and with a sense that identity construction is always partly a fictional process. Part of a larger argument that Web 2.0 features such as "wikis" are changing the way that people, especially young people, think about how knowledge is produced (see Mallan and Giardina, "Wikidentities" in First Monday June 14, 2009).

Zombie cookies A zombie cookie is a cookie illegally planted that remains even after it has been deleted by the removal option on a browser. It continues to gather information about a user's activities usually for the purposes of surreptitious marketing research. Zombie cookies can work across several browsers on the same computer, and can gather information about user login IDs.

Index

Sex acts and digital culture, 141–43
Sex education online, 139–41
Sexual harassment online, 108–09
Sex trafficking, 149–52
Sexism and digital culture, 101–16; and
 video games, 202–211
Silo effect online, 160–61
Silicon Valley Toxics Coalition, 46
Sit-in, digital, 176
Situated knowledge, 6
Slacktivism vs netroots activism, 153, 172
Slow Technology Movement, 74
Social media addiction 94
Social movements and digital media,
 168–78
Social and Public Art Resource Center
 (SPARC), 186
"Social Network Constitution" (Lori
 Andrews), 80–81
Sofia, Zöe, 114
SOPA, internet protest of, 170
Sousveillance (vs. surveillance), 171
Snowden, Edward, 90–91, 177, 182
Starlink (Internet access project), 248
Student Non-violent Coordinating
 Committee (SNCC), 172
Sturgeon, Theodore, 14, 250
Subject position (see also default subject),
 65, 102
Sukey (app), 181
Sunstein, Cass, 160–61
Sunstein, Cass, *Republic.com*, 161
Sunstein Thesis, 160
Superstruct (game), 213
Surveillance and digital culture, 77–100
Surveillance society, 78, 91
Swift, Jonathan, on lies and truth, 161

Take Back the Tech (organization against
 gendered violence), 151
Technocultural analysis, 22–3
Technological determinism, 10–13,
 24, 189
Technological imaginary, 24
Technology for social inclusion, 243–48
Tessera (game), 224
Textual analysis approaches, 14–15
Thoreau, Henry David, 175, 230

Tillerson, Rex, 166
Troll farms (Russian), 90, 160
Turkle, Sherry, 32, 73–74, 129
Trump, Donald, 110; and ending Net
 neutrality 95, 170; as pussy grabber,
 115; racism and Charlottesville riot
 122; voter patterns 123; and fake news
 158–59; and "bullshit" 162
Twitter, and #MeToo movement 115; and
 political disinformation, 155–65; and
 Arab Spring 167–68; ISIS sites on 176;
 and hate speech 183
Twitterature, 231
Twain, Mark, on the swift flow of lies, 161

Vaidhyanathan, Siva, 137
Video games, 191–214; theories of 190–93;
 moral panic around 195–98; as
 art 211–12, 233; for social change,
 212–14;
Virtual communities, 71–73
Virtual reality art, 232–33
Virtual World/Real World, 19–21
Visualizing Emancipation (online
 project), 230

Warschauer, Mark, 105, 124–26, 242–47
Wearable computers, 257
Weblining, 83–84
Wikipedia, 104, 107, 245
Wikidentities, 65
White supremacists: and digital media,
 170; taken off terror list by Attorney
 General Sessions, 183
Witness, The (game), 233
Women's March (2017), 173
World of Warcraft (game), 157
World without Oil (game), 213
Wolfson, Jordan, *Real Violence*, by (virtual
 reality art), 233
Wu, Brenda, 109
Wu, Tim, *The Attention Merchants*, 74

Yes Men, The, 186
Yippies, 185

Zombie cookies, 305
Zuckerberg, Mark 95